DOSTOEVSKY

DOSTOEVSKY

The Years of Ordeal

1850-1859

JOSEPH FRANK

PRINCETON UNIVERSITY

PRESS

Copyright © by Princeton University Press
Published by Princeton University Press, 41 William Street,
Princeton, New Jersey

All Rights Reserved
Library of Congress Cataloging in Publication Data will
be found on the last printed page of this book

ISBN 0-691-06576-4
ISBN 0-691-01422-1 (pbk.)

This book has been composed in Linotron Primer

Clothbound editions of Princeton University Press books
are printed on acid-free paper, and binding materials are
chosen for strength and durability. Paperbacks,
while satisfactory for personal collections,
are not usually suitable for library rebinding

Printed in the United States of America by
Princeton University Press, Princeton, New Jersey

Dedicated to the memory of
Rufus W. Mathewson, Jr.
(1918-1978)
An inspiring Slavist and
a never-to-be-forgotten
friend

CONTENTS

vii

CONTENTS

LIST OF ILLUSTRATIONS

Unless otherwise noted, all illustrations are from *Feodor Mikhailovich Dostoevsky v Portretakh, illyustratsiyakh, dokumentakh*, ed. V. S. Nechaeva (Moscow, 1972).

The present volume is the second in a series dealing with the life and works of Dostoevsky. It will be followed shortly by a third devoted to the next five years of Dostoevsky's life. His literary production was so abundant during this relatively short stretch of time, and Dostoevsky was so intimately involved in all the peripeties of this dramatic moment in Russian history, that it has required a separate volume to depict him adequately at this juncture. This third volume is in the final stages of revision, and should not take too long to appear after the publication of the present one.

The favorable reception accorded my first book was very gratifying, and I should like to thank all those who, whether in public print or private correspondence, expressed their approval. Nothing could be more encouraging to an author engaged in so ambitious an undertaking, whose completion still involves many more years of labor.

This response also reassured me that the method I had chosen to follow—the subordination of Dostoevsky's private life to a depiction of his interconnection with the literary and social-cultural history of his time—answered a widely felt need among those who turn to biographies of great writers because of their interest in them as *writers*. Such an interest cannot be satisfied if most space is given by the biographer to an account of day-to-day existence or events, or if the works are simply dissolved into a running account of the experiences which may (or may not) have served as their genesis. To grasp, so far as possible, the creative process by which life is transformed into art, the experience of the life must be apprehended and organized, without any violation of the historical record, so as to clarify this mysterious mutation. And this can only be done if the life is constantly viewed through the focus of, and in terms of, the work, rather than the more usual way of regarding the work only as a more or less incidental byproduct of the life.

As I now realize, it was not very difficult to maintain such a focus in my first volume, where Dostoevsky's life could largely be followed through his affiliations with the various literary and social-political circles of the 1840s. The present book posed quite a different problem, since Dostoevsky's life during these ten years was spent first in solitary confinement, then in a prison camp in Siberia, and finally as a soldier in one of the Siberian regiments of the Russian Army. He was physically thousands of miles away from the centers of Russian literary activity, and for four years was even cut off from all correspondence with the outside world.

It thus proved necessary to depict him much more in isolation (not social, of course, but cultural) than I had done earlier, and this gave me a good deal of trouble. It proved very difficult to shape the chapters dealing with the prison-camp years according to the perspective that I had chosen, and particularly to interpret the most crucial event of these years—what Dostoevsky called "the regeneration of my convictions"—in such terms. Most earlier writers had just contented themselves with a string of quotations from Dostoevsky that explained nothing, or else followed Freud's psychoanalytic speculations, despite their clear inability, on any close examination, to fit the facts (Dostoevsky exhibited no sense of guilt whatever toward the Tsar-Father but only toward the people). I was thus forced to re-examine the question anew; and this led me to focus on aspects of the situation that had been more or less overlooked, such as the catalytic importance of Dostoevsky's relation to his Polish fellow prisoners. My account, in any case, keeps its eye on the *meaning* these experiences assumed for him, and their determining role both in causing him to reject certain elements of his past and in preparing the way for his future ideological—and hence also artistic—evolution.

Furthermore, Dostoevsky's correspondence, both before and after this period, reveals his desperate eagerness not to lose contact with what was going on in Russian culture; and I place this feature of his life in the foreground of my canvas, to the neglect of a fuller and more picturesque deployment of the available documentation. I might add that this effort led to the unexpected but happy consequence of causing me to explore more intensively than had yet been done certain rather neglected material (such as the correspondence between Dostoevsky and Aleksey Pleshcheev, of which only Pleshcheev's letters have survived). These texts turned out to yield valuable inferential evidence concerning Dostoevsky's reactions to the Russian cultural scene in the mid-1850s, and they thus help to fill out the picture of this obscure period of his life.

Inevitably, however, events such as his first serious love affair and his marriage, which occurred during the years portrayed in this volume, required a fuller biographical treatment than his private life had received in the first. For I did not want to be caught in the same rather absurd position as Boris Eikhenbaum, a critic I greatly admire and whose three-volume work on Tolstoy (unfortunately left incomplete at the time of his death) has served as an inspiration for my own. One of the founders of Russian Formalism, and like all members of this school a ferocious opponent of the confusion of art with life, he later undertook a massive historical study of Tolstoy—but only, as he cautiously explained, on the level of "literary mores" (that is, the literary and social-cultural history of the time). As a result, at the end of a richly detailed discussion in his second volume of Tolstoy's struggles with his school for peasant children and of his theories of pedagogy, Eikhenbaum concludes: "Tolstoy did not become an expatriate, but closed the school, married, and entrenched himself in Yasnaya

Polyana—like a feudal lord in his castle." So much for the marriage! Notwithstanding my immense respect for Eikenbaum, and the refreshing stimulus provided by such jaunty iconoclasm, it seemed to me that one could yield a bit more to "real life" while still retaining the primary interest in "literary mores" that pushed him to so ascetic an extreme.

Work on the present book, in any case, persuaded me that I had drawn too sharp a distinction when I said, in the preface to my first, that "my work is . . . not a biography"; I would still maintain, however, that those who come to my pages seeking "conventional biography" are apt to be disappointed. The critical responses also helped to change my mind, since the first book was invariably taken, not as any attempt to break with biography entirely, but rather as a welcome effort to extend the limits of the genre. Indeed, I am now happy to make my own the observation of a distinguished commentator, who generously spoke of my promising "experiment in fusing biography, literary criticism and social-cultural history." Such a fusion, as I now realize, is exactly what I have been trying to achieve. Whether I have succeeded in doing so here must be left for the reader to judge.

In the preface to my preceding volume, I thanked all those who had aided me in the long and laborious task I had undertaken throughout the many years of working on various drafts. The indebtedness I continue to feel toward Rufus Mathewson, as well as the sense of personal loss caused by his death, is recorded in my dedication. For this second volume, I wish particularly to thank Robert L. Jackson and René Wellek once again, both of whom read the manuscript and gave me criticism and suggestions that have helped to improve it. Nina Berberova also was kind enough to read it, and came to my aid with her intimate knowledge of Russian life and literature. She saved me from making several egregious errors and also suddenly brought me very close to my subject by remarking casually that her grandfather, one of the liberal landowners of the Tver district committee that I mention, had met Dostoevsky during the novelist's stay in that provincial city. Julian Jaynes provided me with material concerning epilepsy, and did me the great favor of putting me in touch with Dr. Gilbert H. Glaser of the Yale Medical School, who took time off to give my remarks on Dostoevsky's epilepsy his professional scrutiny. Both were immensely helpful.

I am grateful also to David Goldstein for checking my footnotes and correcting errors of transliteration, and to Mrs. Rebecca Balinski and Jeannette Mirsky for scrupulous and helpful readings of the galleys. My eagle-eyed copyeditor, Gretchen Oberfranc, pounced on all sorts of lapses that would otherwise have gone unnoticed and made many useful stylistic suggestions. My typist, Carol Szymanski, was inexhaustibly patient, and her interest in the story I was unfolding reassured me that I had managed to preserve a narrative movement in my text. Orest Pelech, the Slavic bibliographer of the Firestone Library of Princeton University, has been invariably informative and accommodating to all my demands on his time and patience. Gaylord Brynolfson volunteered to provide the index of my second volume, as he had done for the first, despite the pressure of his increased duties as a librarian in the above institution.

Both the Guggenheim and Rockefeller Foundations supported my work in the interim between the first and second volumes, and without their financial assistance, which helped me to obtain time off from my teaching duties, who knows how much longer this volume might have been delayed! I deeply appreciate their invaluable help. The Princeton Research Council has been unfailingly forthcoming in defraying the costs of research and typing expenditures.

Finally, as is the custom, a last word must be reserved for my wife, Marguerite. But the expression of my obligations to her is far more than conformity to a professional ritual. Despite the demands of her own academic work, she serves as my first reader and editor, and I rely absolutely on her judgment in matters of organization and style. It is her editorial advice that helps me to untangle and improve my text as I go along, and nobody else can really understand how much more burdensome my task would become if I were not able to obtain her guidance in the course of my work.

Joseph Frank

Princeton, N.J., November 1982

The problem of transliteration is always a difficult one, and I have opted for the simplest solution. For all Russian words, names or otherwise, I use System I in the transliteration chart contained in J. Thomas Shaw, *The Transliteration of Modern Russian for English Language Publications* (Madison, Milwaukee, and London, 1967), 8-9. I have, however, occasionally inserted a "y" to indicate a soft sound where this would not be the natural pronunciation of the transliterated word in English, even though System I does not pay any attention to this feature of Russian. And I have always used English forms, rather than transliteration, where such exist and have become customary (Alexander rather than Aleksandr, for example).

Citations to Dostoevsky's texts in Russian are made to the volumes of the new Soviet edition now in the course of publication: F. M. Dostoevsky, *Polnoe Sobranie Sochinenii* (Leningrad, 1972-); 23 volumes of this planned 30-volume publication have so far been published as this work goes to press. For my quotations from Dostoevsky's short stories and novels, I have used the translations of Constance Garnett because she takes fewer liberties with the literal meaning than more recent translators. However, I have not hesitated to alter her version where this seemed indicated. If no source is given for a translation, I have made it myself.

PART I

The Peter-and-Paul Fortress

O the mind, mind has mountains; cliffs of fall
Frightful, sheer, no-man-fathomed. Hold them cheap
May who ne'er hung there. Nor does long our small
Durance deal with that steep or deep.

Gerard Manley Hopkins

At any rate, our task is set. We must do the job that Dostoevsky himself planned, but failed to carry out: tell the story of the regeneration of his convictions.

Lev Shestov, Dostoevsky and Nietzsche:
The Philosophy of Tragedy.

CHAPTER 1

Introduction

This second volume of the life of Dostoevsky deals with the period between the time of his arrest as a conspirator in the Petrashevsky case and his return to St. Petersburg, ten years later, a changed man both physically and spiritually. Its focus will be on this process of change: its causes in the excruciating experiences he went through, and its consequences, so far as these can already be discerned, in opening up for him the path to future greatness.

The Feodor Dostoevsky taken into custody in April 1849 was fairly well known to the tiny world of Russian literati who, even during the severe military and bureaucratic régime of Nicholas I, were busily laying the foundations for the future glory of Russian literature and Russian culture. Indeed, the most important critic of the time, Vissarion Belinsky, had once enthusiastically predicted that Dostoevsky would someday reach the apogee of his fame when many of his literary competitors, considered to be of equal stature, had long since been forgotten; but this prophetic judgment was quickly reversed in a very few years.[1] By the time Dostoevsky was sent to Siberia, the success of his first novel, *Poor Folk*, had not been repeated by any of his later creations; and he was generally looked on as a writer who, failing to live up to his early promise, had been greatly overpraised. No one could possibly have foreseen the astonishing growth of his talent that would make him one of the dominating figures in modern world literature.

What had attracted attention immediately to Dostoevsky's first novel had been its social and even Socialist character. Belinsky called *Poor Folk* "the first attempt at a social novel we've had,"[2] and Alexander Herzen, in his famous *On the Development of Revolutionary Ideas in Russia*, written five years after Belinsky's comment, cited Dostoevsky's novel as proof that "little by little [our] literary productions were becoming imbued with Socialist inspirations and tendencies."[3] These inspirations and tendencies had taken a good while to come to birth in Russia, and may be said to have been initially stimulated by the crying injustices of serfdom—an institution which had long disturbed the consciences of the best members of educated Russian society, and provided one of the motives for the abortive Decembrist uprising in November 1825.

A new generation had then taken up the same cause, now inspired not by the ideals of liberal republicanism that were mainly (though not exclusively) prevalent among the Decembrists but rather by the Socialist theories that had begun to make their appearance in France during the 1830s. Strongly stirred by his personal contact with the brutalities inflicted on the peasantry, Dostoevsky had also been powerfully affected by his reading of the progressive, humanitarian, and vaguely Utopian Socialist literature (Victor Hugo, George Sand, Eugène Sue, and many others of less renown) that flowed into Russia from France despite all the efforts of the censors to block its entry. Nor should one overlook the new impulse given to Russian literature by Gogol's *The Overcoat* and *Dead Souls*, which were seized upon by Belinsky as splendid native examples of the same "philanthropic" social-literary tendency. The young Dostoevsky was thus well prepared to respond positively when, under the stimulus of Belinsky, the Russian social-cultural climate shifted from Romanticism to Social Realism in the early 1840s; and the signal success of his first book showed how well he had absorbed the lessons of his masters—and of the times. But he did more than participate in a literary movement, or a current of social-political ideas, dedicated to freeing the Russian peasant from enslavement and bringing about a new era of social justice in Russian society. Beginning in the winter of 1848, he also began regularly to attend the meetings of the Petrashevsky circle, a group of young men who gathered at the home of Mikhail Butashevich-Petrashevsky to discuss all those great issues of the day that the muzzled Russian press was forbidden to mention. Thrones were toppling everywhere in Europe in 1848; new rights were being obtained, new liberties being clamored for. It was under the spur of this tensely expectant atmosphere, filled with the excitement created by the news of unexampled victories abroad, that the discussions at Petrashevsky's gradually moved into more dangerous channels and led to an irresistible urge to emulate the prodigies of heroic valor taking place in Europe.

The ever-vigilant ruler of Russia, Nicholas I, only decided to tighten his iron grip even more firmly in the face of this new threat. The arrest of Dostoevsky and the entire Petrashevsky circle occurred as part of the Tsar's endeavor to suppress the slightest manifestation of independent thought which, sympathizing with the revolutions erupting elsewhere, might perhaps lead to similar convulsions closer to home. The last years of Nicholas's reign thus froze Russian society into a terrified immobility, and whatever few traces of independent intellectual and cultural life had been allowed to exist earlier were simply wiped away. To take only one example, the new Minister of Education, Prince Shirinsky-Shikhmatov, eliminated the teaching of philosophy and metaphysics in the universities—whose students, in any case, were now severely limited in number—and the courses in logic and psychology were transferred to professors of theology. T. N.

Granovsky—a famous liberal historian at the University of Moscow, who was one day to sit for the portrait of Stepan Trofimovich Verkhovensky in *The Devils*—wrote to a friend in 1850: "It drives one insane. Good for Belinsky who died in time."[4]

It was in this climate of opinion that Dostoevsky was taken into captivity, tried, and sentenced. Relief for Russian society, however, was to come shortly after Dostoevsky completed his term in prison camp. For the declaration of war against Turkey in 1853 soon led to a conflict, not only with the crumbling Ottoman Empire, but with France and England as well. The superior equipment and efficiency of the European armies, compared with the incompetence of Russian arms, was glaringly revealed in defeat after defeat, despite the acknowledged bravery of the Russian soldiers. Nicholas had sacrificed all other interests to maintaining the military might of his far-flung empire; and the public disclosure of the vanity of his efforts drove him to his grave. He died, a broken man, two years later, while the conflict was still raging, and he was succeeded by his son Alexander II. Russian society heaved a huge sigh of relief, and looked forward to a new era of hope and relative liberalization. The first years of Alexander's reign did much to justify such expectations, and enthusiasm for the new monarch reached a pitch of adoration when he declared his intention to liberate the serfs.

Such was the social-political background against which Dostoevsky's life was being carried on during these years, first as a prisoner both in Petersburg and Siberia, and then as a soldier and officer in the Russian Army. His fate was indirectly shaped by all these momentous events, and his responses to them will enable us to chart the interaction—so important for any adequate understanding of his work—between his personal destiny and the more general concerns shared by his countrymen. And when he finally returned to Russia at the beginning of 1860, amidst the euphoria engendered by the prospect of impending liberation; when his years at hard labor and his desperate struggle to survive were at last triumphantly ended—we shall see that he felt much more intimately identified with the common lot, and the common population, of his vast, sprawling homeland than had ever been the case before. Why this should have been so is the theme of the present volume; and while such an inner evolution may seem paradoxical and enigmatic to some, and frankly pathological to others, our task will be to make it at least comprehensible.

CHAPTER 2

The Petrashevsky Affair

Sometime in late April 1849, a worthy dignitary of the Russian Empire, Senator K. N. Lebedev, set down in his diary (published only in the next century) the following entry: "The whole city is preoccupied with the detention of some young people (Petrashevsky, Golovinsky, Dostoevsky, Palm, Lamansky, Grigoryev, Mikhailov, and many others), who, it is said, reach the number of 60, and this number will no doubt increase with the uncovering of links with Moscow and other cities. The affair is an important one, not in itself, but because it could happen at all. . . . So far as is known (and very little is known), at the home of the young Petrashevsky, a one-time student of the Lyceum [at Tsarskoe Selo] there were gatherings of lovers of discourse and orators, talking now about the peasant question, now about reforms in various departments of government, now about our relation to the Western disorders [i.e., the revolutions of 1848]. The chatterers set down their names in advance to speak, and, in this way, represented something in the nature of a [political] club."[1]

These words give some notion of the excitable rumors sweeping through St. Petersburg in that late spring of 1849—rumors caused by the arrest of the members of the Petrashevsky circle during the night of April 22-23, or rather, as was the custom, in the early morning hours. The order for the arrest had been issued by Nicholas I the day before, just after the Tsar had read the report prepared for him by Count A. I. Orlov, the head of the Third Section of His Majesty's Imperial Chancellery (more familiarly known as the secret police). The Friday night gatherings of the Petrashevsky circle, although no attempt had ever been made to conceal them, had been under observation for more than a year. Normally, an investigation of this kind would have been placed directly in the hands of the secret police; but Nicholas had become dissatisfied with their recent performance, and Count Orlov had agreed to let the Ministry of Internal Affairs take charge. Pursuit of the inquiry was entrusted to I. P. Liprandi, a seasoned official who, having been chief of the military and political police in Paris under the Russian occupation after Napoleon's defeat, was considered uniquely qualified for the task of uncovering subversive plotters.

On taking charge, Liprandi had promptly set up a cabstand opposite Petrashevsky's flat, whose cabmen proved unusually willing to take visitors emerging from the meetings everywhere and anywhere at minimal fees.[2]

When such secret surveillance failed to yield any appreciable results, Liprandi enlisted the services of an ex-student of the University of Petersburg, P. D. Antonelli, with a background and education deemed sufficient to allow him to infiltrate the gatherings and report back on their tenor. Once Antonelli had supplied his superior with enough incriminating evidence, Liprandi passed on the dossier to Orlov for whatever further action should be considered necessary. "I have read through it all," wrote Nicholas in response to Orlov's summary of the findings. "It's an important matter, for even if it were just a lot of idle talk, this would still be criminal and intolerable."[3]

2

As rumors of the arrests began to spread, all Petersburg was asking itself the same question raised by the Tsar. Were the meetings just "idle talk," or did they have a more sinister and determined purpose? Senator Lebedev, who was very well connected, spoke to Liprandi himself and received one reply: "Today I ran into I. P. Liprandi in the Passage [a covered arcade] and he quite freely engaged in conversation about our child-conspirators now in the fortress. He began this affair, and he is very familiar with it as a member of the Commission [set up to examine the books and papers of the suspects]. The affair, in his opinion, is exceedingly important, and should terminate with capital punishment. This is terrible. I did not expect in it anything adult and decisive."[4] Lebedev made an appointment to dine with Liprandi the next day, and the ominous official promised to acquaint him with the documents of the case.

Senator Lebedev was skeptical because, like many others in the small, closed world of Petersburg officialdom, he was personally acquainted with some of the young men under arrest, who belonged to families that he frequented. "Knowing two of them," he writes, "Kolya Kashkin and Vasya Golovinsky [he affectionately uses the Russian diminutive form in writing both names], I (and I repeat this) cannot imagine anything adult, and I attribute everything to unstable enthusiasm." Nor did the evidence he was shown during his visit to Liprandi impel him to change his mind: "I was there and saw the indictment, read the documents and copies along with the confiscated papers, and nonetheless I do not find the importance that some wish to give to this business. Many are involved in it; particularly Petrashevsky and Speshnev. . . . But in all these papers I see only stupidity, schoolboy pranks, petty skylarking."[5]

The notion that the Petrashevsky circle could not be taken seriously as a threat was widely shared, and continued to be held even after the case was concluded. P. V. Annenkov, the shrewdest observer of Russian social-cultural life at that moment, also believed that the Petrashevsky case had been blown up out of all proportion. "The fall of the year now ending," he jotted down in his notebook during the winter of 1849-1850, "was marked by the conclusion, finally, of the inquest into the Petrashevsky conspiracy, which cost all of the society, entirely innocent of conspiracy, so many hardships and terror."[6] Indeed, to a certain extent this opinion was shared even by the Commission of Inquiry set up to examine the evidence—at least if we judge by its refusal to accept Liprandi's view of the danger posed by the Petrashevsky gatherings. In August 1849, Liprandi submitted a memorandum detailing his conclusion that "here was not so much a petty and isolated plot as *the all-embracing plan of an overall movement for change and destruction*." In reply, the Commission of Inquiry politely recognized "the important service rendered by Mr. Liprandi in the prolonged observation of Petrashevsky and other persons" but decided that, "after the most attentive examination of the judgments made by him," it could not agree with them.[7]

Much still remains obscure about the Petrashevsky affair; and the many questions to which it gives rise, unless new documents are discovered, may well remain unanswered. But it is quite probable, from what has been established in the course of one hundred and thirty years, that the truth lies, as it often does, somewhere between the two extremes. Liprandi was wrong in believing that the Petrashevsky circle *as a whole* was "an organized society of propaganda," with its tentacles reaching out into many cities and preparing "minds everywhere for a general insurrection." Mostly it was, as Annenkov had it, just a talk-shop where people came together "merely [to] read their projects for the emancipation of the peasants, for the improvement of shipbuilding and observations on the real internal state of Russia," or even only because they "were fond of his [Petrashevsky's] excellent dinners on those same Fridays."[8] But there *was* within this motley group a small nucleus who were dreaming of the kind of organization that Liprandi spoke of, and who, under the leadership of Nikolay Speshnev, had set about trying to bring it into being. Nor was Liprandi wrong in outlining for the Commission the aims that the members of this society had been discussing—"how to arouse indignation against the government in all classes of the population, how to arm peasants against landowners, officials against their authorized superiors; how to make use of the fanaticism of the [religious] schismatics—but among other groups, how to undermine and dissolve all religious feelings."[9]

The members of this secret group never acknowledged its existence, either then or later; in fact, it remained unknown until revealed by a letter that first came to light in the 1920s. But one member of this secret society, Feodor Dostoevsky, let drop a hint of its presence much earlier to his second wife, who then repeated his words to his first biographer, Orest Miller. Referring to a book published about the Petrashevsky affair in

Leipzig in 1875, Dostoevsky said that the work was "true, but not complete." "I," he explained, "do not see my role in it. . . ." "Many circumstances," he added, "have been completely passed by; an entire conspiracy has vanished."[10] This "conspiracy" was the one that the Speshnev secret society had tried to organize, and which, because of the arrests, had been stopped dead in its tracks before it was really able to begin its work of propaganda. And Dostoevsky knew very well that, if all traces of it had vanished so thoroughly, it was in large measure because he had struggled so staunchly and so successfully to keep them hidden from the Commission of Inquiry.

3

Ten years after that fateful night of April 22-23, when asked to inscribe something in the souvenir-album of the daughter of his friend A. P. Milyukov, Dostoevsky scribbled a graphic account of the circumstances of his arrest—probably because Milyukov and his family were intimately connected with his recollections of those nerve-wracking events. Awakened at four in the morning by an officer in the light-blue uniform of the secret police, who was flanked by an armed guard and the local police official of the district, Dostoevsky sleepily watched the clumsy and semi-comical search of his quarters and the confiscation of his papers. Then he was taken in a carriage, accompanied by the officer and the police official, to the notorious headquarters of the Third Section, close to the Summer Gardens. There he found a good deal of bustle and stir, with carriages arriving every moment from various parts of the city. As he writes slyly, "I met many acquaintances. Everybody was sleepy and silent. Some kind of bureaucratic gentleman, but of high rank, did the honors . . . light-blue gentlemen kept on arriving uninterruptedly with various victims."[11] The atmosphere, all the same, must have been comparatively free and easy, because the prisoners were able to cluster around the official checking the identity of those brought in and could clearly see, marked on the document he was consulting, the name of the secret agent—P. D. Antonelli.

Someone then whispered in Dostoevsky's ear, using a peasant idiom, "Here, grandmother, is your St. George's day," which means something like, "here's a fine fix."[12] April 23 was, in fact, the spring St. George's day in the Russian calendar of saints; another St. George's day occurred in the fall, on November 23. The use of this folk expression, which may well have referred only to the date, was nonetheless peculiarly appropriate in a deeper sense. For its origin has been traced back to the decree of Boris Godunov in 1597 that abolished the right of peasants to change masters on the fall St. George's day.[13] This was the effective beginning in Russian history of the total enserfment of the peasantry; and the idiom enshrines in folk speech the woebegone reaction of the Russian people to their enslavement. It was thus especially relevant to the arrested Petrashevtsy, who were now indeed in "a fine fix" for having wished to make permanent the emancipation once enjoyed by the Russian peasant only on St. George's day.

The consternation provoked in Dostoevsky by his arrest was only heightened when, to his amazement, he saw his younger brother, Andrey, being led in among those taken into custody. Andrey was then a student at a Civil Engineering Institute and had never taken part in any of the Petrashevsky gatherings. Feodor, if we are to believe his version, instantly grasped that Andrey had been arrested by mistake in place of their older brother, Mikhail, who *had* participated actively in the Petrashevsky reunions and also attended the meetings of a smaller group, the Palm-Durov circle. At this point, there is a conflict in the accounts left by the two brothers. In 1856, Feodor claimed in a letter that he had asked Andrey to conceal the error temporarily from the authorities out of concern for Mikhail, who was burdened with a wife and three children: the delay in his arrest would allow him to make some provision for them before disappearing into the maw of captivity. Andrey mentions no such request, recalling only that, before they could exchange a word, they were separated and taken to different rooms.[14] Mikhail Dostoevsky was in fact arrested two weeks later and Andrey released; but by then Mikhail had arranged for his older son to live with A. P. Milyukov, and the family was also helped through the crisis by A. A. Kraevsky, the publisher of *Notes of the Fatherland*. Mikhail had contributed a regular chronicle of internal affairs to this publication, and Dostoevsky's novel *Netotchka Nezvanova* had also just begun to appear in its pages.

The prisoners spent all of the first day, April 23, scattered through the various rooms of the spacious headquarters of the Third Section; and they were, for some unexplained reason, treated with a good deal of courtesy and consideration. Tea, coffee, and breakfast were served, and in the evening a carefully prepared dinner; one of the Petrashevtsy remembered even being offered cigars. "In a word," Andrey Dostoevsky writes, "we were fed splendidly, as guests of the Third Section."[15] At midday, Count Orlov made the rounds of his "guests" and favored them with a little speech. Its substance was that those assembled had unfortunately not known how to use properly the rights and freedoms accorded to them as Russian citizens, and their behavior had forced the government to deprive them of the said freedoms. After careful investigation of their crimes, they would be judged; and the final decision as to their lot would depend on the mercy of the Tsar. No accusations were made or other information offered; nor were the prisoners allowed to converse with each other. Andrey nonetheless managed to scribble a note to the man sitting next to him, who, as it later turned out, had also been arrested by mistake because his family name was the same as that of N. Ya. Danilevsky, later a famous scientist and Pan-Slav theoretician.

At about eleven in the evening, each name was called individually, and one by one the prisoners passed through the office of the second in command of the Third Section, General L. V. Dubelt. Alexander Herzen remembered Dubelt as "an unusual person . . . probably more intelligent than the whole of the Third [Section]," and Herzen noted that "he was always courteous."[16] This last trait is confirmed by Andrey, who was asked politely by the cold and impassive Dubelt to be so kind as to accompany the lieutenant waiting to escort him. A carriage was ready for them in the courtyard, with a noncommissioned officer seated inside, and once the blinds were drawn they set off for an unknown destination. Andrey believed that he was being taken straight to the outskirts of the city, from there to be sent directly to Siberia in a convoy. Instead, after a lengthy circuit, the carriage drew up inside the walls of the ill-famed Peter-and-Paul Fortress.

Built on an island in the Neva, this formidable citadel had been one of the first buildings to rise in the new city of Sankt Pieter Burkh envisioned by Peter the Great. Here Peter installed his headquarters while a vast army of serf-laborers toiled and died to realize his vaulting dream of a great modern metropolis arising in the midst of the Finnish swamps; and for a few years this minuscule tuft of land became the effective capital of the Russian Empire. Deciding that the island would continue to serve as the

1. The Peter-and-Paul Fortress

11

bastion of the royal house of the Romanovs and the final resting place of its members, Peter ordered his Swiss-Italian architect, Domenico Trezzini, to erect a cathedral within the confines of the fortress grounds. Soon a Baroque church began to rise on the spot—a church whose tall and elegant bell tower, crowned with a golden cupola and spire, was one of the most elevated in Russia and could be seen from every part of the city.

Less conspicuous, but no less essential, was a small, maximum–security prison within the fortress complex, which Peter used for the seclusion, torture, and, finally, execution of his son, the Tsarevich Alexis. Later Tsars also found it convenient for the detention of other highly placed personages who, for whatever reason, had incurred the royal displeasure. It was here that Catherine the Great, before shipping him off to Siberia, had imprisoned Alexander Radishchev, who had dared to expose the horrors of serfdom in his *Journey from St. Petersburg to Moscow*. It was here that the Decembrists had languished after their bungled uprising, while each awaited his turn to be taken to the Winter Palace and personally interrogated by the Tsar. The prison very early acquired an evil reputation, and its ill-repute only increased with time. No one had yet managed to escape over its walls—or would ever succeed in doing so—and it was reserved for inmates whose misdeeds were considered a danger to the state.

4

Even though Feodor Dostoevsky did not leave any description of the physical conditions of his incarceration, the memoirs of Andrey Dostoevsky, as well as those of other prisoners, allow us to reconstruct them with some exactitude. The cells differed in size but were quite ample for one person; most had high, vaulted ceilings, and all had windows (in back of an iron grill) whose glass was smeared over, except at the very top, with some sort of oily paste that allowed only a diffuse light to filter through. At night, each cell was lit by a small oil lamp set high on the wall in a window embrasure, whose cotton wick often sputtered and fumed instead of giving off light. The lamp in Andrey's cell smoked so much that it stung his eyes; but when, during his first night, he made a motion to snuff it out, a voice instantly told him to desist.

All cells had a small judas in the door, and the prisoners were constantly under surveillance by guards walking silently in the corridors. The furniture consisted of a cot, a stove of Dutch tiles, a table, a stool, and, in one corner, what Andrey calls "a necessary piece of furniture,"[17] probably a basin and a close-stool. The cot was covered with a straw mattress and a pillow of sacking material without sheets or pillowcase; the only covering was a blanket made of the coarse and heavy woolen cloth used for Army overcoats. The walls of Andrey's cell had recently been scraped to remove the graffiti of previous occupants; other cells still retained traces of the marks made on them by those struggling against apathy and numb dejection.

Most of the accounts of the fortress complain of its dampness, and Andrey writes that "one felt the cold piercing through to the very bones. I never took off the warm overcoat in which I slept."[18] Other prisoners were not so appreciative of the prison garb they were forced to wear. "Cold shivers run all through me," writes the gently nurtured P. A. Kuzmin, an officer of the General Staff included in the roundup and soon released, "when I remember the sensations I felt in putting on my convict's clothes"—made of the roughest material and stained by previous usage—whose contact on his flesh filled him with uncontrollable repulsion.[19] Besides the cold, Andrey was also bothered by the appearance of good-sized rats (not, he is careful to specify, mice) the moment darkness came on; they seemed to materialize from nowhere, and he only slept during the daytime for fear of being attacked. From the presence of such huge rats, he surmised that a granary was probably located somewhere in the vicinity; other accounts do not speak of rats, but cockroaches were plentiful and omnipresent.

Andrey's cell was situated in the Zotov bastion, which was more dilapidated than other sections of the prison. For he recalled the commandant of the fortress, General I. A. Nabokov (the great-great-uncle of the author of *Lolita*),* looking round him with distaste on his first visit and muttering: "Yes, it's bad here, very bad, and we've got to hurry"—meaning, as Andrey learned later, to build new quarters for prisoners.[20] This explains the discrepancies between some details of Andrey's memories and what we learn from others. I. F. Jastrzembski, who was placed in the Alekseevsky Ravelin, wrote later that "all the hygienic conditions there [in his cell] were satisfactory; fresh air, cleanliness, good food, etc., everything was fine."[21] Nor was this remark written in any spirit of retrospective contrition: the remainder of Jastrzembski's memoir gives an indignantly sarcastic account of his interrogation by the Commission of Inquiry. Andrey Dostoevsky also comments favorably on the food, which, if hardly refined, was still solid and nourishing, and was accompanied by as much bread as one wanted, as well as by a jug of water or kvas. Those prisoners who had a little money could have tea brought to them twice a day and buy cigars, cigarettes, and tobacco.

---

* His great-great-nephew Vladimir Nabokov describes him as "one of the heroes of the anti-Napoleon wars and, in his old age, commander of the Peter-and-Paul Fortress in St. Petersburg where (in 1849) one of the prisoners was the writer Dostoevsky, author of *The Double*, etc., [?] whom the kind General lent books." This last (and very literary) detail is either a family tradition or a Nabokovian retouching of history—perhaps his ancestor was actually improving Dostoevsky's deplorable literary taste! So far as my knowledge goes, no confirmation of it can be found in the materials concerning Dostoevsky's imprisonment. Perhaps all it means is that Dostoevsky borrowed books from the prison library. Vladimir Nabokov, *Speak, Memory!* (New York, 1967), 39.

13

2. The Alekseevsky Ravelin

Feodor Dostoevsky was also placed in the Alekseevsky Ravelin, which lies at one tip of the island and was reserved for the most important prisoners. Hence we may assume that Dostoevsky's living conditions were much the same as those that Jastrzembski praises and superior to those afforded his brother. From the account of another prisoner, D. D. Akhsharumov, we know that after June 20 life became much more comfortable for all those under investigation. Old, rough bedding was changed for a new variety of much softer quality; coarse linen was replaced by some of a finer texture; and instead of receiving the rations of the ordinary soldier, as had been the case before, food now came from the officers' mess. Aksharumov was also given a roomier cell with two windows instead of one. According to the authoritative opinion of N. F. Belchikov, "Dostoevsky lived in the Ravelin under the same conditions" as those of Akhsharumov.[22] No complaints about his physical treatment can be found either in Dostoevsky's letters of the time (read by the prison censorship, of course, and hence subject to caution) or in later remarks.

What seems to have been most trying for those imprisoned was, rather than any material deprivation, the silence, the isolation, and the sense of being continually under secret observation. "Solitary confinement," Jastrzembski writes, "had a depressing effect on me. The very thought that I was being held *au secret*, after two weeks of confinement, brought on nervous attacks, fainting, and palpitations of the heart."[23] Akhsharumov, who could hear deep sighs, and sometimes the sound of weeping, from neighboring cells and from the corridor, remarks that these, along with "the silence, the stuffy air, total inactivity . . . exercised a dispiriting effect, which took away courage."[24] Petrashevsky complained that he was being tortured and deprived of sleep by mysterious tappings on the wall and by whispering voices also coming from the wall, which disconcertingly substituted themselves for his own thoughts. Andrey mentions listening to the church bells, which rang every quarter hour, and to the beating of the tower clock as a welcome relief from his own oppressive musings.

Actually, however, the isolation of the prisoners was only relative, since they were visited five times every day. In the morning, about seven or eight o'clock, they were brought some water to wash with, and their toilets were emptied. At ten or eleven, every cell was usually inspected by the commandant of the fortress or one of his subordinates. A midday meal was brought at twelve, dinner at seven in the evening, and a guard came to light the lamp at dusk. Dostoevsky mentions in a letter being taken occasionally for a walk in the small garden of the Ravelin, where there were, as he remarks with a touch of humor, "almost seventeen trees."[25] Except for these welcome distractions, life flowed on "from day to day in idleness," as Andrey writes. "No book, not a sheet of paper, there was nothing! . . . One could only dream and mull over what might lie ahead. The only occupation I could think of for myself was to rise from the cot and to walk up and down, counting each step, stopping when I had reached one thousand, and sitting down to rest. Then I began to do the same thing again. This helped me a bit to chase away gloomy thoughts."[26] No doubt this is how most of the other prisoners spent these first few weeks while waiting to be called up for interrogation.

5

To get to the bottom of the Petrashevsky affair, a Commission of Inquiry was appointed, headed by General Nabokov and including General P. P. Gagarin, Count V. A. Dolgorukov, General Ya. I. Rostovtsev, and General Dubelt. Nabokov, who took no part in the questioning, presided over the Commission only because he was commander of the fortress. The impression he produced on Jastrzembski was that of a rather uncultivated individual, a gruff old soldier "who was firmly convinced that if someone was behind bars in prison, then of course this alone proved that he was guilty and deserved punishment."[27] Such words, however, are not confirmed by his treatment of Andrey Dostoevsky when it became clear to the Commission that the young man had been arrested by error. The other members were willing to allow him to languish in his cell until the formalities for his release had been completed; but Nabokov, better acquainted with the "amenities" of the lodgings he supervised, protested and installed Andrey in his own quarters. It should be recorded, as well, that both Feodor Dostoevsky and Sergey Durov spoke to A. P. Milyukov "with particular warmth . . . of the commandant [Nabokov], who had continually concerned himself with them and, so far as he could, eased their condition."[28]

General Gagarin led the way in conducting the interrogation, even indicating some acquaintance with the incendiary ideas of Fourier, which he had learned about through his son. Feodor Dostoevsky gratefully recalled, many years later, that Gagarin had expressly summoned him to the headquarters of the fortress in order to cheer him with the good news that his brother Mikhail (about whom he had expressed great concern) had been cleared of suspicion and freed. Dolgorukov, later to become head of the Third Section, took no notable part in the proceedings. Despite a bad stammer, Rostovtsev was much more active—as became someone with his checkered career and closeness to the Tsar. Once a member of the dissident Decembrist group of Army officers, Rostovtsev had voluntarily informed Nicholas, two days before the planned date of their armed uprising, that a coup was impending; but as an honorable man he had refused to name any names. All the same, his information had been crucial in enabling Nicholas to take steps to meet the looming crisis and suppress the malcontents. As someone who had once entertained liberal ideas himself, Rostovtsev expressed a certain amount of sympathy for the youthful and woefully misguided Petrashevtsy. But he was also head of a committee in charge of education in military establishments, and he severely reprimanded those among the prisoners (including Dostoevsky, a graduate of the Academy of Engineers) who had shamefully abused what they had learned at such institutions.

Dubelt, representing the Third Section, was sharply attentive to the proceedings and intervened very frequently in barbed and sarcastic tones. He had been greatly upset on learning that the surveillance of the Petrashevsky circle had been carried on for over a year without his knowledge, and he regarded this concealment as a personal insult. It was to satisfy a private vendetta, as well as to protect his bureaucratic interests, that he undertook, at every opportunity, to undermine the importance given to the case by the Ministry of Internal Affairs and by his erstwhile friend and ex-Army comrade I. P. Liprandi. One surmises that he advanced very convincing arguments to persuade the Commission against accepting Liprandi's view that an organized plot had existed; and he is mentioned by several of the Petrashevtsy as having taken a generally "humane" attitude toward them. Jastrzembski, so severe for everyone else, remarks: "I know several instances in which he [Dubelt] did as much as he could to help those accused of political crimes, and I do not know of a single instance in which he destroyed anybody."[29] Annenkov records that Dubelt paid a private visit to the home of one of the prisoners, Balasoglo, and left some money with his hard-pressed wife.[30] Dostoevsky too, perhaps for similar reasons, remarks in the album of A. P. Milyukov's daughter: "I can affirm that Leonty Vasilevich is a very pleasant person."[31]

The procedure of the Commission was to interview the prisoners individually and question them on the basis of the information supplied by Antonelli; they were also asked to answer questions in writing touching on their associations with Petrashevsky and other members of the circle. When contradictions or ambiguities appeared in the various accounts, those concerned were pressed to clarify them, and a direct conflict of testimony led to a face-to-face confrontation in the presence of the Commission. Meanwhile, additional information was being continuously supplied by the group set up to study the papers and documents confiscated at the time of the arrest, and these of course provided some of the crucial evidence. No forcible methods of interrogation were used, nor were the prisoners brutalized in any way; a threat was made to place Speshnev in shackles if he refused to continue to answer questions on specific points, but it proved unnecessary to put that measure into execution. Dostoevsky was called in for questioning several times between April 26 and May 16, and only one rather dubious story is known about his treatment and behavior.

He later told Orest Miller that, as he was replying evasively to some early inquiries, General Rostovtsev turned to him with these words: "I cannot believe that the man who wrote *Poor Folk* can be in sympathy with these vicious people. It is impossible. You are only slightly involved, and I am fully empowered by the Tsar to pardon you if you agree to tell about the whole business." Dostoevsky stubbornly remained silent, and Dubelt, with a slight smile, said to Rostovtsev: "I told you so." Rostovtsev, if we are to believe Dostoevsky's account, then leaped up, exclaimed, "I can no longer bear to look at Dostoevsky," and bolted into another room, whose door he closed behind him with a key. From there he asked: "Has Dostoevsky left yet? Tell me when he goes—I can't bear the sight of him."[32]

N. F. Belchikov, the Soviet Russian scholar who has devoted most attention to Dostoevsky's imprisonment and trial, hesitates to give this rather implausible story any credence; but Rostovtsev's stammer does indicate a high degree of nervosity, and his strange behavior may have been caused by his humiliation at the hands of Dubelt.[33] Whether true or not, the story indicates that Dostoevsky recalled the interrogations as far more grotesque than terrifying, and as having revealed a gratifying acquaintance with his writing on the part of at least one of his judges.

CHAPTER 3

"A Wealth of Life"

During his first conversation with the Epanchin sisters in *The Idiot*, Prince Myshkin tells of his early yearning to know the secret of life and of how he had "dreamed of some great town like Naples, full of palaces, noise, roar, life. . . . But afterwards I fancied one might find a wealth of life even in prison" (8: 51). At the time of his arrest, Dostoevsky too found it almost impossible to imagine the secret of life being discovered except in the midst of the roar and bustle of a large city, if not Naples, then St. Petersburg. But, against all his expectations, he nonetheless managed "to find a wealth of life" within the confines of his prison cell; and what Prince Myshkin merely asserts as a fancy, Dostoevsky knew to be a fact.

"When I found myself in the fortress," he told Vsevolod Solovyev in 1873, "I thought that the end had come, that I would not last three days, and—suddenly I calmed down. Look, what did I do there? I wrote *A Little Hero*—read it, is there any sign of bitterness or torment in it? I dreamed peaceful, fine, good dreams, and then, the longer it lasted, the better it was."[1] Such a statement, of course, should not be taken too much at face value; Dostoevsky's state of mind, not to mention the state of his health, was much more precarious than he later recalled. But he did find unexpected reserves of inner strength that enabled him to endure the trials of captivity without losing heart; and it was this sense of mastery that dominated in his recollection of the event.

What Dostoevsky discovered in prison had a good deal to do with his emotional state just before detention, and we know from his second wife that he was living at this time on the edge of nervous collapse. According to her notes, he told her that, "if not for his [Dostoevsky's] arrest, which broke his life in two, he should have gone mad. An idea had appeared which made a concern for his health, and care about himself, seem like nonsense."[2] What Mme Dostoevsky calls an "idea" was actually her husband's decision to join Speshnev's secret society, whose plan was to set up a printing press, publish propaganda against serfdom, and, ultimately, stir up a revolution among the peasantry and other discontented elements of the Russian population such as the religious dissenters (*raskolniky*).

Most of the other Petrashevtsy had merely indulged in harmless discussions without any thought of subversive activity; many could regard their imprisonment as a terrible mistake, a misunderstanding on the part of the authorities that would soon be cleared up. Twenty-four people known to have visited Petrashevsky, including Mikhail Dostoevsky, were in fact released as innocent in the course of the investigation. Dostoevsky, however, was one of the seven or eight members of the circle who had actually belonged to a secret underground organization with a well-defined revolutionary goal; and there is reliable evidence that, during the last few months before his arrest, he was deeply troubled and emotionally agitated by the risks he had pledged himself to assume.

Dr. S. D. Yanovsky, a close friend of Dostoevsky's as well as his personal physician, noted a distinct change in his mood during the winter and spring of 1848-1849. He became much more touchy, irritable, and quarrelsome than ordinary, and complained more frequently of nervous symptoms such as giddiness. Moreover, he told his doctor vaguely that his increased jumpiness and irascibility were the result of "his intimacy with Speshnev."[3] It is in light of this background that Dostoevsky's curious remark to his wife must be interpreted: no doubt the terror under which he was living had been so great that he later believed his sanity might have snapped if not for the providential accident of his capture. Once that which he had feared most—discovery and arrest—had actually occurred, all his energies could be mobilized for self-defense against a visible and tangible enemy, who proved to be much less terrifying than the indistinct forebodings that had worked up his nerves to a state of near hysteria in the preceding months.

2

Dostoevsky's first letter from the fortress, written on June 20, was addressed to his brother Andrey and forwarded by special permission; perhaps Andrey's mistaken arrest accounts for the leniency of the authorities in this instance. And Dostoevsky's words immediately strike the relatively cheerful note that remains constant throughout this period, continually triumphing over all the ample reasons that he had for dejection. "I hasten to inform you," he says, "that I am, thank God!, healthy, and though bored am very far from despondency. Every condition has its consolation, so don't worry about me."[4] Dostoevsky asks for information about the family of his brother Mikhail, then still a prisoner, and he tells Andrey to write to Moscow requesting help for himself, as well as for Mikhail and his family, from their wealthy Moscow relatives, the Kumanins. This appeal justifies, to a certain extent, Dostoevsky's claim that his first thought on being arrested had been to protect Mikhail and his dependents; if not his immediate and exclusive preoccupation, they were definitely of great concern to him all the same. Dostoevsky had also managed to wangle a loan of ten rubles from somebody in the fortress and hoped Andrey would enable him to repay the debt. Most important of all, though, he wanted to see a copy of the latest issue of *Notes of the Fatherland*. "The third part of my novel [*Netotchka Nezvanova*] is appearing, but without me, without my supervision, so that I didn't even see the galleys. I am worried. What have they printed and haven't they disfigured my novel?"[5] Dostoevsky seems much more concerned with this problem than about his personal predicament and possible fate, and there is no sign of any emotional perturbation at all. Some of the other Petrashevtsy, not so strong-minded, began to go to pieces in captivity as the months wore on and the interrogations continued.

At the beginning of July, the prisoners were given permission to receive books (there was a small library in the fortress, composed largely of religious works) and to correspond with the outside world. By this time Mikhail had been released, and Dostoevsky's letters to him continue to inform us about his physical condition and state of mind, which remain remarkably balanced and positive considering what he reports. "My health is good," he writes on July 18, "except for the hemorrhoids and my nervous troubles, which go *crescendo*. I have begun to have nervous spasms as before, my appetite is poor, and I sleep very little, with painful dreams when I do. I sleep about five hours of the twenty-four, and wake up about four times every night."[6] A month later, the report on his health indicates that it has deteriorated: "I have been living on castor oil for a whole month now and it is all that keeps me alive. My hemorrhoids are terribly inflamed and I have a pain in my chest I never had before. Moreover, my impressionability increases, especially at night; I have long, ugly dreams, and to top it all, I have recently felt all the time as though the floor were heaving under me, and I sit in my room literally as if in a ship's cabin. From all this, I conclude that my nerves are giving way."[7]

Nonetheless, Dostoevsky does not for a single moment surrender to complaint or to debilitating self-pity. "Generally speaking," he writes, "my time goes at an extraordinarily uneven pace—sometimes too fast, sometimes draggingly. Sometimes one almost feels that one is used to this kind of life and doesn't mind it. I try, of course, to drive any seductive thoughts out of my imagination, but occasionally there is no managing them, my old life simply forces itself into my mind, with all its old feelings, and the past comes to life again." The same letter illustrates this undermining intrusion of recollection as Dostoevsky slips into a worried nostalgia, recalling not only the immediate past—when Mikhail too had been a prisoner in the fortress—but also the carefree days of a vacation spent together on the Baltic, and, even farther back, his own school years as a student engineer. "Three months soon will have already passed since our imprisonment; what else is in store for us? Perhaps we shall not see the green

20

leaves this summer.* Do you remember how we were sometimes taken out to walk in the little garden in the month of May [the garden of the Ravelin]? It was just beginning to be green then, and it reminded me of Reval and staying with you there at about the same time of year, and of the garden of the Engineering School. And I always thought you must be making the same comparisons too—how sad it made me!"8

For the most part, however, Dostoevsky struggled more or less successfully against giving way to either retrospective melancholy or gloomy forebodings. In mid-September, he tells Mikhail that his health has not improved at all and that he is anticipating the advent of autumn with misgiving: "Now the difficult autumn months are at hand, and along with them my hypochondria. The sky is now beginning to scowl, and the clear patch of sky from my cell is the guarantee of my health and good spirits." Despite this unhappy prospect, though, Dostoevsky refuses to lose heart: "But meanwhile I am still alive and healthy. And this for me is a fact. So please don't imagine that I am especially badly off. For the moment my health is fine [?]. I expected it would be much worse; and now I see that I have such a reserve of vitality that it cannot be exhausted."9

The vitality that Dostoevsky so fortunately discovered in himself was more than a reserve of purely physical energy; it sprang much rather from his determination not to buckle under despite the pressure of all the forces assailing his mental and psychic stability. "I only wish to remain healthy," he writes Mikhail in the midst of the third month; "boredom is something transitory, and anyhow, *a good disposition depends on myself alone.* Man has infinite reserves of toughness and vitality; I really did not think there was so much, but now I know it from experience".10 One of Dostoevsky's greatest discoveries, in the solitary confinement of his cell, was precisely that of the resiliency and strength of the human spirit when thrown back on its own resources. He may have previously believed in such a power abstractly, but now this belief came to seem irrefutably self-evident and confirmed by his own successful inner struggle against despondency. The self, he knew, possessed powers of resistance that it could exert even under conditions of the extremest distress; man never had to renounce the autonomy of his personality if he chose—finally and stubbornly chose—not to do so.

3
———

Nothing worked more disturbingly on the nerves of the prisoners, in the first weeks of their isolation, than the lack of any occupation or distraction

---

* Leaves flowering in the spring continued to have an important emotive significance for Dostoevsky. "I have a longing for life," says Ivan Karamazov, "and I go on living in spite of logic. Though I may not believe in the order of the universe, yet I love the sticky little leaves as they open in the spring" (14: 210).

that could take their minds off their perilous situation. Jastrzembski remembered how delighted he had been when, after being questioned, he was finally given a few sheets of paper and asked to write a declaration. At last something to do, instead of sitting in endless and idle self-torment! Dostoevsky too, of course, spent a good deal of time occupied with his defense; but this did not really serve the purpose of psychic evasion, and the never-ending preoccupation with the same dangerous issues finally exercised a deadening effect. What he badly needs, he tells Mikhail, is some external mental impressions to revivify him, because the mind requires nourishment just as the body requires food. "Once again thank you for the books," he writes. "They are at least a way of passing the time. It is now very little short of five months that I have been living on my own resources, i.e., on my own mind alone and nothing more. So far the machine has not run down and still functions. However, endless thinking and nothing but thinking, without any external stimulation to renew and support the thought, is burdensome. It is like living within a vacuum pump from which air is always being sucked out. . . . Books may be only a drop in the ocean, but all the same they help."[11]

As a result, the moment he was given access to reading material, Dostoevsky threw himself on whatever was available with indiscriminate eagerness. "I have been able to read a little here: two pilgrimages to holy places, and the works of St. Dimitry Rostovsky," he informs Mikhail. "The last interested me greatly. . . ."[12] It is difficult to imagine Dostoevsky occupying himself with such works earlier; but now, he says, he is "unbelievably glad of any book. . . . Especially so for what might even be the curative effect of having one's train of thought interrupted by other people's ideas, or one's own rearranged on new lines."[13]

The particular interest he expresses in the works of St. Dimitry Rostovsky may indeed indicate the beginnings of such a "rearrangement" of Dostoevsky's ideas. St. Dimitry, the Metropolitan of Rostov, was an obscure seventeenth-century writer who belongs as much to Ukrainian as to Russian literature and whose works include a very popular version of the *Lives of the Saints*. These are based on earlier collections, but St. Dimitry retells the stories in a much livelier and more readable style influenced by Polish and Western European models. He was also a playwright who composed works on religious themes (the birth of Christ, the resurrection of Christ, the ascension of Mary) that were performed in the seminary at Rostov. Much like the Western medieval mysteries in conception, they contained Biblical figures and allegorical personifications representing virtues and vices and other abstract ideas. St. Dimitry ranks as an innovator in the history of Russian drama because he was the first to interweave the main religious episodes with interludes of realistic low comedy which, taken from peasant life, burlesque the solemnity of the central motifs. Dostoevsky

22

was later to mingle exalted religiosity and burlesque low comedy in *The Idiot* and *The Brothers Karamazov*, and he may well have been impressed by this aspect of St. Dimitry's stagecraft.

Regularly renewed in the letters to Mikhail are requests for copies of *Notes of the Fatherland*. "For I, in my role as an out-of-town subscriber," Dostoevsky writes jokingly, "await them [the issues] as an epochal event, like a landowner bored to death in the provinces." He also asks Mikhail for "works of history," and "best of all would be if you sent me the Bible (both Testaments). I need them. But if it's possible to send it, then forward the French translation. And if you could add the Slavonic one as well, that would be the very acme of perfection."[14] Why Dostoevsky particularly needed the Bible at this juncture, and both the French and Slavonic translations to boot, is by no means clear; perhaps he had decided to study it again intensively after reading the works of St. Dimitry and the two pilgrimages. Dostoevsky spoke later of having read and re-read the New Testament in his Siberian prison camp; but he had begun to immerse himself seriously in the sources of the Christian faith a good while earlier. Mikhail did send his brother the Bible, *Notes of the Fatherland*, and a French translation of Schiller's *History of the Thirty Years War*; a volume of Shakespeare was thrown in for good measure. "I particularly thank you for the Shakespeare," Dostoevsky writes delightedly in mid-September. "How could you have guessed?"[15]

4

As we can see, Dostoevsky eagerly pored over every bit of print that he received from the outside world; but what he comments on, in his letters to Mikhail, is the new material appearing in the *Notes of the Fatherland* rather than the classics. Much of what he talks about are translations because, at this period, Russian literature was muzzled by a censorship fiercer than any it had known for a long time, and few Russian writers were now willing to say anything that might be considered in the least provocative. Despite the sporadic incursions of Nicholas I and various other guardians of public morality and order, the period of the 1840s had been one of the most fertile and productive in the brief history of modern Russian literature. But, after the revolutions of 1848 in Europe, the relative tolerance of the past had been reversed, and Nicholas installed what has become known as "the era of censorship terror." A special commission, headed by the notoriously obscurantist Count Buturlin, was appointed to tighten the censorship. And the extent of Buturlin's capacities is indicated in a journal entry of P. V. Annenkov, who cites him as having said "that, if the Gospel were not as widespread as it was, it would be necessary to ban it on account of the democratic spirit it disseminated."[16]

As a consequence, more translations than ever appeared in the Russian periodical press at this time; but to a prisoner avid for any sort of literary provender, the lack of native texts could easily be overlooked. "You say that literature is ill," Dostoevsky writes to Mikhail, whose letter obviously had reflected the prevailing gloom in literary circles. "And yet the issue of the *Notes of the Fatherland* is as rich as ever, of course not in its literary section. There is not a single article that one does not read with pleasure. The section on science [*nauka* in Russian, which includes history and philosophy] is marvelous. *The Conquest of Peru* is a whole *Iliad*, and, in truth, is as good as last year's *Conquest of Mexico* [both by the American historian William Prescott]. Who cares whether it's a translation?"[17] In his next letter, Dostoevsky remarks appreciatively that "the English novel in the *Notes of the Fatherland* is extremely good."[18] The novel in question happens to be Charlotte Brontë's *Jane Eyre*; and while it is no surprise to find Dostoevsky recognizing literary quality when he comes across it, there are some special reasons why *Jane Eyre* might have particularly appealed to him.

In the first place, he was probably struck by its resemblance to his own *Netotchka Nezvanova*, an installment of which had just recently appeared (without the name of the author) and which Dostoevsky never completed because of his arrest. Like Netotchka, Jane is a poor orphan girl of unusual intelligence and character, struggling to make her way despite penury and social prejudice. Dostoevsky would also have responded favorably to Jane's sympathy for the mute and despised lower classes, whose sufferings she has shared, and approved her willingness as a teacher to unlock the doors of learning to their daughters. In addition, *Jane Eyre*, like *Netotchka Nezvanova*, is cast in the first-person form of an autobiography, and there is also some similarity to Dostoevsky's early work (*The Double*, *The Landlady*) in Charlotte Brontë's use of Gothic conventions, not merely for external shock effect, but to suggest nonrational depths of personality.

Nor could the future creator of Raskolnikov have failed to notice how Charlotte Brontë dramatizes Jane's romantic dilemma (whether or not to become the mistress of Rochester) as a conflict between the laws of God and the temptation to seek individual happiness at whatever price. "If at my individual convenience I might break them [the laws of God]," she asks herself, "what would be their worth?"[19] Raskolnikov will not hesitate to reply that the laws of God are worth very little, and he imagines himself capable of breaking them with impunity; but he will find that the burden of having done so is more than he can bear. Finally, there is a marked resemblance between Jane's relation to the blind and mutilated Rochester, at the end of *Jane Eyre*, and the very similar relation between the helpless, feeble-minded Versilov and his all-forgiving peasant wife at the conclusion of *A Raw Youth*.

Dostoevsky responded with equal fervor and enthusiasm to the Russian contributions in *Notes of the Fatherland*, even commenting favorably on a discussion of banks. He was also moved to encomium by an article of his old professor, I. I. Davydov, with whom he had studied literature in Moscow during his last year at Chermak's boarding school in 1837. Davydov was a polymath who, at various times, had taught mathematics, philosophy, and literature; his chief claim to fame was that he had helped to introduce Schelling's ideas into Russia in the 1820s. His article dealt with Homer's *Odyssey*, then being widely discussed in connection with V. A. Zhukovsky's new translation. "I read with great pleasure the second article analyzing the *Odyssey*," Dostoevsky informs Mikhail, "but this second article is much less good than the first by Davydov. That was a brilliant piece; especially that section, where he refutes Wolf, is written with such a deep understanding of the subject, with such fire, that one hardly would have expected it from such a veteran professor. In that article he even manages to avoid pedantry, typical of scholars in general and Moscovite ones in particular."[20]

The well-known theory of the eighteenth-century classicist F. A. Wolf maintained that "Homer" had never existed in fact but was a fictitious personage, whose name had become attached to the final redaction of the two Greek epics. These were not, Wolf argued, the creation of any one writer; rather, they had been woven together from the fragments of a long line of rhapsodes who elaborated various parts of the story. It seems clear that Davydov had defended the Romantic conception of an actually existing Homer as the single creator of the works, and that Dostoevsky agreed with him wholeheartedly. Such agreement, moreover, documents more than an opinion on an obscure point of literary doctrine; it takes us back to a statement made by Dostoevsky years before, in an earlier letter to Mikhail, in which he had asserted that "Homer (perhaps a legendary person like Christ, incarnated by God and sent to us) can be paralleled only with Christ. . . ."[21]

Homer and Christ, in other words, had shared the same God-man status in Dostoevsky's eyes, and his excitement over the article involving the first could scarcely have been unrelated to his devotion to the second. Indeed, the existence of Christ had recently been attacked on much the same grounds, and using much the same type of argument, as Wolf had used to dissolve Homer into a myth. D. F. Strauss, in his epochal *Life of Jesus*—a book that Dostoevsky had withdrawn from the library of the Petrashevsky circle and presumably read—had argued that the Gospels were merely a compilation of the myths of the Jewish people. Jesus himself, if he actually existed as a historical personage, was only one of the many itinerant prophets of those Messianic days around whom the myths had accidentally accumulated. Dostoevsky's comment on Homer thus obliquely confirms his refusal to accept the conclusions of the dominant Left Hegelian ideas which, in the late 1840s, had converted many of the Russian Westerners to atheism.*

Also touching Dostoevsky closely, but in a different context, was another work on which he offers a judgment—his only negative one—Turgenev's play *The Bachelor* (*Kholostyak*). "Turgenev's comedy," he says, "is unpardonably awful. Why does he have such bad luck? Is he really inescapably condemned to spoil every one of his works longer than a printed sheet? I don't recognize him in this comedy. Nothing original: an old, well-worn path. All this was said before him, and much better. The last scene smacks of childish incapacity. Something glimmers here and there, but this something is good only for lack of anything better."[22] Dostoevsky and Turgenev had been friends for a brief period in 1845, and Dostoevsky had inordinately admired—surely with a touch of jealous envy—the elegant, nonchalant, and talented young scion of the gentry who had already given proof that he was destined for a notable literary career. But Dostoevsky's conspicuous vanity, in the first flush of his success over *Poor Folk*, had grated on Turgenev's nerves, and the friction between them finally led to an open break. One might suspect Dostoevsky's negative reaction to be only a reflection of this mutual antagonism; but his personal squabbles with Turgenev never prevented him from appreciating the latter's talent, and Dostoevsky in this instance has some good, objective grounds for his evaluation.

The Bachelor is very far from being one of Turgenev's literary triumphs, and, as V. V. Vinogradov has convincingly shown, the play is strongly influenced by Dostoevsky's own work in both theme and style.[23] The central situation is exactly the same as that of his first novel, *Poor Folk*, but without the social pathos that Dostoevsky exploited by placing his characters in poverty-stricken circumstances. Just as Dostoevsky's Makar Devushkin protects Varvara Dobroselova, so a good-hearted, rough-hewn, middle-aged bureaucrat named Moshkin (the bachelor) takes under his wing a much younger girl who becomes his ward. In *Poor Folk*, a similar situation ends tragically when the girl vanishes into the steppe as the bride of a brutal landowner; but when Marya's fiancé deserts her for reasons of social snobbery, Moshkin proposes himself and is accepted. The play thus concludes with a completely unconvincing happy ending that reverses

* This similarity between the theories of D. F. Strauss and F. A. Wolf has been noted from time to time. Jean Pommier, writing about Ernest Renan, remarks that Renan's conception of Christ was influenced by both writers. Renan, he points out, distinguished Christ as an individual and a private person, about whom we know almost nothing ("the Galilean who bore the name"), from Christ as a type. The latter is of much greater importance for him, and "not only because he has read Strauss." It is also because "his [Renan's] sensibility has inhaled the Romantic theory which served to authorize works like those of F. A. Wolf, as a result of which 'Homer drowns his personality in the bottomless ocean of humanity.' " Jean Pommier, *Un itinéraire spirituel* (Paris, 1972), 27-28.

Dostoevsky's far more persuasive resolution. It is this last scene of proposal and acceptance that, in his view, "smacks of childish incapacity," and he could justly accuse Turgenev of trodding a well-worn path because it was one he himself had smoothed.

5

Dostoevsky's absorption with literature during his months in prison was not confined to the passive role of reader; he also tried, as best he could, to continue actively with the work of creation. "I have some occupation," he tells Mikhail in his first letter. "I have not been wasting my time: I have thought out three stories and two novels; one of them I am now writing, but I am afraid to work too much."[24] The continuation of this letter, and some remarks in a slightly later one, provide precious information on Dostoevsky's state of mind while engaged in composition.

For one thing, Dostoevsky was afraid to write too uninterruptedly, "because of its effect on the nerves, especially when it is done with pleasure (and I have never worked so much *con amore* as now). When I was working in freedom, I was always having to interrupt myself with distractions, but here the tension that follows writing must pass of itself."[25] In the next letter, after describing his sensation that the floor of his cell was rocking like a ship's cabin, he continues: "When I was attacked by similar nervous states in the past, I made use of them to write—I can always do more and better writing in this condition—but now I have to hold back, so as not to finish myself off for good."[26] Dostoevsky, it is clear, composed in a high state of nervous excitement, whose pressure only increased as work progressed; and some break or relaxation was absolutely indispensable to maintain his balance and ability to function.

In prison, he apparently jotted down notes for a number of works including plays as well as prose fiction. None of these plans, however, have survived; the only project he completed was the story now called *A Little Hero* but entitled originally *A Tale of Childhood*. It was given to Mikhail, along with his brother's other papers, after Dostoevsky had been sent to Siberia; eight years later, even before Dostoevsky was certain that he had received permission to publish again, it was printed anonymously in *Notes of the Fatherland*. *A Little Hero* is the story with which Dostoevsky made his reappearance on the Russian literary scene, but it belongs properly with his other works of the 1840s. And even though, as he said to Vsevolod Solovyev, it bears no obvious traces of the gloomy circumstances under which it was written, one can still detect some covert connections between this charming tale and the situation of its author.

The first that springs to mind derives from the tone and setting of the story itself. It takes place in a world that Dostoevsky rarely touches elsewhere, and not at all in the 1840s: the world of wealthy landowners living grandly on their country estates and entertaining a swarm of guests in lavish splendor—the world of Turgenev and Tolstoy rather than of Dostoevsky. This setting is so atypical for him that one cannot help surmising it to be a deliberate attempt to escape imaginatively from the grim fortress, with all the unhappiness it might presage for the future. What a relief to dwell in a climate of elegance, laughter, and beauty, of tender delicacy of sentiment and awakening erotic passion! In this sense, the story's very remoteness from Dostoevsky's actual surroundings may be taken as an expression of his emotive need to seek refuge outside their confines.

Placed in the context of his other work of the 1840s, *A Little Hero* has obvious thematic resemblances both with *Netotchka Nezvanova* (the central figure is a child) and with *White Nights* (which also depicts the awakening of a character to love). The tonality of the frame narrative—eliminated by Dostoevsky in the definitive version of the story published in 1860, and not included in the English translation—also reinforces the relation to *White Nights*. For the story is orginally told as a fragment of the past, and the mature narrator at the outset, remembering his boyhood, speaks in the shy but ardent accents of the sentimental-romantic hero of Dostoevsky's most luminous and ingratiating early story. There are also, however, significant differences between *A Little Hero* and these other works. The child in this case, unlike Netotchka, has not been battered and bruised by life; nor is he, like the young man in *White Nights*, "a dreamer" immersed in the world of Romantic fantasy. He is a perfectly normal and ordinary eleven-year-old boy on the threshold of adolescence, whose adventure simply marks the progression from childhood to youth and early manhood, the time of the awakening of the senses and the pursuit of the opposite sex. The "little hero" falls desperately in love with the beautiful and melancholy Madame M., leaps on the back of an untamable thoroughbred so as not to suffer humiliation in her eyes, and aids in concealing her grand (perhaps even pure) passion for another gentleman from her hateful husband. At the end, he is rewarded with a burning kiss and a lace kerchief as a memento of his boyish ardors.

6
———

The story is thus purely personal, a deft psychological sketch notable in Dostoevsky's work only for the "normalcy" of the passions it depicts. All the same, it contains certain intriguing elements that call for some further comment. There is, for example, the character of Madame M., who is described not only as being beautiful but also as having "mild, gentle features which recalled the serene faces of Italian Madonnas" (2: 273), and whose expression is saddened by some hidden grief. Her character and situation are similar to that of Alexandra Mikhailovna in *Netotchka Nezvanova*, and Madame M. too is distinguished by an instinctive moral sympathy for others. "There are women who are like sisters of mercy in life" (ibid.), writes the mature "little hero" as narrator, and Madame M. was one of them. It is characteristic that he falls in love with her rather than with the "wonderfully good-looking" blonde and high-spirited lady who teases him unmercifully; physical beauty alone will rarely attract a Dostoevsky protagonist, who is usually drawn to those who suffer.

The most developed character portrait is devoted, curiously enough, to Madame M.'s complacent and self-centered husband. Mr. M. is not a sadistic hypocrite like Peter Alexandrovich in *Netotchka Nezvanova*, who, under the guise of tolerant understanding, tyrannizes his helpless wife; rather, Mr. M. is someone pretending to embody a human quality he does not possess and whose outstanding traits are the very opposite of his wife's spiritual sensitivity. Dostoevsky describes him as "before all things a European, a modern man, who sampled the newest ideas and prided himself upon them." But this "Europeanism" turns out to be only a mask for selfishness and cold indifference: "You continually hear from such men that there is nothing they can do owing to certain very complicated and hostile circumstances, which 'thwart their genius,' and that it was 'sad to see the waste of their talents.'" Mercilessly censorious of others, they refuse to recognize any defects in themselves; though they really have "a lump of fat for a heart," they have persuaded themselves—and the rest of the world—"that they are honest men and that their roguery is honesty. . . . Their own priceless personality, their Baal and Moloch, their magnificent *ego* is always in the foreground everywhere" (2: 275-276).

Dostoevsky's attack on Mr. M., at first sight, recalls the opprobrium that he heaps on similar characters in his early stories and in one of his feuilletons of 1847; there is no lack of such jabs at a surface of complacent respectability concealing arrant egoism and personal viciousness. The particular vehemence of the language in *A Little Hero* may be attributed to Dostoevsky's resentment, sitting as he was in prison, against those who cheapened and exploited for their own advantage the social idealism he had courageously tried to put into practice. But there are certain aspects of Mr. M.'s portrait that go beyond a general type and take on an intriguing ideological specificity—for example, his so-called Europeanism. "They [people like Mr. M.] have a particular set of phrases for proclaiming profound sympathy for humanity, for defining what is the most correct and rational form of philanthropy, and for continually attacking romanticism, in other words, everything fine and true, each atom of which is more precious than all their slimy breed. But they coarsely fail to recognize the truth in an indirect, transitional and unfinished form, and they reject everything that is immature, still fermenting and unstable" (2: 276-277).

29

The harshness of such words seems to indicate that Dostoevsky is aiming at a particular target, but it is difficult to identify who (or what) it might be.* Nonetheless, Dostoevsky's defense of "romanticism," it is striking to see, is cast in the same terminology that he employs in his deposition for the Commission of Inquiry. For in that document he calls Utopian Socialism "a science in ferment" and characterizes it as immature and still in a state of transition.† People like Mr. M. hypocritically wish to "rationalize" it in some way, but in doing so they only betray their egoism and the baselessness of their supposed love for humanity. Dostoevsky thus appears to be defending the emotive roots of his own "philanthropy" (a code word for the moral-religious and vaguely Socialist progressivism of the 1840s) against the attempt to "rationalize" what should spring from compassion or fellow-feeling. Egoism and rationalism, in other words, are beginning to become amalgamated in Dostoevsky's sensibility: both are the enemies of genuine sympathy springing from the heart, and they are the attributes of a character preening himself on being "European." This is a cluster of qualities that will become very important for Dostoevsky later, when the pattern will be used, not only to depict a type taken from the ruling strata of Russian society, but also to describe the ravages of European radical ideology among the less affluent intelligentsia.

There are still two other aspects of *A Little Hero* that deserve mention. Even though the main intrigue—the worshipful adoration of the young lad for his beloved—is banal enough, his devotion to her is demonstrated by his concealment of her relation to a more mature lover. In other words, his love consists in accomplishing an act of self-sacrifice to aid a suffering soul and in being able to keep a secret. Might not Dostoevsky have seen himself precisely in some such terms? He had, after all, sacrificed himself to free the suffering Russian people and was still in the midst of a struggle to keep the secret of the conspiracy from the authorities. Whether justified or not, such a conjecture provides a possible glimpse into the source of

---

* A possible clue may be found in one detail of the story: Dostoevsky writes of Mr. M., "He was called a *clever man*," and emphasizes the appellation with italics. Just about a year before, and in an article that Dostoevsky was not likely to forget—it contained a harsh criticism of his story *The Landlady*—Belinsky had spoken of a character in Goncharov's *An Ordinary Story* in the same way. Peter Aduev, he had written, "is a very good man in his way: he is clever, very clever. . . ." There is a certain similarity in the values espoused by Peter Aduev and Mr. M., and Dostoevsky may thus have been sniping directly at this evaluation of the type—as well as indirectly at Belinsky, who was then precisely in the process of "rationalizing" his previous ideas about "philanthropy." V. G. Belinsky, *Izbrannye Filosofskie Sochineniya*, 2 vols. (Moscow, 1948), 2: 491.

† Dostoevsky's exact words to the Commission of Inquiry are as follows: "Socialism is a science in ferment, a chaos, alchemy rather than chemistry, astrology rather than astronomy. It seems to me, however, that out of the present chaos something consistent, logical, and beneficial will be worked out for the common good." For more discussion of this opinion, and for Dostoevsky's extremely judicious evaluation of early Utopian Socialism, see my *Dostoevsky, The Seeds of Revolt, 1821-1849* (Princeton, 1976), 252-256.

the story as a transposition of Dostoevsky's own perilous and (as he certainly felt at the time) heroic situation.

Totally unexpected, but also very intriguing, is the sudden allusion to the Sermon on the Mount that crops up in the midst of one descriptive passage. During a pause, sitting with his fair lady in a forest glade, the little hero becomes aware of nature in all its splendor. "The never ending concert of those who 'sow not, neither do they reap' and are as free as the air they cleave with their sportive wings was all about us. It seemed as though at the moment every flower, every last blade of grass, exhaling its sacrificial aroma, was saying to its creator: Father! I am blessed and happy!" (2: 292-293). The evocation of the birds "free as the air" takes on a special poignancy, coming from the pen of the imprisoned Dostoevsky; but the religious overtones of the text are of equal, if not greater, interest.

Nothing similar to this prayer of nature can be found in any of Dostoevsky's other works of the 1840s, and it may have been an accidental result of his reading both in the works of St. Dimitry and in the Bible; no intrinsic reason would seem to account for the embellishment of this brief pastoral evocation with an allusion to the Sermon on the Mount. But the man who wrote it seems already to have begun groping his way toward that "regeneration" which, in the future, will take him from a revolt against certain social arrangements of God's world—a revolt whose motives he will never cease to regard with a certain sympathy—to a reverent acceptance of its eternal blessedness and beauty.

CHAPTER 4

"Clever, Independent, Cunning, Stubborn"

Whatever the transformation that Dostoevsky may have begun to undergo during his stay in prison, there is no evidence that he abandoned any of the beliefs that had sent him there initially. Twenty-four years later, in the *Diary of a Writer*, he wrote that, "if not all, then at least a considerable majority of us (the Petrashevtsy) would have considered it dishonorable to renounce our convictions" under the pressure of arrest; and these words have since been confirmed, at least so far as Dostoevsky himself is concerned, by the publication of the documents relating to his case.[1] These documents have all been available since the 1930s, but surprisingly little use has been made of them to illuminate his ideas and attitudes at this period.

It has been generally assumed that material of this kind, written in answer to unspecified accusations and attempting to parry the suspicions in the minds of his interrogators, could hardly be accepted at face value. No one can quarrel with such an assumption; but there is no reason, all the same, to discard this mass of evidence as entirely untrustworthy. Much of what Dostoevsky told the Commission of Inquiry represented what he genuinely thought and believed; a good portion falsifies more by what he omits than by what he asserts. Even that part which is questionable—because too obviously self-serving, or in contradiction with other evidence now at our disposal—helps to light up the course of his future evolution. What is important is not so much the probable veracity of this or that isolated statement but the general views that emerge from his attempt at self-defense; and these views anticipate, to a surprising degree, many that have ordinarily been assigned to a much later stage of Dostoevsky's development.

No one scrutinizing what Dostoevsky wrote and said, so far as his words are recorded, can have the slightest doubt about several crucial matters. He did not believe that anything he had done was morally reprehensible; he did not feel even the slightest degree of contrition or remorse; and he tried, as best he could, to protect and defend others as well as himself. Two years after being released from prison camp, in March 1856, Dostoevsky wrote to General E. I. Totleben, an old acquaintance from his days as a cadet in the Academy of Engineers and now a national hero after supervising the fortification of Sevastopol during the Crimean War. "When I went off to Siberia," he told him, "I took with me at least the consolation of having behaved honorably in the investigation, not imputing my guilt to others, and even sacrificing my own interests if I saw the possibility of protecting others from trouble in my deposition. But I held myself in check, I did not confess everything, and for this I was punished more severely."[2]

The mixed Military-Civil Court that sentenced Dostoevsky gauged the severity of its punishment according to whether the accused had exhibited any repentance, or had freely revealed facts otherwise unknown that might have remained undiscovered. Dostoevsky did neither—unlike Speshnev, for example, who told of secret conversations with Petrashevsky and also disclosed the existence of the smaller Palm-Durov circle, which had escaped the vigilance of Antonelli. In addition, Dostoevsky continually tried to shield others in his testimony and to depict whatever might seem suspicious about them in the most harmless light. He had every reason to be proud of his behavior in this harrowing situation, whose strain caused many others to break down and beg for mercy—even though his letter to Totleben indicates that he may have begun to have some regrets about his intransigence. Much later, however, when he had become a notorious opponent of the radicals—who were, in their own eyes, carrying on the revolutionary traditions of the Petrashevtsy—the memory of his uprightness served him as consolation and as psychological support. For Dostoevsky knew inwardly that, even though he had become converted into a supporter of Tsarism, his change of heart had not been accompanied by any betrayal of principle or of his own standards of personal integrity.

2
—————

The most important document that Dostoevsky wrote for the Commission of Inquiry was an "Explanation," which he was asked to submit immediately after the preliminary questioning on May 6. Even though no formal accusations were ever made, the questions put to him indicated the grounds on which he had been taken into custody. Accordingly, he attempted in his "Explanation" to clarify his actions so as to justify, or at least to defend, whatever about them might be considered suspicious and subversive.

From the attitude of his interrogators, it was clear that Dostoevsky's participation in the meetings of the Petrashevsky circle was itself considered a criminal act; and his first concern was thus to minimize such participation as far as possible. In doing so, however, he sticks close to the truth, so far as it can be established. "I did not visit him (Petrashevsky) very often," he writes. "It sometimes happened that I was absent for more than six months."[3] It was only beginning in the fall of 1848, at a time when most of the progressive Russian intelligentsia had been stirred by the revolutions of 1848, that Dostoevsky began to visit Petrashevsky with any regularity. Even then his attendance was sporadic, and during the last few months of the circle's activity he spent much more time at the meetings of the smaller Palm-Durov group; but he said nothing about them in his "Explanation" because their existence had not yet been discovered.

Dostoevsky also described his personal relations with Petrashevsky as being quite distant, and he painted a portrait of the latter that was far from flattering: "He was one of those acquaintances of mine whom I did not value very highly, not having any similarity with Petrashevsky either in character or in ideas. And so I kept up my acquaintance with him only as much as politeness required. . . ."[4] Here again there is no reason to suspect Dostoevsky of evading the truth; people drifted in and out of the Petrashevsky circle quite casually, and occasional attendance did not prove any particular intimacy with the host.

The image that Dostoevsky gives of Petrashevsky is that of a strange and eccentric character, constantly and fussily occupied with what, to others, seemed like futilities, a personage hardly to be taken seriously from any practical point of view. "Over some matter worth nothing," Dostoevsky writes, "he sometimes takes as much trouble as if everything he owned were involved. Another time he hastens somewhere for a half-hour to finish up some minor matter, and to finish with such a minor matter would take at least two years. He is a man eternally bustling about and in movement, eternally busy about something."[5] Such words, tending to undermine any possibility that Petrashevsky's frenetic busyness could constitute any danger to the state, by inference made Dostoevsky's own participation in such activity equally innocuous. Yet the opinion expressed here about Petrashevsky corresponded to Dostoevsky's genuine estimate of his capacities. For he had told his friend Apollon Maikov, just a few months before being arrested, that "Petrashevsky, really, is a fool, a play actor and a chatterer; nothing sensible would ever come out of him. . . ."[6]

Dostoevsky characterizes the meetings of the Petrashevsky circle as equally innocent, much more a social diversion than anything resembling a political conspiracy: "I never encountered any unity in the Petrashevsky group, any tendency, any united aim. I can say positively that it was impossible to find three people in any sort of agreement on whatever point came up for discussion."[7] This account jibes with all the others that were given of the circle by various members, and is also verified by Dostoevsky's actions. It was precisely because he found no unity of any kind among the Petrashevtsy, no common goal that could be translated into any plan of action, that he eventually became a member of Speshnev's secret revolutionary organization.

3

After countering the possibly damning effects of his association with Petrashevsky, Dostoevsky gets down specifically to the accusations that he suspected were being formulated against him in the minds of his judges. First, he tries to dispose of the charge that he had "participated in public discussions at Petrashevsky's" and had spoken there "in a freethinking fashion."[8] Dostoevsky, of course, did not know how much information the Commission might have gathered about inflammatory words he may have uttered on various occasions, and so he begins by casting doubt on the feasibility of judging him by verbal utterances alone. What criterion is being used to evaluate his words? "I say quite sincerely that up to the present the most difficult thing in the world for me has been to define the words: *free thinking, liberal.*" It is impossible, he argues, to judge a man solely on the basis of what he may have said: "Who has seen into my soul? Who has determined that degree of perfidy, harm, and revolt of which I am accused? By what standard has the determination been made?"[9]

In any case, Dostoevsky continues, he had spoken only three times at Petrashevsky's and then on non-political topics. "I do not recall," he asserts enigmatically, "that I ever expressed myself *entirely, as I truly am*, at Petrashevsky's" (italics in text).[10] This astonishing hint to the Commission that he had nourished secret thoughts never uttered at Petrashevsky's was hardly prudent; it might easily have led to further questioning if the Commission had been inclined to pick up the suggestion. To be sure, the sentence may have slipped out inadvertently: the manuscript of the "Explanation" is full of corrections and word changes, and it was obviously written with much uncertainty and under great nervous stress. It may also have sprung, however, from an uncontrollable urge—so similar to that of Raskolnikov fifteen years later—to harry and toy with the guardians of the law by cryptic confessions and to take a malicious pleasure in their obtuseness and incomprehension. Since the Commission never learned of the existence of the Speshnev secret group, it never discovered what Dostoevsky "truly was" at this time of his life.

But Dostoevsky remains on this slippery terrain only for an instant, quickly returning to the much safer ground of attempting to justify what could be considered his "freethinking" and "liberalism." And his tone is one of implicit defiance; he offers no apology of any kind, but much rather an assertion of his *right* to concern himself with matters that could be considered to fall within these forbidden domains. "Yes, if *to desire improvement* is liberalism, *freethinking*, then in this sense perhaps," he concedes, "I am a *freethinker*"—surely words hardly designed to placate his interlocutors! But he hastens to add that, from this point of view, every honest citizen worried about the welfare of his country can also be considered to belong in the same category, and he insists that he never desired "improvements" to be brought about "by force, in a revolutionary manner, stirring up gall and bitterness!"[11] At first he challenges the Commission to prove this latter contention to be false; but then—as if fearing that proof might well be forthcoming—he falls back again on the impossibility of deducing his intimate convictions from his words: "And I am not afraid of evidence because no denunciation in the world can take anything from me or add anything to me; no denunciation can cause me to be other than I am as a matter of fact."[12]

Not content with this rather feeble defense, Dostoevsky then has recourse to what is certainly the most bizarre vindication recorded in the entire annals of the Petrashevsky proceedings. For he maintains that, far from proving any hostility to the régime, whatever inflammatory words he may have uttered should be taken as an exhibition of his trust in the government as the guardian of the rights enjoyed by the citizens of a civilized state! "Does my freethinking consist in having spoken out loud on the subjects about which others think it a duty to keep silent! . . . But I was always offended by this fear of speech, much more apt to be offensive to the government than agreeable to it. . . . This means that one assumes the law does not adequately protect the individual, and that it is possible to be destroyed because of an empty word, an incautious phrase."[13] It is impossible to imagine Dostoevsky advancing such an argument except with bitter irony; no one could believe that the government of Nicholas I was *insulted* by the terrified silence of its citizens and wished them to utter their opinions on social-political topics more vociferously! Once again we catch a glimpse of some of the biting sarcasm that Raskolnikov would one day use to address those who regarded him with suspicion and mistrust.

4
————

Dostoevsky's replies did not stop with such general attempts to deny any wrongdoing; he also tried to answer the more concrete charges that he could imagine being leveled against him. "But of what am I accused?" he asks plaintively. "Evidently, that I have spoken about politics, the West, the censorship, etc. But who has not spoken and not thought about these questions in our time? Why did I study, why did knowledge awaken my curiosity, if I do not have the right to express my opinion or to agree with such opinions as are authoritative in themselves?"[14] This heartfelt outcry bluntly expresses the actual situation of repression under which the Russian intelligentsia suffered; there is no longer any pretense that the fear of speaking out was self-imposed, the result of a regrettable misinterpretation of what the régime desired. And Dostoevsky now goes on to discuss his specific views in a manner that, if somewhat adjusted to make them more palatable to his judges, nonetheless already reveals certain patterns of thought whose constancy entitles us to accept them as his genuine convictions. "In the West," he writes, "a terrible spectacle is taking place, an unexampled drama is being played out. The age-old order of things is cracking and falling to pieces. The most fundamental principles of society threaten to collapse at any moment, and to carry along an entire nation [France] in their fall." This nation is the land from which Russia itself had received the gifts of science, culture, European civilization. Is it surprising that educated Russians should be passionately involved with this great historical drama? "This, after all, is history—and history is the science of the future. . . . Is it possible to accuse me because . . . I consider this crisis, perhaps historically necessary in the life of this people, as a transitory phase (who can decide this now?) and which will lead, finally, to better times."[15] Dostoevsky thus implicitly admits that he may have expressed some sympathy with the revolution that had taken place in France and, a few sentences later, he repeats—underlining the key phrase for emphasis—that in his view "the Western revolution" is "*a historical necessity* of the contemporary crisis in that part of the world."[16]

Dostoevsky has thus already developed that apocalyptic view of Europe on the brink of crisis and collapse that he was to reiterate so many times in the future, and he also draws the same sharp line between Europe and Russia in this respect that was to remain a permanent feature of his thought. Vigorously denying that he considered any such revolution "a historical necessity" for his fatherland, he writes: "But if I spoke about the revolution in France, if I permitted myself to think about contemporary events, does it follow that I am a freethinker, that I have republican ideas, that I am an opponent of autocracy, that I am bent on undermining it? . . . In my eyes, nothing could be more nonsensical than the idea of a republican government in Russia."[17]

Such words offer an excellent illustration of how carefully one must weigh Dostoevsky's testimony to distinguish truth from falsity. For while he clearly *was* "an opponent of autocracy," in the sense of being willing to participate in a conspiracy against it, this does not mean that he was then, or ever would be, a partisan of political democracy or republican ideas. One of the important altercations at Petrashevsky's had focused on whether a dictatorship would be necessary during the turbulent period of revolutionary upheaval; and Petrashevsky, a genuine admirer of republican institutions, had been violently opposed even to contemplating any such possibility. But it was advocated by Dostoevsky's close friend V. A. Golovinsky, whom he had brought to the gatherings shortly before, and Dostoevsky intervened to support Golovinsky's position against Petrashevsky's vehement onslaught. Dostoevsky had no theoretical objections to autocratic rule at all; nor, it might be recalled, had most of the early Utopian Socialists like Fourier, who appealed unsuccessfully to several monarchs to finance the establishment of phalansteries in their countries. If Dostoevsky was willing to oppose autocracy, it was only because his hatred of serfdom had reached a pitch of intensity that swept aside all ancillary considerations.

To buttress his assertion of monarchical loyalty, Dostoevsky sketches a view of Russian history designed to indicate why, even though he may have regarded revolution as a "historical necessity" in France, this did not prove that he believed the same necessity existed for Russia. Relying on an image popularized in Walter Scott's *Ivanhoe* and then given authority by the Romantic historian Augustin Thierry, Dostoevsky describes European history as a more than one-thousand-year-old "very stubborn struggle between society and an authority deriving from a foreign civilization of conquest, force, and repression."[18] European society, in other words, is inherently unstable because it is based on the conquest of one race by another; the ruling class there always remains an alien conqueror to the lower classes whom it governs. This theory was much favored by the Slavophils, who used it as a contrast to reinforce their conviction of the natural harmony reigning between the autocracy and its subjects in Russia. But Thierry's reputation as a liberal also helped to make it acceptable to the progressive Westerners, and one of Alexander Herzen's first publications had been an essay on Thierry that prefaced some translations of extracts from his work.

In Europe, then, revolt was inevitable, and republican institutions were only a natural result of the desire of the lower classes to establish a defense against the alien races who had seized power over them. No such problem existed in Russia, where power was not in the hands of a foreign conqueror, and where, on the contrary, it had been the native autocracy that time and again had saved the country from enslavement and chaos. Russia had twice been rescued, Dostoevsky writes, "solely by the efforts of the autocracy: first from the Tartars, and second in the reforms of Peter the Great, when solely a warmly childlike faith in its great pilot made it possible for Russia to endure such a sharp swerve into a new life."[19] The providential role of the autocracy had been stressed in N. M. Karamzin's *History of Russia*, one of Dostoevsky's favorite books as a boy; and while he may now be advancing this conception as a means of exhibiting his fealty, there is every reason to believe that he was persuaded of its essential truth. For the same view will crop up again and again in his later utterances, and the glorification of Peter the Great by the Russian Westerners made the acceptance of an "enlightened" autocrat perfectly compatible with progressive opinions.

Indeed, the sentences that follow suggest how eagerly Dostoevsky would have welcomed a reforming Tsar willing to save the country again by eliminating the intolerable moral-social blight of serfdom. "Yes," he writes, "who among us thinks of a republic? If reforms are pending, it is clear as day even to those who desire them that such reforms must come from an authority even much more reinforced during this period; otherwise, the matter will have to be dispatched in a revolutionary fashion. I do not think that admirers of a Russian revolt can be found in Russia. Well-known examples are recalled to this day, though they occurred long ago."[20] This menacing reference to the bloody uprisings of Pugachev and Stenka Razin, prefiguring the kind of revolts that might be provoked again unless reforms were made, was hardly calculated to reassure Dostoevsky's judges. But when all hope of such reforms "from above" had been crushed after 1848, it was such reasoning that had persuaded Dostoevsky to participate in the desperate venture organized by Speshnev.

5

If Dostoevsky was still somewhat circumspect in his remarks about the necessity of reforms, he drops all caution when he comes to write about the depredations of the censorship. As a writer, he could legitimately complain of a personal grievance against its strictures—and to have some private and, as it were, *selfish* motive for discontent was far preferable to being considered a revolutionary out of theoretical and disinterested conviction. Dostoevsky thus made no effort to restrain himself in attacking the censorship, even though this was also not without its dangers. Nicholas I had ordered the surveillance of publications tightened in the winter of 1848-1849, and Dostoevsky was thus protesting against measures that, as was well known, had been mandated by the personal authority of the Tsar.*

How difficult to be a writer, Dostoevsky laments, when works are prohibited, "not because anything liberal, freethinking or immoral had been found in them, but because, for example, a story or novel ended too sadly, that it offered too gloomy a picture, even though this picture did not blame or suspect anybody in society, and even though the tragedy occurred in a completely accidental and external fashion." He invites the Commission

---

* The Soviet Russian editor of the valuable book containing the documents of Dostoevsky's case, N. F. Belchikov, cannot restrain an expression of admiration for Dostoevsky's intrepidity on this score. "Dostoevsky's condemnation of the politics of the censorship," he writes, "must be recognized as an act of civic courage." Living under a far more efficient censorship than any prevailing in the worst eras of Tsarism, Belchikov knows whereof he speaks. N. F. Belchikov, *Dostoevsky v Protsesse Petrashevtsev* (Moscow, 1971), 49.

to examine everything he had written himself, both in print and in manuscript, and unearth, if it could, a single word contrary to morality and the established order. "And yet I too have been similarly prohibited precisely because my picture was painted in too gloomy colors."[21] Little does the censorship know, Dostoevsky adds feelingly, how "gloomy" they make the life of the poor writer with their exactions! Not only does he see his time go for naught, but he is then forced, in order to gain a crust of bread, to paint life in the rosiest colors, although plunged himself in the blackest despair.

Dostoevsky tries to blunt the edge of this unsparing assault by again attributing the situation to a "misunderstanding"; but he maintains, all the same, that the fault lies with the censorship, not with the writers. Under the present circumstances, he insists, "whole genres of art have to disappear: satire, tragedy will no longer be able to exist. With the severity of the present censorship, such writers as Griboedov, Fonvizin, and Pushkin would not be able to exist either." Satire, Dostoevsky explains, requires that vice be ridiculed, although it often appears under the guise of virtue; but how can one ridicule anything these days? The censor sees insinuations everywhere, and every phrase, even the most innocent, is suspected of being *"harmful for society"* and is mercilessly excised (italics in text). Yet all this effort is wasted, because, by hiding vice and the somber side of life, "you [do not] hide from the reader that vice and the somber side of life really exist in the world." Further, "is it possible to write only with bright colors? How can the bright side of a picture be visible without the dark side? Can there be a picture without light and shadow together? . . . We are told: describe only heroism, virtue. But we know virtue only through vice; the very conception comes from the fact that good and evil always have lived together side by side."[22]

Since so little is known regarding Dostoevsky's opinions about "the people" before going to Siberia, another passage is particularly precious for disclosing a distinctly disparaging view of the peasantry, as well as for illuminating his conception of the social task of Russian literature. "Literature," he writes, "is one of the expressions of the life of the people, is a mirror of society. With education, with civilization, new ideas appear which require definition and designation in Russian, so as to be available to the people; for the people cannot name them under present circumstances, since civilization does not come from them but from above. Only that social group is able to name them which accepted civilization earlier than the people, i.e., the upper class of society, the class already educated for the acceptance of these ideas. Who formulates new ideas in such a form so that the people can understand them—who, if not those who create literature!"[23] A great social mission thus falls on the shoulders of Russian literature, and this is another reason, Dostoevsky explains, why he has been driven to desperation by the ravages of the censorship.

The condescending attitude expressed here toward "the people" was quite common in the 1840s, even among those Russian Westerners who were most concerned to abolish the glaring injustice of serfdom. The great critic V. G. Belinsky, who was the spiritual leader of the Westerners and launched Dostoevsky's career by his admiration for *Poor Folk*, was quite merciless in his gibes at the backward and unenlightened state of the peasantry. It was only the Slavophils who, at this period, saw any virtues in the life and native customs of the Russian people; but Slavophilism was rejected root and branch by the Westerners, and Slavophil opinions about the people were scarcely given serious consideration. Dostoevsky fully shared this combination of superior magnanimity in the abstract, and sniffish contempt in the concrete, which characterized the Westerners in their relation to the people—an attitude that changed only slightly in the late 1840s under the impact of growing Slavophil influence. Traces of this latter influence can be found in Dostoevsky's own views; but the decisive mutation occurred only when he met the people face to face in Siberia and was forced to realize that all his previous notions about them had been woefully in error.*

If Dostoevsky was drastically to alter his attitude about the people, however, what he says here about the role of Russian literature will remain largely immutable. He always objected to attempts to turn literature into an instrument of social propaganda to the detriment of its function as art; but this does not mean that he refused it an important social role. Quite the contrary, he saw literature as the vehicle of Russian enlightenment— the means through which the new ideas and ideals of civilization were given Russian form and made accessible to society at large. Even later, when Dostoevsky began to feel that European "civilization" could have negative and destructive effects as well, his attention as a writer always remained focused on the impact of European ideas in Russia. For him, the task of Russian literature would continue to be that of informing Russian society about the effect of European ideas on the national psyche,

---

* In this context, it is worth citing another passage in Dostoevsky's "Explanation." "In conclusion," he writes, "I recall my words, repeated by me at various times, that everything of any value in Russia, beginning with Peter the Great, invariably came from above, from the throne; while from below, up to the present, nothing had been manifested except obstinacy and ignorance. This opinion of mine is well known to my acquaintances." Belchikov, *Protsesse*, 101

That such a view of the people was not uncommon among the Russian Westerners is confirmed by P. V. Annenkov, who writes of the 1840s: "Literature and our cultivated minds had long ago relinquished the notion of the people as a human entity ordained to live without rights of citizenship and to serve the interests of others only, but they had not relinquished the notion of the people as a brutish mass without any ideas and with never a thought in its head." P. V. Annenkov, *The Extraordinary Decade*, ed. Arthur P. Mendel, trans., Irwin R. Titunik (Ann Arbor, 1968), 134.

and about the peculiar manner in which European ideas contributed to the formation of certain types of Russian mentality. And he eagerly remained on the alert to detect the new "types" in which such ideas were incarnated—no longer, to be sure, because he wanted to help spread their influence, but rather because he believed it imperative to warn of their dangers.

6
———

The gravest charge that Dostoevsky knew had been made against him was that, at the Petrashevsky gathering of April 15, he had read aloud the exchange of correspondence between Gogol and Belinsky provoked by the former's *Selected Passages from My Correspondence with Friends*. This work had created a huge scandal, primarily because Gogol had taken it upon himself to defend *all* the existing social-political structures of Russia as God-given and sacred, including the institution of serfdom. To make matters worse, the book was written in a suffocating tone of unctuous humility that even some of Gogol's closest friends found repellent—a tone, in addition, completely at odds with the overweening arrogance displayed by the author as he dispensed gratuitous advice right and left to all his correspondents on how best to conduct their lives.

No one was more outraged and indignant than Belinsky, whose critical articles had raised Gogol's *Dead Souls* to the status of a canonical text embodying the ideals of the progressive Westerners in their attack on the abuses of Russian society. Belinsky's negative opinion led to an exchange of correspondence culminating in his famous *Letter to Gogol*—a whitehot burst of rage against, as Belinsky saw it, the betrayer of the cause of humanity. Not only does Belinsky's letter bitterly denounce and demolish Gogol; it is equally violent against all those institutions of throne, state, and church that the erstwhile satirist had taken under his wing. The letter naturally circulated only in handwritten copies, one of which was sent to Dostoevsky from Moscow by a close friend, the young poet Aleksey Pleshcheev. Imprudently, Dostoevsky read it aloud to the Palm-Durov circle and then repeated the performance at Petrashevsky's; even worse, by lending it to others who wished to make copies, he took part actively in its dissemination. It is very likely that the Speshnev group intended to publish Belinsky's *Letter* on the handpress they had just succeeded in assembling at the time of the arrests.

Dostoevsky tries to ward off the incriminating effect of having read the correspondence, including Belinsky's *Letter*, by an ingenious, but hardly convincing, argument: "Yes, I read the article, but can whoever denounced me say to which one of the correspondents I was partial?"[24] Dostoevsky claimed that, since he had read the exchange of letters in a perfectly

42

neutral manner, it was impossible to tell which side he approved or rejected; but he knew that this line of defense was not very persuasive, especially since Belinsky's *Letter* had been greeted with great enthusiasm by the audience. Nor did his supposed neutrality explain why he should have undertaken to read the correspondence at all. To answer this question, which created an *ipso facto* presumption of participation in illegal activity, he blocks in a picture of his personal relations with Belinsky as a way of justifying his interest in the explosive missive.

For about a year and a half, from the late spring of 1845 to the winter of 1846-1847, Dostoevsky and Belinsky had indeed been very close. The influential critic had taken the talented young writer under his wing, and Dostoevsky, for a short while, became a member of that select group of Belinsky's friends known as his *pléiade*. But relations began to cool when Belinsky became highly critical of the turn taken by Dostoevsky's work after *Poor Folk*. "In the literary world," Dostoevsky writes, "very many know of my quarrel and final split with Belinsky." It would have been easy for Dostoevsky to take advantage of this well-known dispute between himself and the most notorious radical of the time, and to pretend to a greater estrangement from Belinsky than he actually felt; but he was unable or unwilling to sink to such perfidy. Instead, he assures the Commission that Belinsky was "the very best of men as a man" and implicitly attributes the break in their relation to the critic's final illness: "But the illness that sent him to his grave even destroyed the man in him. It embittered and hardened his soul, and flooded his heart with gall. His disordered and strained imagination magnified everything to colossal proportions. . . . Such failings and faults suddenly appeared in him of which there had not been a trace when he was healthy."[25] One can well imagine Dostoevsky consoling himself with such a version of his rift with Belinsky, and attributing the latter's wounding rejection of his later work in the 1840s to a distortion of judgment produced by his malady. In any case, Dostoevsky explains his quarrel with Belinsky on purely literary grounds, neglecting to mention the serious ideological disagreements that also existed between them. As a moral-religious progressive influenced by French Utopian Socialism, Dostoevsky considered his social idealism to be an up-to-date version of Christ's messages of brotherly love, and he stubbornly refused to be converted to the atheism advocated by Belinsky in the late 1840s after becoming acquainted with Left Hegelian thought. It is unlikely, however, that the arguments between the two over the immortality of the soul, or whether Christ would have been a leading social agitator in the modern world, would have led to any personal hostility. Both Petrashevsky and Nikolay Speshnev were staunch atheists who made no secret of their convictions, and such views did not prevent Dostoevsky from continuing to maintain good (and, in the case of Speshnev, very close) relations with them. The break with Belinsky probably occurred for the reasons that, touching him more intimately as a writer, Dostoevsky gave to the Commission.

"I criticized him for striving to give literature a partial significance unworthy of it," he writes, "degrading it to the description, if one may so express it, *solely of journalistic facts* or scandalous occurrences [italics in text]. I objected specifically that you do not attract anyone with biliousness, but only bore everybody to death when you clutch at everyone coming and going in the street, seize every passerby by the buttonhole, and begin to preach at him forcibly and teach him reason. Belinsky became angry with me, and finally from coolness it came to a formal quarrel, so that we did not see each other all through the last year of his life."[26] In his last years, Belinsky had indeed expressed a marked preference for a socially didactic literature and tended to give art less importance in itself (even if he did not go quite as far as Dostoevsky's words would indicate). But the "Explanation" probably reports quite accurately what the younger writer's wounded self-esteem prompted him to say during the heat of argument.

Such a version of the facts allows Dostoevsky to explain more or less persuasively why he should have had an interest in Belinsky's *Letter to Gogol* quite aside from its social-political content: "I have long wished to read this letter. In my eyes, this correspondence is a quite notable literary memorial. And Belinsky and Gogol are very notable figures; their relationship is very interesting, especially for me, who was acquainted with Belinsky. . . . I read through the work neither more nor less than as a literary memorial, firmly convinced that it could not lead anyone into temptation, although it is not lacking in some sort of literary value. So far as I am concerned, I do not agree exactly with a single one of the *exaggerations* that it contains" (italics added).[27]

This rather feeble disclaimer is as far as Dostoevsky could go in concealing his fundamental agreement with Belinsky's powerful assault; nor was his final effort to exonerate himself any more forceful. Since his quarrel with Belinsky was a matter of record, why, he asks his judges, do they assume he had read the *Letter to Gogol* with approval? His judges could well have replied that his quarrel with Belinsky, as he insisted himself, had concerned only literature, while the *Letter* was manifestly a social-political document. No doubt aware of the implausibility of his words, which could hardly fail to escape notice, Dostoevsky at this point makes his one and only concession to the perils of the situation and expresses regret at his lack of caution: "I have only now understood that I made a mistake and that I should not have read that work aloud: but then I was not aware of it and even could not suspect for what I might be blamed. I did not suspect that I had committed a sin."[28]

To conclude his "Explanation," Dostoevsky returns to the question of his relations with Petrashevsky and to the latter's ideas. He repeats a good deal of what he already had said about the lack of unity in the circle; and while conceding that he knows Petrashevsky to be an admirer of Fourier, he denies any knowledge of whether the latter wished to propagandize Fourier's ideas. To the Commission's inquiry as to whether Petrashevsky had made any disciples, particularly among the members of the circle who were teachers in various academic establishments in Petersburg, Dostoevsky replied: "I absolutely know nothing of the secrets of Petrashevsky."[29]

Dostoevsky, however, does not rest content with this refusal to answer. Wishing to prove that Petrashevsky could not possibly have done any harm, he proceeds to discuss Fourierism in general for the benefit of the Commission. In the first place, he explains, Fourierism "is a peaceful system; it captivates the soul by its beauty, seduces the heart with that love of mankind inspiring Fourier when he created his system, and surprises the mind with its rigor. It makes converts not by caustic attacks but by its inspiring love for mankind. There is no hatred in this system." Moreover, Dostoevsky adds, "Fourierism does not propose any political reforms; its reform is an economic one. It does not infringe on either government or property, and in one of the most recent sessions of the Chambre des Deputés [in France] Victor Considérant, the representative of the Fourierists, solemnly renounced any attempt to destroy the family."[30] Very unexpected here is Dostoevsky's lyrical glorification of the "beauty" of Fourierism; it reveals how powerfully this Utopian vision of a harmonious and peacefully happy mankind appealed to his sensibility. This mirage of a Golden Age of social justice—inspired by love of mankind, and to be ushered in peacefully rather than by hatred and violence—was always to remain Dostoevsky's social ideal. Later, it was to be the basis of that "Russian Socialism" which, he believed, would transform society purely through the moral-Christian impulses of the Russian spirit.

Indeed, one can discern in embryo many of the elements of this later doctrine already beginning to take shape in Dostoevsky's reflections on Socialism, particularly in his stress on the differences between the situation in Europe and that in Russia. For, despite his warm words of praise for Fourierism, he immediately adds that, "without doubt, this system is harmful, first, if only because it is a system. Secondly, no matter how beautiful, it is, all the same, a Utopia of the most unrealizable kind." As a matter of fact, Dostoevsky affirms that Fourierism is already completely out-of-date, ridiculed and unpopular even in Europe; its advocates there do not see that "they are living corpses, nothing more." But "in Europe, in France, at this time every system, every theory is harmful for society, since a hungry proletariat in desperation seizes on every means, and from every means is ready to make a banner. Over there the moment is one of extremity. There hunger stalks the streets." European socialism is thus seen by Dostoevsky as an artificial attempt ("a system") to cope with the menacing Western problem of a starving proletariat. Whether he actually believed it to be as "harmful" as he pretends may be left undecided; what counts is the diagnosis of the critical situation of Western society that necessarily gave birth to Socialist doctrines.

Once again, as he had done when speaking of republicanism, Dostoevsky sharply contrasts the state of affairs in Europe with that in Russia. "So far as we, in Russia, in Petersburg are concerned," he writes, "one has only to take twenty paces in the street to be convinced that Fourierism on our soil can exist only in the uncut pages of a book, or in a tender, kindly, and dreamy soul, but not otherwise than in the form of an idyll or a poem of this kind in twenty-four rhymed stanzas." Dostoevsky insists that the idea of applying Fourierism in Russia is simply comic, not to be taken seriously, and he assures the Commission that Petrashevsky is too intelligent a man ever to have had any such ridiculous whimsy. "Fourierism, and along with it every Western system, is so unsuited to our soil, so unrelated to our conditions, so alien to the character of our nation— while, on the other hand, it is so much a product of the situation of things there in the West, where the proletarian question is being solved at any cost—that Fourierism, with its relentless necessity, at the present time, among us who have no proletariat, would be killingly funny."[31]

Such words, proffered in such a context, would of course be suspect if we had no further information about Dostoevsky's views; but what he writes corresponds exactly with utterances that he had made quite freely in the Palm-Durov circle. According to Alexander Milyukov, while agreeing that the theories of the Socialists had a noble aim, Dostoevsky had considered them to be only admirable fantasies. "He especially insisted," Milyukov tells us, "that all these theories had no meaning for us, that we should seek the sources of the development of Russian society not in the teachings of the Western Socialists, but in the life and age-old historical structure of our people, where in the *obshchina* [village commune], *artel* [workers' cooperative], and *krugovaya poruka* [mutual tax responsibility] have long existed foundations more solid and normal than all the dreams of Saint-Simon and his school."[32] Even if Dostoevsky's ideas may not yet have acquired the precision given them half a century later in Milyukov's memoirs, it seems plausible that he had already begun to be attracted to a specifically "Russian" solution to the issues posed by European Socialism. All the more so because, as can be seen from his oblique reference to "relentless necessity," he had never been persuaded that Utopian Socialist communities were capable of guaranteeing the freedom of the individual personality. It is instructive to note, as well, that he had already found the *tone* in which he would later depict the Utopian Socialists: they were "killingly funny," and he would never portray them except in some such satirical and parodistic manner.

Dostoevsky terminates his "Explanation" with some observations about his fellow prisoners, and in doing so adopts a tactic that he uses throughout the interrogation—the tactic of attributing their culpable behavior to some defect of character. "I have long nourished the opinion," he remarks confidentially, "that Petrashevsky is infected with some sort of egotism. It was because of self-love that he invited people to his Fridays, and it was because of egotism that they did not bore him to death. Because of egotism he owned many books, and, it seems, took pleasure in having people know that he had hard-to-find books."[33] By this means—anticipating the outlook he would attribute, many years later, to the narrator of *The Devils*—Dostoevsky tries to reduce the social-political activities of the Petrashevtsy purely to the personal motives of egoistic self-display, vanity, or callow bravado. Such a psychological analysis, even if disparaging, is also clearly a method of protecting the people concerned, since faults of character are amenable to correction and improvement and would be seen as far less serious than a principled commitment to revolutionary aims.

8

During the month of June, Dostoevsky was called in four more times for interrogation and was also presented with a further list of questions to be answered in writing. The only other document of importance is the record of his replies, which include emendations and second thoughts that he added in the margins. By this time, the Commission of Inquiry had made considerable progress: it had learned a good deal about what had gone on in the Petrashevsky circle, discovered the existence of the Palm-Durov group, and gotten wind of the plan discussed there to lithograph prohibited texts for illegal circulation. Dostoevsky thus had to pick his way very carefully amidst many dangerous pitfalls, and we can watch him trying not to be trapped in an outright lie, or seeming to hold back information at his disposal, while guarding against any utterance that might prove injurious to himself or to others.

Several of the questions posed in this second document indicate suspicions of an organized revolutionary conspiracy, and with these Dostoevsky was particularly on his guard. He denied that his youthful friend Golovinsky had advocated a revolution in order to obtain the liberation of the serfs, or had envisaged "a revolutionary dictatorship" during the period of turmoil and transition to a new government. Similarly, he denied ever having heard Petrashevsky entertain the idea of revolution and remarked that, if such a revolt were really being planned, it would hardly have been discussed openly at the meetings. Here we have Dostoevsky, the underground conspirator, stealthily giving the Commission the benefit of his experience—certainly with an inner smile of contempt at their ineptitude! His replies to all such questions were invariably evasive or consisted of elaborate circumlocutions intended to confuse the issue entirely. No wonder General Rostovtsev commented that, as a witness, Dostoevsky had been "clever, independent, cunning, stubborn."[34]

The final examination of all the defendants took place before the mixed Military-Civil Court appointed to pass sentence on the accused. Each was summoned into its presence in mid-October, told he was to be judged according to military law (much more severe than the civil code), and asked to submit in writing anything further he wished to add to his testimony. Some of the Petrashevtsy took this opportunity to throw themselves on the mercy of the authorities in a humiliating fashion. To cite only one instance, D. D. Akhsharumov wrote: "I repent everything and ask for pardon, and I write this not because I wish to be spared the punishment I deserve, but out of remorse, with a pure heart; feeling myself gravely guilty toward thee, as my Sovereign, I consider it my duty as a Christian and a subject to plead for pardon. Forgive me, Sire, if it is possible, because of my remorse and in memory of the service of my father."[35]

Dostoevsky, however, maintained his reserve and dignity to the end, and replied in quite another style. "I can add nothing new to my defense," he says, "except perhaps this—that I never acted with an evil and premeditated intention against the government—what I did was done thoughtlessly and much almost accidentally, as for example my reading of Belinsky's letter."[36] These words sound much less like an apology than a self-reproach for having exposed himself so carelessly; nor was Dostoevsky humbling himself unduly when he asserted that he had never acted with an evil intention "against the government." It was not the government of Nicholas I that he abhorred but the horrifying institution of serfdom, which he detested with an implacable and personal hatred rooted in his sense of guilt over the murder of his father by the peasants on the Dostoevsky estate.*

---

* For further details, see the first volume of the present work, *Dostoevsky, The Seeds of Revolt, 1821-1849* (Princeton, 1976), 81-91. My view agrees with that of Sigmund Freud in assuming that Dostoevsky felt a sense of guilt and complicity in his father's murder (if his father actually was murdered, as there is now some reason to doubt; but Dostoevsky believed that he was). However, I attribute this sense of guilt not to an Oedipus complex but rather to the empirical fact that, in the year or two immediately preceding his father's death supposedly at the hands of his peasants, Dostoevsky made inordinate demands on him for extra funds.

CHAPTER 5

The Incident in Semenovsky
Square

The Commission of Inquiry into the Petrashevsky circle completed its work on September 17, 1849, and sent a report of its findings to the Ministry of War for transmission to the Tsar. The report concluded that, while the meetings at Petrashevsky's "were in general notable for a spirit of opposition to the government, and a desire to alter the existing state of things," they had not exhibited "either a unity of action or a common purpose" and "did not belong in the category of a secret society"; nor was there evidence that they had "any sort of connection outside Russia."[1] Despite this reassuring verdict, the Commission decided that twenty-eight of those held in custody were guilty of criminal actions.

To pass sentence on those who had committed crimes (their number was very soon whittled down to twenty-three as a result of various special orders and exemptions), Nicholas took the unusual step of appointing a mixed Military-Civil court on September 25, and he instructed it to judge the accused under military law. The decision of this Court, handed down on November 16, condemned fifteen of the accused, including Dostoevsky, to execution by firing squad; others were given lesser sentences to hard labor and exile; and one was ordered released under strong suspicion and secret surveillance. This judgment was then sent for review to the highest military court, the General-Auditoriat—again a move for which there was no legal precedent—and this gave rise to numerous rumors that ran rife in Petersburg while the case was being tried in strictest secrecy. The Military-Civil Court, it was said, had recommended that all the prisoners be freed for lack of evidence, but Nicholas had sent the case to the General-Auditoriat to ensure punishment. The record of the proceedings, however, does not bear out this tradition.

Nevertheless, the General-Auditoriat, declaring that a judical error had been committed, did rule more harshly than the Military-Civil Court. It pointed out that, under the law used for field courts-martial, no distinction could be made between degrees of guilt; all the prisoners should have been equally condemned to death by execution. Dostoevsky's dossier was also slightly revised by the higher court. Originally, he had been sentenced for having read aloud and circulated Belinsky's *Letter*, and also for having failed to denounce another subversive work, N. P. Grigoryev's *A Soldier's Conversation*, to the authorities. A third charge was now added to the indictment: he had "taken part in deliberations about printing and distributing works against the government by means of a home lithograph."[2]

Once having asserted the full rigor of the law, the General-Auditoriat asked the Tsar to show mercy on various grounds—the repentance of some; the voluntary confessions of others, who had helped the work of the Commission; the youth of most of the prisoners; and the failure of their criminal intentions, which had been nipped in the bud, to lead to any harmful consequences. Instead of death, a list of lesser sentences was appended and submitted for the Tsar's scrutiny and approval on December 11, and he accepted the plea for mercy. It was well-known that Nicholas enjoyed playing the role of all-powerful but clement ruler, and Senator Lebedev confided to his journal that the General-Auditoriat had probably increased the severity of the recommended sentences in order to allow Nicholas more amply to exhibit his forbearance.[3] No mercy, however, was shown to Petrashevsky, whose sentence—exile and hard labor in the mines for life—was simply confirmed. For most of the others (though not all), Nicholas shortened the length of the sentences and eased their conditions.

Dostoevsky, initially condemned to eight years of hard labor, enjoyed a reduction of his period of penal servitude to four years, after which he was ordered to serve in the Russian Army for an indeterminate time. As we know from his own statement, Dostoevsky regarded this latter provision as a special dispensation personally granted in his favor by the Tsar (although the same sentence was also given to Sergey Durov). A convict sentenced to hard labor lost all his civil rights and did not regain them even after having completed his sentence; but Dostoevsky's civil rights would automatically be restored by military service. He believed this to have been the first time that a convict had been allowed to regain his civil rights, "and (it) occurred according to the will of the Emperor Nicholas I, taking pity on his (Dostoevsky's) youth and talent."[4] Whether justified or not, this conviction nonetheless helps to explain some of Dostoevsky's later favorable utterances about Nicholas, which commentators have usually found either totally baffling or have attributed to Dostoevsky's unhealthy penchant for masochistic submission to authority.

Final disposition of the case was made on December 21, and a packet of instructions was sent to the military authorities, on the orders of Nicholas I, regarding the procedure to be followed in announcing the sentences. The law called for a mock execution to be staged when, as in this instance, a sentence of death had been commuted by an act of imperial grace; but this ceremony, in most instances, was just a ritual formality. In this case, however, explicit instructions came from the Tsar that the prisoners were to be told their lives had been spared only *after* all the preparations had been completed for putting them to death. Nicholas carefully orchestrated the scenario on this occasion to produce the maximum impact on the unsuspecting victims of his regal solicitude. And Dostoevsky thus underwent the extraordinary emotional adventure of believing himself to have been only a few moments away from certain death, and then of being miraculously resurrected from the grave.

2

Once their interrogation had been completed in October, the prisoners learned nothing more about the deliberations concerning their case. As the dreary days rolled by with deadening monotony, Dostoevsky was more fortunate than most in being able to occupy his time profitably. "My incarceration had already gone on for eight months," writes D. D. Akhsharumov in his memoirs, "and my weariness and low spirits were overwhelming; I did not occupy myself with anything, I could no longer stir myself to anything; I had ceased talking to myself, moved about the room somewhat mechanically, or lay on my cot in apathy."[5] On the morning of December 22, though, he became aware of an unusual noise and animation in the ordinarily silent corridors of the fortress, whose deathly stillness had been broken only by the peal of the church bells. Looking out of the window of his cell, he noticed a line of carriages emerging from the direction of the church and lining up in the courtyard—so many of them, indeed, that it seemed the line would never end. Suddenly, to his even greater surprise, he saw them being surrounded by squadrons of mounted police. At first Akhsharumov thought that it might be a funeral; but who was being buried so impressively, and why were the carriages empty? Only then did it occur to him that the mysterious bustle and stir might have something to do with the Petrashevsky case, and that he had managed to live to see the day when the tedium of his imprisonment was finally to be relieved.

Meanwhile, he could also hear within the prison the sound of guards noisily scurrying about and opening the cells. His turn came at last, and an officer whom he knew walked in, accompanied by some prison attendants. They handed him the clothing in which he had been seized— light spring clothing, since the arrests had been made in April—as well as some warm, thick socks. He was told to dress and not to fail to put on the socks because it was freezing weather outside; but he received only an evasive answer to his excited questions and was ordered to hurry. Escorted out of the cell and along the corridor to an outside porch, he was placed in the two-seater closed carriage that quickly drew up, and a soldier clambered in beside as escort. Unable to see through the frost-covered window, he scratched at the pane with his fingernail to clear a view as the carriage began to move. Speshnev, who tried to do the same in his carriage, was told to desist or he would be restrained by force. Akhsharumov's guard, while less zealous, remained stubbornly mute and refused to answer questions. But when Akhsharumov went so far as to lower the window and glance outside, one of the mounted squadron rode close to the carriage and shouted for him to shut it again, and his guard hastily complied. From then on, he could catch only dim and distorted glimpses of the awakening city (it was very early in the morning) as the carriage rolled through the streets.

There is no account of Dostoevsky's feelings during this seemingly interminable and enigmatic journey, but they must have been similar to those recorded by others. The excitement of the departure, and all it might portend, produced an invigorating and exhilarating effect; at least it broke the stultifying inertia of the months just passed and the lifeless torpor produced by prolonged isolation. Nor was this mood of relative buoyancy broken by any apprehension about the future. All the evidence indicates that not a single one of the Petrashevtsy imagined they could possibly be condemned to death for whatever "crimes" the authorities might hold against them. Since Dostoevsky has written such unforgettable pages on the horror of a condemned man being taken to the place of execution, one is tempted to imagine him undergoing some such experience at this time; but no more than the others, so far as we know, had he the faintest inkling of what awaited him. Even the cynical Speshnev, who had recommended the use of terror as a revolutionary weapon, told Orest Miller that the idea of being driven to meet a firing squad never crossed his mind.[6]

Akhsharumov calculated that the trip lasted about thirty minutes before the carriage stopped and he was told to step outside. "Looking around, I saw a locality that I was familiar with—the Semenovsky Square. It was covered with newly fallen snow and surrounded by troops formed into a square. On the edges far away stood a crowd of people looking at us; everything was silent; it was the morning of a clear wintry day, and the sun, just having risen, shone like a bright, beautiful globe on the horizon through the haze of the thick clouds."[7] The sight of the sun, which he had not seen for eight months, overwhelmed Akhsharumov with a sudden sense of intoxicating well-being, and for a moment he forgot where he was. But he came to himself when, roughly seized by the elbow, he was shoved forward and told in which direction to move. Only then did he become aware that he was standing in a foot of deep snow and that, dressed in his light clothing, he was bitterly cold.

It was only then, too, that he became aware of a construction, slightly to his left, that had been built in the middle of the square—a four-sided scaffolding, twenty to thirty feet high, hung round with black crape, and with a staircase leading up from the ground. But he was more interested in the sight of a group of his old comrades crowding together in the snow and exchanging excited greetings after their long separation. What struck him, as he came closer, was the terrible change that had taken place in the features of those he knew best: "Their faces were emaciated, exhausted, pale, drawn, several had untrimmed beards and uncut hair. I was especially struck by the face of Speshnev; he had always stood out from the others because of his notable handsomeness, vigor, and flourishing good health. His good looks and flourishing aspect had vanished; his face, once circular, had become longer; it was sickly, pale yellow, with gaunt cheeks, eyes as if sunken and with great blue rings underneath, framed by long hair and a large overgrown beard."[8]

The joyous moment of reunion was very quickly interrupted by the loud voice of a general, obviously in charge of the proceedings, who rode up and ordered them to remain silent. A Civil Service official then appeared, document in hand, and the prisoners were lined up according to the order in which he called their names, Petrashevsky and Speshnev being first on the list. A priest carrying a cross succeeded the official and declared to the assembled prisoners: "Today you will hear the just decision of your case—follow me!"[9] And he led the procession to the scaffolding, not directly, but only after passing in front of the entire array of troops. Several of the Petrashevtsy had been officers in the Petersburg regiments lining the square, and the purpose of the maneuver was to display to the soldiers the degradation of their disloyal superiors. Conversation resumed again as the prisoners stumbled through the snow, and their attention was attracted by some gray stakes rising from the ground on one side of the scaffold. What were they for? Would they be tied to them and shot? Surely not, though it was impossible to tell what might happen—probably they would all be sent to penal servitude. . . . So ran the snatches of talk that Akhsharumov heard while the group was led to the staircase.

3

Once having ascended the platform, the prisoners were separated again by the accompanying soldiers and arranged in two files on each side. Standing beside N. A. Mombelli, another member of the Speshnev secret group, Dostoevsky quickly and incongruously, in a state of agitated febrility, told him the plan of a story he had written in prison (perhaps *A Little Hero*). Suddenly the square resounded with the crisp, metallic sound of soldiers snapping to attention, and the accused were ordered to remove their headgear while their sentences were being read. Most hesitated to obey the order in the biting cold, and the soldiers standing behind them were ordered to rip off their hats. Another Civil Service official, in full dress uniform, then moved along the line so as to face each man while reading to him the list of his imputed crimes and the punishment. It was impossible, according to Akhsharumov, to catch what he said because he spoke so rapidly and indistinctly. But, during the half-hour or so that he was performing his function, one sentence echoed and re-echoed like the tolling of a funeral bell: "The Field Criminal Court has condemned all to death sentence before a firing squad, and on December 19 His Majesty the Emperor personally wrote: 'Confirmed.' "[10]

As the meaning of these words began to sink in, the sun suddenly appeared again through the clouds, and Dostoevsky, turning to Sergey Durov, said, "It's not possible that we'll be executed."[11] In reply, Durov gestured to a peasant cart standing beside the scaffolding, in which were piled up, as he thought, coffins covered with some straw matting (it later turned out that the cart contained convict clothing). From that moment, as Dostoevsky recalled, he was convinced that he was doomed, and he could never afterwards forget the words thrown out so matter-of-factly: "condemned to death by a firing squad." After the official finished, the prisoners were given long white peasant blouses and nightcaps—their funeral shrouds—and helped into them by their military escort. The same priest, now with Bible as well as cross in hand, appeared on the scaffolding again and uttered the following appeal: "Brothers! Before dying one must repent. . . . The Savior forgives the sins of those who repent. . . . I call you to confession. . . ."[12]

In 1873, Dostoevsky wrote that while many of the Petrashevtsy who heard this entreaty may have been troubled by lapses they wished to confess ("those which every man, throughout his life, conceals in his conscience"), they felt no remorse whatever for the deed that had led them to the desperate straits in which they found themselves. "But that action for which we were being condemned," writes Dostoevsky, "those thoughts, those ideas, which ruled our souls—they seemed to us not only not to require repentance, but even to be something purifying, a martyrdom for which much could be forgiven!"[13] Dostoevsky's testimony is confirmed by Akhsharumov, who reports that none of the Petrashevtsy responded to the priest's repeated call to repent (which, under the circumstances, meant a renunciation of their moral-social convictions and not only of their sins as private individuals).

Finally, though, Konstantin Timkovsky stepped forward, muttered a few words, kissed the Bible, and returned to his place. (Timkovsky was a deeply religious person whose faith had been shaken by the "freethinkers" he had met at Petrashevsky's, and who had previously told the Commission of Inquiry that he bitterly deplored his apostasy.) Dostoevsky also recalled that just one person stepped forward to confess, but he told Orest Miller it was Peter Shaposhnikov—the only prisoner who was a simple citizen (*meshchanin*), while everyone else was of noble rank.[14] One suspects Dostoevsky here of giving a little symbolic embellishment to his memory, as he often did, so as to illustrate the innate and instinctive faith of the Russian common man by contrast with his more educated compatriots. The appearance of the priest, in any event, served Dostoevsky as additional proof that the death sentence would be carried out; it seemed inconceivable that such a religious rite would be used only as a "decorative accessory."[15]

But if the Petrashevtsy refused to lend themselves to a public act of contrition, they did not exhibit any hostility to the sacred symbol of the Christian faith in which all had been raised. When the priest moved down the row and held up the cross to their lips, they unanimously—including such confirmed atheists as Petrashevsky and Speshnev—kissed it. Dostoevsky certainly remembered this moment when, in *The Idiot*, he described a condemned man being led to the guillotine: "At that instant, when the condemned man seemed overcome by weakness, the clergyman, with a rapid and silent gesture, placed a small, silver, four-sided cross against his lips. He then repeated this gesture without stopping. Each time that the cross touched his lips, the condemned man opened his eyes, seemed to gain new life for several seconds and find the strength to move his feet. He kissed the crucifix with avidity, hastening to kiss it, as if hastening not to forget to lay hold of something in reserve, just in case. But it is hardly likely that he had a conscious religious feeling at that moment" (8: 56). This last sentence probably translates Dostoevsky's recollection of his own state of mind: there was no awareness of anything specifically "religious" in what he felt, but the kissing of the cross helped him to sustain the ordeal and provided the spiritual "food" he obscurely sensed he might need.

4

What occurred next was the most terrifying of all: the first three men in one of the rows—Petrashevsky, Mombelli, and Grigoryev—were seized by the arm, taken off the platform, and tied to the stakes standing just beside it. In one account—that of F. N. Lvov, which tends to glorify Petrashevsky—the impenitent agitator is supposed to have quipped in going from the platform to the stakes: "Mombelli, lift your legs higher, otherwise you'll go to the kingdom of heaven with a cold."[16] The order was given to pull the caps of the bound men over their heads, but Petrashevsky defiantly pushed his back and stared straight at a firing squad taking aim on the command of its officer. Dostoevsky was among the next three in the row from which the first group had been selected, and he fully expected that his turn would come in a few moments.

What was he feeling at this time? Quite late in life, he told Orest Miller that "he felt only a mystic terror, and was completely dominated by the

3. The Mock Execution of the Petrashevtsy

thought that in perhaps five minutes he would be going to another, unknown life. . . ."[17] He describes his emotions at greater length in that
famous passage from *The Idiot* in which Prince Myshkin tells the Epanchin ladies what he heard from a man who believed he had just five
minutes to live before being executed:

> It seemed to him that, in those five minutes, he was going to lead
> such a great number of lives that there was no place to think of the
> last moment. So that he divided up the time that still remained for
> him to live: two minutes to say good–bye to his companions; two
> minutes for inward meditation one last time; and the remainder to
> look around him one final time. He remembered perfectly having
> fulfilled these dispositions just as he had calculated. He was going to
> die at twenty-seven [Dostoevsky had just turned twenty-eight in 1849],
> full of health and vigor. He recalled that, at the moment of saying
> good-bye, he asked one of his companions a rather indifferent ques-
> tion, and took a keen interest in the reply. After saying good-bye, he
> began the period of two minutes reserved for *inward meditation*. He
> knew in advance what he would think about: he wished to focus his
> attention firmly, and as rapidly and clearly as possible, on what was

going to happen: right now, he was existing and living; in three minutes, *something* would occur; someone or something, but who, where? He thought to resolve these uncertainties during these two final minutes. Nearby rose a church whose golden cupola sparkled under a brilliant sun. He recalled having looked at that cupola and the rays it reflected with a terrible obstinacy; he could not take his eyes away; those rays seemed to him to be that new nature that was to be his own, and he imagined that in three minutes he would become part of them. . . . His uncertainty and his repulsion before the unknown, which was going to overtake him immediately, was terrible. [8: 52]

This passage has been much discussed in Dostoevsky criticism, and it has been debated whether its author was or was not a believing Christian in the face of death. It may seem, at first sight, as if Dostoevsky felt only that he would fuse with the sunlight and become part of nature; but such an interpretation, in my view, is much too literal and simple-minded. In the first place, it is clear that Dostoevsky is haunted by the question of the kind of "new life" he is about to enter—which implies a belief in some sort of immortality, a belief that his consciousness *in some form* would continue to exist. Even if his terror came from the possibility that *no* such "new life" waited beyond the grave, this by no means would indicate that he had reconciled himself to outright extinction; what he describes is an attitude of uncertainty rather than one of either conviction or resignation.

Moreover, even though the church and the sunlight were part of the actual scene as described by other participants, would not Dostoevsky have felt some symbolic relation between nature (the sunlight) and the architectural image of the Christian faith? In *A Little Hero*, composed in the months just preceding, the radiant beauty of a sunlit summer day is given a religious meaning in which "every flower, every blade of grass was exhaling the aroma of sacrifice, was saying to its Creator, 'Father, I am blessed and happy.'" And the image of the sun in *The Idiot* definitely takes on the significance of a symbol of God's majesty and creative power. It is for this reason that the dying young Ippolit, in revolt against the injustice of God's world, decides to read his blasphemous "Necessary Explanation" and to commit suicide only at the break of day, as a supreme insult to the sublimity of God embodied in the rising sun.

The Idiot, of course, was written twenty years after the incident on Semenovsky Square, and it may seem hazardous to deduce Dostoevsky's state of mind from the evidence it provides. Luckily, however, there is one account by someone who stood with him on the scaffold—an account surprisingly neglected—which provides valuable confirmation of the view offered above. F. N. Lvov, in a document written between 1859 and 1861 (hence with relatively fresh recollections), depicts Dostoevsky's behavior in the following words: "Dostoevsky was quite excited, he recalled *Le dernier jour d'un condamné* of Victor Hugo, and, going up to Speshnev, said: 'Nous serons avec le Christ' [We shall be with Christ]. 'Un peu de poussière' [A bit of dust]—the latter answered with a twisted smile."[18]

Nothing could better illustrate the difference between Dostoevsky's tormented and uncertain faith—tortured by fear, like Hugo's condemned criminal, but clinging, all the same, to the promise proclaimed by the God-man Christ—and the stoicism of a confirmed atheist like Speshnev, ruefully accepting that after death he would be nothing but dust. What Dostoevsky felt when he was five minutes removed from certain death was not the despair of total extinction but a terror of the unknown—the same "mystic terror" that had overcome him during his nervous attacks in the mid-1840s, and which he had described as being similar to "the anguish of people afraid of the dead."[19] It is precisely because Dostoevsky could not help believing in some sort of life after death that he was so terrified by its impenetrable mystery.

The suspense of waiting for the firing squad to pull the trigger—Akhsharumov recalls it as having been "terrible, repulsive, frightening"[20]—lasted about a minute, and then the roll of the drums was heard beating retreat. Not having served in the Army, Akhsharumov did not understand the meaning of the signal and thought it would coincide with a volley from the rifles; the ex-officer Dostoevsky knew immediately that his life had been spared. The next moment the firing squad had lowered their rifles and were no longer taking aim; the three men at the stake were untied and returned to their places. One of them, Nikolay Grigoryev, was white as a sheet, all the blood having been drained from his face; he had already shown signs of mental derangement in prison, and the mock execution ceremony finished him off entirely; never recovering his senses, he remained a helpless mental invalid for the rest of his days. Meanwhile, an aide-de-camp arrived on the scene at a gallop carrying the Tsar's pardon and the real sentences. These were read to the astonished prisoners, some of whom greeted the news with relief and joy, others with confusion and resentment. The peasant blouses and the nightcaps were taken off, and two men—looking like executioners, and dressed in worn, multicolored caftans—climbed the scaffolding. Their assigned task was to break swords over the heads of the prisoners, who were compelled to kneel for this part of the ceremony; the snapping of the sword signaled exclusion from civilian life, and they were then given convict headgear, soiled sheepskin coats, and boots.

Now outfitted in the garb appropriate to their lowly status, the condemned men were still lacking one essential item—their shackles. These were dumped in the middle of the platform with a grinding crash that made the planking vibrate, but only Petrashevsky was led forward by two blacksmiths, who, fastening the chains on his legs, began to close them with a large hammer. At first standing patiently while the work was going on, Petrashevsky finally seized one of the heavy hammers and, sitting on the floor, began to rivet the shackles with his own hands. "What impelled him to do violence to himself, what he wished to express in this fashion, is difficult to say," writes Akhsharumov, "but we were all in an unhealthy frame of mind or in a state of exaltation."[21] Such a scene would have been much more understandable to Dostoevsky, with his intuitive comprehension of masochism as the self-assertion of a personality driven to desperation by helplessness and humiliation. A peasant cart then pulled up with a troika of horses and a gendarme perched beside the driver as an escort, ready to transport Petrashevsky on the first leg of his journey into exile; but he protested that he wished to say goodbye to his friends before departing. When the commanding general acceded to his request, Petrashevsky embraced each in turn and bowed deeply to them all when through. The unaccustomed weight of his shackles impeded him from climbing into the cart, and he had to be aided before sinking heavily into his seat and being driven away. His sentence provided that he be dispatched to Siberia immediately; the others were to follow in the course of the next several days.

5

The remaining prisoners were taken back to the fortress in the carriages that had brought them and were examined by a military doctor to ascertain if their prolonged exposure to the cold had left any ill effects. On returning to his cell, Dostoevsky immediately seized pen and paper to write a letter to Mikhail—a letter not only moving in itself, but also one of the most valuable documents for comprehending the moral-spiritual consequences of the ordeal he had just sustained. The effects of this ordeal can, of course, hardly be overestimated, and the quotations from *The Idiot* indicate how clearly Dostoevsky remembered all its details. There are numerous ways in which the Dostoevsky of the 1840s differs from his post-Siberian *alter ego*; but first and foremost is a new grasp of existence profoundly shaped by this confrontation with death. It is from this moment that the primarily secular perspective from which Dostoevsky had previously viewed human life sinks into the background; and what comes forward to replace or absorb it are the ultimate and agonizing "cursed questions" that have always plagued mankind—the questions whose answers can be given, if at all, only by religious faith. Dostoevsky's novels would later manage to create a remarkable fusion between these two dimensions of human awareness; indeed, it is this union of uncommon social sensitivity with agonized religious probings and questionings that gives his work its properly tragic character and its unique place in the history of the novel.

Not everything in Dostoevsky's letter, to be sure, is equally memorable. Poured out in the fever of the moment, it mingles penetrating glimpses into the recesses of his soul with requests for aid, last-minute instructions, and a sober factual account of what had just occurred. Notable is the deep love it exhibits for his older brother and his family; they were, he assures Mikhail, in his thoughts during his (presumed) last moments, "and only then did I know how much I loved you, my dear brother!"[22] The truth of these words is confirmed by Dostoevsky's entire behavior throughout the remainder of his life, and particularly after his brother's death in 1864. He also asks Mikhail to say goodbye to close friends—the Maikov family, Dr. Yanovsky—and to get in touch with all the members of their own family, both in Moscow and elsewhere, so as to bring them his parting greetings. He leaves all his belongings in prison to Mikhail (except the Bible, which he wishes to keep), and he urgently asks his brother to send him whatever funds he can scrape together. Dostoevsky did not yet know whether he would be sent to Siberia in a convoy on foot or with a smaller party in carriages; in either case he would need money to buy whatever comforts could be obtained on the road. "Money is now more necessary for me than air," he explains.[23]

Of course the agonizing question of the future preoccupies him, and he oscillates between fear and hope while wondering whether he will ever be able to resume his literary career. "Can it be that I will never again take my pen in hand? I think it will be possible in four years. . . . My God! How many forms, still alive and created by me anew, will perish, extinguished in my brain or dissolved like poison in my bloodstream. Yes, if it's impossible to write I will die. Better fifteen years' imprisonment with pen in hand!" But Dostoevsky clings desperately to the lifeline provided by service in the Army and tells Mikhail: "Don't grieve over me. Know that I am not downhearted, remember that I have not given up hope. In four years my lot will be easier. I will be a soldier—and that's different from a convict. . . ."[24]

What Dostoevsky dreads most is that his health will break down under the sheer physical strain of the trials he is about to face: "Will my body hold out? I don't know. I am leaving in ill health. I have scrofula. But maybe it will!" Despite such concerns, Dostoevsky assures Mikhail that he has never been in a better mental or emotional state: "Never before have I felt welling up in me such abundant and healthy reserves of spiritual life as I do now."[25] Dostoevsky repeats again later that he is afraid not of the vicissitudes ahead but simply of the capacity of his body to continue to function. "My life in prison," he says in a significant admission, which reveals that his past life had been far from puritanical, "has already sufficiently destroyed in me those fleshly demands that are not entirely pure; I did not spare myself before.* Now, deprivation means nothing to me, and this is why I am not afraid that any kind of material hardship will destroy me. That won't happen! Oh, only let me be healthy!"[26]

Nothing is more astonishing about Dostoevsky's letter than the sense of buoyancy it exhibits, the rush of inner force and spiritual vitality that he reports as sustaining him. Unquestionably, this access of psychic vigor springs from the incredible miracle of having been granted the gift of life when he had been absolutely certain that it would be snatched away from him the next instant. "I cannot recall when I was ever as happy as on that day," Dostoevsky told his second wife many years later. "I walked up and down my cell in the Alekseevsky Ravelin and sang the whole time, sang at the top of my voice, so happy was I at being given back my life."[27] Such happiness is expressed in the letter with truly ecstatic exuberance, and it clearly overwhelmed Dostoevsky with the impact of a revelation. As a result, all of his past life is seen in a new perspective and re-evaluated in the light of the dazzling truth he has finally been vouchsafed.

Even Dostoevsky's agonies over being deprived of the ability to write are now somewhat mitigated when measured against what he has received in return: "Yes! Truly! That head which created, and lived the highest life of art, which had become conscious and accustomed to the highest life of the spirit, that head has already been struck from my shoulders. Memory remains, and the forms created by me not yet given body. They will poison me, true! But I still have my heart and the same flesh and blood, and these too can live, suffer, desire and remember, and that, after all, is also life. *On voit le soleil!*"[28] This last phase ("One sees the sun") is a snatch of Hugo's *Le dernier jour d'un condamné*, whose details had surged back into Dostoevsky's memory as he stared death in the face; and the letter shows how accurately he remembered the very words of the text. For the citation forms part of the frantic reflections of Hugo's "condemned man" as he awaits execution by the guillotine and desperately tells himself that life under any conditions, no matter how harsh, is preferable to extinction. At least—*on voit le soleil*!† Unlike the diarist of Hugo's

---

* Very little is known about Dostoevsky's private affairs during the 1840s, and no reliable information exists concerning his sex life. A glimpse into what this may have been, however, is contained in a letter written shortly after the first enormous success of *Poor Folk*, when he was luxuriating in the euphoria of his newly acquired fame. "The Minnas, Claras, and Mariannes, etc., have become as beautiful as they can possibly be," he writes, "but cost an awful lot of money. Just a few days ago Turgenev and Belinsky scolded me severely for my disorderly life." If Dostoevsky is not just pretending to be a man of the world so as to impress his older brother Mikhail, these words would indicate that he was frequenting some of the fashionable ladies of the evening reigning at that time in the Petersburg *demi-monde*. F. M. Dostoevsky, *Pisma*, 1: 85; November 16, 1845.

† In recalling this passage from Hugo, Dostoevsky slightly altered the wording of the original. The text reads as follows: "Oh my pardon! my pardon! perhaps I will be pardoned. The king is not angry with me. Let my lawyer be summoned! Quickly, my lawyer! I agree to hard labor.

story, Dostoevsky would still happily continue to see the sun, and the immensity of this simple fact throws everything else—even the wreck of his literary ambitions—into the shade.

It is not only his commitment to literature that Dostoevsky suddenly beholds from this new point of view; everything in his previous life is also severely judged as he turns back to contemplate it from, as it were, the edge of eternity: "When I look back on my past and think how much time I wasted on nothing, how much time has been lost in futilities, errors, laziness, incapacity to live; how little I appreciated it, how many times I sinned against my heart and soul—then my heart bleeds. *Life is a gift, life is happiness, every minute can be an eternity of happiness* [italics added]! *Si jeunesse savait* [If youth only knew]! Now, in changing my life, I am reborn in a new form. Brother! I swear that I will not lose hope and will keep my soul and heart pure. I will be reborn for the better. That's all my hope, all my consolation!"[29]

Such words try to convey some of the blinding truth that Dostoevsky now understood for the first time—the truth that life itself is the greatest of all goods and blessings, and that man has the power to turn each moment into an "eternity of happiness" once the scales have fallen from his eyes. Dostoevsky was never to forget the wave of renewal that swept over him at this moment; nor would he ever abandon the hope that he could communicate to others the same conviction of infinite possibility that had thrilled through every fiber of his own being. It was this rapturous apprehension of life, and this ambition, that he will later impart to Prince Myshkin, although with a sadly ironic awareness of how "idiotic" such an aspiration would seem to those immersed in the preoccupations and passions of worldly existence.

Powerless to change the past, Dostoevsky's rejuvenated sense of the boundless wonder of life nonetheless served to steel him for the trials of the future and to provide him with an armor of spiritual invulnerability. For if one considers the sheer gift of life itself to be a miracle and a blessing, if one believes in man's power to turn each moment into an "eternity of happiness," then one also believes in his capacity to overcome all the harsh and oppressive circumstances that trammel his earthly lot. Hence Dostoevsky reassures Mikhail: "I am neither downhearted nor discouraged. *Life is life everywhere, life is in ourselves, not in the exterior* [italics added].

Five years at hard labor. Five years at hard labor, nothing more be said—or twenty years— or for life, branded with a hot iron. But a pardon from execution!

"A convict, that's someone who can still walk, someone who comes and goes, someone who sees the sun [*Un forçat, cela marche encore, cela va et vient, cela voit le soleil*]."

It is this last phrase that Dostoevsky cites, changing the "cela" to "on"; but the text hauntingly conveys what his thoughts must have been once the sentence of death had been pronounced. See Victor Hugo, *Bug-Jargal, Le dernier jour d'un condamné, Claude Gueux* (Paris, 1942), 279. For a fascinating study of the influence of this work on Dostoevsky's novels, see V. V. Vinogradov, *Poetika Russkoi Literatury* (Moscow, 1976), 63-75.

I shall have human beings around me [in Siberia], and to be a *man* among men and to remain one always, not to lose heart and not to give in no matter what misfortune may occur—that is what life is, that is its task, I have become aware of this. This idea has entered into my flesh and blood."[30]

To struggle to preserve one's humanity, "no matter what misfortune may occur," is thus now the primary task of life; "the exterior" is firmly relegated to a secondary status, and absolute priority is assigned to the obligation of the individual to uphold his human integrity under all circumstances. During the 1840s, many among the progressive intelligentsia had begun to argue that free will and moral responsibility were outmoded ideas because, as Belinsky told Dostoevsky, they had no meaning in "a society organized so vilely that one cannot help committing crimes . . . (and) is pushed into crime for economic reasons."[31] Dostoevsky had always refused to accept this dismissal of individual moral obligation; but it had been exceedingly difficult for him to support his opposing position in personal debate with the choleric critic. What had then been only a theoretical preference, however, now entered, as he rightly said, into "his flesh and blood"; it had become an "idea-feeling," so deeply interwined with his emotions that no argument would ever be able to dislodge or even shake it in the future.

No passage in Dostoevsky's letter, though, is more poignant and more precious than his description of the morally purifying effects of what he believed would be his last moments on earth. "If anyone remembers me as nasty," Dostoevsky tells Mikhail, "or if I quarreled with anybody, if I produced an unpleasant impression on anyone—ask them to forget, if you happen to meet them. There is no gall and rancor in my soul; I should so much like at this moment to love and to embrace just someone from among those I knew. This is a consolation, I experienced it today, saying goodbye to those dear to me before death" (he had embraced Sergey Durov and Aleksey Pleshcheev, who had stood next to him).[32] What Dostoevsky had felt, in these climactic instants, had thus been a need to forgive and be forgiven, and a desire to embrace others in a gesture of unconditional and heartfelt love. Such values had of course not been absent from Dostoevsky's moral sensibility in the past; but now, in his hour of greatest need, they had taken on an immensely heightened significance as the supreme human consolation. And if the values of expiation, forgiveness, and love were destined to take precedence over all others in Dostoevsky's artistic universe, it was surely because he had encountered them as a truth responding to the most anguishing predicament of his own life.

Indeed, it is Dostoevsky's piercing sense of the awful fragility and transiency of human existence that will soon enable him to depict, with a powerful urgency unrivaled by any other modern writer, the unconditional and absolute Christian commandment of mutual, all-forgiving, and all-embracing love. For Dostoevsky's morality is similar to what some theologians, speaking of the early Christians, have called an "interim ethics," that is, an ethics whose uncompromising extremism springs from the lurking imminence of the Day of Judgment and the Final Reckoning: there is no time for anything but the last kiss of reconciliation because, quite literally, there *is* no "time." The strength (as well as some of the weakness) of Dostoevsky's work may ultimately be traced to the stabbing acuity with which, above all, he wished to communicate the saving power of this eschatological core of the Christian faith.*

6

On December 24, 1849, three days after the grisly pageant enacted in Semenovsky Square, Mikhail Dostoevsky was informed, as Feodor's closest relative in Petersburg, that his brother would begin his long and hazardous journey to Siberia that very night. Mikhail hastened to convey the information to Alexander Milyukov, and both went to the fortress to say farewell to the departing prisoner. Such a privilege was reserved only to immediate family; but Milyukov appealed directly to General Nabokov for permission, counting on "his kind heart and leniency,"[33] and permission was granted. It is owing to this infraction of the rules that we possess an account of Dostoevsky's condition and state of mind just before departing for exile and hard labor.

When Feodor Dostoevsky, accompanied by Durov, was ushered into the room where Milyukov and Mikhail Dostoevsky were waiting, both prisoners were already wearing the sheepskin coats and felt boots provided them to confront the glacial cold of the Russian winter. The physical effect of eight months of imprisonment apparently had been less severe on Dostoevsky than on most, and Milyukov was agreeably surprised at how little his friend seemed to have changed. Commenting on Dostoevsky's intense concern for the welfare of his brother and his family, Milyukov was also struck by the note of faith and hope in the future, the unshakable conviction of his ability to survive, that marked his entire behavior. "Looking at the farewell of the brothers Dostoevsky," he observes, "everyone would have remarked that the one suffering the most was remaining in freedom in Petersburg, not the one who was just on the point of traveling to Siberian

---

* The eschatological importance of the presumably brief "interim" between the First and Second Coming for the interpretation of the ethics of Jesus was brought into prominence by the book of Albert Schweitzer, *The Quest of the Historical Jesus*, published in German in 1906 and first translated into English in 1910. It has since gone through numerous editions. For a penetrating critical discussion of its thesis, see Reinhold Niebuhr, *The Nature and Destiny of Man*, 2 vols. in 1 (New York, 1955), 2: 47-52. Niebuhr's comments in this context on the relation between eschatology and history are also very relevant for the interpretation of Dostoevsky, but not yet at this point in his career.

katorga. Tears rose in the eyes of the older brother, his lips trembled, but Feodor Mikhailovich remained calm and consoled him."[34]

Some of the words that Milyukov cites also reveal the expectations with which Dostoevsky approached his impending exposure to convict life. "Stop, brother," he said at one point, "you know me, I am not going to my grave, you are not accompanying my burial—and there are not wild beasts in *katorga* but people, perhaps better than I am, perhaps worthier than I am. . . ."[35] Such words are the only documentation we have so far as Dostoevsky is concerned; but some other evidence throws a vivid light on the all-important question of what he, as well as the other Petrashevtsy, expected to encounter among the people with whom they would share their captivity. In the documents that Petrashevsky wrote for the Commission of Inquiry, we find the following remarkable and touching reverie:

> Perhaps fate . . . will place me side by side with a hardened evildoer, who has ten murders on his soul. . . . Resting at a way station and dining on a piece of stale bread . . . we begin to talk—I tell him how, and for what reason, I suffered misfortune. . . . I tell him about Fourier . . . about the phalanstery—what and why things are that way there, and so forth. . . . I explain why people become evildoers . . . and he, sighing deeply, tells me about his life. . . . From his story I see that circumstances crushed much that was good in this man, a strong soul fell under the weight of misfortune. . . . Perhaps, at the end of the story, he will say: 'Yes, if things were arranged your way, if people lived like that, I would not be an evildoer' . . . and I, if the weight of my shackles allows me, extend a hand to him—and I say—'let's be brothers'—and, breaking my piece of bread, I give it to him, saying: 'I am not used to eating very much, you need it more, take it and eat.' With this, a tear appears on his roughened cheek and . . . before me appears . . . not an evildoer, but my equal in misfortune, perhaps also in the beginning a person badly misunderstood. . . . The act of humanization is completed, and the evildoer no longer exists.[36]

Such "philanthropic, Utopian dreams of Petrashevsky," as a Soviet Russian critic has justly remarked, "expressed the general state of mind and convictions of the circle. And though Dostoevsky was hardly so romantic in inclination, evidently he too, despite instinctive doubts and forebodings, must have imagined something similar."[37] All the more so, we may add, since Dostoevsky's early writings had led to the rise of a literary tendency known as "sentimental Naturalism," whose creations stressed the human worth hidden in the lives of the most humble and downtrodden elements of society—even when these unfortunates could hardly be considered exemplars of virtue in any conventional sense.

Dostoevsky's words may thus be taken as a more laconic expression of the same roseate fantasies articulated by Petrashevsky, a reaffirmation of the philanthropic aspect of his moral-social convictions of the time. Nonetheless, in the suggestion that the convicts might even perhaps be "worthier" than himself, Dostoevsky was unconsciously speaking better than he knew. For what was uttered only as a consolatory possibility in 1849, and was surely not accepted literally either by Dostoevsky or by those he was attempting to reassure, would one day become the basis of a view of the Russian people that he would not hesitate to proclaim to the entire world.

PART II

Katorga

CHAPTER 6

First Impressions

Dostoevsky disliked writing letters, and usually made the effort only under the pressure of some necessity or in response to the impulse of a particular moment. He rarely used his correspondence as a form of personal stock-taking, or as a means of communicating his ideas and summing up the events of his life in an orderly fashion. One of the few exceptions to this generalization is the letter he wrote his brother Mikhail on February 22, 1854, just a week after being released from prison camp. Dostoevsky had not received a single word from his family in four years, even though occasional correspondence was permitted; he himself had sent one letter through official channels, as well as another privately with a returning traveler. Why Mikhail failed to respond to either is not clear; perhaps, as Dostoevsky surmised, he had been misinformed that correspondence was forbidden, and had been reluctant to pursue the matter any further. In any case, the complete loss of contact with his family inspired Dostoevsky to compose a letter unusual for its objective narrative of events and its documentary value.

Picking up the thread of his life at the moment of departure for Siberia, it recounts the impressions gathered on the eighteen-day journey, the major incidents marking his arrival at the first way station, Tobolsk, and it also contains a valuable account, brief but indelibly etched, of the conditions of life in the prison camp. With the help of other information, this document will serve to provide a first summary view of Dostoevsky's crucial four-year ordeal. In succeeding chapters, using the *House of the Dead* as a primary source, we shall continue to explore this period of his life in more detail and depth, and attempt to give a plausible and coherent account of what he later called "the regeneration of my convictions"—an event of incalculable consequences for his future.[1]

2

"Do you remember how we parted, my dear, my dearest," he writes to Mikhail. "As soon as you had left me, the three of us, Durov, Jastrzembski, and I, were taken to be put in irons. At exactly 12 o'clock, i.e., exactly as it became Christmas Day, I put on shackles for the first time. They weighed about ten pounds and were extremely uncomfortable to walk in. Then we were put into open sledges, each separately, with a gendarme, and in four sledges, with a government courier in the lead, we set out from St. Petersburg.

"My heart was heavy and filled with a kind of vague confusion of many different emotions. A sort of restlessness gnawed at my heart with a dull pain. But the fresh air revived me, and since one usually feels some vitality and courage before every new step in one's life, I was essentially quite tranquil and watched St. Petersburg attentively as I was carried past the festively lighted buildings, saying goodbye to each one individually. We were taken past your flat and I saw that Kraevskys' was all lit up. You had told me that the children had gone there with Emilya Feodorovna, and now at this house I became terribly sad. I took my leave, as it were, of the children. I hated to leave them, and afterwards, even years later, how often I thought of them, almost with tears in my eyes!"[2]

Dostoevsky then goes on to give further details of the journey, and some glimpses into his own state of mind and that of his companions. "After eight months of confinement, sixty versts of winter traveling had made us so hungry that it does my heart good to remember it. I was cheerful, Durov chattered without ceasing, and Jastrzembski foresaw extraordinary terrors in the future."[3] The courier in charge of the convoy proved to be a humane and kindly man who made sure they were transferred to covered sledges, in view of the extreme cold, and even paid half of the expenses for the prisoners (presumably from a government allowance) when they were unmercifully gouged at the posting stations. "It was a sad moment when we crossed the Urals," Dostoevsky recalls. "The horses and sledges had foundered in the drifts. A snowstorm was raging. We got out of the sledges—it was night—and stood waiting while they were dragged out. All around us was the snow and storm; it was the frontier of Europe; ahead was Siberia and our unknown fate, while all the past lay behind us—it was so depressing that I was moved to tears."[4]

On January 9 the party reached Tobolsk, once the capital city of western Siberia and, at that time, the main distribution center in which prisoners arriving from European Russia were sorted out and dispatched to their final destinations. The prison, built on the top of a steep hill rising above the banks of the Irtish River, was set in the midst of other military and administrative installations inside a fortress complex. A winding road led up to this citadel from the lower town, where lived most of the native Khirgiz and Tartar population, intermingled with a motley assortment of Russian and German traders and adventurers (mostly gold prospectors). As Dostoevsky's party climbed slowly up to their temporary destination, one of the first sights to greet their eyes was the town's most ancient and notorious exile, the famous Uglich bell, located just off the main road along which they were proceeding.

At the discovery of the death of Crown Prince Dimitry, suspected of having been murdered by his guardian, Boris Godunov, the bell had rung to summon the inhabitants of Uglich to pour out and avenge the boy's death. The new Tsar, Boris, later ordered the offending bell to be publicly flogged and mutilated, and it was exiled to Siberia in perpetuity with the injunction that it never ring again. But the people of Tobolsk had long since housed the Uglich bell in a small belfry, and its deep-voiced sonority called them to prayer. There it stood along the roadside, a constant reminder to later exiles of the despotic, capricious, and all-encompassing authority of the Russian Tsars, as well as of the ultimate futility of many of their sternest ukases.

Dostoevsky's reception in Tobolsk illustrates some of the moral incorporated in the subversive survival of the Uglich bell. "We arrived in Tobolsk," he continues, "on January 11 [a slight error in dating], and when we had been brought before the authorities and undergone a search in which all our money was taken from us, Durov, Jastrzembski, and I were removed to a separate room. The others, Speshnev and the rest, who had arrived before us, were in a different section of the prison, and during the whole time there we hardly saw them. I wish I could tell you in detail of our six days in Tobolsk and the impressions they left on me, but this is not the right place. I will only say that the sympathy and lively concern we met with blessed us with almost complete happiness. The exiles of the old days (that is, not they themselves but their wives) looked after us as though we were their own flesh and blood. What wonderful people, tried by twenty-five years of sorrow and self-sacrifice! We had only a glimpse of them, for we were strictly confined. But they sent us food and clothing, they consoled us and gave us courage."[5]

3

Dostoevsky's letter is short on details of his stay in Tobolsk; but we can fill them in more fully from other accounts. Jastrzembski also left a description of their arrival and of his first glimpse of convict-clerks, branded on cheeks and forehead, who were sorting mail in the chancery to which Dostoevsky's group was taken. In reply to Jastrzembski's naive question as to whether a samovar could be obtained, the official in charge simply laughed. "All this seemed to forebode nothing good," he continues. "We were taken into a room. A narrow, dark, cold dirty room. . . . Here there were plank beds, and on them three sacks filled with straw instead of mattresses and three pillows of the same kind. It was pitch-black. Outside the door, on the threshold, could be heard the heavy tread of the sentinel, walking back and forth in a 40 degree frost." Their room was separated only by a partition from another, which held other prisoners awaiting trial, and they could hear "the rattle of bottles and glasses, the exclamations of people playing cards and other games, and what insults, what curses. . . ."[6]

All three travelers were in a lamentable state after their weeks on the road. "Durov's fingers and toes were frostbitten, and his feet had been badly damaged by the shackles. Dostoevsky, moreover, had broken out with scrofulous sores on his face and in his mouth while still in the Alekseevsky Ravelin. The edge of my nose was frostbitten."[7] Terribly dejected by the gloomy prospect of even further suffering looming ahead, Jastrzembski decided to commit suicide—a decision, he says, for which his solitary imprisonment in the Ravelin had been an excellent preparation. Whether he kept his resolution to himself is not clear; but since, even on the road, he had expressed fear of "extraordinary terrors in the future," his melancholy state of mind was hardly a secret to his companions. What occurred on this occasion shows us Dostoevsky's ability to keep up his own courage as well as to aid and comfort others. To be sure, the external situation had a good deal to do with changing Jastrzembski's mood. It turned out that one of the officers of gendarmes at Tobolsk was an old acquaintance, who provided him and his friends with a candle, matches, and some hot tea, "which seemed to us sweeter than nectar. Some excellent cigars suddenly turned up in Dostoevsky's possession [he had evidently succeeded in concealing them during the search]. . . . We spent a good part of the remainder of the night in friendly conversation. The sympathetic, gentle voice of Dostoevsky, his tenderness and delicacy of feeling, even some of his capricious sallies, quite like a woman, had a soothing effect on me. I gave up any extreme decision. Dostoevsky, Durov, and I were separated in the Tobolsk prison, we wept, embraced, and never saw each other again."[8]

If Dostoevsky was instrumental in bringing solace to Jastrzembski and in persuading him not to lay violent hands on himself, the same function was performed for Dostoevsky by the wives of "the exiles of the old days," (that is, the Decembrists) whom he mentions in his letter—although he had scarcely approached the state of total despondency to which Jastrzembski had been reduced. Immediately on their arrival, the Petrashevtsy became aware of the benevolence of the exiled Decembrists; and their welcome gifts provided Dostoevsky's first contact with the peculiar conditions of Siberian society, which helped so much to ease the lot of political prisoners, whether Russian or Polish, during the last years of the régime of Nicholas I. One hundred and twenty Decembrists, all of good (and some of the very best) family, had been sent into exile in 1825. All had long since served their sentences at hard labor. Not allowed to reside in European Russia, they had remained in Siberia and formed part of the very small educated and cultivated upper strata of society composed of the higher ranks in the Army and the bureaucracy. Many of them had relations at court; some were independently wealthy; and all were treated with marked consideration by the officials coming from Petersburg. New arrivals were only too happy to mix with people of their own class and breeding in this still wild frontier territory, otherwise peopled only by uncouth and enterprising freebooters out to make a fortune and by a mixture of Asiatic nomads still living their age-old tribal existence. The Decembrists, through their connections, were thus able to exercise a considerable influence despite their suspect status as ex-rebels, and their wives and children were unceasingly active in charitable work among the convicts.

4

On the last day that Dostoevsky and Durov spent in Tobolsk, three Decembrist wives arranged, through their contacts, to visit them in the quarters of one of the officers. It was a moment he was to remember all his life, and one that he refers to again, in the same grateful and reverential tone, fourteen years later in his *Diary of a Writer* (1873): "When we [the Petrashevtsy] sat in prison in Tobolsk, awaiting our further fate in the transportation section, the wives of the Decembrists pleaded with the overseer of the prison and arranged a meeting with us in his quarters. We saw these sublime sufferers, who had voluntarily followed their husbands to Siberia. They gave up everything, position, wealth, family ties, sacrificed everything for the highest moral duty, a duty which nothing could impose on them except themselves. Completely innocent, during twenty-five years they bore everything to which their husbands had been condemned. The meeting lasted an hour. They blessed us as we entered on a new life, made the sign of the cross, and gave us a New Testament—the only book allowed in prison. It lay under my pillow for four years during penal servitude. I read it sometimes, and read it to others. With it, I taught one convict to read."[9] Each copy of the holy book contained, in its binding, ten rubles in bank notes.

The three women who came to talk with Dostoevsky were Mme Muravyeva, Mme Annenkova, and Mme Fonvizina. The only native Russian of the three, and the most important of all for Dostoevsky, was Natalya Fonvizina, a remarkable woman of considerable intellectual culture and profound religious faith. "Her intense religiosity," writes M. D. Frantseva, daughter of the government prosecutor in Tobolsk and a close friend of the family, "was displayed not only by observing the external forms of ceremonial ritual, but in a deep development of religious interests; she lived an inner, religious life in the full sense of the word. She read all sorts of religious books; not to speak of the Bible, which she knew almost by heart, she read the works of the Fathers of the Orthodox Church and the writers of the Catholic and Protestant churches, and also knew German philosophy. . . ."[10] Four years later, Dostoevsky would set down one of the few statements of his own religious credo in a letter to Natalya Fonvizina.

It was during this hour-long meeting that Dostoevsky first heard about the terrible Major Krivtsov, the commandant of the prison camp at Omsk, and was warned to be on his guard against him. Dostoevsky describes him in his letter as "a scoundrel whom few could equal, a petty barbarian, an intriguer and a drunkard, the most repulsive creature imaginable."[11] Natalya Fonvizina was related to Count Gorchakov, the Governor-General of Siberia, and promised to speak to him on Dostoevsky's behalf; Mme Annenkova, of French origin, also told him about her son-in-law Konstantin Ivanov, an officer in the Military Engineers at Omsk, about whom Dostoevsky was to say later that "he has been like a brother to me.[12] Letters were also sent to the three daughters of Count Gorchakov, then on a visit to their father, enlisting their intercession on behalf of the Petrashevtsy. Even though all this activity did not spare Dostoevsky and Durov from being treated like ordinary convicts and assigned to hard labor, it made Krivtsov a little more cautious in dealing with them than he otherwise might have been.

On the morning of the departure of Dostoevsky and Durov for Omsk, Mme Fonvizina and Marie Frantseva rode out in advance to meet them on the way for a last encounter. "The cold was frightful," writes the latter in her memoirs. "Having gone out in a sledge very early, so as not to miss

4. Natalya Fonvizina

the departing prisoners, we got out of our vehicle and walked ahead on purpose up the road for a verst because we did not want the coachman to be a witness to our farewells; particularly since I had to give in secret to the gendarme a letter for my close friend, Lieutenant Colonel Zhdan-Pushkin, in which I asked him to look after Dostoevsky and Durov. . . . At last we heard the distant tinkle of bells. Quickly, a troika appeared out of the edge of the forest [and] . . . Dostoevsky and Durov leaped out of their Siberian sledge. The first was a thin, not very tall, not very good-looking young man; the second, about four years older than his companion, had regular features, large, dark, and pensive eyes, dark hair, and a beard covered with snow and frost. They were dressed in convict half-coats and fur hats with earflaps; heavy shackles made a resounding noise on their feet. We said goodbye to them quickly, fearing that some passing travelers might chance on us with them, and had time only to tell them not to lose heart, and that kind people would look after them even where they were going. I gave the letter I had ready for Pushkin to the gendarme, who conscientiously delivered it to him in Omsk."[13]

Unfortunately, the gendarme also carried another letter, which he delivered just as conscientiously—a secret letter from the commandant at Tobolsk to the one at Omsk. It contained instructions, originating from the Tsar himself, that the two deportees were to be treated as "prisoners in the full sense of the word; according to their sentence, the improvement of their condition in the future should depend on their conduct, on the clemency of the monarch, and by no means on the indulgence of those in immediate authority over them; a trustworthy official should be appointed to maintain a strict and unceasing vigilance."[14] In these faraway outposts of the Russian Empire, such instructions were more apt to be honored in the breach than in the observance, and there is no evidence that any such petty bureaucrat was ever appointed. All the same, such orders made it more difficult to come to the aid of the political prisoners; there was always the chance that some zealous underling, eager to gain advancement, would denounce any favoritism to the headquarters of the Governor-General. Moreover, the amount of leniency that could safely be exercised depended on how the attitude of the Governor-General and his entourage would be gauged. In this respect, Dostoevsky and Durov were unfortunate: Mme Fonvizina quarreled with Gorchakov for personal reasons shortly after their arrival in the camp, and this quickly became known in the tight little world of the higher bureaucracy.

5
———

Dostoevsky's letter also contains an unvarnished description of his years in prison, his first immediate expression of what had affected him most strongly during the period of time that was to reshape so many of his ideas and values. "I had already become acquainted with convicts in Tobolsk," he says, "and here in Omsk I settled down to living with them for four years. They were coarse, ill-natured, cross-grained people. Their hatred for the gentry knew no bounds, and therefore they received us, the gentlemen, with hostility and malicious joy in our troubles. They would have eaten us alive, given the chance. Judge, moreover, how much protection we had, having to live, to eat and drink and sleep with these men for several years, without even the chance of complaining of the innumerable affronts of every possible kind. 'You are noblemen, iron beaks that used to peck us to death. Before, the master used to torment the people, but now he is lower than the lowest, has become one of us'—that's the theme on which they played variations for four years. One hundred and fifty enemies never tired of persecuting us; it was a pleasure for them, an amusement, something to do, and if anything at all saved us, it was indifference, moral superiority (which they could not but recognize and respect), and unyielding resistence to their will. They always acknowledged that we were superior to them. They had no understanding of our crime. We ourselves were silent on the subject, and so we could not understand each other, and we had to endure all the persecution and vindictiveness toward the gentry class for which they lived and breathed.

"Things were very bad for us. A military prison is much worse than a civilian one. I spent the whole four years in the prison behind walls and never went out except to work. The work they found for us was heavy (not always, of course), and I was sometimes completely exhausted in foul weather, in damp and rain and sleet, and in the unendurable cold of winter. Once I spent four hours on urgent work, when the mercury froze and there was perhaps about 40 degrees of frost. My foot became frostbitten.

"We lived on top of each other, all together in one barrack. Imagine an old, dilapidated, wooden construction, which was supposed to have been pulled down long ago, and which was no longer fit for use. In summer, intolerable closeness; in winter, unendurable cold. All the floors were rotten. Filth on the floors an inch thick; one could slip and fall. The little windows were so covered with frost that it was almost impossible to read at any time of the day. An inch of ice on the panes. Drips from the ceiling, draughts everywhere. We were packed like herrings in a barrel. The stove took six logs at once, but there was no warmth (the ice in the room barely thawed), only unendurable fumes—and this, all winter long. There in the barracks the convicts washed their clothes and the whole space was splashed with water. There was no room to turn around. From dusk to dawn it was impossible not to behave like pigs, for after all, 'we're live human beings.' We slept on bare boards and were allowed only a pillow. We spread our sheepskin coats over us, and our feet were always uncovered all night. We shivered all night. Fleas, lice, and black beetles by the bushel. In winter we wore short sheepskin coats, often of the most wretched quality, which hardly gave any warmth, and on our feet half-boots—just try to walk around with them in the freezing cold. The food they gave us was bread and cabbage soup with a quarter of a pound of beef in it; but the meat was minced up and I never saw any of it. On holidays, thin porridge almost without fat. On fast days, boiled cabbage and hardly anything else. I suffered unbearably from indigestion and was ill several times. You may judge whether we could have lived without money, and if I had had none I should certainly have died; and nobody, no convict, whoever he was, could have borne such a life without it. But everybody worked at some-thing, sold it, and thus had a kopek or two. I drank tea and sometimes bought a piece of meat to eat, and this was my salvation. It was impossible not to smoke tobacco as well, for one might have choked in that atmos-phere. All this was done by stealth.

"I often lay ill in the hospital. Disordered nerves have given me epilepsy, but the fits occur only rarely. I have rheumatism in the legs besides. Apart from this I feel fairly well. Add to all these amenities the almost complete impossibility of possessing a book (and if you get one you read it on the sly), the eternal hostility and quarreling around one, the wrangling, shout-ing, uproar, din, always under escort, never alone, and all this for four years without change—really, one may be pardoned for saying that things were bad. Besides all this, the eternal threat of punishment hanging over one, shackles, the total stifling of the soul, there you have an image of my existence. . . ."[15]

Dostoevsky then leaves the past to return to the present and the pressing needs of his situation; but he shifts again a few pages later to further reflections on his life in the prison camp. And now he gives, if not a totally different, then at least a greatly modified version of his relation to some of his fellow convicts. "Men, however, are everywhere men," he writes. "In four years in prison I came at last to distinguish men among criminals. Believe me, there are deep, strong, beautiful characters among them, and what a joy it was to discover the gold under the coarse, hard surface. And not one, not two, but several. It is impossible not to respect some of them, and some are positively splendid. I taught a young Circassian (sent to hard labor for highway robbery) reading and writing and Russian. What grat-itude he heaped on me! Another convict wept at parting from me. I used to give him money—but was it very much? His gratitude, on the other hand, was unbounded. And meanwhile my own character became worse; I was capricious and impatient with them. They respected the condition of my soul and bore all without a murmur. And by the way: What a store of types and characters from the people I have carried out of the prison camp! I have lived closely with them, and so I think I know them thor-oughly. How many stories of tramps and bandits, and in general of the entire dark and miserable milieu! Enough for whole volumes! What a wonderful people."[16]

Dostoevsky's letter evokes the physical conditions of his imprisonment much more honestly than he would be allowed to do later by the censorship in *House of the Dead*. And the seeming contradiction between the two views of his fellow convicts illustrates the process of discovery that took place between the beginning of his imprisonment and the end—by which time he had succeeded in penetrating beneath the shocking and abhorrent surface to a much more accurate understanding of the psychic and moral depths. Indeed, the transition from one to the other view already furnishes the ground plan that he will later use to structure his prison memoirs.

6

On arriving in Omsk, Dostoevsky obtained his first glimpse of the fearsome and hated Major Krivtsov. "He began by roundly abusing the two of us," he says in his letter, "Durov and myself, as fools because of our crimes, and promised to punish us with corporal punishment at the first offense."[17] This incident is later recounted in *House of the Dead*, where Dostoevsky depicts the major more fully: "His [the major's] spiteful, purple, pimply face made a very depressing impression: it was as though a malicious spider had run out to pounce on some poor fly that had fallen into its web." After ordering the heads of the newly arrived prisoners to be shaved and confiscating all their property and personal clothing (except, for some reason, white underlinen), he concluded with the following threat: "Mind you behave yourselves! Don't let me hear of you! Or . . . corpo-ral pu-nishment. For the least misdemeanor—the lash!" (4: 214).

Whether or not Dostoevsky ever was flogged as a convict has been a subject of unceasing speculation; rumor to this effect was widely current in his lifetime and continued to circulate after his death. It seemed to be confirmed by the testimony of Dostoevsky's old friend, Dr. Riesenkampf, with whom he had shared an apartment in Petersburg in the 1840s and who later served on the staff of the Omsk Military Hospital. Riesenkampf claimed to have learned on the spot that Dostoevsky had been flogged on the orders of Krivtsov. "You cannot imagine," he wrote after Dostoevsky's death, "the horror of the friends of the late [Dostoevsky], who witnessed how, as a result of the punishment, and in the presence of his personal enemy Krivtsov, Feodor Mikhailovich, with his nervous temperament and his vanity, was struck down in 1850 for the first time with epilepsy, which then returned every month."[18]

Dostoevsky himself makes no mention of such an incident in his letter and even says specifically of Krivtsov: "God saved me from him."[19] Baron Wrangel, who became Dostoevsky's confidant shortly after the latter's release from prison camp, and whose sympathy with the ex-prisoner's plight would surely have overcome any reticence, categorically rejects any allegation of flogging: "I can testify, from the words of F. M. Dostoevsky himself, that neither in *katorga*, nor during the course of his unlimited term of service as a soldier, was he ever touched by so much as a finger, either by the officers or by his fellow convicts and fellow soldiers. Everything that has appeared on this point in the press is a pure invention."[20] Most conclusive of all, perhaps, is that Dostoevsky's Polish fellow prisoner, Szymon Tokarzewski, does not mention any such episode in his memoirs. Exiled for plotting to regain Polish independence, Tokarzewski paints a merciless picture of the ferocity and brutality of camp life and particularly of Krivtsov. To his jaundiced and quite comprehensibly anti-Russian eyes, the major was typical of the wayward inhumanity of Russian oppression; nor would Tokarzewski have wished to spare Dostoevsky, with whom he quarreled about politics. One may be sure that he would have cited this further example of Russian barbarism and savagery with relish if it had ever occurred.

The origin of Riesenkampf's certainty, however, is probably an incident recounted in the memoirs of P. K. Martyanov, one of the few reliable sources of information about Dostoevsky's prison years. According to Martyanov, Major Krivtsov did, on one occasion, issue an order for Dostoevsky to be punished by the lash. Making one of his impromptu inspections of the prison (he was nicknamed "eight-eyes" by the convicts because he seemed to see and know everything that went on, either through his own observation or through informers), Krivtsov discovered Dostoevsky lying on a pallet in the barracks at a time when he should have been at work. As it happened, Dostoevsky had been excused because of illness and allowed a day of rest; this was explained to Krivtsov by the noncommissioned officer on guard duty, one of a group of ex-naval cadets, all of good family, who had been demoted because of minor acts of insubordination and exiled to Siberia as punishment. But the furious Krivtsov, livid with rage, shouted that Dostoevsky was being protected and commanded that he be flogged immediately.

Preparations were being made to carry out the order when the commandant of the fortress, General de Grave, hurriedly arrived on the scene. He had been summoned by a messenger from the ex-naval cadet, who, like his fellows, was lenient toward the convicts in general and the political prisoners in particular. Not only did the general, known for his decency, countermand Krivtsov's order on the spot, but he also gave him a dressing-down in public for having illegally tried to punish a sick convict.[21] This event was well-known to the Omsk circle of Dostoevsky's protectors, but by the time the story had reached Riesenkampf it had probably become embellished with all the extra details provided in his version. The horrible deed, in other words, had not been averted but actually committed, and Dostoevsky had supposedly suffered the shattering consequences for the rest of his life—to the everlasting shame of Tsarist despotism.

It may be assumed, then, that Dostoevsky was never flogged, and the attempt to attribute his epilepsy directly to a nervous shock brought on by such an incident must be rejected. One understands, all the same, the impulse to link the appearance of his fearful malady with the terrible stresses to which he was exposed by his sentence; there is a certain poetic truth, even if not a literal one, in making such a connection. For the entire sequence of events beginning with his mock execution, followed by the exposure to prison camp conditions and the constant terror of being at the mercy of Krivtsov's drunken rages, certainly contributed to the outbreak of Dostoevsky's epilepsy. The first genuine attack, so far as can be determined, occurred sometime in 1850, and was characterized seven years later in a medical report as having been marked by shrieks, loss of consciousness, convulsive movements of the face and limbs, foam at the mouth, raucous breathing, and a feeble, rapid, and irregular pulse. The same report states that a similar attack recurred in 1853; since then, the seizures had continued on the average of once a month.

There has been a good deal of discussion as to the exact date when Dostoevsky's epilepsy first appeared, and the question has become especially complicated for two reasons. One is that Dostoevsky suffered from some unspecific "nervous ailment" in the later 1840s that was probably a warning signal of his later affliction; and the two illnesses are often confused, even though Dostoevsky states, time and again, that the symptoms of the first vanished during his Siberian years. The second complication is the widespread credence given to Sigmund Freud's famous article, "Dostoevsky and Parricide," which asserts that Dostoevsky's first epileptic symptoms were caused by "something terrible, unforgettable, and agonizing in childhood." The only evidence cited by Freud for this conclusion, however, refers to the (presumed) murder of Dostoevsky's father in 1839, when the writer was eighteen years old; nor is there any reason to believe that he was overcome by an epileptic attack at this time either.* Dostoev-

* Lack of documentary evidence is no obstacle to zealous Freudians. Dominique Arban, in a supposedly scholarly study of Dostoevsky's pre-Siberian years, simply invents a "primal scene" out of whole cloth to support the Freudian view. She depicts Dostoevsky at the age of seven, awakened one night by his mother's outcries, entering his parents' bedchamber, and being struck down by his first epileptic seizure at the sight of his father beating his helpless and pleading mother. Not a shred of proof can be offered to support this flight of the psychobiographical imagination. But, as David E. Stannard has remarked of other such efforts, "the most common approach in psychoanalytic work is to do precisely" what Dominque Arban has done here—"to read back from adult characteristics to assumed or 'reconstructed' childhood experiences." For more details, see the appendix to my *Dostoevsky, The Seeds of Revolt, 1821-1849* (Princeton, 1976), 379-391; Dominique Arban, *Les années d'apprentissage de Fiodor Dostoievski* (Paris, 1968), 31-32; David E. Stannard, *Shrinking History* (New York, 1980), 73.

sky's letter is the only firsthand document available, and it is clear that he speaks of his epilepsy as an entirely *new* phase of his old ailment ("disordered nerves")—the worsening of a condition whose initial symptoms may have shown up in Petersburg but only became truly epileptic in Siberia. This is exactly how he described it to Baron Wrangel, a year or two after he wrote the letter to his brother Mikhail. "The first sign of his illness, as he (Dostoevsky) affirmed," Wrangel writes, "had already appeared in Petersburg, but it developed in *katorga*."[22] In view of his medical history, Dostoevsky could not consider his epilepsy as entirely unexpected; but he always alludes to his Siberian seizures as an affliction of which he had had no previous experience.

7

Major Krivtsov was unquestionably a despicable petty tyrant and sadistic bully who enjoyed torturing the convicts under his control simply to display his authority. Sometimes, as Dostoevsky recounts and Tokarzewski confirms, he would invade the barracks at night and awaken the convicts, exhausted after a day of hard labor, because they were lying on their right sides or their backs and he decreed that the only permissible sleeping position was on the left side.† Nonetheless, his savage anger at what he considered Dostoevsky's malingering, even if it would have exploded at any convict caught under similar circumstances, was strengthened by his awareness that Dostoevsky *was* being partially "protected." Konstantin Ivanov, adjutant to the general of the Engineering Corps, arranged for Dostoevsky, so far as possible, to be assigned only the lightest kind of labor—painting, turning the wheel of a lathe, pounding alabaster, shoveling snow during the long Siberian winters. He also, at one point, assigned Dostoevsky to clerical work in the chancellery of the Engineering Corps; but this order was soon countermanded by the staff officer on duty, an ambitious careerist who had the ear of Governor-General Gorchakov and exercised a good deal of influence. Probably aware that Dostoevsky's protectors were no longer in good grace with Gorchakov, he informed Ivanov that clerical work was not suitable for political prisoners condemned to hard labor.

Dostoevsky, however, did not take this incident too badly; he felt that fairly taxing labor outdoors was necessary to combat the noxious effects

---

† Describing the senseless tyranny of Major Krivtsov, Tokarzewski remarks that, while he sometimes ordered floggings for genuine offenses, "in most cases it was for nothing. To be sentenced to the 'sticks,' it was enough to sleep on the right side. Yes, this is not a joke—it is the purest truth! Vaska [another convict nickname for Krivtsov] frequently erupted into the barracks at night, and whoever on the plank bed slept on the right side was flogged. Vaska justified this punishment by saying that Christ always slept on his left side, consequently everybody was required to follow his example." Dostoevsky does not supply this last detail. Szymon Tokarzewski, *Siedem lat Katorgi* (Warsaw, 1907), 127.

of the pestilential atmosphere in the barracks, and he sought it out after a time. "Being constantly in the open air, working everyday until I was tired, learning to carry heavy weights—at any rate I shall save myself," he writes. "I thought: I shall make myself strong, I shall leave the prison healthy, vigorous, hearty and not old. I was not mistaken; the work and exercise were very good for me" (4: 80). Sergey Durov, on the other hand, apparently avoided manual labor whenever he could; and though scarcely older than Dostoevsky, he emerged four years later an ailing and broken old man barely able to stand on his feet. The one description of Dostoevsky's appearance in the prison camp by an eyewitness stresses his air of sturdiness and physical vigor: "F. M. Dostoevsky looked like a strong, thickset, stocky working man, well-trained and adapted to military discipline."[23] Dostoevsky's years as a cadet in the Academy of Engineers probably accounts for this latter impression.

All the same, Dostoevsky's health would probably have suffered more than it did if not for the kindness and humaneness of the head of the fortress hospital, Dr. Troitsky, toward the political prisoners. Dostoevsky's first stay in the hospital may have been caused by his epileptic attack, or because he collapsed from exhaustion while engaged in clearing snow; but he returned there frequently, even when not ailing from any specific complaint. Dr. Troitsky would pass the word along through the ex-naval cadets (affectionately called *moryachki*, "the little sailors," by the convicts) that space was available. Dostoevsky would then show up to be entered on the books as "convalescing" and take a much-needed respite from the incessant noise and turmoil of the barracks. The hospital afforded him relative quiet and comfort, the luxury of a bed, and nourishing food, tea, and wine supplied either from hospital rations or the doctor's own kitchen. Major Krivtsov certainly knew about Troitsky's favors to the "politicals"; but since the hospital was an Army installation, not part of the prison, there was little he could do. And while both the general of Engineers and General de Grave were very well aware that Dr. Troitsky was playing fast and loose with the strict application of the sentence passed on the Petrashevtsy, they preferred to close their eyes to such infractions with a warning to the doctor to be very careful.

8

Such a warning, as it turned out, was by no means superfluous; one of the physicians in the hospital finally denounced his superior's suspicious favoritism toward the political prisoners in a letter to Petersburg. An investigation into the charges was ordered, and a legal official dispatched from Tobolsk to carry on the inquiry. But since he received no cooperation from the local authorities, the informer could not produce any witnesses to substantiate the charges he had made. When Dostoevsky was asked whether he had written anything, either in the prison or in the hospital, he replied that, while he had not actually set pen to paper, he was gathering material. Pressed to explain where this material could be found, he retorted: "In my head."[24]

In desperation, the investigator decided on a sudden search of the convicts' quarters. Since this required the permission of the commandant, General de Grave had time secretly to pass the word along to the prisoners, who, hastening to remove everything illegal and forbidden, obligingly left a few barely concealed items to reward the searcher. He turned up a pot of pomade, a bottle of eau de cologne, a torn woman's shirt, women's stockings, and some children's toys. The prize, however, consisted of a few sheets of writing paper, on which he eagerly pounced in the hope of having at last unearthed some incriminating evidence of forbidden literary composition. The sheets did, in fact, contain a literary work—but not of a kind he had anticipated. It turned out to be a prayer, addressed to the Almighty, pleading for divine intercession to exorcise the presence of Satan, who had, it would appear, returned to earth from the nether world in the shape of Major Krivtsov. Whether Dostoevsky took any part in the composition of this bit of gallows humor is not recorded; but his literary talents would hardly have gone unused.

As a matter of fact, Dostoevsky did much more than gather material in his head; he kept a notebook in the hospital in which he jotted down phrases and expressions used by the convicts and typical of their salty and picturesque peasant language. These precious pages he confided to the care of the medical assistant, A. I. Ivanov, who returned them to him on his release; and Dostoevsky kept the scribbled sheets, sewn together by hand into a little notebook, until his dying day. To have carried them on his person, or to have kept them in the barracks, would have been too risky—not only because they might have been lost or stolen (everything was stolen that could bring in a kopek or two, and *everything*, as Dostoevsky learned to his amazement, could be sold), but also because, if found by the major, they might have provided the long-sought justification for a flogging. Besides noting phrases and proverbs, Dostoevsky also preserved the texts of songs later included in *House of the Dead*. Certain sentences, which contain names and dates, are evidently mnemonic devices intended to recall the stories or incidents he was not able to set down in full. Dostoevsky made ample use of all this material in the book that directly emerged from his prison-camp days, as well as in many of his novels, where locutions first noted in Siberia are incorporated to enliven the text. Students of ethnology, Russian folklore, and linguistics have since found Dostoevsky to be a very accurate observer and recorder of peasant mentality and prison jargon.

The existence of the *Siberian Notebooks* reveals Dostoevsky's grim determination, despite all the deprivations and exhausting demands of prison-camp life, to carry on his literary career and never to give up hope that it would some day be resumed. "I cannot find the expressions to tell you," he wrote his friend Apollon Maikov, "what torture I suffered because I was not able to write."[25] In the one encounter during these years where he could speak freely to someone from the metropolis, what he inquired about most eagerly was the literary scene from which he had been so roughly torn away. This conversation took place in the winter of 1853, and it was carried on with Evgeny Yakushkin, the son of an exiled Decembrist family who, after completing his studies in Russia, had returned on a mission to Siberia in his capacity as a land surveyor.

Passing through Omsk, and knowing that Dostoevsky was a prisoner there, Yakushkin asked an officer friend in the fortress to arrange a meeting. The next day, convict Dostoevsky was assigned to clear the snow in front of one of the houses serving as quarters for passing officialdom, and he was invited inside by the occupant, a young man in the uniform of the Corps of Land Surveyors. "I remember," Yakushkin writes in a letter many years later, "that Dostoevsky's appearance made a terribly painful impression on me when he walked into the room in his convict clothes, wearing shackles, and with his sickly face bearing the traces of a serious illness." Relations were quickly established after the first moment, and the two eagerly spoke "of what was going on in Russia, of current Russian literature. He asked me about some of the new writers who had just appeared and spoke of his difficult situation in a convict battalion."[26] Yakushkin, pressing a small sum of money on Dostoevsky, also willingly agreed to take a letter back to Mikhail that was written on the spot, and he was delighted when Dostoevsky said that the meeting had brought him back to life. This manifestation of interest and sympathy reassured the erstwhile writer that he was still remembered, and had not, like the heroine of his own *Poor Folk*, vanished into the steppe without leaving a trace.

9

Dostoevsky's last two years in prison camp were painful enough, but much less of a hardship than those preceding. In the first place, Major Krivtsov was arrested, tried for misconduct, and forced to resign from government service; with him went the reign of terror he had established. Dostoevsky had the satisfaction of seeing the ex-major in town, after these events, a broken and disconsolate figure, "a civilian wearing a shabby coat and a cap with a cockade in it" (4: 218). Once Krivtsov was gone, "everyone seemed to breathe more freely and to be more confident; . . . all knew that in case of need one could have things out with the authorities and that the innocent would not be punished for the guilty except by mistake" (4: 219). Governor-General Gorchakov too, whose mistress (the wife of a well-rewarded Army general) shamelessly collected graft hand over fist, also fell from favor and was replaced. In the spring of 1853, Dostoevsky's friends in the Omsk Engineering Command, trying to take advantage of the new and more favorable climate that prevailed, petitioned for the status of Dostoevsky and Durov to be changed so that the prisoners would no longer have to wear shackles; but the Ministry of War notified Omsk that the Tsar had not seen fit to grant their request.

Despite this setback, the external conditions of Dostoevsky's imprisonment nonetheless took a sharp turn for the better. "I enjoyed more privileges toward the last than in the early years of my life in prison," he notes in *House of the Dead.* "I discovered among the officers serving in the town some acquaintances and even old schoolfellows of mine . . . through their good offices I was able to obtain even larger supplies of money, and even to have books" (4: 229). Who these old schoolfellows were remains unknown—but they could only have been classmates from the Academy of Engineers, now posted to service in Siberia. Nor, except for two titles—Russian versions of *The Pickwick Papers* and *David Copperfield*—do we know the books to which Dostoevsky finally had access. The two novels of Dickens were lent him by the *moryachki*, who were surprised, however, that, unlike Durov, he exhibited little interest in their stock of French works by Alexandre Dumas, Eugène Sue, and Paul Feval. The impact of his reading of Dickens, though, appears to have left a profound moral trace; years later he would see Mr. Pickwick as one of the precursors of his own Prince Myshkin, "a perfectly good man," the embodiment of a Christian ideal mocked and ridiculed in the world. Most important, Dostoevsky's situation was also eased because he had at last been able to establish friendly relations with some of the peasant-convicts, and this provided a welcome relief from his oppressive sense of living in a world surrounded only by enmity and hatred.

He was released from prison in February 1854—not at all to genuine freedom, but to serve as a lowly private in the Russian Army for an indeterminate period. All the same, the presentiment of the difficulties lying ahead could not suppress the immense joy of his long-awaited delivery. For years he had paced in solitude every evening round the stockade of the prison camp, counting another paling each day to mark the gradual expiration of his sentence; at last the great moment had finally arrived! But no words can surpass the restrained pathos with which he depicts the mingled sorrow and happiness of this never-to-be-forgotten event— the implicit regret over a bitter past, and the tremulous anticipation of the uncertain but infinitely alluring future. "The fetters fell off. I picked them up. I wanted to hold them in my hand, to look at them for the last time.

5. The Stockade around the Omsk Prison Camp

I seemed already to be wondering that they could have been on my feet a minute before. 'Well, with God's blessing, with God's blessing!' said the convicts in coarse, abrupt voices, in which, however, there was a note of pleasure. Yes, with God's blessing! Freedom, new life, resurrection from the dead. . . . What a glorious moment!" (4: 232).

CHAPTER 7

A World of Moral Horror

No period of Dostoevsky's life is more difficult to depict satisfactorily than the interval of these prison years. Not that there is any lack of material—on the contrary, his correspondence, the memoirs of contemporaries, and the full-scale account given years later in *House of the Dead* would seem to provide ample documentation. Despite such an apparent abundance of evidence, there is still a lingering mystery about exactly what occurred that is very difficult to pierce. Neither in *House of the Dead* nor in his letters does Dostoevsky, the great psychologist, ever analyze his inner state of mind except in the vaguest terms; nowhere does he overtly provide the information that might help us to understand the specific modality of his transformation. Once or twice in his letters, to be sure, Dostoevsky approaches the brink of such a self-analysis and self-avowal; but he always retreats at the very last moment: "But my soul, heart, mind—what has grown, what has ripened, what has been discarded together with the weeds, that can't be communicated and recounted on a sheet of paper. . . . In general, prison has taken away many things from me and brought many others."[1] This is as far as Dostoevsky ever goes in baring the secrets of his psyche; and such words merely tantalize curiosity without providing any genuine illumination.

Only one other passage, written twenty-five years later, goes beyond vague generalities of the kind just quoted. Reminiscing, in his *Diary of a Writer* (1873), "on the regeneration of my convictions," Dostoevsky remarks that it had in fact been a lengthy affair. "It did not occur so quickly," he writes, "but gradually—and after a long, long time."[2] Whether this means that the "regeneration" overlapped the immediate prison years still remains unclear; but such an inference seems warranted by the emphasis of Dostoevsky's words. If so, this would suggest that Dostoevsky did not emerge from prison camp with a fixed and firmly defined set of new convictions to replace those he had abandoned. It is much more plausible to see him, at first, gradually trying to make human sense out of his exposure to a whole range of new impressions that had clashed with his preconceived notions, and only subsequently coming to understand in a more self-conscious fashion how this experience had changed his ideas. Such explicitly formulated "ideas" would have begun to take shape when Dostoevsky, making contact once again with Russian social-political and cultural life in the mid-1850s and early 1860s, found it necessary to define a position amid the abrupt transformations and epochal events of these agitated years.

The same passage in the *Diary of a Writer* is also valuable because it points to a major motivation for whatever changes did occur. It was not, Dostoevsky says, the hardships of exile and forced labor that had altered his ideas and those of others like him among the ex-Petrashevtsy; they had not been broken by the sheer physical burdens of their cruel destiny. "No, something different . . . changed our outlook, our convictions and our hearts. . . . This something different was the direct contact with the people, the brotherly merger with them in a common misfortune, the realization that [we had] become even as they, that we had been made equal to them, and even to their lowest stratum."[3] Such words, we have seen, gild and idealize a "merger" that was far from having been as "brotherly" as Dostoevsky wished his readers to believe; but he is unquestionably pointing to something crucial in the process of his transformation all the same, even if he does so in terms that are manifestly misleading. For what he highlights in the words just quoted is the *end product* of the process he went through; the "brotherly merger" only resulted from a complex inner struggle whose details Dostoevsky neglects to mention here, though it forms one of the dominating *leitmotifs* of *House of the Dead*.

Whatever happened to Dostoevsky in *katorga* should of course not be seen in isolation from the momentous events that immediately preceded his departure. The months of isolation and stubborn self-defense in the Peter-and-Paul Fortress; the confrontation with death and with the tormenting mystery of life beyond the grave during those ultimate moments on the scaffolding; the meeting at Tobolsk with the wives of the Decembrists, those moving witnesses to the sublime reality of self-sacrifice and Christian charity—all these left their indelible traces. His prison solitude had proven to him that the autonomy of the human personality could be a living reality; the agonizing expectation of the end had given a new transcendent (and no longer exclusively social and secular) significance to his Christian beliefs; and he had seen the moral essence of these beliefs movingly incarnated in the benevolent visitors to his place of captivity. Such experiences certainly helped to transform Dostoevsky, but they were not of such a nature as to clash sharply with his earlier convictions; they acted rather to accentuate the more purely moral-religious aspects of his previous world-view, while detaching them from their connection with any doctrine of social-political action. It was only when he arrived in the prison camp, and was forced to live cheek-by-jowl with the peasant-convicts, that some of his earlier opinions were directly challenged; only then did he begin to realize to what extent he had been a dupe of illusions about the Russian peasant and the nature of Russian social-political reality.

Consequently, there is some justification for the priority that he assigns to his encounter with the Russian people in bringing about the transformation that occurred. For it was this encounter that led to the collapse of his entire psychic-emotive equilibrium and called for a desperate effort to find some means of adjusting to the unsettling truths that assailed him on every side. Dostoevsky's remarkable response to this challenge constitutes the hinge on which his regeneration turned; and once this response was made, his convictions were gradually altered to conform to the new vision he had acquired of his companions in misfortune.

2
―――――

Many things remain uncertain and conjectural about Dostoevsky's four years of internment in the prison camp; even the question of how to read the book he wrote about that period of his life, *House of the Dead*, poses something of a problem. For, clearly, it is as much poetry as truth: Dostoevsky rearranged his experiences in conformity with a dominant artistic purpose, and his account can in no way be accepted as an innocent reproduction of his day-to-day existence. All the same, his aim was to communicate the objective correlatives of what he knew to be the inner "truth" of his own moral-spiritual mutation; and the "reality" of this mutation can hardly be called into question.

No matter, then, how much Dostoevsky may have embellished or pointed up his memories and observations of the past, such "improvements" all went in the direction of imparting as much artistic and symbolic pregnancy as possible to this profound alteration of his sensibility. Hence the incidents and events he writes about—even if they were accompanied by many others that he neglects to mention, or are compressed into a time span different from their actual duration—may be accepted as at least accurate in substance, if not in form, and used as biographical material. The same is true of the thoughts and feelings of his narrator—who is not, however, supposed to be Dostoevsky himself. In the present context, though, we shall neglect the artistic devices that Dostoevsky employs and focus rather on whatever clues he provides that help us to grasp the underlying motives of his regeneration. A study of *House of the Dead* as a literary work will be reserved for the next volume, when we reach the years in which it was finally composed.

Any proper understanding of Dostoevsky's prison years must take, as its point of departure, one indisputable certainty: the first period of his life there, extending perhaps for over a year or longer, plunged him into a mood that may be considered one of traumatic shock. And, despite Dostoevsky's denial, the physical rigors of the prison régime could hardly have failed to affect his general psychic state. It is true that he was not broken by the hardships he had to sustain, and did not change his convictions to ease his lot or to curry favor. How could he have done so, since he never breathed a word about such changes to anyone and mentioned them in only the most general terms even to his brother? But it would be ingenuous to imagine that the harsh conditions of the life he describes in his letter, where he notes repeated illnesses as a result of the unaccustomed strain on his organism, did not influence his state of mind in any way. To be sure, Dostoevsky had not been wealthy and had scarcely lived in the lap of luxury; but he had been accustomed to the normal amenities of civilized Russian upper-class life. Torn from this relatively comfortable milieu, he was forcibly thrown into a situation of extreme deprivation that stretched his physical stamina to the utmost. It was only natural that the grueling hardships he now had to confront should have reacted on his sensibility, and colored all his impressions with an exceedingly dark hue.

Nor should one forget either the constant terror in which Dostoevsky lived of being shamefully chastised at the orders of Major Krivtsov. On first setting foot in the camp, he had been threatened by a flogging for the slightest infraction of the regulations, and he lived in shrinking fear that this threat would be carried out. Krivtsov had not hesitated to order a flogging for the Polish noble Z (Zochowski), about whom Dostoevsky writes with great sympathy; having himself escaped such punishment only by the skin of his teeth, he was obviously obsessed with dread that he would not be so lucky a second time. This constant anxiety certainly accounts for the morbid curiosity with which, as he admits, he questioned others about their sensations on being flogged. "I wanted to know with precision in certain cases," he writes, "how great it [the pain] was, to what, finally, it could be compared. *I do not really know why I wanted so much to know. I recall only one thing: it was not a vain curiosity. I repeat, I was terribly upset and shaken*" (italics added). And he could not listen to the information he solicited without "my heart leaping into my throat, and beating strongly and violently" (4: 153-154).

The specter of being subjected to such indignity, and the gnawing doubt as to whether he would be capable of conducting himself bravely, is enough to account for the symptoms of nervous excitement invariably stimulated by such conversations. But Dostoevsky was not only reacting to an instinctive concern about himself; he was also exhibiting the same sort of visceral response to the routine brutality of Russian life that had marked him from the very first. As an adolescent, the sight of a government courier phlegmatically beating his peasant driver on the back of the neck had come to him as a terrible flash of insight into the true nature of Russian society; it was from this moment that he began to hate the power that gave one human being the right so to violate another.[4] A. I. Savelyev, who knew Dostoevsky as a cadet and as a newly commissioned Officer of Engineers, attributes his refusal to remain in military service to his revulsion against the daily punishment of disobedient soldiers and convicts in work parties that he was forced to witness while stationed in Kronstadt Fortress.[5] Savelyev exaggerates the importance of this motive in Dostoevsky's decision; but if he does so, it is surely because Dostoevsky must have expressed his sentiments with such vehemence. Fellow members of the Petrashevsky circle also testified to his furious indignation whenever he heard about any incidents of flogging, or other types of corporal punishment inflicted on peasants or soldiers (and most Russian soldiers were of peasant origin). Dostoevsky himself was now living under the frightening shadow of what he had always found so intolerable for others, and of what, in the past, he could never even hear spoken of without an outburst of rage. The helplessness and hopelessness of his position could only have filled him with a bitterness all the more rankling because it had to be so severely repressed.

3
———

Such circumstances, however, provide only the general framework within which Dostoevsky's crisis occurred. They must, of course, be taken into account, but it would be a mistake to give them too much importance; they were only contributing factors and not the essential cause. After all, the loathsome living arrangements of the camp and the sadistic tyranny of Major Krivtsov would have been more or less what Dostoevsky might have expected to find, even though the reality (unlike his reaction to solitary confinement in the Peter-and-Paul Fortress) proved far more harrowing than he had probably imagined. What he had not anticipated at all, though, was to discover so little to choose between his reception at the hands of Krivtsov and the treatment he received from his fellow convicts. What Dostoevsky had expected cannot be known with certainty; but we have cited both the innocent lucubrations of Petrashevsky and Dostoevsky's words in his final interview just before departing. He was not, he had told his brother Mikhail consolingly, being sent to a jungle to live among wild beasts; he would be among people, among other human beings like himself, perhaps even better than himself. Even allowing for some attitudinizing under the stress of the moment, such words would indicate a hope that was cruelly deceived.

Fully to grasp what this hope may have been, we should keep in mind that Dostoevsky's image of the people had been decisively shaped by the philanthropic and humanitarian ideas of the 1840s in Russia, and nourished by his reading of the French social novel of the 1830s (Hugo and

George Sand in particular), with its strong overtones of Socialism and "progressive" Christianity (the two had not yet become separated). As Maxime Leroy has pointed out, such works were steeped in "a divinization of the people" and took for granted that "they are good, they are moral; better than the wealthy, more moral than the wealthy."[6] No French writer of the time conveyed this "divinization" more expressively than the Christian radical Abbé Lamennais, whose *Paroles d'un croyant* was translated into Russian, with Dostoevsky's encouragement, by Milyukov himself and read at one of the meetings of the Palm-Durov circle. "It is my profound conviction," Lamennais wrote in another work, "that today the people, the true people, ignorant, ragged, living every day on the labor of that day, are still the healthiest portion of society, and among whom one finds the most good sense, the most justice, the most humanity."[7] Dostoevsky's own *Poor Folk*—and indeed, most of his writing of the 1840s—are imbued with much the same conviction. And if we take his remark to his brother seriously, it would indicate that, upon leaving to share the fate of the people in the prison camp, he had fully expected to find there a heart-warming confirmation of such views.

What he found instead was a cruelty and brutishness that, under the shock of the first impact, did not differ by a jot from the worst excesses of the miserable Krivtsov. Indeed, one of the first incidents that Dostoevsky records in *House of the Dead* proved to him, in an appalling fashion, that it was not only Krivtsov who might do violence to his person. He and Durov, having arrived the day before, had gone into the spacious prison kitchen to buy a glass of tea; this luxury was not included in the prison rations, but the cook supplied the convicts with whatever supplement to the ordinary fare they could afford to purchase. As the two sat and contentedly sipped their tea, surrounded by others busily eating what they too had bought, the two newcomers pretended not to notice the baleful glances cast in their direction by the peasant-convicts. Suddenly, they were accosted by the drunken Tartar Gazin. A giant of a man, who became ugly when he drank, he sneeringly asked the two "gentlemen" where they had obtained the funds for their "treat," and whether they had been sent to Siberia to enjoy themselves by drinking tea. When both remained silent in face of this nasty provocation, Gazin seized a huge bread tray lying nearby and held it menacingly over their heads. It might have come crashing down the next moment; but whether by accident or design (Dostoevsky does not decide) someone rushed in to tell Gazin, a large-scale vodka smuggler, that his stock had been stolen, and the Tartar hurried off with no damage being done. This ominous incident, though, left no doubt in Dostoevsky's mind that he was equally exposed to outrage at the hands of his fellow prisoners, and that there was little to choose between them and the routine ferocity of the Krivtsovs.

Actually, such direct threats to life and limb, so far as Dostoevsky was concerned, happily proved to be the exception rather than the rule. But the menace, even if it never materialized, was always palpable; and Dostoevsky was given ample proof, in the way the prisoners treated each other, that the menace *could* turn into mayhem at any moment. Of one convict he writes: "He liked to steal very much, and was frequently beaten for that by the others; but who among the others had never stolen and who then had never been beaten for that?" (4: 146). Beatings were also customary when convicts became drunk and unruly to a degree that might have created a disturbance, provoking "eight-eyes" to discipline the barracks as a whole. Gazin was a very serious offender of this kind, as Dostoevsky had good reason to know, and sometimes even lunged at people with a knife when inflamed by vodka. What would happen next was witnessed by Dostoevsky many times: "A dozen men from his barracks rush at him all together and begin to beat him. One cannot imagine anything more terrible than this rain of blows: he is beaten on the chest, the heart, the pit of the stomach, the groin; he is beaten tirelessly and brutally, and one stops only when he is unconscious and resembles a corpse" (4: 41).

Even when not forced to be a sickened eyewitness to such savage spectacles, which he detested with every fiber of his being, Dostoevsky was constantly reminded of them by the oaths, insults, menaces, and threats that flew back and forth and testified to the constant irascibility of his fellow inmates. It seemed to him as if some bloody brawl was always about to break loose, though in most cases, to his initial surprise, matters would end after a volley of the most scurrilous abuse. "To exchange insults, to strike with injurious words," he remarks, "was permitted. It was even a bit of a distraction for everyone. But fights are not always tolerated [by the others] and it is only in exceptional cases that the adversaries come to blows" (4: 25). All the same, blows were used to stop fights that might cause trouble; and there was hardly a moment when the menace of violence was not hanging in the air.

Life in the barracks was thus a never-ending, rasping assault on Dostoevsky's sensibility at one of its sorest points; there was no escape, as he wrote in his letter, from "the eternal hostility and quarreling around one, the wrangling, shouting, uproar, din. . . ." Or rather, as we know, there was luckily one means of sporadic refuge—a flight to the hospital, even though this sanctuary carried the risk of infection and meant confinement in a fetid ward without a chance of getting a breath of fresh air. "And yet, especially at the beginning," Dostoevsky writes, "I often went to the hospital, sometimes being ill, sometimes simply to stay in bed; I was fleeing from the prison. Life was unbearable there, more unbearable than the hospital, *morally unbearable*" (4: 164-165; italics added).

Such moral revulsion was not only a result of the ferocity prevailing in the relations of the prisoners with each other. It was also considerably increased by what Dostoevsky very quickly learned of the appalling depravity that reigned among them, and which certainly far surpassed anything he could have foreseen. Dostoevsky had depicted people who lived in misery; but those who were truly vicious had always come from the upper class or had worked to serve its vices. He was evidently unprepared to find among the peasant-convicts a moral degeneracy he had attributed previously only to their betters; or, if he had suspected anything of the kind, its reality proved far more intolerable than he could have anticipated. For, as he wrote about being suddenly plunged into the midst of convict life, "I was astonished and upset, as if until then I had not suspected or heard anything about all that, and yet I knew it and had learned about it. *But the reality makes quite a different impression than what one learns from books and hearsay*" (4: 65; italics added). Censorship would not permit him, of course, to speak too plainly about the mores of the convicts, but there is very little that he does not manage to convey.

The drunken sprees on illegal vodka are described in considerable detail, and it has even been suggested that Dostoevsky's informed exposé of the methods used by the smugglers complicated the task for later generations of camp inmates. Prostitution, both female and male, is clearly alluded to, explicitly in the case of the former (women were available in Omsk, and guards could be bribed to overlook absences from work parties in town), more circuitously, though still unmistakably, for the latter. Nothing astonished Dostoevsky more, however, than the universal prevalence of thievery—the fact that "generally speaking, [the convicts] stole from each other dreadfully" (4: 18). And no wonder he was astonished, having written a touching little story, *An Honest Thief*, in which a hopeless drunkard, so as to obtain a bit of vodka, steals a pair of breeches from a friend almost as destitute as himself and dies of heartbreak and remorse for having done so. No such heartbreak could be observed in the prison camp, as he very quickly became aware. "Some of the convicts hung about me suspecting that I had money with me," he writes, recounting the events of his first day. "They began making up to me at once, began showing me how to wear my fetters, got me—for money, of course—a box with a lock on it for me to put away the precious belongings already served out to me, as well as some underclothes I had brought with me to prison. Next day they stole it from me and sold it for drink. One of them became most devoted to me later on, though he never gave up robbing me at every convenient opportunity" (4: 25).

The equitable calm of this last sentence hardly conveys the furious surge of indignation that surely swept over Dostoevsky on discovering the theft, and his dismay at finding himself at the mercy of men lacking the most elementary principles of honesty—men for whom "friendship" did not exclude incessant larceny. Clearly, this was a world in which the ordinary norms of morality had ceased to exist; and such a conclusion seemed confirmed by his failure to observe any signs of repentance or remorse among the peasant-convicts for their crimes, either in the past or in the present. "In the course of several years," Dostoevsky observes, "I never saw a sign of repentance among these people; not a trace of despondent brooding over their crimes, and the majority of them inwardly considered themselves absolutely in the right. This is a fact. No doubt vanity, brag, bad example, false shame are responsible for a great deal of this. On the other side, who can say that he has sounded the depths of these lost hearts, and has read what is hidden from all the world in them? Yet surely it would have been possible during all those years to have noticed something, to have caught some glimpse which would have borne witness to some inner anguish and suffering in those hearts. But it was not there, it certainly was not there" (4: 15).

Dostoevsky thus concludes that "crime cannot be interpreted from preconceived conventional points of view," and that "the philosophy of it is a little more difficult than is supposed" (4: 15). Here he is unquestionably conveying his own first, bewildered reaction to what he was now confronting in the prison camp. For was it not he himself who had harbored such "preconceived conventional points of view"? Had he not imagined, as we may infer, that he would find the peasant-convicts bowed down by the weight of their sins? A brief glance at some of his early works will clarify why it is very likely that he should have entertained such a guileless misconception.

Dostoevsky consistently portrays lower-class characters (not peasants, to be sure, but people with a similar subaltern status in Russian society) who are consumed by guilt and remorse over their timid and insignificant velleities of rebellion. Makar Devushkin (*Poor Folk*) is terrified at the "freethinking" ideas that flit through his mind as a feeble protest against his humiliating condition; Golyadkin (*The Double*) is driven into schizophrenia by his temerity in refusing to accept a social rebuff from his office superior. The ravishingly beautiful heroine of *The Landlady*, Katerina, who comes from a merchant background, is evidently meant to be taken as a symbolic image of the Russian people; and Dostoevsky depicts her as suffering under a crushing burden of guilt cunningly kept alive by the sinister Murin, who maintains his power by playing on her fears of eternal damnation. It may be presumed that Dostoevsky expected to encounter a state of mind corresponding to such preconceptions, if perhaps in a less strikingly sensational guise, in the prison camp. But instead of a conscience whose manifestations could even be considered excessive, considering what the lower classes were forced to endure in Russian society, he was shocked to discover no traces of any moral misgivings at all.

The environment in which Dostoevsky found himself thus filled him with consternation and horror, and he makes no bones about stating his reaction to it in *House of the Dead*. In a passage describing the long winter evenings, when the convicts were locked in early and had several hours to spend together before being overcome with sleep, he gives vent to the bitter misanthrophy that assailed him in these early days. For he paints a grim picture and utters a harsh judgment: "noise, uproar, laughter, swearing, the clank of chains, smoke and grime, shaven heads, branded faces, ragged clothes, everything *defiled and degraded*. What cannot man live through? Man is a creature that can become accustomed to anything, and I think this is the best definition of him" (4: 10; italics added). One commentator has taken these last words as another of Dostoevsky's frequent tributes to the providential elasticity of the human spirit; but they seem to me quite the opposite. Are they not rather a sarcastic thrust at the abysmal depths of defilement in which the peasant-convicts—but not, clearly, Dostoevsky himself—had learned to exist and even to feel at home?[8]

5
———

By this time, it should be self-evident why Dostoevsky did not make any effort, as hostile critics have sometimes suggested he might have done, to explain the nature of his crime to the other inmates. (Whatever the disagreements between Durov and Dostoevsky, to which we shall come presently, the former made no such effort either and presumably arrived at a comparable estimate of the situation.) It was evidently impossible for Dostoevsky to have spoken directly of this matter in *House of the Dead*; but passages of the book help to throw some light on it all the same. One of the first things that Dostoevsky was told, by a prisoner who had once been an Army officer, was that the peasant-convicts "do not like the gentlemen, especially political prisoners, they will eat them alive, and that's understandable. First of all, you are another breed, different from what they are, and then, they were all serfs or soldiers. Judge for yourself if they can like you" (4: 28). Elsewhere, another remark even more directly applies to Dostoevsky's decision to keep silent. "If I had begun to try and win their good-will by making up to them," he writes, "being familiar with them . . . they would at once have supposed that I did it out of fear and cowardice and would have treated me with contempt" (4: 77).

As a result, Dostoevsky did not seek any closer contact with the peasant-convicts and decided to remain aloof; but nothing appears to have taken him more by surprise than the discovery of their innate and instinctive hostility. Why this should have come as such a revelation poses something of a problem; after all, given the nature of Russian society, why should any other reaction have been expected? Why should Dostoevsky, who believed that his own father had been murdered by his serfs, and who certainly knew of other instances of peasant discontent, have imagined that he would be greeted with friendly acceptance? One possible reason is that, in view of the equality of conditions reigning in the camp, Dostoevsky had assumed that easier relations between the peasants and the "gentlemen" would automatically be brought about. Such an expectation seems to be implied by an observation like the following, which of course confirms the opposite: "The ex-nobles in the camp were regarded, as a general rule, darkly and without friendliness," Dostoevsky observes. "Even though they have been deprived of all their privileges of caste, and are assimilated in every respect to other prisoners, these latter never recognize them as comrades. This happens even without any conscious prejudice, but simply, in all sincerity, unconsciously" (4: 26).

Another reason, however, was probably the disparaging view of the Russian peasant that was common to the Russian Westerners—the view we have seen reflected in Dostoevsky's testimony before the Commission of Inquiry. For while the peasant would certainly strike back at personal injury and mistreatment, he was generally considered too primitive and intellectually undeveloped to take any conscious objection to his own status and condition. In a famous article on Peter the Great, which may be considered a manifesto of the ideology of the Russian Westerners, Belinsky had written in 1841 that "the Russian *muzhik* is still semi-Asiatic, but in his own way: he loves pleasure, but conceives it to be exclusively in the flowing bowl, in eating and lying on the sleeping shelf of his stove. When the harvest has been a good one and he has bread in plenty he is happy and contented; thoughts of the past and future do not disturb him! For men in their natural state, apart from satisfying their hunger and similar wants, are incapable of thinking."[9] If Dostoevsky held some such opinion of the *muzhik*, we can understand why the evidence of a certain social-political consciousness among them should have come as such a jolt. It was the beginning of his realization that the Russian peasant, far from living completely in the moment and responding to stimuli only on the level of immediate need, was quite capable of thinking and had a well-developed, independent outlook of his own.* For the moment, though,

---

* Such a view of the peasant, it might be noted, was by no means restricted to Russian Westerners; it was common throughout Europe as well up through the third quarter of the nineteenth century and, in some countries, even beyond. Balzac, for example, wrote that peasants lived "a purely material life that approaches the savage state." Jerome Blum has culled citations illustrating the same conviction from a number of other novels of various countries. See his extremely informative article, "Fiction and the European Peasantry: The Realist Novel as a Historical Source," *Proceedings of the American Philosophical Society*, 2 (1982), 128 and passim.

what affected Dostoevsky most was the reflection of this self-consciousness in the implacable enmity of the peasant-convicts toward the nobles in general, and himself in particular.

6

From the very start, Dostoevsky became uneasily aware of this hostility through the "dark looks" cast in his direction; and the meaning of such looks was confirmed during the incident in the prison kitchen with Gazin. No effort was made by the others to intervene on behalf of the nobles, as would certainly have been done if other peasant-convicts had been threatened in a similar fashion. "Not one word in our defense!" Dostoevsky observes. "Not one shout at Gazin, so intense was their hatred of us!" This is only the first of many occasions when Dostoevsky learned the truth of the words uttered by one of the Polish prisoners, also a political detainee, whom Dostoevsky had naively asked why the peasant-convicts had seemed to resent his tea even though many of them were also eating their own food. The prison-hardened Polish noble replied: "It is not because of your tea. They are ill-disposed to you because you were once gentlemen and not like them. Many of them would dearly like to insult you, to humiliate you. You will meet with a lot of unpleasantness here" (4: 32).

Such predictions were borne out a few days later, when Dostoevsky was sent on his first assignment with a work party. Unskilled at manual labor, he found that "everywhere I was in the way, everywhere I was pushed aside almost with abuse. The lowest ragamuffin, himself a wretched workman, who did not dare to raise his voice among the other convicts who were sharper and cleverer than he, thought himself entitled to shout at me on the pretext that I hindered him if I stood beside him. At last one of the smarter ones said to me plainly and coarsely: 'Where are you shoving? Get away! Why do you poke yourself in where you are not wanted!' " As a result, Dostoevsky continues, "I had to stand apart, and to stand apart when all are working makes one feel ashamed. But when it happened that I did walk away and stood at the end of the barge, they shouted at once: 'Fine workmen they've given us; what can one get done with them? You can get nothing done' " (4: 76).

The impact of such experiences on Dostoevsky can only be appreciated if we recall the image of his character as we know it from the pre-Siberian period of his life. For he had been notorious in Petersburg literary circles as a person of extreme nervous susceptibility and pathological sensitivity, quite unable to control himself in face of the slightest suggestion of opposition or hostility. His relations with the other young writers of the Belinsky *pléiade*, at first friendly and even cordial, were quickly poisoned by his unhappy proclivity to take offense at every passing remark; and by the end of the 1840s he had acquired an unenviable reputation as being socially intolerable and morbidly suspicious. Even though one should not take the character of the underground man as a portrait of his author, there is still a good deal of resemblance between Dostoevsky's personality and the exacerbated, self-defensive prickliness of the underground man's responses to those other human beings in whose midst, willy-nilly, he is forced to live. In short, the thin-skinned and excruciatingly vulnerable Dostoevsky, ready to flare up at the slightest pinprick to his self-esteem, was now caught in a nightmare of humiliation from which there was no escape, and which he simply had to learn how to endure.

It would have been no consolation for Dostoevsky that such ill-will was not directed against him personally but included all the other nobles as well. Indeed, this lack of discrimination only made it harder to bear, since in his own case he could hardly help smarting under its crying injustice. Over and over again in *House of the Dead* he returns to confirm the heartache inflicted by this relentless class hatred. Indeed, he came to consider, as the most agonizing of all the torments of camp life, this awareness of being eternally ringed by enemies, eternally alienated from the vast majority by a wall of animosity that nothing he could do would ever cause to crumble. An ordinary peasant-convict, he explains, "within two hours after his arrival . . . is on the same footing as all the rest, is *at home*, has the same rights in the community as the rest, is understood by everyone, and is looked on by everyone as a comrade. It is very different with *the gentleman*, the man of a different class [italics in text]. *However straightforward, good-natured and clever he is, he will for years be hated and despised; he will not be understood, and what is more he will not be trusted* [italics added]. He is not a friend, and not a comrade, and though he may at last in the course of years attain such a position among them that they will no longer insult him, yet he will never be one of them, and will forever be painfully conscious that he is solitary and remote from all." (4: 198).

Such words attest to Dostoevsky's recognition that he would have to steel himself to survive in the midst of outright enmity or, in the best of cases, confront an attitude of commiserating contempt. A peasant-convict named Petrov, an ex-soldier reputed (and justly, in Dostoevsky's opinion) to be the most dangerous and determined man in prison—though he was much less quarrelsome and pugnacious than many others who paraded their fearsomeness—was one of the few men of his class to seek an acquaintance with Dostoevsky. It was he who stole Dostoevsky's Bible, even while fussing over him tenderly in the famous bath scene of the book and coming to visit him every day for an amicable chat. Petrov, who could read, had an inquiring mind, and he pumped Dostoevsky for all sorts of information—sometimes concerning French politics, sometimes whether the people in the antipodes really walked on their heads. But while Petrov's gregariousness was a welcome relief, it was accompanied by a condescension of which Dostoevsky was fully aware.

"I had the impression," he writes, "that in general he considered me as a sort of child, almost as a new-born baby, incapable of understanding the simplest matters. . . . It seemed to me that he had decided, without worrying his head about it, that it was impossible to talk to me as with other men, and that outside of books I understood nothing and was even incapable of understanding anything, so that there was no reason to bother me with that" (4: 86). Dostoevsky was certain that, even when stealing from him, Petrov pitied him at the same time because he was not able to defend his own belongings. "He said to me himself one day," Dostoevsky recalls, "that I was 'a man with a good heart,' and 'so simple, so simple, that it makes one feel sorry for you' " (4: 87). Such an attitude of superior scorn, without the pity exhibited by Petrov, was the reigning one among those convicts who were not openly aggressive toward Dostoevsky; and their relative tolerance did little to allay his estrangement or to ease the painfulness of his position.

7

During his first year or so of life in the prison camp (it is difficult to date such matters precisely), Dostoevsky could find no way of alleviating the crushing despondency caused by the physical, psychic, and moral weight of the situation he describes in *House of the Dead*, and he freely acknowledges his mood of bitter self-recrimination. " 'This is the end of my wanderings: I am in prison!' I was continually repeating to myself. 'This is to be my home for many long years. . . . And who knows? Maybe when I come to leave it many years hence I may regret it!' I added, not without an element of that malignant pleasure which at times is almost a craving to tear open one's wounds on purpose, as though one desired to revel in one's pain, as though the consciousness of one's misery was an actual enjoyment" (4: 56).

Dostoevsky describes such masochistic self-hatred as being among his first reactions to his new environment; but similar surges of feeling continued to recur so long as he regarded everything around him with loathing. An outside observer portrays him as looking like "a wolf in a trap." "His pale, wasted, sallow face, covered with dark-colored freckles, never lit up with a smile, and his mouth opened only for fragmentary and brief replies regarding business or service matters. His cap was pulled down over his forehead to his eyebrows; he looked fierce, withdrawn, unfriendly; his head drooped and his eyes remained fixed on the ground."[10] The desperation of Dostoevsky's loneliness is movingly conveyed in one scene, where

he sketches his gratitude, on returning from work, at being greeted joy-
ously by the prison dog, Sharik, whom nobody caressed except himself:
"And I remember that it was positively pleasant for me to think, as though
priding myself on my suffering, that there was only one creature in the
world who loved me, who was devoted to me, who was my friend—my
faithful dog Sharik" (4: 77).

No one can say with exactitude what was going on in the depths of
Dostoevsky's mind and heart all through these excruciating months; but
this time of withdrawal marked the beginning of a searching revision of
all his earlier ideas and convictions. "In my spiritual solitude," he writes,
"I reviewed all my past life, went over it all to the smallest detail, brooded
over my past, judged myself sternly and relentlessly, and even sometimes
blessed fate for sending me this solitude, without which I would not have
judged myself like this, nor viewed my past life so sternly" (4: 220). As
we see, Dostoevsky tells us strictly nothing about the content of these self-
accusatory musings; but some pages in his prison memoirs hardly can be
read except as an Aesopian exposure of the blindness of his folly as an
apprentice revolutionary conspirator.

These pages, which compose part of the chapter called "The Complaint,"
begin by describing how, one day, Dostoevsky noticed that most of the
other convicts had assembled in the courtyard of the prison at an unusual
time. Thinking that perhaps he had failed to pay attention to some command, Dostoevsky immediately fell in as if for a roll call. But, to his astonishment, his accustomed presence in the ranks was now greeted with
a hail of jeers and insults, and he was told in no uncertain terms to leave
the group. Bewildered by this unexpected assault, and hesitating to obey
the shouts coming at him from all directions, he was finally taken by the
arm—politely but firmly—and led away to the camp kitchen. There, looking on at the rumpus, were gathered a handful of peasant-convicts and
all the other gentlemen, who promptly told him that a "complaint" had
been organized against Major Krivtsov because of a recent worsening in
the quality of the food. What had happened then became clear: the peasant-convicts had spontaneously and unanimously refused to let a gentleman join the ranks of their protest.

The complaint, as it turned out, was easily crushed by the infuriated
major, who simply ordered some of the protestors to be flogged at random;
but the treatment that Dostoevsky had received remained as a rankling
and admonitory recollection. "I had never before been so insulted in prison,"
he writes, despite all the other humiliations inflicted upon him, "and this
time I felt it very bitterly" (4: 203). Never before had he so much desired
to be accepted by the others as one of their number; never before had he
been so roughly repulsed. Moreover, the full implications of this rejection

were driven home even more tellingly when, that same afternoon, he made some inquiries about the incident.

Contrary once again to what he had expected, he noticed that the peasant-convicts exhibited no signs of resentment or displeasure against those who had remained indifferent to their cause. Baffled by this puzzling tolerance, he spoke about it to Petrov:

"Tell me, Petrov," said I [Dostoevsky], "are they angry with us?"
"Why angry?" he asked as though waking up.
"The convicts angry with us—the gentlemen."
"Why should they be angry with you?"
"Because we did not take part in the complaint."
"But why should you make a complaint?" he asked, as though trying to understand me. "You buy your own food."
"Good heavens! But some of you who joined in it buy your own food too. We ought to have done the same—as comrades."
"But . . . but how can you be our comrades?" he asked in perplexity.
[4: 207]

The social-political implications of this interchange, as they sank into the consciousness of the erstwhile revolutionary conspirator who had once hoped to stir up a peasant revolution, hardly need belaboring. Clearly, the notion that peasants would have accepted the leadership of gentlemen in any struggle to obtain freedom had been the sheerest delusion. And one should also notice that, at the time of this incident, Dostoevsky presumably had not yet lost those rebellious moral-social impulses whose incitation had originally led him into the ranks of the Petrashevtsy. Whether he would have knowingly remained with the protestors, if he had been allowed to do so, remains an unanswerable question; but that he felt a moral obligation to join their cause is unmistakable.

The full significance of his conversation with Petrov, however, only emerges if we note the terms in which Dostoevsky describes Petrov elsewhere in the book. For he is depicted as one of those types from the Russian people who "come conspicuously to the front and take a prominent position at the moment of some violent mass movement or revolution, and in that way achieve all at once their full possibilities." In other words, Petrov was a natural revolutionary, exactly the type of peasant to whom the Speshnevites had wished to appeal—those who, as Dostoevsky writes, "are the first to surmount the worst obstacles, facing every danger without reflection, without fear . . ." (4: 87). Such a man, he now realized, found it impossible to understand how he and a gentleman (and one with whom he was on good terms) could unite as comrades in a social protest. Never again would Dostoevsky believe that the efforts of the radical intelligentsia could have the slightest effect in stirring the broad masses of the Russian people, and history was to prove him right during his lifetime—if not, to be sure, half a century after his death.

Moreover, not only was any cooperation between the people and the intelligentsia impossible, but the leaders thrown up from among the people themselves—those leaders who place themselves at the head of the discontented masses in times of trouble—can only guide them to disaster. For such "agitators and ringleaders," who take command among "gangs of workmen, companies of soldiers, etc." (in other words, the cadres of any conceivable Russian popular uprising), are invariably "spirited men eager for justice, and in perfect simplicity and honesty persuaded of its inevitable, direct and, above all, immediate possibility." They "are no stupider than their fellows, in fact there are some very clever ones among them, but they are *too ardent* to be shrewd and calculating" (italics added); it is not such leaders who have the capacity to control and direct a successful mass movement. "If there are men who are capable of skillfully leading the masses and winning their cause, they belong to a different class of popular heroes and natural leaders of the people, *extremely rare among us*. But these agitators and ringleaders of whom I am speaking now almost always fail, and are sent to prison and penal servitude in consequence" (4: 201; italics added).

Such words obviously ring the death knell for the possibility of any social change in Russia through revolutionary agitation. The people would never follow the intelligentsia, and their own leaders can only charge ahead on the road to self-destruction: "Through their zeal they [the leaders] fail, but it is their zeal that gives them their influence over the masses" (4: 201). These are surely some of the melancholy conclusions that Dostoevsky began to draw as he judged his own past "sternly and relentlessly"; and he would certainly have recalled, while doing so, the famous concluding lines of Pushkin's *The Captain's Daughter*, a novel set in the midst of the bloody Pugachev uprising in the eighteenth century. Indeed, Pushkin's words may be used to express the point of view to which Dostoevsky had now come round himself: "God save us from seeing a Russian revolt, senseless and merciless. Those who plot impossible upheavals among us are either young and do not know our people, or are hardhearted men who do not care a straw either about their own lives or those of others."[11]

CHAPTER 8

A Russian Patriot

The collapse of his political hopes alone would not have been enough to throw Dostoevsky into that state of inner turmoil and moral-spiritual crisis by which he was assailed. Surely he berated himself unmercifully for the hopeless naiveté of the social-political adventure on which he had so recklessly embarked; but he was not essentially a political being—like Petrashevsky and Speshnev, for example—and he tended later to regard his involvement in revolutionary activity as more or less a biographical accident. Nor was this view merely an apologetic afterthought in soberer years; he had been terribly uneasy about his commitment even while carrying it through, and had spoken, in fatalistic terms, of having been trapped into political activism by his "Mephistopheles"—Speshnev—almost as if against his will. Politics did not really engage the deepest level of his personality; and even though his treatment during the complaint had been particularly humiliating, it was only a further, if more wounding, example of the endemic hostility of the peasant-convicts. What disturbed him much more profoundly was the larger issue posed by his own response to such hostility.

For Dostoevsky was deeply troubled, not only by his abusive treatment at the hands of his fellow convicts, but more unnervingly by his own horrified recoil at their appalling conduct and behavior. Both what they had turned out to be, and how he had reacted to them, came to him as a shocking revelation; and he reveals the extent of his dismay in a passage directly addressed to the readers of *House of the Dead*—members of the educated class like himself largely inspired by much the same humanitarian sentiments about the people. Everything that such readers believe they know about the peasants, he tells them, is woefully mistaken; they have invariably dealt with peasants in the ordinary course of social life, and the impressions gathered from such contacts are totally misleading. One only learns what peasants are *really* like "when the *gentleman* by force of circumstances is completely deprived of his former privileges and is transformed into a peasant. You may have to do with peasants all your life, you may associate with them every day for forty years, officially for instance, in the regulation administrative forms, or even simply in a friendly way, as a benefactor or, in a certain sense, a father—you will never know them really. It will all be an optical illusion and nothing more. I know that all who read will think I am exaggerating. But I am convinced of its truth. I have reached this conviction, not from books, not from abstract theory, but from reality, and I have had plenty of time to verify it" (4: 198-199).

The self-reflexive irony of such words shows the clean sweep that Dostoevsky initially made of all his previous notions about the peasant, to whom he had unquestionably stood, at least by intention, in the role of a benefactor, if not a father. And this benevolent attitude had now been replaced by a loathing of everything around him, but most of all of the peasant-convicts. "The misery of all that first year in prison was intolerable," he writes, "and it had an irritating, bitter effect on me" (4: 178). Nor is there any doubt as to the major cause of this misery: "The dislike with which as a 'gentleman' I was continually regarded by the convicts during my first few years became intolerable, *poisoning my whole life*" (4: 176; italics added). Still, such words only characterize Dostoevsky's victimization and its corroding effects; but he records another response plainly in a letter to Mme Fonvizina shortly after his release. "There were moments [in prison camp]," he confesses, "when I hated everybody I came across, innocent or guilty, and looked at them as thieves who were robbing me of my life with impunity. The most unbearable misfortune is when you yourself become unjust, malignant, vile; you realize it, you even reproach yourself—but you just can't help it."[1]

As a result of encountering the "obstinate, irreconcilable hatred" of his fellow convicts, Dostoevsky himself thus became irrepressibly "malignant" and "vile" toward them; this was his reaction to the first collision of contact. His emotions thus underwent a total reversal from his previous humanitarian fellow-feeling; and the biting sarcasm with which, in the future, he will portray all such instances of tenderhearted "Schillerism" may be seen as the artistic consequence of this initial, negative phase of the "regeneration of [his] convictions." Indeed, it is hardly possible to exaggerate the importance of this destruction of Dostoevsky's humanitarian faith in the prison camp; but there is also some danger in placing it too exclusively at the center of interpretative attention. For while Lev Shestov has also rightly stressed the great significance of this psychic-emotive shift, he has gone on to argue that Dostoevsky never really overcame the "hatred of mankind" that swept over him during these prison years—a hatred which, as Shestov sees it, breaks forth later in the vitriolic tirades of the underground man against all those "sublime and beautiful" ideals to which the youthful Dostoevsky had once so innocently pledged his faith. "Dostoevsky not only burned all that he had formerly worshipped," Shestov contends, "he trampled it in the dirt. He not only hated his earlier faith, he despised it."[2]

For Shestov, as a result, the humanitarian note that still continues to sound in certain scenes of *House of the Dead*, and the ethos of love and forgiveness preached by the later Dostoevsky, are simply a timorous concealment of the terrifying truth about man whose full force even Dostoevsky did not have the audacity to confront. "But the truths of the prison camp," Shestov argues, "whatever he might do to arrange and embellish them, retain all too evident traces of their origin."[3] Shestov's view thus coincides with my own in its emphasis on the crucially unsettling effects of the prison camp upheaval on Dostoevsky's sensibility; but we part company when he indicts the writer as "false" and "insincere" for not being courageous enough to retain this embittered egoism as the final word of wisdom. One should at least do Dostoevsky the justice of accepting the full range of his emotions and beliefs, and not measure him, as Shestov does, by the alien standard of Nietzsche.

Shestov, of course, says nothing about how Dostoevsky solved his moral-spiritual crisis; nor could he have been expected to do so, since, in his opinion, no genuine resolution ever took place. But Dostoevsky *did* manage to find a way out of his torturing and hate-filled psychic entrapment, and he went through an experience exhibiting all the characteristics ordinarily noted in cases of conversion—whether religious, as in the past, or, more recently, involving questions of political allegiance. Before describing what occurred in detail, however, we must first turn back to survey other aspects of Dostoevsky's situation in the prison camp that are crucially connected with the process of his regeneration.

2

Up to this point, we have focused solely on the picture given in *House of the Dead* of Dostoevsky's relations with the peasant-convicts; but there were also fellow prisoners of his own class with whom he was on better terms, although these acquaintances did very little to ease his heartache and anguish. "That first summer I wandered about the prison in almost complete loneliness without a friend. . . . I had comrades too of my own class but their comradeship did not ease my heart of its oppression," he writes. "I hated the sight of everything and I had no means of escape from it" (4: 199). Nothing further is said—or, at least, nothing explicitly—that helps to clarify the puzzling question as to why such friendships should have proven so unsatisfactory. There were, as we know, twelve other prisoners of the noble class in the Omsk camp while Dostoevsky was serving his sentence, even though he lists only eleven and refuses to include Durov (for reasons we shall come to in a moment). Three of these were Russian, and what Dostoevsky tells us about them indicates abundantly, if obliquely, why he took so little comfort in their presence at his side.

One was an ex-officer of the Russian Army in the Caucasus whom

Dostoevsky calls Akim Akimich but whose real name was Yefim Belikh. Once the commander of a frontier outpost, he was serving a sentence for having taken the law into his own hands by executing a local tribal chieftain. Technically, this chieftain had been at peace with the Russians; but the zealous officer, suspecting him of having treacherously attempted to burn down the Russian fort, decided to act on his own initiative. Akim Akimich befriended Dostoevsky from the moment he arrived, served as his guide and mentor during the first crucial days, and could hardly have been more helpful and accommodating; but Dostoevsky could never feel any real sympathy for him or establish any sort of intimacy. For Akim Akimich was an utterly prosaic person, so conditioned to subordination that obedience with him had become inclination and second nature; he was perhaps the only prisoner, Dostoevsky remarks, perfectly content with his lot. "He was a good-natured man . . . but I confess," Dostoevsky writes, "sometimes, especially at first, he produced in me an intense depression which still further increased my misery. . . . I longed sometimes for a living word, however bitter or impatient or spiteful." Nothing came forth, however, except details of the routine of Army life, which Akim Akimich dwelt on with loving devotion, "and all in the same even, decorous voice like the dripping of water." At times, Dostoevsky admits, "I (and always quite suddenly) began, I don't know why, almost to hate Akim Akimich and I cursed the fate which had put me with my head next to his own on the common bed" (4: 208-209).

Another Russian convict of the noble class is referred to only as a "parricide." His real name was D. I. Ilinsky, and he is a figure of some importance in Dostoevsky's career: his history later furnished the novelist with the main plot of *The Brothers Karamazov*, and his personality probably also provided some of the character traits for Dimitry Karamazov. Ilinsky was an ex-officer suspected (but only on circumstantial evidence) of having killed his father to obtain his inheritance and then of burying the corpse in a shallow ditch covered with planks. The murdered man "was dressed and tidy, the gray head which had been cut off had been put on the body, and under the head the murderer had laid a pillow" (4: 15-16). Ilinsky was, as Dostoevsky saw him, "an unaccountable, feather-brained fellow, irresponsible in the highest degree, but by no means stupid," who was always "in the liveliest, merriest spirits" and steadfastly continued to deny his guilt (4: 16).

What fascinated Dostoevsky was the clash between Ilinsky's buoyant behavior and the gravity of his presumed crime, compounded by the almost mocking cynicism displayed in the arrangement of the murdered corpse. For Ilinsky seemed entirely oblivious of any wrongdoing, and he would even refer to his "late father" unaffectedly in the course of conversation. Dostoevsky remarks that "such savage insensibility seems impossible" and was perhaps the product of "some constitutional defect, some mental and bodily monstrosity not yet understood by science" (4: 16). As a result, he did not give entire credence to Ilinsky's guilt, although the evidence seemed overwhelming as he heard the story told by those who knew all the details.

Years later, while writing the final draft of his prison book, Dostoevsky learned that Ilinsky had been released as innocent: a criminal arrested for another crime had confessed to the murder of the elder Ilinsky. So Dostoevsky's psychological intuition, based on his observation of Ilinsky's character, had been vindicated against all the "facts" that pointed to the prisoner's guilt. Razumikhin, in *Crime and Punishment*, will use exactly the same kind of observation to argue that the young and carefree peasant house painter Nikolay could not have killed the old pawnbroker and her sister. For just a few moments after the established time of the crime, Nikolay had been seen rolling around the courtyard of the tenement in a friendly rough-and-tumble with his working partner. And Dimitry Karamazov will show, by the human qualities he exhibits amidst all his roistering and carousing, that he could not have killed his loathsome father, despite the mountain of evidence piled up against him. But while Dostoevsky never forgot the ex-ensign, or the moral of his mistaken conviction, Ilinsky was hardly the type of person with whom the writer could have had very much in common.

The third Russian noble, mentioned only by the initial A., was Pavel Aristov, an extremely sinister character against whom Dostoevsky had been warned by his friends in Tobolsk. The reality of Aristov turned out to be even blacker than Dostoevsky had foreseen; he was "the most revolting example of the depths to which a man can sink and degenerate, and the extent to which he can destroy all moral feeling in himself without difficulty or repentance" (4: 62). Wishing to obtain funds to lead a life of wild debauchery, Aristov had denounced a number of perfectly innocent people to the secret police as political conspirators, and he continued turning up more "subversives" so long as he was supplied with money. After a certain period, however, even the Third Section became suspicious, and Aristov was eventually sent to prison camp for embezzlement and false denunciations.* There he had ingratiated himself with Major Krivtsov and served as a spy and informer on the peasant-convicts. Dostoevsky was literally aghast at encountering in the flesh someone of Aristov's ilk, who surpassed his most livid fantasies of the evil that a human being could

---

* Aristov achieved some local fame in Petersburg by his hoodwinking of the secret police. An account of his exploits is also given in the valuable *Diary* of A. V. Nikitenko, an important official of the censorship for many years and a professor of Russian literature at the University of St. Petersburg who, born a serf, was a moderate progressive in his political views. He notes that seventy entirely innocent people were arrested as a result of Aristov's denunciations while the latter was engaging in riotous orgies with the money furnished by the Third Section. See Aleksandr Nikitenko, *The Diary of a Russian Censor*, abridged, ed., and trans. by Helen Saltz Jacobson (Amherst, Mass., 1975), 120.

deliberately and knowingly tolerate and perpetrate. "All the while I was in prison," he declares, "A. seemed to me a lump of flesh with teeth and a stomach and an insatiable thirst for the most sensual and brutish pleasures" (4: 63).

To make matters worse, Aristov was by no means a repulsive degenerate whose appearance and behavior would have unmistakably betrayed the abysmal depravity of his character. On the contrary, "he was cunning and clever, good-looking, even rather well-educated and had abilities." What made Aristov's presence literally intolerable for Dostoevsky was his self-conscious and gloating manner of glorying in his own infamy: "And how revolting it was to me to look on his everlasting mocking smile! He was a monster; a moral Quasimodo" (4: 63). Dostoevsky is thus finally driven, in order to find a term of comparison, to fall back on Hugo's misshapen character in *Notre Dame de Paris*—equally deformed in violation of the norms of human life but the obverse of Aristov, since the original Quasimodo was a monster in body but not in soul. And just as Dostoevsky did not forget Ilinsky, so too Aristov remained an ineradicable memory: the first references in Dostoevsky's notebooks to the character of Svidrigailov, the cynically derisive aristocratic debauchee in *Crime and Punishment*, are entered under the name of Aristov.[4] More immediately, Dostoevsky held Aristov responsible for deepening and darkening the crisis of values brought on by prison-camp life. "He poisoned my first days in prison," Dostoevsky explains, "and made them even more miserable. I was terrified at the awful baseness and degradation into which I had been cast. . . . I imagined that everything here was as base and degraded. But I was mistaken, *I judged of all by A*" (4: 64; italics added).

3

Even though Sergey Durov was also in the camp along with Dostoevsky, he is not mentioned in the chapter entitled "Comrades" devoted to fellow convicts of the noble class. This neglect of Durov, which has aroused considerable comment, can be partly explained in terms of literary strategy: to have spoken of Durov with any degree of accuracy would immediately have revived memories of the Petrashevsky case and thus made publication of the book impossible. Moreover, Dostoevsky's aim was primarily to acquaint his readers with the denizens of the prison-camp world, to introduce them to a strange, unexplored milieu hitherto shrouded in dreadful secrecy; a lengthy portrait of Durov would manifestly not have fit into such an intention. But even if Durov had been delineated more extensively, this would not have noticeably changed the picture that Dostoevsky provides of his own tormented solitude. For there is evidence that the two ex-

Petrashevtsy no longer saw eye to eye on various matters, and that some cooling off had occurred in their former friendship.

From the memoirs of one of the ex-naval cadets friendly to the political prisoners, it appears that when Dostoevsky and Durov were invited together to the guardhouse they refused to speak to each other and sat grimly apart at opposite ends of the room: "They cordially hated each other from the bottom of their hearts, avoided each other's company, and, during the entire period of their sentence in the Omsk prison, did not exchange a single word."[5] Whether such testimony should be accepted as conclusive is highly doubtful; relations between Dostoevsky and Durov, however they may have behaved before third parties on some occasions, were never as implacably hostile as these words indicate. On leaving the prison camp in February 1854, they peacefully spent a month together at the home of Konstantin Ivanov; and a year later Dostoevsky instructed a friend in Omsk, where Durov had remained, to "greet Durov for me, and wish him all the best on my behalf. Assure him of my affection, and of my genuine devotion to him."[6]

Nonetheless, there is good reason to believe that the two men drifted apart during the years of their imprisonment, even if they continued to respect each other personally and did not break off all contact. For Durov had remained largely unchanged by his prison-camp ordeal (although his health suffered very badly), and he emerged from *katorga* the same harsh critic of the Russian régime as when he entered. Both men must have become aware of a growing divergence in their points of view as Dostoevsky's opinions slowly began to alter; and Durov's presence must have been for Dostoevsky a constant reminder of all the errors and illusions he was now so bitterly regretting. To see and speak to him only turned the knife in Dostoevsky's aching wound, and brought back a past whose folly he was just truly beginning to understand. No, here once more Dostoevsky could not find any source of solace or relief; his old comrade and erstwhile friend only served further to augment his wretchedness.[*]

4

The Omsk stockade also contained eight Polish nobles, all sent to Siberia for having participated in one or another plot to gain independence for

---

[*] Some recent research has produced new evidence that Dostoevsky's failure to mention Durov in *House of the Dead* was not caused by any deep-seated enmity. For one of the first things that Dostoevsky did on returning to Petersburg was to try and obtain financial help for the ailing Durov, then living in Odessa. Elected a member of the Literary Fund, established to aid needy writers and scholars, Dostoevsky submitted a request for a grant-in-aid to Durov (which was presumably awarded) on March 28, 1860. The Soviet Russian scholar who has unearthed this information in the files of the Literary Fund also comments: "This intercession for [Durov] by Dostoevsky, who himself had been given permission to live in the capital only under police surveillance, was an act of considerable courage." P. B. Zaborova, "Dostoevsky i Literaturnyi Fond," *Russkaya Literatura*, 3 (1975), 158-170.

their homeland from the Russian crown. Only three of these were well-educated in Dostoevsky's opinion, and with two of these three he seems to have been on greater terms of intimacy than with any other of the upper-class convicts. Few other inmates of the *House of the Dead* are described in the laudatory terms that he lavishes on the Polish prisoners with whom he became friendly. Of M., whose full name was Alexander Mirecki, Dostoevsky says, "I got on well [with him] . . . from the first," and he calls Mirecki "a man of very strong and very noble character." Another Polish noble, B. (Joszef Bogusławski), Dostoevsky considered to be "a very kind-hearted and even great-hearted man"; though he eventually broke off relations with all the Poles, he says of B.: "I never ceased to love him." These are words, one presumes, that Dostoevsky did not use lightly, and they stand out as a sudden splotch of radiant color in the surrounding darkness, illuminating the unusual degree of cordiality existing between Dostoevsky and these two Polish exiles. He also speaks very appreciatively of Szymon Tokarzewski, whose own memoirs of his imprisonment in Omsk have already been mentioned, and whom Dostoevsky found to be "kind-hearted and manly, a splendid young fellow," even though "he was not an educated man" (4: 209).

As we know from Tokarzewski, the two Russian political exiles were greeted with rapturous warmth by the Poles, overjoyed at last to find men like themselves in the camp rather than common-law criminals. "When the two men [Dostoevsky and Durov] arrived in Omsk and settled with me under one roof," he writes rather pathetically, "it seemed to me that I saw two still lights shining in the gloomy Northern sky."[7] Such exalted expectations, however, were grievously disappointed on closer contact; the initial friendship with Dostoevsky was gradually transformed into coolness, and then, at least on the Polish side, into positive antipathy. "The best of them [the Poles]," writes Dostoevsky, reacting to this situation, "were morbid, exceptional and intolerant to the last degree. With two of them I gave up talking altogether in the end" (4: 209). Nothing is said about the reasons for such a change of heart, although Dostoevsky does remark of Mirecki that "politics was what interested him the most" (4: 217). Politics did indeed interest all the Polish exiles with whom Dostoevsky was closest, and it was largely, though not exclusively, disagreements over politics that ultimately led to their rift with Dostoevsky and his verdict as to their "intolerance." For they refused to tolerate his ideas regarding the relations between Russia and Poland, while he just as staunchly rejected their claims to the right of independence from Russian domination.

The Poles had naturally expected Dostoevsky, as a certified enemy of Tsarism, to sympathize with the cause of Polish independence; such an attitude would have been taken for granted—and with good reason—in a Russian progressive then and later. But Dostoevsky turned out to be such a rabid and obstreperous Russian patriot that the Poles were taken completely aback, especially since, as Tokarzewski remarks, "judging by his traits and his name it was possible to recognize his Polish origin." One suspects that Dostoevsky, perhaps informed of this opinion about his ancestry by way of a compliment, responded with the insulting remark that Tokarzewski records: "He used to say that if he ever found out that a single drop of Polish blood flowed in his veins, he would immediately have himself purged of it."[8]

More important, though, was the virulent Russian nationalism that Dostoevsky displayed when the talk turned, as it obviously did, to the sacred cause for which the Polish prisoners were suffering their cruel punishment: "How painful it was to listen to this conspirator, this man sentenced to prison for the cause of freedom and progress, when he confessed that he would be happy only when all the nations would fall under Russian rule. He never admitted that the Ukraine, Volynia, Podolia, Lithuania, and finally the whole of Poland were countries seized by Russia, but affirmed that all these regions of the globe had forever been the property of Russia; that the divine hand of justice had put these provinces and countries under the sceptre of the Russian Tsar because they would never have been able to exist independently and that for a long time they would have remained in a state of dark illiteracy, barbarism, and abject poverty. The Baltic provinces, in Dostoevsky's opinion, belong to Russia proper; Siberia and the Caucasus he put in the same category. Listening to these arguments we acquired the conviction that Feodor Mikhailovich Dostoevsky was affected by insanity."[9]

Tokarzewski's memoirs were published after Dostoevsky's death, and with full knowledge of the writings in which he had not only satirized Polish characters in a quite vindictive fashion but had also trumpeted his Great Russian nationalism in the flaming tirades of the *Diary of a Writer*. It is quite likely that, even though Tokarzewski's book is based on notes taken at the time, some of the animosity aroused by Dostoevsky's later work was incorporated into the final redaction of his own. Indeed, what Dostoevsky is supposed to have said on some occasions sounds so trivial and absurd that it is difficult to give it much credence. (For example, he is accused of refusing to believe that the Poles had gotten up a subscription to translate Sue's *The Wandering Jew* in 1844, presumably because he thought Polish culture to have been so backward!) Also, it is hard to recognize the admirer of Schiller, Hugo, Balzac, George Sand, Dickens, and Shakespeare in the Dostoevsky who is supposed to have said that "the literatures of other nations in comparison with Russian literature are simple literary parodies."[10] On the other hand, we have the remark of Belinsky in the mid-1840s, reported by Mme Panaeva, "that when he [Dostoevsky] gets worked up he doesn't know what he's saying"; and the additional comment of Mme Panaeva herself that "Dostoevsky, pushed to the wall [in discussion], sometimes defended with passion the most ridiculous views."[11]

What Tokarzewski reports may well represent such uncontrollable flare-ups—now even less manageable because of increased physical and nervous debility—and should not be taken as considered opinions. But, regardless of what Dostoevsky may or may not have said in such altercations, the fact that they took place is beyond dispute; and there is no reason to question Tokarzewski's account of Dostoevsky's political views. Always a staunch Russian patriot, he had exhibited touches of xenophobia even at the very height of his acceptance of pro-Western ideas in the 1840s. Never had he gone as far as some members of the Petrashevsky circle, including his close friend Valerian Maikov, in rejecting the idea of nationality as an antiquated and obscurantist prejudice; and one can even detect an incipient touch of Slavophilism in his conviction that Russia was destined to follow a historical path quite distinct from that of Europe.

Dostoevsky keeps silent about such political arguments in *House of the Dead* (censorship would have made it impossible to speak of them, even if he had wished to do so), but he does touch on another bone of contention with his erstwhile Polish friends that probably grated on his nerves in an even more abrasive fashion. For Dostoevsky was greatly upset by the Polish abhorrence of the Russian peasant-convicts, whom they looked down upon with supreme contempt and refused to regard as anything but criminal riffraff.

"The convicts particularly disliked the Poles even more than those who had been Russian gentlemen," Dostoevsky comments, at his first mention of the Polish group. "The Poles (I am speaking only of the political prisoners) were elaborately, offensively polite and exceedingly uncommunicative with them. They never could conceal from the convicts their aversion for them, and the latter saw it very clearly and paid the Poles back in the same coin" (4: 26). Later, Dostoevsky elaborates on the Polish disdain: "They saw in the convicts nothing but their brutality, could not discern any good quality, anything human in them, and had indeed no wish to do so" (4: 210). Such a portrayal is confirmed by Tokarzewski's account of how he behaved on first entering the barracks where Dostoevsky was to join him later. "Oh my God, how monstrous these figures appeared to us," he says of the Russian inmates. "And these shapes of men or of the damned approached us and extended their hands, hands so many times covered with blood, so many times soiled by offense and crime. And we were obliged, though with horror and revulsion, to offer them our hands. I pulled away my hand and, pushing everyone aside, I entered the barracks with my head held proudly aloft."[12]

Such was the Polish attitude—and Dostoevsky would have had to be considerably more obtuse than he was not to have realized that it was also his very own. For does he not say plainly that he believed all the peasant-convicts to have been so many Aristovs? And what can this mean except that he too regarded them, for a time, with the same unutterable contempt as the Poles? Yet the intensely patriotic Dostoevsky soon found himself engaged in defending his country, and presumably the majority of its inhabitants, against the only educated people in the prison camp whom he personally liked and respected and who had helped to relieve, at least momentarily, his numbing loneliness. But how could he argue on behalf of Russia without, at the same time, overcoming his violent repugnance for that portion of the Russian people existing all around him in flesh and blood and whose life he was condemned to share? One can well understand why this tangle of idea-feelings should have proven to be, as we shall soon see, the catalytic agent sparking Dostoevsky's conversion experience. For his disputes with the Polish exiles only sharpened and intensified his inner crisis—the crisis initially caused by the destruction of his humanitarian faith in the people—to an unbearable pitch of psychic malaise. Nothing was more emotionally necessary for Dostoevsky than to find some way of reconciling his ineradicable love for his native land with his violently negative reactions to the loathsome denizens of the camp.

5

It is one of the anomalies of *House of the Dead* that Dostoevsky does not include an account of his conversion experience in its pages. Why he failed to do so is difficult to say; perhaps his fear of the censorship influenced his decision, perhaps the incident was too intimate and personal, involved too much psychological exposure, to have blended properly with the objective narrative tonality that he wished to preserve. Nor, of course, would he have been able to handle it with the same freedom as he does later, when he no longer had to conceal the political reasons for his sentence. In any case, it was only twenty-six years later, in an article of his *Diary of a Writer* (1876) entitled "The Peasant Marey," that Dostoevsky supplied the missing pages from his prison memoirs which help to pierce the enigma of "the regeneration of [his] convictions." This regeneration involved essentially a new shift of feeling in relation to the Russian people, a recovery of his faith in them, but a faith that differed considerably from that of the past.

Dostoevsky's article appeared in the February 1876 issue of *Diary of a Writer*, the second number of his new publication, and it had been preceded the month before by a blistering exposé of the vices running rampant among the Russian people. Drunkenness was eating away at their moral fiber, wife-beating was an accepted practice defended by the peasants in the courts, the people would rather save the pothouse than the church in case of a village fire. "Everywhere there seems to be soaring some sort of a drug, as it were the jimson weed, some itch for debauch," writes Dostoevsky. "The people have become affected with an unheard-of perversion of ideas, and a wholesale worship of materialism."[13] No Russian Westerner of the 1840s could have castigated the people more harshly than does Dostoevsky at this late stage of his career, when he had long since become known for his fanatical belief that the salvation of Russia lay precisely in the sturdiness of their moral-religious convictions. For the moment, though, he found himself emotively immersed in the mood that had swept over him during the first phase of his prison-camp years. And it was this temporary resurgence of his ancient hostility—the hostility that had made him so "unjust, malignant, and vile" in the prison camp—which called forth, as antidote, the reply published in the next number of his *Diary*.

To counter the disconcerting effect created by his previous article, where, as he concedes, he had depicted the people as "coarse and ignorant, addicted to drunkenness and debauch," and as "barbarians awaiting the light," he dredges up from memory the incident in the prison camp that had once rescued him from despair under the weight of the same disillusioning impressions. The missing pages of his prison memoirs, in other words, emerge under the stimulus of the very same crisis that he had been forced to wrestle with many years before; and the recollection of the peasant Marey reveals how he succeeded, at that time, in restoring his psychic-emotive equilibrium. Is it not for this reason that, as he says, he wishes to "relate an anecdote" about his past to the reader, "just a remote reminiscence which, for some reason, I am quite eager to recount precisely here and now, in conclusion of our treatise on the people"?[14] His eagerness becomes perfectly comprehensible once we realize that, after having risked plunging his readers into the same despair that he had once faced himself, he was preparing to impart to them the vision of the people whose radiance had led to his own regeneration.

The importance of this article has of course long been recognized; but, so far as my knowledge goes, no one has bothered to examine it in the light of our present knowledge of the psychology of conversion and to explore all the physical, mental, and emotive pressures that converged on Dostoevsky at this critical time. Only by doing so, however, may we hope to supplement his own reticences in more than a speculative fashion, and advance a step further in the comprehension of this mysterious and decisive episode.

CHAPTER 9

The Peasant Marey

The problem of conversion from one set of beliefs and ideas to another has usually been discussed in the context of religious history, where it is illustrated very dramatically in the lives of such founders of the Western religious tradition as St. Paul and St. Augustine. Until fairly recently, most treatments of the topic have been either edifying on the one hand or mocking and incredulous on the other. Conversions were attributed directly to divine intervention by believers; or they were dismissed as priestly shams and impostures, and as manifestations of mental illness, by the skeptical partisans of enlightenment.

Only with the rise of historicism in the late eighteenth century, which began to explore sympathetically the workings of the poetic and mythical imagination, has it become possible to transcend the old oppositions and to approach the question in a more detached and impartial fashion. No judgment was passed on the truth or falsity of the beliefs involved in conversion; but the subjective process by which it came about was explored, and its psychological consequences were accepted as sufficient to explain its necessity and validity for the convert: this was the spirit in which William James wrote his still unsurpassed *Varieties of Religious Experience*. More recently, the study of conversion has shifted from the field of religion to that of politics (or rather, the parallels between the two have been noted) in connection with the use of brainwashing techniques; and there now exists a considerable quantity of neuropsychiatric literature devoted to analyzing the psycho-physical mechanisms by which conversions are obtained. Both these approaches can help to throw some light on what occurred in the case of Dostoevsky.

2

Many writers—encouraged, it must be admitted, by the drift of some of Dostoevsky's own remarks—have maintained that his prison-camp regeneration involved essentially the recovery of his religious faith, lost during the mid-1840s as a consequence of his encounter with Left Hegelian atheism. Such a view, however, uncritically accepts Dostoevsky's misleading version of the facts of his life, which he subtly distorted for the purposes of his polemics with the Russian Populists of the 1870s.[1] To be sure, Dostoevsky was quite familiar with all the Left Hegelian arguments against religion that had been freely voiced in the Belinsky *pléiade* as well as at the gatherings of the Petrashevsky circle. He had unquestionably been troubled and discomfited by such attacks on the divinity of Christ; but there is no evidence, as has been remarked already, that he ever gave way to them entirely. He always remained much closer to the French Utopian Socialists, who, while rejecting official religion as embodied in their own Roman Catholic tradition, regarded their radical social ideals as the application of the divinely inspired Christian doctrine of love to the modern world. As Maxime Leroy has noted, "there is truly something religious in the spirit of the first Socialists, in particular the Communists, who almost unanimously considered themselves as the continuators of the teachings of early Christianity";[2] and it was this type of Socialism that exercised the greatest influence on Dostoevsky's mind and imagination.

Since Dostoevsky had always remained in some sense a Christian (even if an unorthodox one, who accepted the Socialist shift of the Christian message from the heavenly to the earthly paradise), his conversion in the prison camp should not be seen as that of a strayed ex-believer returning to Christ. The epilogue to *Crime and Punishment*, often taken as a faithful account of Dostoevsky's regeneration, has been used to buttress such an interpretation; but while it contains many details identical with those in *House of the Dead* and the later article on "The Peasant Marey," Dostoevsky reshapes this material to suit the thematic and ideological needs of his novel. Raskolnikov's theory is a dramatization of ideas that first came to the fore in the Russian culture of the mid-1860s, and his views can in no way be identified with those of Dostoevsky serving his term in prison camp between 1850 and 1854. Indeed, a close reading of the epilogue reveals how careful Dostoevsky was to present Raskolnikov's atheism *only* as a projection of the enmity felt toward him by the peasant-convicts, not as an objective datum asserted and guaranteed by the narrator. When it is the turn of Raskolnikov at Lent to take the sacrament, "he went to church and prayed with the others. Out of this, *he himself did not know why*, a quarrel arose one day; they turned on him in fury" (italics added). It was then that the others shouted: "You're an atheist! You don't believe in God!" (6: 419). The text, however, does not bear out this charge at all, if we can judge from Raskolnikov's willingness to join in the religious ceremonies and to pray without any inner hindrances or reservations.

Dostoevsky's conversion, then, cannot be considered to involve religious faith in the strict sense, although it unquestionably turned on beliefs with strong religious associations and implications and took place under circumstances highly charged with religious emotion. But in any event, as we know from William James, the process of conversion can occur in relation "to any sort of mental material, [which] need not necessarily assume the religious form."³ It always occurs, however, when the person in question is beset by a severe inner conflict and has become what James calls "a divided self," that is, someone suffering from a state of inner confusion and chaos that must be resolved if he or she is to continue to function. "Unhappiness is apt to characterize the period of order-making and struggle," he remarks. "If the individual be of tender conscience and religiously quickened, the unhappiness will take the form of moral remorse and compunction, of feeling inwardly vile and wrong, and of standing in false relations to the author of one's being and appointer of one's spiritual fate."⁴ Dostoevsky was unquestionably "a person of tender conscience and religiously quickened"; he was certainly unhappy; and he did feel "inwardly vile and wrong"—the words are almost the same as those of his letter to Mme Fonvizina—for standing in "false relations" to the supreme moral authority that he accepted. For he could not help but labor under a crippling burden of guilt because of his violent antipathy toward the peasant-convicts—an antipathy he knew, in the depths of his conscience, to be a betrayal of that compassion for the people long since accepted by him as the essence of Christ's teaching.

At the same time, Dostoevsky was living under conditions that had subjected him, both physically and mentally, to unendurable stress. The effects of such stress on the nervous system have received much attention since Pavlov's researches on conditioned reflexes; and the application of Pavlov's views in neuropsychiatry to human beings (not only for purposes of brainwashing, but also to relieve severe cases of shock and depression) have demonstrated to what extent excessive physical and emotional stress can disrupt established patterns of response in the nervous system. Hunger, fatigue, illness, acute tension caused by fear, physical and mental abuse, extreme humiliation—all these factors, dislocating the conditioned reflex patterns of the brain, make the subject receptive to the formation of new patterns and hence amenable to new ideas. Dr. William Sargant, an eminent English neuropsychiatrist, has pointed out the similarity of the techniques used in brainwashing with the results obtained by Methodist and Fundamentalist revivalism in the past and present, by snake-handling cults in the southern United States, by voodoo ceremonies in Haiti, and by ecstatic religious rituals celebrated all over the world. All these religious practices bring on a nervous exhaustion that leads to a "transmarginal inhibition" of the brain functions and often provokes temporary collapse. Old patterns of brain behavior and response are wiped out, and the person or group becomes extremely susceptible to new impressions and suggestions, which, in some cases, reach what Pavlov calls "the ultraparadoxical phase." At this extreme, there is a complete reversal of the ideas and attitudes of the past and a "conversion" to a whole new set of opposing convictions.⁵

The hardships of prison-camp life, no matter how well Dostoevsky may have adapted to them in the long run, exposed him to precisely the kind of stress that leads to disruption of the brain functions; a trained brain-washer could not have managed things better. In addition, a crucial component of brainwashing is the arousal in the subject of the very same sense of guilt stressed by William James. "Brain-washers use a technique of conversion," according to Dr. Sargant, that depends "on the fomenting in the individual of anxiety, of a sense of real or imaginary guilt, and of a conflict of loyalties, strong and prolonged enough to bring about a state of collapse."[6] By a series of chance events, then, dependent both on the hazards of his fate and on his previous ideas and ideals, Dostoevsky was unwittingly placed in the perfect physical and psychological situation for a conversion to have taken place. And while no literal "collapse" occurred, the same effect as a collapse—the elimination of old patterns of brain response to clear the way for the new—was produced by the onset of his epileptic seizures.

These began, so far as we know, in 1850, and then resumed, at a monthly rate, in 1853; there may also have been sporadic recurrences between those two dates; and such attacks would have greatly heightened Dostoevsky's nervous fragility and psychic-emotive malleability. Epilepsy, clinically speaking, is the overloading of the brain with stimuli to the point of convulsion; it is an illness that produces exactly the state of "transmarginal inhibition" of which Pavlov spoke. Electric shock therapy "is simply the artificial inducement of an epileptic fit,"[7] and such treatment is used to unsettle whatever brain patterns are causing psychopathic behavior so as to allow for healthier ones to take their place. Whatever their frequency or severity, Dostoevsky's attacks could only have had the effect of making him highly and continuously receptive to a remolding of his previous beliefs and values.

3

The incident that Dostoevsky described in his "Peasant Marey" article took place during "the second day of Easter Week"[8]—and this immediately poses a problem of chronology. Was it the first Easter he spent in the camp or the second? He speaks of being twenty-nine years old, and this would tend to confirm the first dating in 1850; but there is some reason to suspect the accuracy of this version. For Dostoevsky attributes to this event a transformation in his attitude toward the peasant-convicts which, if we are to believe *House of the Dead*, could not possibly have occurred so quickly.

Dostoevsky arrived in Omsk late in January 1850; by Easter he would have been there only about two and one-half months; and if we credit his statement that, after this time, he began to look at his fellow convicts in a new light, then it is difficult to understand why in his memoirs he should have portrayed this process as being so much lengthier. "During the *first year*," he declares explicitly, "I failed to notice many things in my misery. I shut my eyes and did not want to look. Among my spiteful and hostile companions I did not observe the good ones—the men who were capable of thought and feeling in spite of their repellent outer husk" (4: 178-179; italics added). It would seem plausible, then, to place the peasant Marey episode during the *second* Easter in camp. Whether sooner or later, however, a fundamental change *did* take place, and Dostoevsky recalled it as having been motivated by his memory of the peasant Marey, one of his father's serfs whom he had known as a boy.

Dostoevsky tells us nothing in the article itself about the Easter week ceremonies in the camp; but there is some information in *House of the Dead* that cannot be neglected as a setting and a prelude. During Lent all the prisoners were divided into seven groups, one for each week of the Lenten fast. Each group took the sacrament in turn, and Dostoevsky was in the group scheduled for the sixth week, shortly before Easter itself; the prisoners, relieved of work, went to church during that week two or three times a day. "I very much liked the week of the preparation for the sacrament . . .," Dostoevsky writes. "It was long since I had been to church. The Lenten service so familiar to me from the far-away days of my childhood in my father's house, the solemn prayers, the prostrations—all this stirred in my heart the far, far-away past, bringing back the days of my childhood. . . ." The convicts stood at the back of the church, as the peasants had done in Dostoevsky's youth, and he remembered how he, from his privileged position, had once watched them "slavishly parting to make way for a thickly epauletted officer, a stout gentleman, or an overdressed but pious lady. . . . I used to fancy then that at the church door they did not pray as we did, but they prayed humbly, zealously, abasing themselves and fully conscious of their humble state" (4: 176).

The Easter preparations thus naturally evoked memories of the religious pieties of Dostoevsky's childhood—the days when his faith had been untroubled and serene—and of his sense even then that the peasants were more truly Christian in their devotions than the arrogant ruling class who shoved them aside so callously. And it was also during this Lenten week that, perhaps for the first time, Dostoevsky found it possible to identify emotionally with the peasant-convicts. "The convicts prayed very earnestly and every one of them brought his poor farthing to the church every time to buy a candle, or to put in the collection. 'I, too, am a man,' he thought, and felt perhaps as he gave it, 'in God's eyes we are all equal. . . .' We took the sacrament at the early mass. When with the chalice in his hands the priest read the words '. . . accept me, O Lord, even as the thief,' almost all of them bowed down to the ground with the clanking of chains, apparently applying the words literally to themselves" (4: 177). Such impressions certainly began to weaken Dostoevsky's notion that the convicts were so many cruder replicas of Aristov; nor should we overlook the possible effects of the Orthodox Easter service itself, which, in celebrating the central mystery of the resurrection of Christ, places strong emphasis on the brotherly love and mutual forgiveness that should unite all the faithful in joy at the miraculous event. It is customary in the Orthodox ritual for all members of the congregation to embrace and kiss at the climax of the Easter service.*

4

By the second day of Easter week, then, Dostoevsky had gone through a long period in which his most exalted feelings had repeatedly been aroused; and it was thus all the more infuriating to witness the appalling spectacle that he saw around him. "It was the second day of the 'holiday' in the camp; the prisoners were not taken out to work, many were drunk, cursing and quarrelling flared up from one moment to the next on every side. Ugly, filthy songs; gambling groups squatting underneath the plank bed; convicts beaten half to death, by common consent, because of having been too rowdy, and lying on the plank bed covered with sheepskins until they revive and wake up; knives already drawn several times—all this, on the second day of the holiday, tormented me to the point of illness."9 What finally impelled him "to run out of [the barracks] like a madman" was that "six robust peasants, all together, threw themselves on the drunken Tartar Gazin, in order to subdue him, and started beating him; they beat him furiously—a camel could have been killed with such blows, but they knew that it was difficult to kill this Hercules, so they beat him without fear."10

Unable to bear this horrifying sight a moment longer, Dostoevsky rushed outside into the bright, sunlit day, with a blue sky radiant overhead. He began to walk, as he often did, in the open space between the stockade and the buildings; but the beauty of the day could not calm the indignation raging in his breast. "Finally," he recalls, "my heart was inflamed with

---

* It may be objected that all these details, taken from Dostoevsky's depiction of the *first* Easter festival in the prison camp, should not be used in relation to the peasant Marey incident occurring during the *second* Easter. It seems to me, however, that the portrayal of Easter in *House of the Dead* also refers to the second year, and that the observations and feelings he sets down would scarcely have been those recorded only a few months after his arrival.

Dostoevsky, as a matter of fact, condenses chronology quite freely in order to obtain a greater artistic unity. We know from other sources that the Christmas theatricals also took place during the second year of Dostoevsky's stay, although he gives the impression that they followed hard on the heels of the first month. As Pierre Pascal has remarked, "It must be admitted that, if Dostoevsky has truthfully depicted facts, he arranged them with a certain liberty in response to his literary preoccupations." F. M. Dostoevsky, *Récits de la Maison des Morts*, trans. Pierre Pascal (Paris, 1961), lxxvii.

rancor"; and just at this instant he happened to meet one of the Polish prisoners, Mirecki, strolling in the same isolated walkway and evidently for the same reasons. "He looked at me gloomily, his eyes flashed and his lips began trembling: *'Je hais ces brigands* [I hate these bandits]!'—he muttered through his clenched teeth, in a half-strangled voice, and passed by."[11]

The effect of these words was to make Dostoevsky abruptly turn on his heel and go back to the barracks, even though, barely a quarter of an hour before, he had bolted out in a frenzy. He does not explain this strange reversal of direction; but by now we should be able to understand what he chooses to leave unsaid. Mirecki, as it were, had been able to read his mind: the Pole had voiced the very poisonous thoughts, had exhibited the same anger, seething within Dostoevsky himself; and this had given him a terrible jolt. It made him aware, or at least raised to the surface, the extent of his alignment with the Poles against his fellow Russians; and he returned to the barracks as a secret gesture of solidarity with his countrymen. All the same, still finding it impossible to support the sight of the pandemonium going on indoors, Dostoevsky lay down on his few inches of plank bed and pretended to be asleep. He often adopted this stratagem because "people will not bother a sleeping person," and, in this posture, he could think and dream undisturbed. "But now I could not dream: my heart was beating agitatedly, and I could hear Mirecki's words ringing in my ears: *'Je hais ces brigands!'* "[12]

As Dostoevsky's text clearly indicates, the severity of his inner conflict was reaching a peak; this was why he found it so difficult to blot out the present, as he had so often been accustomed to do, and allow his subconscious to wander freely in the past. All through his four years in camp he had employed this technique of involuntary association, which probably served somewhat the same purpose as psychoanalysis or drug therapy in releasing repressed memories and thereby relieving his psychic blockages and morbid fixations. This technique also served the additional and reassuring function of keeping alive his artistic faculties under conditions where he was forbidden to put pen to paper. "It used to begin with some speck," he writes of these associations, "some trait—at times almost imperceptible—and then, gradually, it would grow into a complete picture— some strong and solid impression. I used to analyze these impressions, adding new touches to things long ago outlived, and—what is more important—I used to correct, continually to correct them."[13] In this fashion, Dostoevsky managed to exercise his visual imagination and to polish and refine scenes and characters as he might have done in writing his stories and novels.

What emerged in this case, however, was the memory of a long-forgotten incident of his childhood—a period of his life just revived in his subconscious by the Easter preparations and ceremonies. And the experience in question had involved the same emotions of shock, fright, and fear that had been aroused by the prison-camp orgy. Wandering through the forest one day on his father's scruffy little "estate," the nine-year-old Dostoevsky suddenly thought he heard a shout that a wolf was roaming in the vicinity. The wood was in fact criss-crossed with ravines, in which wolves sometimes appeared, and Dostoevsky's mother had warned him to be careful. The frightened boy ran out of the wood and toward a peasant plowing in a nearby field, one of his father's serfs whom he knew only as "Marey." The surprised Marey halted work to soothe the terrified child, white-faced and trembling, and assured him that no one had shouted and no wolf was near. Dostoevsky recalled Marey smiling at him gently "like a mother," blessing him with the sign of the cross and crossing himself, and then sending him home with the reassurance that he would be kept in sight. "All this came back to me suddenly, I do not know why," Dostoevsky writes, "with surprising clarity and in full detail. I suddenly opened my eyes, straightened up on the plank bed and, I recall, my face still retained its gentle smile of recollection."[14]

Dostoevsky never spoke to Marey again after this single contact, and he insists that he had completely lost consciousness of the incident. "And suddenly now—twenty years later, in Siberia—I was recalling that meeting, so distinctly, in every detail." Of course, Dostoevsky remarks, "anyone would have cheered up a child"; but he refuses to remain content with such a commonplace reflection. For he is certain that "here, in this lonely encounter, something entirely different had occurred, and he [Marey] could not have looked at me with an expression gleaming with more genuine love if I had been his only son. And who forced him to do so? He was our peasant serf, and I, after all, the son of his owner; no one would know how kind he had been and reward him for it. . . . The encounter was isolated, in an empty field, and only God, perhaps, saw from above what deep and enlightened human feeling, what delicate, almost womanly tenderness, could fill the heart of a coarse, bestially ignorant Russian peasant serf not yet expecting, nor even suspecting, that he might be free."[15]

And abruptly, as a result of this comforting memory, Dostoevsky finds that his whole attitude toward his fellow convicts has undergone a magical transformation. "I remember, when I got off the plank bed and gazed around, that I suddenly felt I could look on these unfortunates with quite different eyes, and suddenly, *as if by a miracle*, all hatred and rancor had vanished from my heart. I walked around, looking attentively at the faces that I met. That despised peasant with shaven head and brand marks on his face, reeling with drink, bawling out his hoarse, drunken song—why, he may be that very Marey; after all, I am not able to look into his heart" (italics added). The very same evening Dostoevsky met Mirecki again; and by this time he felt inwardly secure, capable now of facing the earlier indictment with a twinge of superior pity for the poor, unhappy Poles. "He could not have had any memories of any Mareys, and any other opinions about these people other than: '*Je hais ces brigands.*' No, these Poles had much more to endure than we did!"[16]

5

The characteristics of a conversion experience, according to James, are three in number. "The central one is the loss of all worry, the sense that all is ultimately well with one, the peace, the harmony, *the willingness to be*, even though the outer conditions should remain the same." Secondly, there is "the sense of perceiving truths not known before"; and finally, "a third peculiarity of the assurance state is the objective change which the world often appears to undergo," so that "an appearance of newness beautifies every object." This latter singularity is often accompanied by "hallucinatory or pseudo-hallucinatory phenomena, *photisms*, to use the word of the psychologists," and James cites numerous examples, the most famous being St. Paul's vision of Christ on the road to Damascus and Constantine's cross in the sky at the battle of the Milvian bridge.[17] Nothing of this sort happened to Dostoevsky; the world around him could hardly be said to have suddenly become tinged, in any self-evident way, with the beauty and the glory of God. But he did experience the inner peace, the harmony and tranquillity of which James speaks, even though nothing had changed externally; and he distinctly had the sense of perceiving a truth which, if perhaps glimpsed dimly before, had never been so lucid and so momentous.

Moreover, even in the absence of any "photisms," Dostoevsky believed that he could at last see through the surface of the world to a beauty hitherto concealed from the eyes of his moral sensibility. For he uses this very figure to express the new truth he had grasped as a result of the peasant Marey recollection. "Owing to circumstances," he writes, "almost throughout the whole history of Russia, the people have been so addicted to debauch, they have been subjected to so much depravity and seduction, to so much torture, that it is really surprising how they have managed to succeed in preserving the human image, not to speak of its beauty. Yet they did preserve also the beauty of their image." It was this "beautiful image" that Dostoevsky could now discern; he had finally learned how to separate "his beauty [that of the Russian peasant] from the alluvial barbarism," and "to discover diamonds in this filth."[18]

What occurred to Dostoevsky, then, bears all the earmarks of a genuine conversion experience; and it also involves, as we see, a recovery of faith.

But it is not faith in God or Christ that is in question; rather, it is a faith in the Russian common people as, in some sense, the human image of Christ. And this aspect of Dostoevsky's regeneration—the fact that it centers primarily on his relations with the people—must be strongly stressed in face of the only serious alternative explanation. In his enormously influential essay on Dostoevsky, Freud has argued that his arrest, the mock execution, and then his imprisonment triggered a masochistic need to submit to the punishment of the Tsar-Father as a means of relieving the unconscious guilt caused by Dostoevsky's repressed Oedipal desire to commit parricide. But there is not the slightest empirical evidence to prove that Dostoevsky submitted to or sought punishment from the Tsar-Father; his unyielding conduct throughout the interrogation, when directly confronted with authority figures representing the Tsar, indicates the exact contrary. It was only from the people that Dostoevsky sought absolution, both because of the immediate sense of guilt engendered by the complexities of his prison-camp sentiments, and, farther back, because of his acceptance of a share of the guilt in his father's presumed murder. For Dostoevsky felt obscurely that his exorbitant demand for funds had contributed to bringing on those exactions by his father that may have driven the peaceful peasants to desperation. Since it was against the people that Dostoevsky had doubly sinned, it is by them that he wished to be forgiven; and the peasant Marey memory fulfilled this precise function.

6

Dostoevsky thus resolved his gnawing mental and spiritual anguish, his sense of guilt, and the tangle of his conflicting loyalties by what can only be called a "leap of faith" in the moral beauty of the Russian peasantry, its infinite capacity to love and forgive those who had for so long sinned against it. Each Russian peasant was now a potential Marey, who had managed to preserve in his soul the highest and most sublime of the Christian virtues. In this way, under conditions of nervous tension, psychic division, and physical exhaustion similar to those in which sharp and sudden alterations of belief frequently occur, Dostoevsky underwent a striking change of heart. And while it may seem, at first sight, as if he had merely restored the foundations of his earlier faith—returning, in effect, to his philanthrophic convictions of the 1840s—what happened was really quite different. For the ostensible reversion to his starting point took place under a complex of circumstances that endowed his view of the people with an entirely new significance.

For one thing, its focus had now specifically become the *Russian* common people, and it was thus newly charged with an intense nationalistic animus. It had been necessary for Dostoevsky, at all costs, to identify with the peasant-convicts as Russians in answer to the contempt of the Poles, and to consider whatever virtues he could detect in them as uniquely national ("he could not have had any memories of any Mareys"). Moreover, a sharp alteration had also occurred in the old class superiority of the Russian Westerner, who had prided himself on assuming the role of benefactor and father to the people. All the galling circumstances of prison-camp life, from Dostoevsky's obvious incompetence at manual labor to the principled rejection and hostility he had encountered, had wiped away all traces of the condescension implicit in his previous philanthrophy. No longer could he regard the people only as the worthy and presumably grateful recipients of *his* charity, or relieve his sense of guilt by his intended magnanimity on their behalf. It was now *they* who had acquired the right— a right he recognized as fully justified by their long history of suffering— to pass judgment and to forgive. And finally, if the Russian people did possess the extraordinary moral capacities that Dostoevsky now finds in them, these had become visible to him as a result of the purifying influences of the religious emotions of his childhood; they were intimately and indissolubly linked with the Orthodox faith that he and the peasants shared. Hence his recovery of faith in the people was also a rediscovery of Orthodoxy, or at least an estrangement from his previous "progressive" Christianity, whose doctrines he could well castigate as the fatal source of all his old illusions.

An essential feature of such doctrines had been a naively optimistic glorification of the people as an inexhaustible fount of moral virtue; but such an image could hardly continue to be valid for Dostoevsky in its old sentimental, idyllic, quasi-Rousseauian form. This form had been destroyed by the reality of living under the menace of "that despised peasant with shaven head and brand marks on his face, reeling with drink, bawling out his harsh, drunken song"—and only too ready to brandish his fist and use it if anyone crossed his path! Yet Dostoevsky persisted in believing in the sterling moral essence of precisely *this* peasant, in violation of the evidence of his senses and rational faculties. And to sustain this belief required the support of a faith that did not shrink back from the paradoxical, the irrational, the impossible, a faith that was willing unblinkingly to accept both the ugliness and the savagery and, at the same time, to search for—and find—the saving spark of humanity concealed underneath the hideous exterior. One might say that, just as Dostoevsky's faith in the miracle of the Resurrection had been quickened and revived by the Easter ceremonies, so his faith in the Russian people had been renewed by the "miracle" of Marey's resurrection in his consciousness. No doubt the leap required to accept Christ's triumph over death played its part in stimulating the similar leap that transformed his vision of the peasant-convicts. The features of the two, in any case, would remain blended together forever in Dostoevsky's sensibility, and eventually lead to that literal "divinization" of the Russian people he was one day to proclaim.

Long ago, in the days of his youth, Dostoevsky had written a boyishly enthusiastic letter in which he had spoken of Christ as having been incarnated by God and sent to earth in order to provide the modern world with "the organization of its spiritual and earthly life." And he had singled out, as the best temporal embodiment of Christ's message in his own time, "the childlike Christian tendency" in the poetry of Victor Hugo.[19] Now he would abandon this cosmopolitan allegiance and, in the future, discover the true teaching of Christ only in the world of the peasant Marey.

CHAPTER 10

A New Vision

Dostoevsky's imagination always tended toward dramatic climaxes and sudden, sharp shifts of feeling, and his characters are invariably caught in moments of tension or crisis in their lives. Accordingly, whenever he publicly wrote about his own life, he portrayed it in much the same fashion. His article about the peasant Marey catches one such moment, depicts its resolution ("all hatred and rancor had vanished from my heart"), and ends with the edifying implication that Dostoevsky had now become a new man. It would be a mistake, however, to take this version too literally, and to confuse his skillful rendering of an incident from his biography with the actual contours of his spiritual evolution.

Whether the peasant Marey episode occurred exactly in the manner he describes, and just how much he "improved" it artistically in the retelling, is impossible to know for certain. But the truth of the experience it is meant to convey, whatever form this episode may have originally assumed, indisputably lay at the root of the moral-spiritual mutation that began to occur in Dostoevsky's outlook. The dazzling moment of insight that he depicts, however, was very far from being stabilized, and the process of regeneration it initiated, as he said himself, took "a long, long time." No doubt there were inevitable backslidings into the old attitudes and a renewed struggle to regain the inspiration of the consoling faith. But, all through this period, Dostoevsky was learning how to see the peasant-convicts with new eyes, freed at last from the rankling bitterness that had blinded him in the past. For until then, as he admits, "everything around me was hostile—and terrible, for though not everything was really so, it seemed so to me. . . . Of course there was a great deal I did not notice then; I had no suspicion of things that were going on in front of me" (4: 56-57).

The function of the peasant Marey episode had thus been to clear Dostoevsky's sight, and to allow him, as he believed, to observe what was happening around him accurately for the first time. Many episodes in *House of the Dead* recount this process of re-education, which is of course one of the book's dominant themes; but since the focus of the text is impersonal and collective, rather than confessional and personal, this process is never depicted directly. It must be inferred from suggestions and side remarks—such as reactions of surprise on the part of the narrator, and his occasional injunctions to the reader to pay special attention to one or another observation. Such clues give us an insight into how Dostoevsky's own perceptions were gradually being altered, and enable us to follow some of the ways in which his convictions were regenerated.

2

An obvious example of such a change of perspective can be found in Dostoevsky's account of how he overcame his ingrained certainty—the certainty of a Russian Westerner—that the Russian peasant was a bungling, incompetent worker. Evidence that he entertained such a view can be found in one of his early stories, where a young and liberal bureaucrat—obviously the author's spokesman—remarks that a retired Army veteran, trained in the European discipline of the Russian military, knows how to work because "skill, know-how and sharp wits are present in him to a greater degree than in the peasant." The veteran "doesn't like to holler bloody murder, like a *muzhik* in trouble, but does everything himself, without whimpering and in an orderly fashion" (2: 422).

These were the ideas that Dostoevsky brought to his first assignment with a work party; and he immediately discovered what appeared to be a glaring confirmation of such a contemptous judgment. Entirely unskilled at manual labor himself, he nonetheless writes that "it was totally provoking [to whom? and for what reason?] to see a sturdy crowd of stalwart men who seemed utterly at a loss on how to set to work." Their job was to remove some of the unbroken beams of wrecked barges in the Irtish River; but "as soon as they began to take out the first and smallest beam, it appeared that it was breaking, 'breaking of itself,' as was reported to the overseer by way of apology." No better proof could have been furnished of peasant incapacities, which instinctively aroused Dostoevsky's upper-class ire, although he had no personal interest in the task being done properly.

But while the work party killed time and waited for new tools, another overseer came along and set the convicts a limited "task": if they finished before the normal workday was over, they could return to barracks earlier. Suddenly everyone set to work with a will; this was obviously what the peasants had been waiting for. "There was no trace of laziness, no trace of incompetence. The axes rang; . . . *to my astonishment* [the beams] came up now whole and uninjured. The work went like wildfire. Everyone seemed wonderfully intelligent all of a sudden," the job was finished half an hour before quitting time, and "the convicts went home tired but quite contented" (4: 75; italics added). So much for the proverbial ineptitude of the *muzhik*—obviously an age-old peasant strategy of resisting orders through sabotage and masking insubordination as clumsiness!

A very similar eye-opener was provided by the skill and talent exhibited at the Christmas theatricals by some of the peasant performers. It is difficult for us now, after more than a century of nationalism, fully to grasp the depth of contempt felt by the Russian Westerners for their own folk culture, which they tended to regard only as the barbarous survival of an uncivilized past. Belinsky, for example, consistently denigrated all attempts to assign any value to folk poetry, and declared of Pushkin's "The Bridegroom" that "in all Russian folk songs taken together there is not more of the folk essence than in this one ballad!"[1] In other words, such folk material had to be filtered through a sophisticated Russian-European sensibility in order to take on any true literary quality. If we assume, as is likely, that Dostoevsky had shared some such point of view, then we can better appreciate his unexpected delight in the peasant-convict orchestra—two violins, three homemade balalaikas, two guitars, a tambourine, later joined by three accordions—which performed at the festivities. "Upon my word," he writes, speaking as an inveterate concert-goer, "I had no idea till then what could be done with the simple peasant instruments. The blending and harmony of sounds, above all, the spirit, the character of the conception and rendering of the tune in its very essence were simply amazing. For the first time I realized all the reckless dash and gaiety of the gay dashing Russian dance songs" (4: 123).*

Indeed, Dostoevsky now reverses Belinsky's judgment when he comes to speak of the vaudeville skit, *Filatka and Miroshka*, staged by the peasant-convicts with Dostoevsky's assistance (although he only hints at his own participation). He had seen this skit many times in Petersburg, and he finds the convict actor playing the role of Filatka—an ex-soldier named Baklushin, who was a natural comic and mimic—to be superior to any he could recall. "Filatka acted by Baklushin was really splendid. He played the part with amazing precision. . . . I can say positively that the city actors were inferior to Baklushin in the portrait of Filatka. By comparison with him they were too much of *paysans*, and not real Russian peasants" (4: 124). The professional actors, schooled in European traditions and conventions, were unable to convey the true Russian peasant as instinctively embodied by Baklushin; and Dostoevsky's use of the French word conveys his sense of the false and artificial gloss imparted by this European admixture. No doubt he too, at the time he saw the theatricals, had begun

---

* Writing of the efforts made by the French humanitarians after 1830 to encourage poets from the working class, Paul Bénichou remarks: "Among contemporaries, it was George Sand who, by the articles in the first issues of the *Revue Indépendante* and the prefaces to various collections, took the most interest in such productions. But, in truth, no one dreamed then of a supposedly original proletarian poetry, as was the case later; one was happy with the accession by the workers (among them some women workers too) to a poetry whose model was provided by authors from the cultivated classes." This attitude was even more the case in Russia, so far as the arts were concerned, and accounts for Dostoevsky's delighted surprise. Paul Bénichou, *Le temps des prophètes* (Paris, 1977), 407.

to feel that he had hitherto known the Russian peasant only under the deforming guise of the *paysan à la Rousseau* encountered in the pages of George Sand and, even earlier, in those of Karamzin and Radishchev.

3

No aspect of life in the house of the dead proved more difficult for Dostoevsky to fathom than the peasant-convicts' relation to the upper-class—a relation containing far more intricacies than he could possibly have suspected in advance. We have seen that, naively expecting to be received on a footing of friendliness, he had been brutally repulsed by bitter class hatred; but while it was out of the question for a gentleman ever to be accepted among the peasants as one of themselves, Dostoevsky discovered that peasant attitudes were far more complex than he had at first realized. For it *was* possible to overcome, or at least to mitigate, the hostility of the peasants to some degree if one understood their view of the world and took this into account in dealing with them.

"My first question on entering the prison," Dostoevsky writes, "was how I should behave, what attitude I should take up before these people" (4: 76). Very probably, since Dostoevsky himself stresses the inner solitude of his first year or two, this question really answered itself up through the period of the peasant Marey experience. His recoil from the peasant-convicts must have been so forceful that, as with the Poles, any contact with them remained formal and perfunctory. Meanwhile, however, since Dostoevsky did not remain entirely oblivious to what was taking place around him, he observed much that ran counter to his preconceptions. He was much struck by a certain insistence among the peasant-convicts, for example, that he preserve the norms of behavior appropriate to his class status. As a liberal and progressive humanitarian, Dostoevsky tried to behave as democratically as possible at first, and to place himself in all particulars on the same level as the peasants; but he discovered that, far from being taken as a gesture of good will, this attempt only made him appear ridiculous.

"According to their ideas . . . ," he remarks, "I ought even to [have kept] up and respect[ed] my class superiority before them, to turn up my nose at everything, to play the fine gentleman in fact. . . . They would, of course, have abused me for doing so, *but yet they would have privately respected me for it*" (4: 76; italics added). Dostoevsky comments that for him to have behaved in this fashion was impossible because "I was never a gentleman according to their notions"—that is, someone who insisted on all the privileges conferred by rank and status (4: 76-77). Yet he could not escape entirely, despite his protestations, and he enjoyed the services of what was in effect a body servant, to whom he paid a miserable pittance.

This desire of the peasants to have status norms preserved was also evident in their attitude toward the officers who ruled over them. Those who managed to gain their respect and even affection never did so by overtly attempting to step over the class barriers; and Dostoevsky clearly indicates how unexpected a discovery this was for him: "I must mention another strange thing: the convicts themselves do not like to be treated too familiarly and *too* softly by their officers [italics in text]. They want to respect those in authority over them, and too much softness makes them cease to respect them. The convicts like their commanding officers to have decorations, too, they like him to be presentable, they like him to be in favor with some higher authority, *they like him to be strict and important and just*, and they like him to keep up his dignity. The convicts prefer such an officer: they feel that he keeps up his own dignity and does not insult them, and so they feel everything is right and as it should be" (4: 91; italics added).

The peasant-convicts thus instinctively preferred officers to behave according to their rank; but they were genuinely fond of those who, even while doing so, did not vaunt their superiority or look down on those below them with haughtiness and disdain. Dostoevsky noted with curiosity that the convicts always spoke fondly of a Lieutenant Smekalov, even though he had administered the same merciless floggings as all the others. "Yet the fact is that even his floggings were remembered among the convicts with love and satisfaction—so successful was the man in pleasing them! And how? How did he gain such popularity? . . . Smekalov knew how to behave so that they looked upon him as one of themselves, and this is a great art, or more accurately an innate faculty, which even those who possess it never think about. . . . *They don't despise, they don't scorn the people under their control*—in that, I think, lies the explanation. There is no sign of the fine gentleman, no trace of class superiority in them; and my word! what a keen scent the people have for it. . . . They are ready to prefer the sternest man to the most merciful if the former has a smack of their homespun flavor" (4: 150; italics added).

Dostoevsky picks out the same character traits in a Lieutenant-Colonel G., who commanded the Engineer Corps at Omsk for a brief period and quickly became beloved. "He could not see a convict without saying something kindly and good-humored to him, without making a joke or laughing with him, and the best of it was there was no trace of the authoritative manner in it, *nothing suggestive of condescending or purely official kindness*. He was their comrade and completely one of themselves. But although he was instinctively democratic in manner and feeling, the convicts were never once guilty of disrespect or familiarity with him" (4: 215; italics added).

It is evident that Dostoevsky admired this mysterious faculty, which worked miracles in alleviating the habitual animosity displayed by the convicts; and his own attitude resembles that of such officers. He guarded the proper social distance required by peasant norms of propriety, but tried to manifest the easy availability to friendlier relations that could overcome mistrust. "I had made up my mind to behave as simply and independently as possible," he explains, "not to make any effort to get on intimate terms with them, but not to repel them if they desired to be friendly themselves; not to be afraid of their menaces and their hatred, and as far as possible to affect not to notice. . . . On the other hand, I did not want to shut myself off from them by cold and unapproachable politeness, like the Poles did" (4: 76-77).

In the long run, Dostoevsky's tactics yielded the results he desired, and he managed to acquire that intermediate position which preserved his pride, respected peasant attitudes, and yet worked to surmount their in-grained enmity. "Nothing is harder than to win people's confidence (especially such people), and to gain their love," Dostoevsky writes. It was "nearly two years in the prison before I could succeed in gaining the good-will of the convicts"; but, as he records with satisfaction, "in the end most of them grew fond of me and recognized me as a 'good man' " (4: 26). Such a triumph, of course, was of great importance in enabling Dostoevsky to cope with the psychic burden of the remainder of his prison term; but it also has a much larger significance as well. For it persuaded him once and for all that, although peasant mentality could not conceive of any society other than the one already in place and consecrated by time, the hatred engendered by existing class relations could be overcome as he had seen it vanish for himself and a few others in the house of the dead. And this is why he insisted so vehemently later that true social progress in Russia would come about not through attempts to change the social-political system (all such attempts, in any case, being doomed in his opinion to inevitable failure), but rather from a moral mutation in the attitude of the upper class toward the people.

4
___

Dostoevsky's growing ability to sympathize with the peasants' conception of the world also made him aware of some of the morally positive aspects, as he saw them, of their inbred refusal to pretend to "equality" with their social superiors. Such an awareness is expressed very strikingly in his description of the Christmas theatricals, a key event in the transformation of his own feelings—and one that may well have contributed to the more spectacular regeneration that occurred probably a few months later. For it was here that Dostoevsky first suddenly saw the peasant-convicts themselves "regenerated" by their sincere and ingenuous enjoyment of the experience of the theater.

"All faces expressed a simple-hearted expectation. . . . A strange light of pure, childlike joy, of pure sweet pleasure, was shining on those lined and branded brows and cheeks, on those faces usually so morose and gloomy, in those eyes which sometimes gleamed with such terrible fire" (4: 122-123). During the performance, "they gave themselves up to their pleasure without reserve," and, at the end, dispersed merry and satisfied; "they praised the actors, they thanked the sergeant. . . . Everyone was unusually contented, even as it were happy, and fell asleep not as on other nights, but almost with a tranquil spirit—and why, one wonders? These poor people were only allowed to do as they liked, ever so little, to be merry like human beings, to spend one short hour not as though in prison—and they were morally transformed if only for a few minutes . . ." (4: 124, 129-130).

A great impression was also made on Dostoevsky by the way he was treated on arriving at the performance. Ordinarily, he was handled roughly and unceremoniously by the others; far from being shown any special consideration, he was either studiously ignored or, on work assignments, gruffly shoved aside as a hindrance rather than an aid. But now, on entering the military ward that served as a theater, Dostoevsky was astonished by the respect and even deference he received; a front-row seat was immediately provided, although the crush in the small space was "incredible" and convicts were standing, sitting on beds, and even watching from behind the impromptu stage. One reason, he explains, was that "Petrov had told me naively that I should have a front place partly because I should subscribe more," that is, contribute more to the plate passed around to reward the actors. But Dostoevsky refuses to accept this mercenary motive as the deeper meaning of his reception; or, rather, he sees this practical aim as part of the deeper meaning that he unravels. For the convicts' treatment of him, he maintains, was prompted by their sense that his superior knowledge of the stage entitled him, in this instance, to special respect. "They looked upon me as to some extent a theater-goer, a connoisseur who had frequented performances very different from this; they had seen Baklushin consulting me all this time and treating me with respect; so on this occasion I had the honor of a front place." (4: 121-122).

Dostoevsky was thus deferred to according to the peasant-convicts' estimate of his genuine superiority to them in theatrical matters, and despite his manifest inferiority to them in all other realms of prison-camp life. "The convicts could laugh at me, seeing that I was a poor hand at their work. Almazov could look with contempt upon us as 'gentlemen' and pride himself in front of us on knowing how to burn alabaster. But, mixed with their persecution and ridicule, there was another element: we had once been gentlemen; we belonged to the same class as their former masters, of whom they could have no pleasant memories. But now at the theatricals they made way for me." For Dostoevsky, such deference was evidence not of any kow-towing to authority (and how could it be, since the peasants could easily have brushed him aside like a fly?) but rather of a sense of dignity that did not allow them to exercise their power in a domain outside their competence. "Even those who liked me least were (I know for a fact)," Dostoevsky asserts, "anxious now for my approval of the theatricals, and without the slightest servility they let me have the best place . . ." (4: 121).

The same interpretation is offered of Petrov's remark about Dostoevsky's presumed larger contribution to the fund for the actors. It was true that he would give a greater amount, and thus the actors would be more amply rewarded; but it was not for money that he had been accorded priority. It was rather out of a general desire of the audience to offer the greatest possible reward to those who had given them all so much pleasure. Interpreting the subconscious behavior of the convicts, Dostoevsky casts it in the form of the following (fictitious) thoughts: " 'You are richer than I am, so you can stand in front, and though we are all equal, you'll give more; and so a spectator like you is more pleasing to the actors. You must have the first place, for we are all here not thinking of the money, but showing our respect, so we ought to sort ourselves of our own accord.' " And Dostoevsky adds: "How much fine and genuine pride there is in this! It is a respect not for money, but for oneself!" Indeed, as Dostoevsky remarks in an afterthought: "I can't remember one of them [the peasant-convicts] demeaning himself for the sake of money" (4: 121-122).

This episode took on a crucial symbolic significance for Dostoevsky and, if it actually preceded the peasant Marey incident, may be considered its moral-social prefiguration. For it reveals the same ability on the part of the peasant-convicts to overcome their instinctive vindictiveness against their former masters for the sake of a higher value. And the moral drawn from these events by Dostoevsky was that "the highest and most striking characteristic of our people is just their sense of justice and their eagerness for it. *There is no trace in the common people of the desire to be the cock of the walk on all occasions and at all costs, whether they deserve to be or not.* One has but to take off the outer superimposed husk and look at the kernel more closely, more attentively and without prejudice, and some of us will see things in the people that we should never have suspected. There is not much our wise men could teach them. On the contrary, I think it is the wise men who ought to learn from the people" (4: 121-122; italics added).

Once again we are at the source of what was to become one of the most cherished and deeply held convictions of the post-Siberian Dostoevsky. For was he not later to proclaim, with accents of prophetic passion, that the Russian peasantry was imbued with a sense of moral rectitude that could serve as a shining example to its "betters"? And while such an idea was often ridiculed by his opponents, it was too firmly rooted in the redemptive emotions of these prison years for Dostoevsky ever to question its validity. One can also see how the same refusal of the peasants to assert their unconditional right to equality in all areas of life, their willingness to cede priority when it was justified according to their outlook, could have led him to conclude, as he told his friend Baron Wrangel shortly after being freed, that "a political overturn in Russia was inconceivable *for the time being*, premature, and even to think of a constitution on the Western model was ridiculous given the ignorance of the peasant masses" (italics in text).²

Indeed, whatever the social-political issues that Dostoevsky became involved with in the future, he would always approach them in a state of mind predetermined by such ineradicable memories. Never would he forget how he and others had managed to win the affection of the peasant-convicts, or the impressive sense of "dignity" he had discerned in their refusal to assert brute power over him at the theatricals. Such experiences, he firmly believed, had given him a unique insight into the hidden depths of the Russian social psyche. "In short," he informs Mikhail in that first letter already quoted so extensively, "I have not wasted my time [in prison camp]. I have learned to know if not Russia then at least her people, to know them well, *as perhaps few know them*. There, that is what I pride myself on a little bit. It is, I hope, pardonable" (italics added).³

5
—————

In the early days of his prison term, Dostoevsky tried to console himself by reflecting, certainly with an edge of masochistic sarcasm, that the denizens of the camp were probably composed of the same mixture of good and bad as people in the world outside. "Even as I thought this," he continues, "I shook my head at the idea, and yet, my God! if I had only known at the time how true it was" (4: 57). At first, he had looked on the vast majority of the other inmates as so many replicas of the evil and vicious Aristov; but then, inspired by the peasant Marey vision, he had rejected this first reaction and striven to take a more favorable view. Once he did so, he found that his initial response had been entirely mistaken, and that, as with so much else in camp life, he had allowed himself to fall victim to his automatic upper-class responses.

At first glance, it may seem disconcerting to find Dostoevsky declaring that there were many "good" people even among a group of men who, in most cases, had committed at least one murder. And this, indeed, has led to a very widespread and popular misconception. One often reads that, after a certain point, the distinction between right and wrong began to blur for Dostoevsky himself, and that he came to admire criminals for their "strength" (as Stendhal had done earlier and Nietzsche was to do later). Such an opinion, however, cannot stand up to a close and unbiased reading of Dostoevsky's text. He never justifies crime as such, and even takes trouble explicitly to reject the view of those who may be inclined to do so. "There are points of view, in fact," he concedes, "from which one is almost brought to justify the criminal. But in spite of all possible points of view everyone will admit that there are crimes which always and everywhere from the beginning of the world, under all legal systems, have unhesitatingly been considered crimes, and will be considered so as long as man remains human. Only in prison have I heard stories of the most terrible, the most unnatural actions, of the most monstrous murders told with the most spontaneous, childishly merry laughter" (4: 15). Dostoevsky is probably referring here to the fearsome Gazin, who was reported by the other convicts to have been a bloodthirsty sadist "fond of murdering small children simply for pleasure" (4: 41).

It is thus totally erroneous to depict Dostoevsky as harboring any secret sympathy for crime and criminality as manifestations of a grandeur "beyond good and evil"; he never surrendered his conviction that man's humanity depends on the acceptance of a moral code preserving the boundary between the two. But this did not mean that all murders were necessarily committed for the same reasons, or that all murderers were sadists and perverts. And the more Dostoevsky came to know some of his fellow convicts, the more he came to understand that some so-called crimes had been prompted by reasons he could not fully condemn. Some, he discovered, had been mistakes or accidents, and the motives behind them were not at all indications of moral baseness or infamy. Others, the prevailing conditions of Russian life being what they were, had often been an individual's only means of defense against intolerable abuse, his assertion of dignity and self-respect in face of unbearable humiliation or his outraged protest against injustice.

In the first group, those who had landed in *katorga* by mischance, we can place Akim Akimich, the Daghestan Tartar Aley (whom Dostoevsky paints with glowing colors), and the woebegone Sushilov, the convict who became Dostoevsky's body servant and was rewarded from time to time with a few kopeks. Akim Akimich, it is clear, could not be considered a criminal at all; in killing the treacherous local chieftain he had merely been carrying out what he conceived to be his supreme duty as a Russian officer. Nor could Aley really be considered a criminal either, even though, along with his older brothers, he had taken part in the murder of an Armenian merchant and his bodyguards and the plundering of their caravan. Aley had simply obeyed the commands of his older brothers to accompany them without knowing the purpose of their foray; he had been a victim of his unquestioning obedience to familial authority, which he revered out of the highest principles of morality. "He was pure as a chaste girl," Dostoevsky writes, "and any ugly, cynical, dirty, unjust or violent action in the prison brought a glow of indignation into his beautiful eyes, making them still more beautiful" (4: 52). When Aley, a Mohammedan, learned to read Russian from the New Testament under Dostoevsky's guidance, he was strongly moved by the injunction of Jesus to "forgive, love, not hurt others, love even your enemies" (4: 54). Aley's enthusiastic words about Jesus went straight to Dostoevsky's heart, and surely helped to strengthen the latter's conviction of the universal appeal of Christ's teaching of all-forgiving love.

Dostoevsky gives a considerable amount of space in *House of the Dead* to Sushilov, and uses him as the prime example of how difficult it had been at first to see the peasant-convicts as they really were. He may have been so taken aback by his original misapprehension because Sushilov, who seems to step right out of one of his own stories, should presumably have been clear to him at a glance. Why this inoffensive peasant had been sent to resettle in Siberia remains unknown; probably as a result of a bit of bad luck, but hardly anything that could be considered a crime. Along the way, though, having been placed in a convoy with much more serious offenders, he had been hoodwinked into changing places (a frequent practice) with a convict sentenced for capital crimes, who had first plied him with vodka and then paid him with a silver ruble and a red shirt. Not realizing what he had done until it was too late, Sushilov thus landed incongruously in the "special division" reserved for the most desperate criminals with indefinite sentences. "Sushilov was a pitiful fellow," Dostoevsky tells us, "utterly spiritless and humbled, hopelessly downtrodden, though no one used to ill-treat him, but he was downtrodden by nature" (4: 59). Extremely devoted to Dostoevsky, he neglected some little task one day and was rebuked with the remark that, after all, he was being paid for his work. For several days afterwards he seemed depressed, and, when Dostoevsky offered him some money again, refused to take it. Instead, running outside, he struck his forehead against the stockade and broke into tears because Dostoevsky had not understood that he served him out of personal affection, not because of money. So even the wretched Sushilov was capable of nurturing the finest feelings of disinterested human devotion!

6

Weak-willed and harmless people such as Sushilov were the exception rather than the rule in camp; and Dostoevsky also came to gain a new insight into others of a quite different and much more refractory stamp. These too, he came to recognize, were very far from being morally degenerate or humanly irredeemable. Dostoevsky could not of course dwell too openly on the reasons for their crimes, but time and again he slips in details that speak for themselves. Petrov, the most dangerous man in camp, had been a soldier who "once, before he came to prison . . . had been struck by the colonel at drill. Probably he had been struck many times before, but this time he could not put up with it and he stabbed the colonel openly, in broad daylight, in the face of the regiment" (4: 84).

Luka Kuzmich, whom nobody in the camp took seriously, even though he tried to give himself the airs of a desperado, had been first arrested for the insignificant offense of being a tramp. But he decided to "lay out" the major in charge of his prison because "the food was bad; the major did as he liked with them [the other prisoners]," and he terrified everyone else by shouting "I am Tsar, I am God too" when he made his appearance on the scene. Luka got a knife ready, threw the major into a rage by replying that there was only one God and one Tsar "set over us by God Himself," and then plunged his weapon up to the hilt into the major's belly. After setting down this story, Dostoevsky takes time out to explain to the reader, carefully limiting his comments only to the past, that unhappily "many similar expressions were not uncommonly used in old days by many commanding officers," and had led to similar results. "This insolence of self-glorification, this exaggerated idea of being able to do anything with impunity," he observes, "inspires hatred in the most submissive of men and drives them out of all patience" (4: 89-91).

Similarly, the gentle and good-looking homosexual Sirotkin, unable to accustom himself to the rigors of Army life, had been hounded and persecuted by one officer in particular. After first clumsily attempting to escape his misery by committing suicide, he killed his tormentor in a fit of baffled rage. Dostoevsky also found it difficult to look on the good-natured Baklushin as a hardened criminal, and believed his story that he had only intended to frighten the elderly German he had murdered. His purpose had been to scare him off from marrying, against her will, the pretty German girl who had confessed her love for the feckless and penniless Russian soldier. But the insistence of the righteous German burgher that Baklushin would not "dare" to shoot him provoked the Russian beyond endurance. Still, such a crime of passion would have drawn him only a relatively light sentence if he had not objected to being abused in court by his captain, whom he rebuked for insulting him "before the mirror of justice"—the transparent prism, surmounted by the imperial two-headed eagle, that was placed on the table of each Russian tribunal. Baklushin's concern for the dignity of the court and his refusal to accept contumely landed him in the special division.

These are only a few examples of the criminals whom Dostoevsky found it more and more difficult to condemn out of hand. One daring passage in *House of the Dead* even contains a general exculpation of many others whose personal histories he does not spell out in detail: "There are men who commit crimes on purpose to be sent to penal servitude, *in order to escape from a far more penal life of labor outside.* There he [the convict] lived in the deepest degradation, never had enough to eat and worked from morning to night for his exploiter . . ." (4: 43; italics added). Such convicts had found penal servitude far more preferable to life as a serf under a merciless landowner, and Dostoevsky says nothing to indicate any disapproval of such a choice. It is in the context of such considerations that we must place one of the most famous passages in the book, often cited and still more often misinterpreted. "After all," Dostoevsky declares, "one must tell the whole truth; these men were exceptional men. Perhaps they were the most gifted, the strongest of our people" (4: 231). Not, however, because they were criminals, but because their crimes sprang from a strength of character and, frequently, a defense of instinctive moral principles, exhibited under circumstances where others would have been completely crushed.

Dostoevsky's increasingly acute awareness of the moral difference between one crime and another became, as he explains, the cause of a "thought which haunted me persistently all the time I was in prison, a difficulty that cannot be fully solved." This difficulty was simply that the same crimes, under the law, received much the same punishment; yet the reasons for which they had been committed, morally speaking, were infinitely varied. "One may have committed a murder for nothing, for an onion; he murdered a peasant on the high road, who turned out to have nothing but an onion." (As a prison proverb had it, "A hundred murders and a hundred onions [each worth a kopek] and you've got a ruble.") "Another murders a sensual tyrant in defence of the honor of his betrothed, his sister or his child. Another is a fugitive [i.e., a runaway serf], hemmed in by a regiment of trackers, who commits a murder in defence of his freedom, his life, often dying of hunger; and another murders little children for the pleasure of killing, of feeling their warm blood on his hands, of enjoying their terror, and their last dove-like flutter under the knife. Yet all of these are sent to penal servitude." Variations in the length of sentences do not cope with the problem because "there are as many shades of differences as there are characters"; and Dostoevsky, admitting defeat, finally resigns himself to the impossibility of an answer: "It is in its own way an insoluble problem, like squaring the circle" (4: 42-43).

Such words anticipate Dostoevsky's later pronounced distaste for legal formalities of any kind, which stick to the letter of the law and rarely leave room for any probing of the heart and mind of the individual criminal. It is only a gifted and sensitive eccentric, like the investigating magistrate Porfiry Petrovich in *Crime and Punishment*, who can truly grasp the tangle of motives that stir Raskolnikov; but he is clearly an exception. Dostoevsky was eventually to pour all his anguish over this issue into his portrayal of the investigation of the putative crime of Dimitry Karamazov, with its regard only for the "facts" and its total neglect of Dimitry's own words and responses.

For the moment, however, we can see how this growing apprehension of human diversity among his fellow convicts enormously increased the range of Dostoevsky's philanthropic convictions of the 1840s—but without causing him to blur the distinction between good and evil. What had been a pitying sentimentalism toward weak and basically unassertive characters now took on a tragic complexity as Dostoevsky's sympathies with the unsubjugated peasant-convicts stretched the boundaries of official morality to the breaking point. More important than the crime itself were the motives, the human situation, from which it emerged. And if the pathetic Sushilov points back to Dostoevsky's literary past, then his increasing respect for so many of his prison companions looks forward unmistakably to the future.

7

If Dostoevsky's attitude toward the peasant-convicts was thus much affected by his increasing familiarity with the causes of their crimes, it was also greatly influenced by what he could observe of their instinctive acceptance of, and reverence for, the Christian moral code. To be sure, he could never detect any personal contrition or remorse among them, although he refused to foreclose the possibility: "Who can say that he has sounded the depths of these lost hearts?" And he also came to understand, or at least to develop a theory, as to why the conscience of the peasant could not be judged in the same terms as that of a member of the upper class. From the peasant point of view, crimes against their superiors were not crimes at all; they were simply another episode in the eternal class war carried on between the two groups. "The [peasant] criminal knows and never doubts that he will be acquitted by the verdict of his own class, who will never, he knows, entirely condemn him (and for the most part will fully acquit him), so long as his offence has not been against his equals, his brothers, his fellow peasants" (4: 147). The lack of repentance for such crimes did not mean, as he had all too hastily concluded, that the peasant-convicts were devoid of all moral sensibility; quite the opposite turned out to be true. We have already seen the peasant-convicts exhibiting their devotion during the Easter service; and Dostoevsky offers many other examples of how the values of the Christian faith, pervading camp life, helped to mitigate some of its ruthlessness and inhumanity.

All the convicts, as Dostoevsky had learned to his sorrow on the first day in prison, stole from each other shamelessly and incessantly. But almost all, after a while, gave their money for safekeeping to a Starodubovsky Old Believer, imprisoned for having set fire to an Orthodox church. Dostoevsky portrays this martyr for the old faith, who won universal trust because of his saintly qualities, in words that anticipate his depiction many years later, in *A Raw Youth*, of the Russian peasant pilgrim Makar Ivanovich: "He was merry, often laughing . . . with a gentle candid laugh, in which there was a great deal of childlike simplicity" (4: 34). Similarly, the elderly Polish prisoner Z. (Zochowski), who was flogged on arriving at the camp, gained the convicts' respect because he did not cry out under the lash and, when the beating was finished, immediately kneeled down to pray. Genuine religious piety always appealed to the convicts, who never mocked or derided anyone displaying it, and all of them exhibited comparable sentiments at one time or another. On a peasant-convict's name day, which was a celebration in honor of his patron saint, all who could afford it indulged themselves with a feast and a drunken spree; but Dostoevsky also notes that "on his name day the convict set a candle before the icon and said his prayers as soon as he got up" (4: 35).

Dostoevsky, as we know, found the human atmosphere of the prison barracks at most times to be nerve-racking and oppressive; he was thus all the more favorably impressed with the change that occurred, at least for a brief moment, during the religious holidays. Of Christmas he writes: "The great festivals of the church make a vivid impression on the minds of the peasants from childhood upwards. They are the days of rest from their hard toil, the days of family gatherings. . . . Respect for the solemn day had passed into a custom strictly observed among the convicts; very few caroused, all were serious and seemed preoccupied, though many of them really had nothing to do. But whether they drank or did nothing, they tried to keep up a certain dignity." If anyone upset the prevailing mood, "even by accident, the convicts set on him with outcries and abuse and were angry with him as though he had shown disrespect for the holiday itself." "This state of mind in the convicts," Dostoevsky adds, "was remarkable and positively touching" (4: 105). It would certainly have been touching—and also a great relief—to observe such manifestations of decorum in the midst of the unbridled behavior that was customary.

Dostoevsky also understood the important role played by the peasants' Christianity in maintaining the convict, whatever his crime may have been, within the human community as one of its members. "Apart from their innate reverence for the great day," he says, "the convicts felt unconsciously that by the observance of Christmas they were, as it were, in touch with the whole of the world, that they were not altogether outcasts and lost men, not altogether cut off; that it was the same in prison as amongst other people" (4: 105). Nor was this by any means an illusion on their part; the religious holidays usually brought forth an outpouring of moral solidarity with the convicts in the form of charity. "An immense quantity of provisions were brought, such as rolls, cheesecakes, pastries, scones, and similar good things. I believe there was not a housewife of the middle and lower class of the town who did not send something of her baking by way of Christmas greetings to the 'unfortunates' and the captives" (4: 108). Dostoevsky is careful to exclude the upper, educated class from such participation in the Christmas spirit; and he remarks elsewhere that "the higher classes in Russia have no idea how deeply our merchants, tradespeople and peasants concern themselves about 'the un-fortunates' " (4: 18).

In this context, once again, Dostoevsky stresses the mollifying effect on the behavior of the peasant-convicts of their basic acceptance of the Chris-tian moral code. "All [the gifts] were accepted with equal gratitude without distinction of gifts or givers. The convicts took off their caps as they re-ceived them, bowed, gave their Christmas greetings and took the offering into the kitchen. When the offerings were piled up in heaps, the senior convicts were sent for, and they divided all equally among the wards. There was no scolding or quarreling; it was honestly and equitably done." The division in Dostoevsky's barracks was carried out by Akim Akimich and another convict, who "with their own hands gave each convict his share. There was not the slightest protest, not the slightest jealousy; all were satisfied; there could be no suspicion of an offering being concealed or unfairly divided" (4: 108). What a contrast with the usual bickering and perpetual pilfering of each other's belongings!

Alms-giving from the population reached a peak during the religious holidays; but it was continual all through the year, and sometimes took the form of money handed to the convicts as they shuffled through the streets of Omsk in a work convoy. The first time Dostoevsky received alms in this way was "soon after my arrival in prison." A ten-year-old girl—the daughter of a young soldier, who had seen Dostoevsky in the Army hospital when she came to visit her dying father—passed him walking under escort and ran back to give him a coin. " 'There, poor unfortunate, take a kopek, for Christ's sake,' she cried, overtaking me and thrusting the coin in my hand. . . . I treasured that kopek for a long time" (4: 19). This last assertion is literally true: Dostoevsky's second wife confirms that he kept it as a memento for many years and was very upset when it was lost through some oversight.[4] What this incident came to mean to him may be seen in *Crime and Punishment*, where Raskolnikov cuts off his ties with humanity, and indicates his rejection of all impulses of sympathy and pity, by the symbolic gesture of throwing into the Neva a twenty-kopek piece given to him as charity by a little girl.

8

Dostoevsky thus came into contact, in this immediate and touching fashion, with such deeply humane, Christian aspects of Russian lower-class life; and he could observe the happy effects of at least the remains of the same emotions in the behavior of the peasant-convicts. Certainly these manifestations served as a precious confirmation of the peasant Marey vision; even more, they suggested that the humanitarian, philanthropic ideals of his earlier work, which he had formerly seen as having been brought to Russian life by the progressive ideology of the Russian Westerners, were actually embodied in the instinctive moral reflexes of the much-despised and denigrated Russian peasant. It is thus little wonder that Dostoevsky was later to become such a virulent opponent of all those who aspired to replace Christian values by other notions of morality. To do so, he was passionately convinced, would undermine the basic moral foundations of Russian life as he had come to know them—under circumstances where the survival of *any* kind of morality could only be considered a miracle! Nor should one forget that the most truly vicious man in the camp, the blackest and most infamous scoundrel, was the well-educated Aristov, whose cynicism knew no bounds and who was entirely free of any trace of the traditional moral restraints.

By the end of his prison term, then, Dostoevsky had swung round full circle in his estimate of the majority of his fellow inmates; and though his sense of estrangement as a gentleman could not be completely overcome, he was now able to identify himself with the others, morally and emotionally, to a far greater extent than he had ever thought possible. Such a sense of identification was also augmented by a further upsurge of the same patriotic and nationalist sentiments that had provided so important a stimulus for his regeneration.

The Crimean War, which broke out in 1853, raged all through the last year of his prison term. But the relations between Russia and Turkey (the latter supported by France and England) had already been tense and troubled for several years, and echos of this hostility had certainly filtered through the walls of the prison stockade. Initially, the cause of the conflict had been a quarrel over the rights of Eastern Orthodox Christians as opposed to those of Roman Catholics in Palestine; and there is some evidence that this issue may have entered into Dostoevsky's envenomed disputes with the Roman Catholic Polish prisoners.* In any case, he emerged

---

* In Tokarzewski's memoirs, there is one anecdote concerning Dostoevsky that clearly involves issues raised by the Crimean War. "He [Dostoevsky] stated even that Constantinople

from the camp firmly persuaded that his new rapport with the peasant-convicts was intimately linked with his own love for his native land. "I assure you," he writes to Apollon Maikov in 1856, "that I am so close by blood to everything Russian that even the convicts did not frighten me: they were the Russian people, my brothers in misfortune, and I had the happiness more than once to discover a greatness of soul even in a bandit precisely because I was able to understand him: for I was also a Russian."[5]

should long ago have belonged to Russia, as well as the whole of European Turkey, which he thought would very soon become the flower of the Russian Empire. Once Dostoevsky recited to us his poem, an ode describing the inevitable entry of the victorious Russian Army into Constantinople. The ode was indeed beautiful. However, none of us was earnest in his praise of it, and I asked him: 'And haven't you an ode for the return trip?' He boiled with rage, and springing at my face he called me an ignoramus and a barbarian."

No such ode is known among Dostoevsky's writings, but Tokarzewski may have been referring to an early draft of "On European Events in 1854," which Dostoevsky had possibly begun to write while still in the prison camp (see pp. 181-183). See also Wacław Lednicki, *Russia, Poland and the West* (New York, 1954), 275.

CHAPTER 11

"Monsters in Their Misery"

Dostoevsky's years in the house of the dead exposed him to an extraordinary range of human (and inhuman) personalities, among whom genuine saintliness rubbed elbows with the basest depravity. Nearly everyone had, at some crucial instant, stepped outside the bounds of normal social life to commit a violent act that had decided his destiny once and for all. The stories Dostoevsky heard all around him rivaled the most desperate deeds of the Gothic novels and Romantic literature that had filled his youthful imagination; yet such stories were part and parcel of the prosaic, squalid existences of perfectly commonplace Russians. It is thus hardly surprising that Dostoevsky's great works should later be marked by the same combination of Romantic extravagance set in the quotidian midst of Russian daily life. And if, more than any other novelist, Dostoevsky was able to lift his melodramatic murder plots to the level of high tragedy, one reason was surely that he had lived through experiences and had been plunged into a world where the sensations of melodrama were more than merely a literary convention. He had felt them racing through his own pulses, and had gathered them from the lips of people with whom he was forced to share his daily routine.

The effect of such exposure on Dostoevsky's imaginative grasp of human experience was of course enormous; and his portrayal of character was later to take a qualitative leap in depth and scale that may be directly attributed to this cause. There was, however, one particular aspect of camp life that became the most distinctive hallmark of his genius. *House of the Dead* contains a remarkable series of analyses, which, focusing on the unconscious urges of the human psyche, describe its irresistible need to assert itself and affirm its native dignity. This need was so imperious that, unable to find normal outlets under the repressive conditions of the prison camp, it burst forth in all sorts of irrational, absurd, and even self-destructive forms—in actions that at first glance seemed totally senseless and inexplicable. Always preoccupied with the deformations of character caused by lack of freedom, Dostoevsky had explored this theme in his early stories; but there he had barely scratched the surface. Life in prison camp gave him a unique vantage point from which to study human beings living under extreme psychic pressure, and responding to such pressure with the most frenzied behavior. Once Dostoevsky had mastered himself

146

sufficiently to be able to contemplate his environment with lucidity, he began to understand even *such* sense-defying conduct as the product of a genuine human need—no longer as the monstrous perversities of a collection of moral Quasimodos wholly beyond the human pale.

In fact, we cannot truly understand Dostoevsky's later world-view if we separate his perceptions and values too sharply from the context of psychic constraint in which they were remolded. For Dostoevsky was persuaded that no human order could ultimately prove viable unless it acknowledged—and offered some relief for—these irrepressible demands of the human spirit.

2

It has often been said that Dostoevsky discovered the "evil" of "human nature" in the prison camp, and that this discovery frightened him into an acceptance of a supernatural faith as the sole bulwark of morality against the inherent corruption of mankind. One can argue that there are enough evil people in Dostoevsky's early stories to cast doubt on the novelty of any such discovery; and such a view hardly accords with the evidence of *House of the Dead*. If any discovery was made, it was rather exactly the opposite: Dostoevsky found that most of the peasant-convicts were far better people than he could possibly have believed at first. All the same, there is just enough truth in this interpretation to make it seriously misleading as it stands, and one should not reject it simply out of hand. If limited and qualified in the proper fashion, it does point to an essential aspect of Dostoevsky's evolution. But this aspect should not be generalized too hastily or, in particular, conceived of in a framework alien to the tradition of Dostoevsky's inherited religious assumptions.

To begin with, since Dostoevsky himself stresses so strongly the injustice of applying a single rule to the immense moral differentiation between one individual and another, it is surely mistaken to saddle him with any overriding theory of human nature. Nor can Dostoevsky's religious faith, or his sense that such faith was a genuine necessity of the human spirit, be attributed primarily to a fear of the consequences of unregenerate human wickedness; after all, he had believed in Christ long before such a fear had presumably begun to exist. It should also be stressed that the doctrine of original sin, which holds human nature irremediably enthralled by evil, has much less force for an Eastern Christian than for a Roman Catholic or Protestant. As the theologian Ernst Benz has pointed out, "The consciousness that man was imprinted with the image of God is so dominant [in Orthodoxy], that the idea of original sin could never become established within the Orthodox Church in its blunt Western form." Orthodoxy conceives of sin as a "damaging" or a "tainting of the image of

God; but it cannot rob man of his original nobility."[1] Such a view accords much more closely with what Dostoevsky found in the house of the dead than does the Western Augustinian dogma of man as ineluctably evil. All this being said, however, it is still true that Dostoevsky became aware of an abyss of frightfulness in some individuals surpassing anything he had known before. And while the bulk of his fellow convicts still remained human because of their traditional Christianity, there were some who, having lost all sense of any distinction between good and evil, seemed to belong to another species.

The most glaring example of such a loss was of course Aristov. Gazin too, whose appearance gave Dostoevsky the impression that he was "looking at a huge, gigantic spider of the size of a man" (the spider is very frequently Dostoevsky's image for absolute evil), also belongs among those who fascinate him by their horror (4: 40). Another appalling individual was the bandit chief Korenev, not a prisoner in the camp, but a convict whom Dostoevsky had seen during his stay in Tobolsk. "He was a wild beast in the fullest sense of the word," Dostoevsky writes, "and when you stood near him you felt instinctively that there was a terrible creature beside you, even before you knew his name." What struck Dostoevsky most, and filled him with dread, "was the spiritual deadness of the man. The flesh had so completely got the upper hand of all spiritual characteristics that at the first glance you could see from his face that nothing was left but a fierce lust of physical gratification—sensuality, gluttony" (4: 47).

Quite the opposite in temperament, but equally terrifying, was another bandit chief named Orlov, about whom Dostoevsky had heard "marvelous stories" before he turned up in the Army hospital during one of Dostoevsky's stays. Orlov "was a criminal such as there are few, who had murdered old people and children in cold blood—a man of terrible strength of will and proud consciousness of his strength." Far from having lost his humanity, like Korenev, because of subjugation by the lusts of the flesh, Orlov for Dostoevsky "was unmistakably the case of a complete triumph over the flesh. It was evident that the man's power of control was unlimited, that he despised every sort of punishment and torture, and was afraid of nothing in the world." He was, clearly, a person of extraordinary self-possession, and Dostoevsky notes being "struck by his strange haughtiness. He looked down on everything with incredible disdain, though he made no sort of effort to maintain his lofty attitude—it was somehow natural" (4: 47).

Tremendously excited by *House of the Dead* when he first came across it, Friedrich Nietzsche could well have seen Orlov as one of the incarnations of his Superman; and what Dostoevsky tells us of his own conversations with the famous brigand remarkably anticipates the Nietzschean distinction between master and slave morality.* For when Dostoevsky began to question Orlov about his "adventures," the latter became aware that his interlocutor "was trying to get at his conscience and to discover some sign of penitence in him." Orlov's only response was to glance at Dostoevsky "with great contempt and haughtiness, as though I had suddenly in his eyes become a foolish little boy, with whom it was impossible to discuss things as you would with a grown-up person. There was even a sort of pity for me to be seen in his face. A moment later he burst out laughing at me, a perfectly open-hearted laugh free from any hint of irony . . ." (4: 48).

Dostoevsky and Orlov left the hospital at the same time, with Orlov impatient to undergo the second half of a punishment by the "sticks" (that is, running the gauntlet of a regiment) from which he was not to return alive. When he shook hands with Dostoevsky, the latter took this gesture as "a sign of great confidence on his part." Nonetheless, Dostoevsky concludes, "he could not really help despising me, and must have looked upon me as a weak, pitiful, submissive creature, inferior to him in every respect" (4: 48). It is impossible to read these words without thinking of Raskolnikov's impassioned dialectic in *Crime and Punishment*, which, although nourished by ideologies that had not yet made their appearance on the Russian social-cultural scene, certainly draws much of its vitality from such a recollection. And Raskolnikov may well be seen as a conscience-

---

* How Nietzsche viewed *House of the Dead* may be gathered from the following passages from *The Will to Power* (Book III). The first erroneously depicts Dostoevsky as supporting one of the chief aims of Nietzsche's own work: "To return a good conscience to an evil human being—has this been my spontaneous [*unwillkürlich*] effort? And the evil human being precisely insofar as he is the *strongest human being*? Here one should bring in the judgment of Dostoevsky about the criminals in the prison camp." A second fragment, however, comes much closer to Dostoevsky's own point of view: "In almost all the crimes [described by Dostoevsky], qualities come to the fore which should not be lacking in any man. Not unjustly did Dostoevsky say that the inmates of the Siberian prison camp made up the strongest and best portion of the Russian people."

Both citations are given in the excellent article of Wolfgang Gesemann, "Nietzsche's Verhältnis zu Dostoevsky auf dem europäischen Hintergrund der 8oer Jahre," *Die Welt der Slaven*, 2 (July 1961), 129-156. This article surveys all the factual material concerning Nietzsche's relation to Dostoevsky and contains the relevant citations from the correspondence and works. A discussion of the Dostoevsky-Nietzsche problem can also be found in V. V. Dudkin and K. M. Azadovsky, "Dostoevskii v Germanii (1846-1921)," *Literaturnoe Nasledstvo*, 86 (Moscow 1973), chap. 3, 678-688.

For the attempt to equate Dostoevsky with Nietzsche, or to view him as secretly sympathetic with Nietzsche's doctrines, see the highly influential book by Lev Shestov, "Dostoevsky and Nietzsche: The Philosophy of Tragedy," in *Essays in Russian Literature, The Conservative View: Leontiev, Rozanov, Shestov*, ed. and trans. Spencer E. Roberts (Athens, Ga., 1968), 3-183. A sharp and convincing refutation of such an interpretation, which draws on new material recently discovered in the Nietzsche archives (some notes he took of *The Devils*), is offered by G. Fridlender, "Dostoevskii i Nitsshe," in *Dostoevskii i Mirovaya Literatura* (Moscow, 1979), 214-254. Fridlender's argument, by no means a novel one, goes back at least to Georg Brandes, who told Nietzsche himself that Dostoevsky represented the very slave morality against which the German thinker was philosophizing with a hammer. Nietzsche agreed, and replied in a letter (November 20, 1888): "I treasure him, all the same, as the most valuable psychological material I know—I am exceedingly grateful to him, however much he always grates against my deepest instincts." Cited in Gesemann, 142.

stricken member of the intelligentsia—exactly like Dostoevsky himself at this moment—who had tried to whip himself up into behaving like an Orlov, but who ultimately finds it morally impossible to sustain the awful consequences of his deeds.

Nor would it have seemed implausible to Dostoevsky that a Raskolnikov could become an Orlov, at least temporarily, under the force of circumstance. Such a possibility—as Dostoevsky makes clear in his remarkable reflections on flogging and torturers in *House of the Dead*—lies slumbering in every human breast; any acceptance of or habituation to cruel and inhuman practices can lead to a total blunting of moral feeling. He cites, as an example, an officer he knew who was "good-natured, even honest and even respected by society, who yet could not with equanimity let a man go until he screamed out under the lash, till he prayed and implored for mercy"; such was the ritual response, and the officer felt personally insulted until it was forthcoming (4: 155). "Anyone who has once experienced this power," Dostoevsky comments, "this unlimited mastery of the body, blood and soul of a fellow man made of the same clay as oneself, a brother in the law of Christ—anyone who has experienced this power and full license to inflict the greatest humiliation upon another creature made in the image of God will unconsciously lose the mastery of his own sensations.... I maintain that the very best of men may be coarsened and hardened into a brute by habit" (4: 154). Hence, by implication, the importance of maintaining intact a Christian conscience that could serve as an inner barrier against a similar deadening of the moral sensibility. And if Dostoevsky later became such an intransigent enemy of the radicals of the 1860s, it was less because he rejected their social-political aims than because he feared that the ethical doctrines they were proclaiming would destroy this all-important defense against moral stupefaction.

3

If we are to judge from the evidence of his book, nothing fascinated Dostoevsky more, during his years in the house of the dead, than the evidence it provided of the immense power of the irrational, volitional, and emotive needs of the human spirit. Indeed, the tendencies of Dostoevsky's ideas, his intimately personal awareness of the limits of reason, and his entire creative orientation—all had prepared him to make the most of his unique opportunity to observe the human psyche reacting to extremes of coercion and oppression much greater than any he could have envisaged earlier.

Dostoevsky had always been inclined to a certain theoretical irrationalism, and, as a very young man, he had defended art rather than philosophy as the highest form through which the cognition of eternal truth could be attained. (Since his brother Mikhail advanced the opposite point of view, their youthful exchange reflects the competing influences of Schelling and Hegel in the Russian culture of the 1830s and 1840s.) He had also been subject to attacks of what he called "mystic terror," which filled him with fear at the apprehension "of something that I cannot define, something ungraspable and outside the natural order of things, but which yet may take shape this very minute, as though in mockery of all the conclusions of reason, and come to me and stand before me as undeniable fact, hideous, horrible and relentless" (3: 208). Such accesses of indeterminate fear made him aware of a sharp "inward division" between reason and the psychic-irrational, and of the impotence of the former to exercise any effective control over the latter. As a writer, Dostoevsky's best early work had centered precisely on the emotive needs and impulses of the psyche, with its insistent demands for recognition and the right to self-assertion. Since such demands were sternly denied by the dominant social conditions of Russian life, the psychological misfits whom Dostoevsky had portrayed were all understood by him to be victims of such conditions. But he no longer had to imagine the dangerously explosive potential of these needs, which, when suppressed, produced the disastrous consequences he could see occurring before his very eyes. It is little wonder that he now came to understand, as never before, the all-pervasive power of such irrational drives of the human personality, and the ease with which, inevitably, they overcame all the so-called reasonable components of human behavior.

House of the Dead is so rich in illustrations of this power of the irrational, and they are so varied in their nature and importance, that one scarcely knows where to begin. But let us start with Dostoevsky's remarks on the psychically unsettling effects of the communal life imposed on the convicts. Kept herded together, they could never really escape from each other's presence; and Dostoevsky was convinced that this closeness contributed, more than most were consciously aware, to their excessive restlessness and irritability. "I am certain," he affirms, "that every convict felt this torture, though of course in most cases unconsciously." As for himself, perhaps the worst "torture in prison life, almost more terrible than any other . . . [was] *compulsory life in common*" (italics in text; 4: 20-22). Elsewhere, he repeats: "I could never have imagined, for instance, how terrible and agonizing it would be never once for a single minute to be alone for the [four] years of my imprisonment" (4: 11).

The truth of these words is proven by an important letter that Dostoevsky wrote, almost immediately after his release, to Mme Fonvizina: "It is now almost five years that I have been under guard among a crowd of people, and I never had a single hour alone. To be alone is a normal need, like eating and drinking; otherwise, *in this enforced communism one turns*

into a hater of mankind. The society of other people becomes an unbearable torture, and it was from this that I suffered most during those
four years" (italics added).[2] It is striking to see how early Dostoevsky
identifies his prison-camp existence with life in one of those ideal Socialist
Utopias (Fourier, Cabet) that so many of his friends in the Petrashevsky
circle had once admired. He had, to be sure, never fully accepted such
Utopias himself, but his rejection has now become viscerally rooted in this
overwhelming sense of the need for the personality to defend itself against
psychic encroachment. Moreover, the exasperation arising from an inability to ward off such pressure has the effect of sweeping away all the
reasonable distinctions which could (and should) be made between the
personal qualities of various individuals: all are lumped together in a surge
of hatred with the same indiscriminate loathing.

A much more dramatic, and personally injurious, illustration of the
power of irrational impulse over human behavior is provided by Dostoevsky's remarks about prisoners awaiting punishment by flogging or beating.
"To defer the moment of punishment . . . convicts sometimes resorted to
terrible expedients: by stabbing one of the officials or a fellow convict they
would get a new trial, and their punishment would be deferred for some
two months and their aim would be attained. It was nothing to them that
the punishment, when it did come, two months later, would be twice or
three times as severe . . ." (4: 144). One of the patients in the hospital had
drunk a jug of vodka mixed with snuff to delay his punishment, and died
from the effects (Dostoevsky used this detail in his novella, *The Village of
Stepanchikovo*, written while still in Siberia). Commonplace prudence, as
we see, has been swept away by a fear too elemental to master.

4

Such examples, to be sure, still remain within a "normal" range of reaction
to the coercive conditions of camp life. They illustrate, in one way or
another, the triumph of emotive impulsions over more reasonable responses; but they do not exceed the limits of understanding, and their
irrational component is still motivated by comprehensible causes. This is
not the case, however, with other types of behavior, where the cause is
so slight as to be entirely incommensurate with the effect, or where no
immediate cause is perceptible at all. Dostoevsky's true genius reveals
itself when he turns to explore these aberrant extremes, and intuits the
deep human significance of what, from the point of view of an ordinary
observer, could only have been considered as extravagant folly or even
madness.

A peculiar and mysterious feature of peasant-convict life, for example,
was the general attitude toward money. It was, Dostoevsky points out, "of

vast and overwhelming importance" in prison, although the convict was fed and clothed and presumably needed nothing more. In fact, though, money allowed him to obtain all sorts of forbidden luxuries—extra food, tobacco, vodka, sexual pleasure—which helped to make life much more endurable. One would thus assume that the convicts hung on to their money for dear life and used it very sparingly; but exactly the opposite turned out to be the case. Instead of hoarding their money carefully, every convict who managed to scrape together a sufficient sum would invariably, on his name day or a religious holiday, squander it gloriously on a drunken fling. And so, after amassing the money "with cruel effort, or making use of extraordinary cunning, often in conjunction with theft and cheating," the convict throws it away with what Dostoevsky calls "childish sense-lessness."

But this, he hastens to add, "does not prove that he [the convict] does not appreciate [money], though it may seem so at first glance." On the contrary, "if he throws it away like so much rubbish, he throws it away on what he considers of even more value." And what is more precious for the convict than all the material benefits he can obtain from money? "Freedom or the dream of freedom," Dostoevsky replies. For one must realize that "the word convict means nothing else but a man with no will of his own, and in spending money he is showing a will of his own." By drinking and carousing, by breaking the rules of prison discipline and bullying his companions in misery, the convict is "pretending to his companions and even persuading himself, *if only for a time*, that he has infinitely more power and freedom than is supposed"; in other words, "he can persuade himself of what is utterly out of the question for the poor fellow" (4: 65-66; italics in text). Nothing is more important for the convict than to *feel* that he can assert his will and thus exercise his freedom; there is no risk he will refuse to run, no punishment he will not endure, for the sake of this temporary (and illusory) but infinitely precious satisfaction.

Here Dostoevsky is no longer simply stressing the dominating role of irrational elements in human behavior; now the need of the human personality to exercise its will, and hence to experience a sense of autonomy while doing so, is seen as *the strongest drive* of the psyche. To fulfill this drive, men will sacrifice all other goods and values; and if they are unable to satisfy it in any way (the drunken orgy is at least an outlet), the results can be disastrous. As if to prove the point, Dostoevsky follows the above passage with a discussion of what sometimes happens to model prisoners who have behaved irreproachably for many years and are, as a result, the joy of the authorities.

One day, such "a convict with no apparent reason suddenly breaks out, as though he were possessed by the devil, plays pranks, drinks, makes an uproar and sometimes positively ventures on serious crimes. . . ." The baffled authorities, who thought they knew him, can only "look at him and marvel"; but Dostoevsky understands what has occurred. "And all the while possibly the cause of this sudden outbreak, in the man from whom one would least have expected it, is simply the poignant hysterical craving for self-expression, the unconscious yearning for himself, the desire to assert himself, to assert his crushed personality, a desire which suddenly takes possession of him and reaches the pitch of fury, of spite, of mental aberration, of fits and nervous convulsions. So perhaps a man buried alive and awakening in his coffin might beat upon its lid and struggle to fling it off, though of course reason might convince him that all his efforts would be useless; but the trouble is that it is not a question of reason, it is a question of nervous convulsions" (4: 66-67).

Nor is this sort of outbreak only a result of the extreme constraints of prison life; similar conditions exist outside, and many of the convicts had landed in the camp precisely for having revolted against them. Each had been a peasant, house serf, soldier, or workman who had long led a quiet and peaceable life, bearing the burdens of his lot with patience and resignation. "Suddenly something in him seems to snap; his patience gives way and he sticks a knife into his enemy and oppressor." Such an act, Dostoevsky remarks, is "criminal but [still] comprehensible"; what sometimes follows is much less so. For now the same quiet and peaceable person often begins to kill indiscriminately "for amusement, for an insulting word, for a look, to make a round number or simply 'out of my way, don't cross my path, I am coming!' The man is, as it were, drunk, in delirium. It is as though having once overstepped the sacred limit, he begins to revel in the fact that nothing is sacred to him . . ." (4: 87-88). Such criminals often had the worst records, but they were by no means the most determined and desperate characters; once the fit was over, they calmed down very quickly, and their original nature reasserted itself. The explanation used for the model prisoners obviously applies here as well, although Dostoevsky himself does not make the explicit connection.

Such descriptions of personalities suppressed beyond endurance, who break out in hysterical frenzy and revolt against their subjugation, are among the most impressive passages in the book; and the imagery that Dostoevsky uses to analyze their behavior allows us to catch some of the internal process through which he transformed his private neuroses into a fecund source of psychological insight. For he himself had been haunted by the fear of being buried alive, and had left letters at one time requesting that, if he appeared to die in his sleep, his interment should be deferred for several days to allow for the possibility of error. No doubt he had imagined, time and again, the horror of waking up in the tomb, and this fearful fantasy is now projected into the situation of the human personality—buried alive in the coffin of all the constrictions both within and outside the prison walls that stifle and suffocate its life. Man will react against such entrapment with exactly the same fury as in Dostoevsky's nightmare, and will commit the wildest and most inhuman follies when stirred by such an irrepressible human need. Here we are obviously at the source of what was one day to become the revolt of the underground man; but this work could be written only after Dostoevsky had become convinced that, in the world envisaged by the radical ideology of the 1860s, the situation of the human personality would become identical with what he had seen and felt in the prison camp.

5

Irrational and hysterical outbreaks of the kind we have been dwelling on were the exception rather than the rule of prison life. For the most part, everything went smoothly and routinely; and Dostoevsky even goes out of his way to comment scornfully on the excessive fear of Russian convicts invariably displayed by those who have anything to do with the breed. He attributes the dread they inspire to their external appearance (the fetters, the convict clothes, the heads shaven in bizarre patterns, the branded faces), as well as to a vague presentiment of the seething mass of resentment pent up behind the prison walls. "Everyone who comes near the prison feels that all this mass of people has been brought together not of their own free will, and that, whatever measures are taken, a live man cannot be made into a corpse; he will remain with his feelings, his thirst for revenge and life, his passions and the craving to satisfy them." Nonetheless, Dostoevsky emphatically affirms "that there is no need to fear convicts. A man does not so quickly and so easily fly at another with a knife" (4: 44-45).

Many details of *House of the Dead* contribute to help us understand how the peasant-convicts managed to maintain their psychic equilibrium; and here again emphasis is placed on the prevalence of irrational components over other aspects of convict behavior. One of the most important forces making for stability in *katorga* was the work the convicts performed; but Dostoevsky sharply distinguishes between forced labor and work done by the convicts on their own. As we know, the convicts preferred to be given a "task" rather than simply to work the regulation number of hours; the assignment of a "task" would incite them to work much harder so as to gain a little extra free time and, in doing so, acquire some slight degree of control over their lives. In general, and for this very reason, everyone hated the *forced* labor and found it particularly burdensome, even though Dostoevsky was surprised to find it so relatively light. Many peasant-convicts had worked much harder in civilian life; and Dostoevsky admits to realizing "only long afterwards . . . that the hardness, the penal character of the work lay not in its being difficult and uninterrupted but in its being *compulsory*, obligatory, enforced" (4: 20).

The same contrast is highlighted even more strongly when Dostoevsky compares forced labor with the occupations of the convicts after-hours. Most of them were skilled craftsmen who earned a little money by exercising their trades and selling the products to the local population. Such work was not formally forbidden by the authorities; but the tools necessary to perform it *were* forbidden because they could be used as weapons. Yet all the convicts had such tools in their possession, and Dostoevsky surmised that "in some cases the authorities shut their eyes" to this infraction of the rules. For they understood intuitively that such work was an important safety valve for the prisoners, who needed some emotional relief from their suppressed resentment against forced labor. "If it were not for his own private work to which he was devoted with his whole mind, his whole interest," Dostoevsky writes, "a man could not live in prison" (4: 16-17).

Of course such labor brought in extra money; but more important were the psychic benefits of this "private work"—that is, a self-imposed task, freely performed and into which each individual could pour himself *as* an individual. "Without labor, *without lawful normal property* man cannot live; he becomes depraved and is transformed into a beast. . . . Work saved them from crime; without [private] work the convicts would have devoured one another like spiders in a glass jar" (4: 16-17; italics added). The social-political implications of this assertion are perfectly obvious, and constitute a flat rejection of the moral basis of Utopian Socialism (or any other kind), which views private property as the root of all evil. The prison camp convinced Dostoevsky that private work, which guarantees the individual a sense of self-possession and moral autonomy, was fundamental for maintaining the human psyche on an even keel; such private work offered a relatively "normal" means of instinctive self-preservation against the destructive forces of prison-camp life.

But just as the human personality could be driven to totally irrational crime and self-destruction, so too it had a totally irrational inner self-defense against reaching a state in which its only recourse was to such desperate extremes. And this self-defence, quite simply, is the human capacity to hope. Hope was an ever-present force in convict life, and Dostoevsky describes a great range of its varieties. Many convicts, like himself, had been sentenced to relatively short terms, and quite naturally all their thoughts were given to anticipating the great day of their release. "From the very first day of my life in prison," Dostoevsky says, "I began to dream of freedom." In the case of many other convicts, "the amazing audacity of their hopes impressed me from the beginning." It was as if prison life were not part of a convict's existence, and he was emotionally unable to accept it as such. "Every convict feels that he is, so to speak, *not at home*, but on a visit. He looks at twenty years as though they were two, and is fully convinced that when he leaves prison at fifty-five he will be as full of life and energy as he is now at thirty-five" (4: 79).

Even convicts condemned to life sentences continued to hope for a change of luck—a sudden order from Petersburg, say, that would send them to the mines and limit their terms, though there was not the slightest reason to believe that any such miraculous event would occur. Dostoevsky attributes the incessant restiveness of the convicts to this latent and obsessive sense of expectation, which served, all the same, to keep them from going berserk. "This everlasting uneasiness, which showed itself unmistakably, though not in words, *this strange impatient and intense hope*, which sometimes found involuntary utterance, at times so wild as to be almost like delirium, and what was most striking of all, often persisted in by men of apparently the greatest common sense—gave a special aspect and character to the place. . . . It made one feel, almost from the first moment, that there was nothing like this outside the prison walls" (italics added). For the Dostoevsky of the 1840s, the term "dreamer" had meant a highly educated member of the intelligentsia incapacitated for the moral-social tasks of real life by the illusory delights of the Romantic imagination; but now he uses it to characterize the convict state of mind as a whole. "Here all were dreamers, and this was apparent at once" (4: 196).

To illustrate the incredible power of the faculty of hope, Dostoevsky has recourse to one of his most hallucinatory evocations. He recalls having seen convicts chained to the wall in the Tobolsk prison, and who were kept like that, unable to move more than a distance of seven feet, for five and sometimes ten years. And yet all were well-behaved and quiet, and "everyone is intensely anxious for the end of his sentence. Why, one wonders? I will tell you why: he will get out of the stifling dark room with its low vaulted roof of brick, and will walk in the prison yard . . . and that is all. He will never be allowed out of the prison. He knows those who have been in chains are always kept in prison and fettered to the day of their death. He knows that and yet he is desperately eager for the end of his time on the chain. But for that longing how could he remain five or six years on the chain without dying or going out of his mind? Some of them would not endure it at all" (4: 79-80).

It is the capacity to hope, then, which keeps men alive and sane even under the most ghastly conditions. "When he has lost all hope, all object in life," Dostoevsky writes, in a piercing phrase, "man often becomes a monster in his misery." He mentions only two cases of prisoners whom he judged to be without "hope." One was the saintly Old Believer whom the convicts trusted with their money; but though, in Dostoevsky's estimation, he "had lost all hope" and "his inner misery was terrible . . . he

157

had his means of escape, his solution—prayer, and the idea of martyrdom" (4: 197). Another prisoner, very devout but not a member of any of the dissenting sects, "used to read the Bible" constantly, and finally decided to seek "a means of escape in a voluntary and almost artificial martyrdom": he threw himself at the hated Major Krivtsov with a brick in an unsuccessful effort to kill him. Dying in the hospital a few days later, unable to recover from his punishment, he declared that he had acted "without malice, simply to 'accept suffering' " (4: 197). This story, which Dostoevsky heard at second-hand, made a profound impression on him, and both "martyrs" later took on a symbolic value as evidence of how thoroughly the Russian people had absorbed the ideal of the crucified and humiliated Christ—the kenotic ideal so typical of Russian Christianity, which, as G. P. Fedotov has written, is founded on "the evaluation of suffering as a superior moral good, as almost an end in itself."[3]

The ideal of martyrdom could thus sustain even someone who had lost all hope, or lead to a calculated gesture of self-sacrifice; but the vast majority of the convicts, wrapped in their incessant dream of freedom, fortunately never reached such a state of total despair. All the same, Dostoevsky's imagination at this point could not resist taking the eschatological leap that was to become so characteristic for him—the leap to the end condition of whatever empirical situation he is considering—and so, in order to dramatize the supreme importance of hope for human life, he deliberately *invents* a situation in which it is systematically destroyed. Such a passage, the most haunting in the book, appears in the midst of his analysis of the differing reactions to free and to forced labor.

Bad as it is, even forced labor was still not utterly intolerable to the convicts because it made sense and could be seen to serve some useful purpose; it was part of a comprehensible world in which even their hope for freedom, their hope for the unforeseeable and the unpredictable, might still conceivably come to pass because chance and caprice were also a part of human life. But what if the convicts were knowingly and deliberately set to work at a task that was totally useless and hence totally inhuman? Dostoevsky answers this question in sentences that knife through to the quick of his religious convictions:

> The idea has occurred to me that if one wanted to crush, to annihilate a man utterly, to inflict on him the most terrible of punishments so that the most ferocious murderer would shudder at it and dread it beforehand, one need only give him work of an absolutely, completely useless and irrational character. Though the hard labor now enforced is uninteresting and wearisome for the prisoner, yet in itself as work it is rational; the convict makes bricks, digs, does plastering, building; there is sense and meaning in such work. The convict worker some-

times grows keen over it, tries to work more skillfully, faster, better. But if he had to pour water from one vessel into another and back, over and over again, to pound sand, to move a heap of earth from one place to another and back again—I believe the convict would hang himself in a few days or would commit a thousand crimes, preferring rather to die than to endure such humiliation, shame and torture. [4: 20]

One has only to transpose the terms of this passage slightly in order to see its crucial metaphysical implications. Not to believe in God and immortality, for the later Dostoevsky, is to be condemned to live in an ultimately senseless universe; and the characters in his great novels who reach this level of self-awareness inevitably destroy themselves because, refusing to endure the torment of living without hope, they have become monsters in their misery.*

6
———

House of the Dead is probably the least read, and certainly among the least *carefully* read, of Dostoevsky's longer works, and it is usually treated far too cursorily by his interpreters and commentators. The matrix of the later Dostoevsky is already contained in its deceptively objective and noncommittal pages, and their careful scrutiny, in my view, can make comprehensible much that has called forth the most extravagant and farfetched speculation. It is thus *House of the Dead* that provides the proper context within which to gloss one of the most disputed passages that Dostoevsky ever wrote.

Contained in his frank and moving letter to Mme Fonvizina shortly after being released, this passage offers a revealing glimpse into Dostoevsky's

---

* What Dostoevsky could only imagine as a nonexistent possibility in the nineteenth century has actually been put into practice in the twentieth. His intuition about the destructive effects of completely senseless labor has been confirmed in an eyewitness account of the reaction of a group of Hungarian Jewish prisoners in a German concentration camp when commanded to perform such labor as an "experiment in mental health" conceived by S.S. "medical experts." Eugene Heimler, who survived to become an English psychiatric social worker, has described the incident.

The prisoners, up to that time, had been working in a synthetic fuel factory, but this was bombed and completely destroyed in August 1944. The commandant of the camp then "ordered a few hundred of us to move sand from one end of the factory to another [could the "experts" have been reading Dostoevsky?], and when we had completed this task we were ordered to move it back to the original place. At first we thought that our guards must have made a mistake, but it soon became clear they had not. From then on, day after day, week after week, we had to carry sand to and fro, until gradually people's minds began to give way. Even those who had been working steadily in the factory before it was bombed were affected, for the work had some use and purpose, even if it was for the Germans, but in face of a completely meaningless task people started to lose their sanity. Some went berserk and tried to run away, only to be shot by the guards; others ran against the electrified wire fence and burnt themselves to death." The commandant remarked "jokingly" one day that "now there is no more need to use the crematoria." Eugene Heimler, *Mental Illness and Social Work* (Harmondsworth, 1967), 107-108.

wrestlings with the problem of faith. By this time, his erstwhile benefactress had returned to Russia and was living under surveillance in a village that Dostoevsky knew very well because it was located on the road leading from Moscow to the property of his family in the countryside. "I must have gone up and down that road at least 20 times, and I can clearly envisage the place of your refuge, or of your new imprisonment," he writes. The touch of bitterness in this last phrase becomes even more explicit as the letter proceeds. Dostoevsky has gathered, from the tone of his correspondent, that her return home has overwhelmed her with feelings far more of sadness than of joy. "I understand that," Dostoevsky assures her, "and I have sometimes thought that if I returned to my country one day my impressions would contain more of suffering than of gladness." He believes such a reaction to be inevitable, and explains why: "I think that on returning to his country each exile has to live over again, in his consciousness and memory, all of his past misfortune. It resembles a scale on which one weighs and gauges the true weight of everything one has suffered, endured, lost, and what the virtuous people have taken from us."

After thus linking the sadness of return with the exile's rankling animosity toward "the virtuous people," Dostoevsky offers Mme Fonvizina the consolation against such bitterness that he has found himself in his religious faith. What he is about to say, his words suggest, has helped to master the surges of his own moods of melancholy and anger. "I have heard many people say that you are a believer, N.D. . . . It's not because you are a believer, but because I myself have lived and felt that [her mood of dejection] that I will tell you that at such moments one thirsts for faith as 'the parched grass,' and one finds it at last because truth becomes evident in unhappiness. I will tell you that I am a child of the century, a child of disbelief and doubt, I am that today and (I know it) will remain so until the grave. How much terrible torture this thirst for faith has cost me and costs me even now, which is all the stronger in my soul the more arguments I can find against it. And yet, God sends me sometimes instants when I am completely calm; at those instants I love and I feel loved by others, and it is at these instants that I have shaped for myself a *Credo* where everything is clear and sacred for me. This *Credo* is very simple, here it is: to believe that nothing is more beautiful, profound, sympathetic, reasonable, manly, and more perfect than Christ; and I tell myself with a jealous love not only that there is nothing but that there cannot be anything. Even more, if someone proved to me that Christ is outside the truth, and that *in reality* the truth were outside of Christ, then I should prefer to remain with Christ rather than with the truth."[4]

The exegesis of this passage has caused a river of ink to flow, but far too often with a current that moves much too rapidly away from Dostoevsky and into the vast sea of theological and philosophical speculation about the great "eternal questions" that he broaches. Not that such questions are alien to him; but we should always remember that his answers, as first revealed in this crucial letter, originate in the two most momentous experiences of his prison years. One is the peasant Marey vision and its spiritually regenerating consequences, whose inspiration helped him to achieve those moments of inner tranquillity and loving identification with others during which he could formulate his *Credo*. The other, contained in his new grasp of the centrality and power of the irrational as a force in human life, resulted in his unambiguous choice of Christ over "the truth."

To be sure, what Dostoevsky says about the beauty and perfection of Christ could well have been written anytime earlier in his life. He had been deeply disturbed—indeed, on the point of tears—when, during a conversation in 1847, Belinsky had attacked and denigrated Christ with the new Left Hegelian arguments then just being introduced to the Russian Left; but for Dostoevsky, at that time, Christ had been the God-man whose message of brotherly love and spiritual equality he had looked on primarily as a doctrine of social transformation. The ideal and the message of Christ had now come to mean something far more intimate and personal, something far more deeply intertwined with the most anguishing needs of his own sensibility. Faith in Christ had supported him at the moment he had confronted death; it had proven to be a crucial link between himself and his fellow Russians, both inside and outside the prison camp; and it had rescued him from the ghastly prospect of living in a universe without hope. All of Dostoevsky's doubts as "a child of the century"—and he had been familiar with them long before meeting Belinsky—had simply been overpowered by his new comprehension of the psychic-emotive demands of the human spirit. Such doubts could no longer shake his faith because everything in the house of the dead had spoken against them, and had proclaimed the feebleness and paltriness of reason when confronted by the crisis situations of human existence.

It has often been questioned whether Dostoevsky's *Credo* should be taken at face value. Does not his acceptance of the possibility that the truth might be outside Christ betray an atheism he was not honest enough to acknowledge? Can a person with such an admittedly ineradicable skepticism truly be considered a believing Christian? Such a question, of course, can never be answered satisfactorily, and it would be impossibly presumptuous to set out here to assess the degree of sincerity of Dostoevsky's religious convictions. All the same, a few pertinent considerations may be ventured by way of conclusion.

The clash between reason and faith has been a constant of the Christian tradition ever since St. Paul (who knew very well that his faith was "foolishness to the Greeks"); and a line of Christian thinkers, running from Tertullian and St. Augustine to Luther, Pascal, and Kierkegaard, has dwelt on the opposition between reason and revelation. Dostoevsky is closest of all to the great Danish defender of the faith, who, confronting the full impact of the Left Hegelian critique of religion as the self-alienation of the human spirit, chose to *accept* this critique and to separate faith off entirely from human reason.

Like Dostoevsky, and even more rigorously, Kierkegaard decided to take his stand with the irrational of faith against reason and to push the opposition between the two to the point of paradox. Faith, he said, is "subjective certainty," which he defined as "objective uncertainty . . . grasped with the apprehension of the most passionate inwardness."[5] Some words in Kierkegaard's notebooks further help to illuminate the subjective, existential aspect of that "most passionate inwardness" on which Dostoevsky also fell back to compensate for the "objective uncertainty" of his own belief to Christ. "Whether I have faith," Kierkegaard wrote, "can never be ascertained by me with immediate certainty—for faith is precisely this dialectical hovering, which is unceasingly in fear and trembling but never in despair; faith is exactly this never-ending worry about oneself, which keeps one alert and ready to risk everything, this worry about oneself as to whether one truly has faith—and look! precisely this worry about oneself is faith."[6] No better description can be given of the ever-insecure, ever-unstable balancing point of Dostoevsky's own faith, which, as we see it spontaneously expressed in his *Credo*, will always remain perilously poised in "dialectical hovering" above the abyss of doubt.*

* In an interesting and persuasive article comparing Coleridge's *The Rime of the Ancient Mariner* and *Crime and Punishment*, Richard Gill makes some illuminating remarks on what he calls the "typical post-Renaissance strategy" of such an emphasis on the irrationality of faith. "From Pascal to Kierkegaard and his followers among twentieth-century religious existentialists, such a choice, or 'leap of faith,' has provided a *modus vivendi* for the sincere Christian assailed by modern varieties of scepticism. Yet this anti-intellectualist approach to faith, while it became a prevailing strategy, was not without its risks, as Kierkegaard himself recognized. To acknowledge the impossibility of intellectual certitude in matters of ultimate belief is to remain susceptible to the anguish of doubt and to admit the need for vigilance and rededication. This is all the more evident with respect to both Coleridge and Dostoevsky particularly because the mode of thought most natural to the ambivalent temper of each one was dialectical. Both display a remarkable openness and even fascination with opposition and contradiction; where their coreligionists might strive for the comfort of settled beliefs, both gave the rationalist adversary his due, to the point of admitting him within the gates." Gill then goes on to cite the passage from Dostoevsky's letter to Mme Fonvizina used above as evidence for "this dialectical tension between [his] religious needs and intellectual doubts . . ." See Richard Gill, *"The Rime of the Ancient Mariner* and *Crime and Punishment*: Existential Parables," *Philosophy and Literature*, 5 (Fall 1981), 145.

PART III

First Love

CHAPTER 12

A Thirst for Knowledge

Dostoevsky was released from the Omsk stockade on or about the fifteenth of February 1854, and became, in the most obvious and literal sense, a free man. But the freedom for which he had waited so long and impatiently was still quite minimal, and the immediate future presented only the dreary prospect of serving for an indefinite length of time in the Russian Army. As he remarked sadly in his letter to Mme Fonvizina: "In the overcoat of a soldier, I am just as much of a prisoner as before."[1] For reasons of health he was allowed to remain in Omsk for a month, and both he and Durov lived during this time at the home of the hospitable Konstantin Ivanov and his wife. In mid-March he made the journey to Semipalatinsk and joined the ranks of the regiment to which he had been assigned—the 7th Line Battalion of the Siberian Army Corps.

Dostoevsky's letters give us a graphic picture of his plight as a lowly soldier, and are sometimes painful to read because of the abjectness to which he is reduced by the difficulties of his position. Completely dependent on the good will and even charity of others, he was forced to humble his pride and continually plead for help. What made his situation even worse was the conviction that he had emerged from prison camp with new powers as a writer, and that, if only allowed to utilize his talents, all his problems could be solved at one stroke. It was, however, to be a long and arduous struggle, requiring the aid of friends reaching up to the immediate entourage of the Tsar himself, before Dostoevsky could return to the literary life and re-establish his claim to eminence in the teeth of skepticism and even outright hostility.

2

Dostoevsky's relation to his older brother, Mikhail, had always been very close, and he had confided in him as to no one else during his pre-Siberian years. They also shared common memories of the Petrashevsky circle; and in his first letter, sent by personal courier, Dostoevsky does not fail to pass along the information he had obtained through the Siberian grapevine about their mutual acquaintances. "All of our exiles are getting on well enough," he writes, detailing the news that has come his way. Of greatest interest are his observations about Petrashevsky and Nikolay Speshnev.

"Petrashevsky is as devoid of common sense as ever," he remarks bitingly, confirming the opinion he had long held of this erratic personality. What he says of Speshnev prefigures the hypnotic effect produced by the future Stavrogin on those with whom he came into contact. "Speshnev is in Irkutsk province, and he has conquered everyone's respect and affection. What a marvelous destiny that man has! Wherever and however he appears, the simplest, most ignorant and ordinary people immediately surround him with devotion and esteem."[2] Dostoevsky also asks Mikhail whether, in Petersburg, he had received any word about Aleksey Pleshcheev, the only one of the Petrashevtsy with whom Dostoevsky was later to renew more than casual relations.

Mikhail was the one member of his family on whom Dostoevsky believed he could count for help, and, while in prison, he had been deeply disturbed because not a line of any kind from Petersburg had arrived to maintain some contact between them. Dostoevsky was terribly afraid that this indicated some cooling in feeling which augured ill for his future. Suspecting, in his pessimistic moments, that Mikhail might leave him in the lurch when he most needed assistance, his letters are filled with expressions of misgiving; but these are immediately followed by elaborate self-reproaches for having been capable of harboring such unworthy forebodings. "Write and reply [to me] immediately . . . ," he enjoins his brother, "write in detail and at length. I am now like a branch lopped off from all of you—and I want to grow back again, but I am not able to. *Les absents ont toujours tort.* Is it possible that this must happen to us too? But don't get upset, I have faith in you."[3]

Dostoevsky's suspicions, as it turned out, were quite unjustified. Several weeks before his release, Mikhail had presented to the Third Section a letter containing fifty rubles for his brother; but this did not arrive until the first week in March. Dostoevsky had also been worried by advertisements he had seen in newspapers with Mikhail's name prominently displayed as a manufacturer of cigarettes. In 1852, the Dostoevsky family property had been sold to Dr. A. P. Ivanov—the husband of Vera, Dostoevsky's second sister—and the purchase price distributed among the children (excluding Feodor Mikhailovich, who had sold his share in 1845). With the money received from this sale, Mikhail had opened a small cigarette factory; and his unexpected transmutation from poet, short-story writer, and literary journalist to businessman caused Dostoevsky considerable apprehension. Would Mikhail be as ready and willing to aid him as he had hoped? Or would he insist, in return for financial succor, that his brother pursue the more "practical" course that Mikhail had chosen himself?

For all these reasons, we can well understand why Dostoevsky should have insisted that Mikhail, in his reply, "set out in the most precise fashion

everything important that has happened to you in the past four years."
But while imposing this task on his brother as an inescapable obligation,
Dostoevsky shrinks from submitting to the same sort of exposure himself.
"What is most important?" he asks musingly. "And what really, in these
last years, has been most important for me? When I think about it, I see
that I shall say nothing in this letter. How can I convey to you everything
in my head and in my mind, everything of which I have become convinced
and on which I take my stand. I won't attempt this. Such a task is absolutely
impossible. I don't like to do anything by half, and just to say something
halfway is totally meaningless."[4] One can only regret that Dostoevsky stuck
so stubbornly to his resolution and, being incapable of telling all, resigned
himself to telling nothing; but this decision strikes a note that sounds
repeatedly throughout his correspondence of these years.

It would be unduly cynical not to take at face value Dostoevsky's assertion of his emotional need to reintegrate himself as a member of the
family community once again. At least with Mikhail, however, he makes
no attempt to conceal that he has a very practical purpose in mind when
he asks for a full report on all his relatives and on the exact state of Mikhail's
finances. What he wishes to discover is whether or not he can count on
them for support in the battle he is determined to wage to regain his lost
literary reputation. For the major motif in Dostoevsky's letter, after the
past has been accounted for, is precisely his grim determination to fight
his way back into Russian literature. He knows this will involve a long
and difficult campaign, during which his ability to survive will depend on
the help he can muster from family and friends. "I need money," he tells
Mikhail bluntly. "*I have to live, brother. These years will not have passed
without bearing their fruits. . . .* What you spend for me—will not be lost.
If I manage to live, I will return it with interest . . . and now I will no
longer write trifles. You will hear of me being talked about."[5] Not only
does Dostoevsky passionately reaffirm his literary vocation, but he rightly
foresees that his prison-camp years have opened up before him a whole
new horizon of literary creation.

3

No time was wasted by Dostoevsky in embarking on a two-pronged campaign to restore himself as both a Russian citizen and a literary notable.
He urgently asks Mikhail to approach the authorities in St. Petersburg
and persuade them, if possible, to transfer him from Siberia to a corps on
active service. The Russian Army in the Caucasus was then engaged in
battle against Turkey, and Dostoevsky probably believed that his chances
of obtaining a full pardon in the future might be enhanced if he were to
exhibit his loyalty by serving in a combat zone.

A further request to Mikhail, made in even more pressing terms, was for the dispatch of books. It had been difficult for Dostoevsky to obtain books, and dangerous to read them, under the tyrannical and capricious reign of Major Krivtsov. Even later, after the major had been toppled, Dostoevsky's entire relation to literature had been too painful and problematic to allow him to pick up a book lightly. Whenever he did so, he was inevitably tormented by the question of whether he himself would ever be able to resume his place in Russian literature. The first book he looked at after a long interval, he writes in *House of the Dead*, "made a great, strange and peculiar impression upon me . . . and I am sure that to many people [these impressions] would be utterly unintelligible" (4: 54-55).

Dostoevsky promised "to speak of these impressions more particularly" later in his text; and in the last few pages, just before describing his release, he recalls "the strange and agitating impression of the first book I read in prison"—which turns out to have been, not literally a book, but one of the Russian "thick" periodicals containing literary works, criticism, and social commentary. "It was as though news had come to me from another world," he explains; "My former life rose up before me full of light and color, and I tried from what I had read to conjecture how far I had dropped behind. Had a great deal happened while I had been away? What emotions were agitating people now? What questions were occupying their minds? I pored over every word, tried to read between the lines and to find secret meanings and allusions to the past; I looked for traces of what had agitated us in my time. And how sad it was for me to realize how remote I was from this new life, how cut off I was from it all. I should have to get used to everything afresh, to make acquaintance with a new generation again" (4: 229).

Such a reaction helps to explain why Dostoevsky took so little interest in the popular light reading offered by the *moryachki* and why, in writing to Mikhail, he so evidently and frantically wished to make up for lost time. Indeed, he begs Mikhail to send him what would constitute, in effect, the contents of a small research library. "I still have some money," he says, "but no books at all." As one might expect, Dostoevsky asks for the dispatch of "the magazines of this year, at least *Notes of the Fatherland*"; yet, while obviously concerned to come abreast of the latest trends in Russian literature, he seems even more anxious to plunge back into the past in a very serious and systematic fashion. "But here is what is indispensable: I need (badly need) ancient historians (in French translation) and the moderns—that is, Vico, Guizot, Thierry, Thiers, Ranke, etc., the economists, and the Church Fathers. Select the cheapest and handiest editions. Send them right away. . . . Understand only that the very first book I have need of is a German dictionary."[6]

A few paragraphs later, Dostoevsky again stresses his need for books and adds a few more to his list. "Send me the Carus,* Kant's *Critique of Pure Reason*, and if you are able to send things clandestinely, slip Hegel in without fail, *especially Hegel's History of Philosophy*. My entire future is tied up with that."[7] Dostoevsky repeats several times that Mikhail should inquire whether it was permitted to send him books; but, even if not allowed, they should be shipped to an assumed name (Mikhail Petrovich), or through the brother of Konstantin Ivanov and addressed to the latter. From Dostoevsky's instructions to Mikhail, whom he warns to burn his letter, it is clear that he is terrified of getting into trouble; but so great is his desire for books that he is willing to run the risk of violating regulations in order to obtain them. Whether he actually received all he requested is impossible to ascertain. More than a year later, no books had yet arrived from Mikhail, although the latter had turned over a consignment to a mutual friend, E. I. Yakushkin, for shipment. Some may have reached their destination in the late spring of 1855, when Dostoevsky thanks Mikhail for the receipt of a package. But Dostoevsky could hardly have obtained everything he asked for: at that time he was sharing a cottage with Baron Wrangel, who refers to "the pitiful stock of our books," and pictures Dostoevsky rereading each of them a countless number of times.[8]

Dostoevsky's letter also reveals that he had already managed to spot some of the rising new stars on the literary horizon. "How do you stand with relation to literature and in literature?" he asks Mikhail anxiously. "Are you writing anything? What's new at Kraevsky's, and what are your relations? I don't like Ostrovsky; as regards Pisemsky, I haven't read him, and Druzhinin makes me sick. I'm enthusiastic about Evgeniya Tur. I like Krestovsky."[9]

A. N. Ostrovsky, soon to become the most famous Russian playwright of the mid-nineteenth century, had just started to make an impact with his depictions of Moscow merchant life, and Dostoevsky's opinion of him would shortly become much more favorable. Aleksey Pisemsky, whose name Dostoevsky had no doubt seen in critical articles, created a stir between 1851 and 1854 by a whole series of novels and short stories. Druzhinin was already well-known for his *Polinka Saks* (1847), a novel following in the footsteps of George Sand and dealing tolerantly with a wife's infidelity; but Dostoevsky is probably referring to Druzhinin's literary *feuilletons*, which enjoyed a passing vogue in the literary doldrums

---

* The translation given here of this letter does not conform to the wording of the Russian edition of Dostoevsky's correspondence. There, the word marked by an asterisk is printed as "Coran" and has usually been taken to designate the sacred book of the Muslim religion. A recent article by Professor Jean Drouilly, who asked S. V. Belov, a well-known Soviet Russian specialist of Dostoevsky, to check the text, reveals that the word is not "Coran" but "Carus" and that the original transcription was in error. See F. M. Dostoevsky, *Pisma*, ed. A. S. Dolinin, 4 vols. (Moscow, 1928-1959), 1: 131 (February 22, 1854); Jean Drouilly, "Une erreur dans l'edition russe de A. S. Dolinin des lettres de F. M. Dostoevsky," *Études Slaves et Est Européennes* 19 (1974), 118-120.

of the 1850s.* Tur and Krestovsky were both women writers, and Dostoevsky's liking for Tur was only partly shared by Turgenev, who devoted
an important article to her in *The Contemporary* (1850). Dostoevsky is
also concerned about his own work and inquires whether Mikhail has
received the manuscript of *A Little Hero* from the authorities. "If you have
it, don't do anything with it, and don't show it to anyone," he advises. Also,
"who is the Chernov who wrote a *Double* in 1850?" he asks possessively,
clearly keeping an eye on his literary property.[10]

4

Dostoevsky had wide-ranging intellectual interests and was much better
read than has generally been thought; but the prevailingly erudite nature
of the reading matter he asked for is still rather surprising. Why not, for
example, more novelists and poets? The answer, very probably, is that he
was mulling over several projects that he hoped would speed his rehabilitation. One was an "article on Russia," which he mentions in a letter two
years later (1856), although by this time the idea has been abandoned. It
would have been, he tells Wrangel, "a real political pamphlet," but he has
given it up because "I doubt whether, despite the most patriotic ideas, I
will be permitted to begin by publishing a pamphlet."[11] The historians and
economists he requested would have provided background for such a
project, and he wanted to obtain them at the earliest possible moment.

The same letter refers to another project on which he was then engaged
and which, he claims, is "the result of ten years of reflection. I had already
entirely conceived it in Omsk, down to the very last words. . . . Certain
chapters will include entire pages of the pamphlet. It is concerned, in sum,
with the mission of Christianity in art." Dostoevsky intended to call this
work *Letters on Art* and to dedicate it to Her Highness Maria Nikolaevna,
the daughter of Nicholas I, who was then President of the Academy of
Fine Arts. "I wish to demand the authorization to dedicate my article to
her," he explains, "and to publish it without signature."[12] (The permission
to publish, even if anonymously, would set a valuable precedent and make
it easier to break down future bureaucratic barriers.) If Dostoevsky had
thought about such an article in the prison camp, he would have wished
to obtain material for it immediately on his release; and the works of the
Church Fathers would have supplied him with information on both theology and the attitude of the early Church toward art. So far as Kant and
Hegel are concerned, they indicate Dostoevsky's desire to deepen the foun-

---

* Dostoevsky's dislike of Druzhinin's *feuilletons* was expressed more publicly, though less
directly, a few years later in *The Village of Stepanchikovo*. The odious Foma Fomich, whose
literary taste is a grotesque medley of pretentiousness and ignorance, considers them the very
acme of wit and sprightliness (Druzhinin's name is not mentioned, but the reference is
unmistakable). See *PSS*, 3: 70, 512.

dations of his own thinking, and also involved another plan to break into print again by translating.

That Dostoevsky was thinking of translating is indicated by his request for a German dictionary "as the very first book I have need of," and probably also by his demand, the following month, for "any work on physiology" as well as for a textbook on physics. For if he wished to be sent such scientific texts, it was because he intended to set to work on "Carus"—the famous German physician, physiologist, painter, and man of letters, Carl Gustav Carus. Dostoevsky had asked Mikhail to send him "Carus," meaning by this Carus's once-famous treatise on psychology, sometimes considered a precursor of psychoanalysis, *Psyche, zur Entwicklungsgeschichte der Seele* (1846).* In a letter written ten months later (November 1854), shortly after meeting Dostoevsky, the young Wrangel tells his father that he and his new-found friend intend "to translate Hegel's *Philosophy* [?] and the *Psyche* of Carus."[13] The offhand way in which Dostoevsky makes his request, referring only to the name of the author, assumes that Mikhail will know the particular work he desires. Where and how Dostoevsky came across the book remains unknown; but he had been in the habit of borrowing medical works, especially those concerned with mental illness, from the library of his own physician and friend, Dr. Yanovsky. And since Carus, who had published a three-volume *System der Physiologie*, utilizes the results of such research in his less specialized *Psyche*, Dostoevsky might well have wanted easy access to Russian equivalents for the technical vocabulary of scientific German.

Dostoevsky had thus clearly thought of translation as an unobtrusive means of returning to literature, and perhaps also as a welcome supplement to his meager income as a lowly private second class. Raskolnikov scorns such a paltry prospect in *Crime and Punishment*, but his more practical friend Razumikhin manages to keep body and soul together with humble literary drudgery of this kind, even though, as he admits, "my German is sometimes very weak, so that I am reduced to making up most of it myself, comforting myself with the idea that it is probably an improvement" (6: 88-89). The state of Dostoevsky's German could hardly have been very much better, although he had been perfectly capable, as a young man, of judging the accuracy of his brother's translations of Schiller.[14] But Baron Wrangel, who subscribed to newspapers in French and German, tells us that, while Dostoevsky eagerly read one that came from Brussels, he scarcely cast a glance at the *Augsburger Allgemeine*

* See Lancelot Law Whyte, *The Unconscious Before Freud* (New York, 1960), 149. Whyte speaks of *Psyche* as a "landmark" in the study of the unconscious, and notes that Freud had several works of Carus in his library (it is not clear if these included *Psyche*). "While the conflicts which were Freud's main concern were relatively neglected by Carus . . . [he] had a vivid sense of the importance of the sexual functions, unconscious as instinct and conscious as voluptuousness, in relation to the mind as a whole."

Zeitung because "he did not know German, and did not like the language."[15] No doubt this is why Dostoevsky instantly enlisted the aid of his friend, who came from a family of Baltic barons and for whom German would have been as much of a native tongue as Russian.

5

It seems likely, in view of Wrangel's reference to it a year later, that Dostoevsky had received a copy of *Psyche*, although it is impossible to be certain. But even if it did not reach him, he was unquestionably familiar with—and greatly taken by—its contents; and this tells us something about the cast of his own ideas. For what Dostoevsky would have admired in Carus, whose scientific and medical credentials were impeccable—he was professor at the Dresden Medical Clinic and court physician to the ruling house of Saxony—was a mind totally abreast of the very latest theories of biology and physiology, but who continued to interpret them in the old-fashioned terms of Schelling's *Naturphilosophie*. Dostoevsky had come into contact with Schelling's ideas while still a schoolboy; and this Idealist view of the universe, which refused to look on the world simply as a soulless mechanism ruled exclusively by physical laws, left a deep and lasting impression on his youthful mind. He would thus have been immediately sympathetic to Carus, who saw both nature and human life as originating in a Divine Idea and considered the individual soul to be immortal because it shared in the eternity of this Divine creative principle.*

Back in the mid-1840s, when Dostoevsky had been disputing with Belinsky about free will, moral responsibility, and Christ, the ardent Westerner Belinsky had adduced Littré's physiology as an argument in favor of atheism and the acceptance of materialism and determinism. To support his opposing point of view, Dostoevsky would have eagerly seized on Carus's book as proof that one could be up-to-date, "scientific," and a prominent physiologist to boot without abandoning a belief in some sort of supernatural principle or in the precepts of Christian morality. For Dostoevsky could find in Carus a glowing tribute to the fundamental tenet of this morality—the law of love—supported by a quotation from the New

---

* Carus has more or less fallen into oblivion in modern times, but nonetheless continues to have a few admirers. Ludwig Klages re-edited *Psyche* in 1926, and Albert Béguin devoted an enthusiastic chapter to him in his magisterial study of German Romanticism, *L'Âme romantique et le rêve* (Paris, 1939), bk. III, chap. 8.

Elsewhere, Béguin has written that the works of Carus "contain a psychology of the unconscious which, in many respects, anticipates and in others surpasses the results of modern science. He owes to Goethe and Schelling an organic and 'vitalist' conception of the universe, to the philosophers of nature (Schubert, Oken, Steffens . . . etc., who are all inspired more or less by Novalis and go back through him to Böhme and Paracelsus) the idea of the Fall and of the future Age of Gold. But he strips these modish theses of their astrological and magical language." This latter trait is probably what endeared him to Dostoevsky. See Albert Béguin, *Création et destinée*, ed. Pierre Grotzer, 2 vols. (Paris, 1973-1974), 1: 55-56.

Testament. It is the law of love, running through all of nature and beginning with sexual differentiation, that for Carus first stirs in mankind the impulse to devotion and self-sacrifice, and hence to the ultimate conquest of egoism. Moreover, the action of this law on lower levels paves the way "for the unconditional surrender to the godly that hovers above all consciousness, in a word, to *the love of God.*" Carus depicts this law of love in nature with accents that anticipate, by forty years, those of Father Zosima in *The Brothers Karamazov*. Man is morally educated and developed, as Carus sees him, not only by the effects of sexual love but also by "a love for everything in creation, the earth on which we grow and which nourishes us, the stars that light our way, the air that we breathe, the plants and the trees, the animals . . . ," etc.[16]

Dostoevsky, as we know, had been led by his prison experiences to a greatly deepened awareness of the power of the irrational in human existence; and this would only have confirmed what he had previously learned from Carus. For Carus announces, in his very first sentence, that the main theme of his book is precisely to emphasize this power of the irrational and the unconscious: "The key to the understanding of the essence of the conscious life of the soul lies in the region of the unconscious."[17] By "unconscious," though, Carus refers not only to psychic life but to all of nature, which he also considers to be endowed with soul-life and to differ from the psyche only in degrees of consciousness and self-consciousness. And while the higher forms of consciousness are indispensable for the full development of the personality and the human spirit, Carus constantly emphasizes that they must be kept in equilibrium with the unconscious forces of existence if they are not to become unbalanced. One can see in this proto-Jungian schema some analogy to, and certainly an encouragement for, Dostoevsky's ideology of *pochvennichestvo*, elaborated only a few years later and calling for the fusion of an intelligentsia inspired by Western ideas of rationalism and enlightenment with the unconscious moral forces slumbering in the still-uncorrupted bosom of the Russian people.

In this connection, Carus makes continual reference to the danger of a hypertrophy of the intellect on the higher levels of consciousness; and he considers the act of suicide, in certain cases, to be an expression of the very fullest and highest development of the freedom of self-consciousness (though hastening to add that such an act can almost never be justified in individual cases). Nonetheless, a fully self-conscious suicide, even in the very act of destroying its own life—destroying, that is, the unconscious basis of its own existence—affirms the freedom of self-consciousness. Using a quotation from Shakespeare's *Julius Caesar* to drive home the point, Carus acknowledges that such an act attains a certain sublimity.[18] Many of the suicides or thoughts about suicide in Dostoevsky's novels are motivated by a similar conception, and personal self-destruction is shown as the effect of a pathological overdevelopment of self-consciousness.

Another thematic link with Dostoevsky's creations can be found in Carus's comparison of moral evil to a state of physical illness; both are deviations from the normal condition of the unconscious forces that regulate the health of an organism. But, just as nature has means of restoring its own equilibrium in the case of physical illness, so the moral consciousness has its own "unconscious" means—the human "conscience"—which works to restore the moral health of the personality.[19] This image of conscience as a natural and instinctive regulator of the human psyche, whose distortion or perversion leads to a literal "sickness" of the self, was to become one of the major themes of the great works of Dostoevsky that lie ahead.

Carus, it might be mentioned, also believed that visions and premonitions probably had some objective meaning because all of nature was one vast organism, and the relations between its parts on various unconscious levels was far from having been completely explored. Dostoevsky would thus have found confirmation in Carus for his own belief in signs and portents, which Wrangel remarks on with some humor. "He suddenly became superstitious," his friend writes of one difficult moment in Dostoevsky's courtship of his first wife, "began to tell me about clairvoyants, and since, twenty-two years old as I was, I had my own romance at that time, he dragged me to some old woman telling fortunes with beans."[20] Carus also affirmed the reality of various mysteriously "magnetic" connections between individuals; but while such connections are often hinted at by Dostoevsky, he carefully refrains from giving them any more than atmospheric importance.

Many other points of contact can be (and have been) noted between Dostoevsky's works and Carus's ideas, but they are not concrete enough to be more than suggestive.[21] More than any specific "influence," however, Dostoevsky's interest in Carus and in the ideas of *Psyche* reveals a permanent bent of his own mind. For he will always continue to exhibit an eager curiosity about learned works that, while displaying a full awareness and mastery of the latest positions of modern science and philosophy, continue to take up the task of defending idealism and a religious worldview.

CHAPTER 13

Private Dostoevsky

Whatever plans Dostoevsky may have had for intellectual and literary activity quickly had to be abandoned in face of the grim necessities of his existence. His lengthy letter to Mikhail was written during his brief period of recuperation in Omsk; and his leisure ended when he left the hospitable home of the Ivanovs, whose tact, kindness, and generosity he praises to his brother with heartfelt words. "I would have died for good if I had not found people here," he confesses. "K. I. I[vanov] has been a veritable brother to me. He did everything for me that he could. . . . I owe him 25 silver rubles. But how can one repay that welcome of the heart, that constant readiness to comply with every wish, the brotherly care and concern. And he was not alone. Brother, there are many noble people in the world."[1]

The three-day journey to Semipalatinsk, where he was to begin his military service, also left an unforgettable memory. Just a year before Dostoevsky's death, a friend jotted down his account of "how happy he had been when, after leaving *katorga*, he went off to be settled. He walked on foot with the others, but they met a wagon train transporting rope and for several hundred versts he rode on those ropes. He said that he had never been so happy in his entire life, and had never felt so well as when he was sitting on those rough and uncomfortable ropes, with the sky above him, vast spaces and pure air around him, and with freedom in his soul."[2] Those three days of unalloyed bliss were the last that Dostoevsky was to experience for a very long time.

2

Semipalatinsk turned out to be, as Baron Wrangel describes it, "a half-city, half-village,"[3] sprawling amidst the ruins of an ancient Mongol town located on the steep right slope of the Irtish River. Most of the houses were one-story constructions of wood; only the single Orthodox Church, forced to compete with seven mosques, was built of stone; and a huge covered marketplace sheltered the caravans of camels and packhorses that conducted the flourishing trade between Russia and Central Asia. On the opposite bank of the river could be seen the large felt tent dwellings of the half-nomad Khirghizes, who, if they had houses at all, used them only for winter quarters.

6. Streets of Semipalatinsk. Drawings by George A. Frost, who accompanied
George Kennan on his trip through Siberia

The American newspaper correspondent George Kennan, who visited Semipalatinsk in 1885, found that "from almost any interior point of view it [the town] presents a peculiar gray, dreary appearance, owing partly to the complete absence of trees and grass, partly to the ashy, weatherbeaten aspect of its unpainted log-houses, and partly to the loose, drifting sand with which its streets are filled." Russian officers with whom Kennan talked still called the place "The Devil's Sand-box," exactly as they had done in Wrangel's hearing thirty years before. The mosques and the camels, side by side with the white-turbaned and white-bearded mullahs, made Kennan think "of a Mohammedan town built in the middle of a North African desert."[4] Semipalatinsk was also still part of a border region on the edge of the steppe, and incursions by raiding parties of Mongols and hostile Khirghizes into the area were no means uncommon, although a garrison town would not have been directly threatened.

During his first months, Dostoevsky again had to face the problem of adjusting to life in common with a group of men drawn largely from the Russian peasantry. Army barracks were much like the prison camp, with plank beds for sleeping and food impossible to stomach; nor was he yet able to obtain what he had told Mme Fonvizina he desired above everything else in the world—"books, the possibility of writing, and *to be alone for several hours every day*" (italics added).[5] Still, Dostoevsky was left in peace by his fellow soldiers and even treated kindly by them. Unluckily, he was relentlessly persecuted by the sergeant of his company, who had been told by one of the officers not to show any leniency toward the ex-convict. Despite the physical toughening of his years at hard labor, Dostoevsky also found that the process of adapting to Army life was wearisome and extremely exhausting. But he took a certain pride in fulfilling the obligations of his military service, and he accepted what he had to endure with stoic resignation, as a justified consequence of his own mistakes. "I am not complaining; this is my cross and I have deserved it," he penitently writes to Mikhail.[6]

Dostoevsky's neighbor on the plank bed was a seventeen-year-old Jewish cantonist, N. F. Katz (a cantonist was the son of a soldier in one of the Russian military colonies), who of course had no idea that the gloomy and painstaking fellow soldier he came to know was a person of any consequence. But Katz, the butt of continual abuse by the others in the barracks, was very grateful for the gentleness and kindness shown by Dostoevsky, who always behaved toward him without the slightest trace of superiority or condescension.

"I see Feodor Mikhailovich before me as if it were now," he told an inquirer many years later; "he was of average height, with a flat chest; his shaven, sunken cheeks made him look sickly and older than he was. He had gray eyes, and a serious, morose expression. None of us soldiers in the barracks ever saw a real smile on his face. It sometimes happened that a regimental joker, for the amusement of his comrades, played some humorous trick, and all of us absolutely split our sides with laughter; but Feodor Mikhailovich would only curl the corner of his mouth, and so faintly that it was scarcely noticeable. His voice was soft, low, pleasant; and he spoke distinctly, without hurrying. He never said a word to anyone in the barracks about his past. In general he talked very little. The only book he had was the New Testament, which he looked after carefully and, clearly, valued very highly. In the barracks he never wrote anything; and of course a soldier then had very little free time. Dostoevsky rarely left the barracks, and mostly sat by himself sunk in thought."[7]

What Dostoevsky was brooding over, while plunged in such dispirited reflections, appears very clearly in his letters. Writing to his younger brother, Andrey, about the horrors of the prison camp, he remarks sadly that "my release from prison appeared to me formerly as a bright awakening, the resurrection to a new life . . . but in my new life I have encountered so many new difficulties that, really, I can hardly turn around."[8] One such "difficulty," which we learn about only through Katz's recollections, must have filled Dostoevsky with unbearable revulsion. He was forced, like the other soldiers, to take his place in the ranks while those condemned to punishment ran the gauntlet of the regiment and were beaten with "sticks." Nor was it possible to evade taking part in this cruel ceremony; an officer walked up and down the line to guarantee that each soldier did his duty, and those who did not swing vigorously and accurately were punished themselves in the same fashion. No wonder Dostoevsky was to speak out so strongly against corporal punishment just a few years later in *House of the Dead*, and to declare that "a society which looks indifferently on such a phenomenon is already contaminated to its very foundations" (4: 154).

3

Once again the providential intervention of the indefatigably charitable Ivanovs came to Dostoevsky's rescue. Through the good offices of some of their cultivated friends in the higher Army echelons at Semipalatinsk, he was given permission to live by himself in town. At last he would be able to snatch every day a few hours of that solitude he had so desperately craved in the prison camp! He found modest lodgings situated near the barracks, in a spot more bare and desolate than ordinary even for grim Semipalatinsk. His one-room cottage, owned by an elderly widow, was fairly large, but dark and with a low ceiling; the furnishings were of the simplest; and hordes of cockroaches, according to the fastidious Wrangel, roamed freely over the table, bed, and walls.

Dostoevsky's housekeeping needs were taken care of by the elder daughter of the family, twenty-two years old and the widow of a soldier, who clearly found him attractive, looked after him lovingly, and seemed to be constantly in his quarters. Wrangel recalls taking tea with Dostoevsky in the summer out-of-doors one day and being casually joined, as he puts it discreetly, by the housekeeper *en grand négligé* (just a smock tied at the waist with a red sash, and nothing else). One cannot help wondering whether, after four years in the prison camp, Dostoevsky could really have resisted taking advantage of such readily available female charms. Nothing would have been simpler or more natural, and we know that he exhibited a keen personal interest in the affairs of the family. For he tried, unsuccessfully, to persuade the mother not to allow the very attractive younger daughter, sixteen years old, to supplement the family income by occasional prostitution with the Army garrison.

Gradually, the presence of an ex-convict named Dostoevsky, who had formerly enjoyed some literary notoriety, began to be known among the more literate members of the Russian community in Semipalatinsk. Educated men were at a premium in that part of the world, and exiles of all kinds (mostly Poles) were employed as tutors to supplement or even replace the scanty public education available to Russian children. Like his fictitious narrator Goryanchikov in *House of the Dead*, Dostoevsky was soon approached to tutor the offspring of various families; and in this fashion he began to strike up closer relations with various households.

The wife of the commander of Dostoevsky's company, Mme Stepanova, looked on him kindly, and so did her husband, a confirmed drunkard whose weakness for the bottle had resulted in his banishment to the Siberian wilderness. Stepanov was a poet as well as a soldier (the combination was not infrequent in Russia) and was very happy to make the acquaintance of another literary man. Literature proved a great leveler of class barriers, and Stepanov did not hesitate to ask Dostoevsky to correct his verses. Dostoevsky also became acquainted with the commander of his battalion, the good-natured and knock-about Lieutenant-Colonel Belikhov, who had worked his way up from the ranks and was thus not at all a stickler for the social forms.

This worthy officer, who liked to keep abreast of what was going on in the world, found reading a very tedious chore; and so he invited Dostoevsky to come and read to him from newspapers and magazines. The arrangement proved so satisfactory that the humble private, wrapped in his ill-fitting Army greatcoat, was often asked to stay for dinner. Belikhov was a simple soul whose tastes ran to cards and the fair sex, and whose choice rarely strayed beyond the wives and daughters of his soldiers; so affable was he that his subordinates did not begrudge him this occasional amusement. Unhappily, like the father of Katerina Ivanovna in *The Brothers*

Karamazov, he was one day to stretch his resources a little too far, embezzle Army funds at his disposal, and honorably shoot himself rather than face disgrace. It was at the home of Belikhov, one evening, that Dostoevsky first met Alexander Ivanovich Isaev and his wife, Marya Dimitrievna.

4
—

Isaev was another of those incorrigible and appealing Russian drunkards whom Dostoevsky had already portrayed in such a figure as old Pokrovsky (*Poor Folk*), and whom he was to immortalize, probably utilizing some of his memories of Isaev, in the elder Marmeladov, Sonya's father in *Crime and Punishment*. By the time Dostoevsky came across him, Isaev had gone to pieces quite badly. Once a schoolmaster, he had come to Semipalatinsk as a customs official, but for some obscure reason—perhaps drink, perhaps the exacerbated pride of a drunkard—he had resigned his post. The Isaev family, which included a seven-year-old son, Pasha, was thus living in hand-to-mouth fashion while the breadwinner nominally sought other employment. Meanwhile, what little money he and his wife could scrape together was squandered by Isaev in drinking bouts with his cronies among the riffraff of the town.

Many of the local families had closed their doors to the Isaevs, not so much because of Alexander Ivanovich's tippling (hard drinking was a venial sin in the Russian social catechism), but because of the disreputable company that he frequented. Dostoevsky, Wrangel tells us, was infinitely charitable with regard to all sorts of human foibles and fallibilities; and what he says about Isaev's character after the latter's death confirms Wrangel's words. Writing to Mikhail, Dostoevsky remarks that Isaev had "suffered from much undeserved persecution at the hands of local society. He was as careless as a gipsy, self-centered, proud, but he could not discipline himself and, as I have said, had sunk very low. And yet he was highly cultivated and the kindliest of persons. . . . He was, despite all the dirt, exceptionally noble."[9] It was not, however, the husband who soon drew Dostoevsky to spend all his time at the Isaevs but the wife, destined to become the first great love of his life.

Marya Dimitrievna's family name was Constant and indicated her French ancestry; her father had once been director of the high school in Astrakhan and was at that time head of the quarantine for travelers arriving in that port city on the Caspian Sea. All of his daughters had been carefully educated in a private *pension*, and Mme Isaeva's intellectual and spiritual capacities were unmistakably a cut above those of the average Semipalatinsk Army or bureaucratic spouse. "Marya Dimitrievna was about thirty years old," writes Wrangel; "a quite pretty blonde of medium height, very slim, with a passionate nature given to exalted feeling. Even then an ill-omened flush played on her pale face, and several years later tuberculosis took her to the grave. She was well-read, quite cultivated, eager for knowledge, kind, and unusually vivacious and impressionable. She took a great interest in Dostoevsky and treated him kindly, not, I think, because she valued him deeply, but rather felt sorry for an unhappy human being beaten down by fate. It is possible that she was even attached to him, but there was no question of being in love."[10]

Wrangel believes that she knew Dostoevsky had "epilepsy" from the very beginning of their relation; but this is highly doubtful. Certainly, like everyone else in town, she was aware that he had an "illness," but he himself was as yet uncertain about its diagnosis. "I have already spoken to you of my illness," he writes Mikhail. "Bizarre attacks, resembling epilepsy and yet not being epilepsy."[11] More reliable is the information that she saw him as being "direly in need of resources, and that she said he was a man 'without a future.' Feodor Mikhailovich took the feeling of pity and sympathy as mutual love, and fell head over heels in love with all the fire of youth."[12]

5

Dostoevsky's amorous passions, seriously inflamed for the first time in his life, provided an additional incentive for him to use whatever means he could to resume his literary career. The first groping step in this direction was taken through the only contact he had been able to make. In May 1854, Lieutenant-Colonel Belikhov, commander of the 7th Siberian battalion of the line, presented to Lieutenant-General Yakovlev, chief of staff, a poem by the ex-convict, Private Second Class Dostoevsky, entitled "On European Events in 1854." Belikhov respectfully requested that his superior obtain permission for this patriotic effusion to be published in the *St. Petersburg Gazette*; and Lieutenant-General Yakovlev, taken off guard by such an unorthodox poetic offensive, dispatched the poem to the all-powerful Third Section for a final decision.

So far as the record shows, Dostoevsky had never written any poetry before, and would never do so later (except for the very funny parodies included in his novels). The poems he wrote were thus a means of attracting attention, or of trying to do so, and should not be taken too seriously as contributions to the Russian Muse. The first of his poems is clearly influenced by Pushkin's famous "To the Calumniators of Russia," written by the great poet in response to the French manifestations of sympathy for Poland during the uprisings of 1830. The "events in Europe" to which Dostoevsky refers were the alliance of England and France with Turkey in the Crimean War—an alliance cemented just two months before Dostoevsky dispatched his poem through official channels. Even when he had been glorifying the achievements of Peter the Great in the 1840s, Dostoevsky had not been able to suppress a certain anti-European animus from creeping into his words; and the Crimean War crystallized once and for all his latent anti-Western xenophobia. The result is evident in the poem, which expresses for the first time many of the sentiments that Dostoevsky would later continue to propound in his journalism.

Written in the old-fashioned form of the celebratory or triumphal ode, the verses are filled with many of the clichés of the war propaganda of the time. They celebrate, with appropriate solemnity, the grandeur and might of Russia, revive the memories of its glorious past (particularly the triumph over the massed might of Europe in 1812), and predict the inevitable victory of Russian arms. All the same, Dostoevsky manages to inject into these well-worn motifs a note unmistakably his own—an emphasis on Russia's ability to endure catastrophe and suffering and to emerge from such suffering strengthened and fortified. "But know this, that in the final torment / We shall be able to find the strength to endure our suffering!" (2: 403). Premonitory of the later Dostoevsky as well is the affirmation of Russia's providential mission in world history, as yet here confined only to the East but soon to be extended to Europe as well:

> Unclear to you is her [Russia's] predestination!
> The East—is hers! To her a million generations
> Untiringly stretch out their hands,
>
> . . . .
>
> And the resurrection of the ancient East
> By Russia (so God has commanded!) is drawing near.
>
> [2: 405]

Another frequent motif in the official patriotic poetry was the scandal of nominally Christian nations such as France and England joining with the Mohammedan infidel to fight against fellow Christians. Dostoevsky gives this theme a particularly vivid twist by depicting it as a new crucifixion of Christ. Jesus is now no longer, as he had been in the Utopian Socialist poetry of the 1840s, a symbol of oppressed and downtrodden humanity persecuted by the wealthy and the powerful of the world. Instead, he is a specifically Russian and Orthodox Christ, crucified by the so-called Christian nations of Europe that have joined with the Turks to keep the Orthodox Slavs of the Turkish Empire in submission:

> Just look—He is crucified right now,
> And His sacred blood flows again!
> But where is the Jew, crucifying Christ now,
> Selling once again His Eternal Love?
>
> . . . .

Christians with the Turks against Christ!
Christians—the defenders of Mohammed!
Shame on you, apostates of the Cross,
Extinguishers of the divine light!

[2: 405]

Such words have a ring quite different from the conventional rhetoric and, whatever the stiltedness of their form, give voice to a genuine sense of betrayal. Henceforth, Dostoevsky will find it impossible ever to believe that Christian values and true Christian faith have continued to exist in the hearts and minds of the people of Europe, and of France and England in particular.

Despite the unimpeachable character of its sentiments, Dostoevsky's poem never managed to make its way into public print. On arriving in Petersburg, it was scrupulously placed in the capacious archives of the Third Section—and remained there until disinterred in 1883, two years after his death! No answer to Yakovlev has ever been found, and Dostoevsky presumably never heard a word about the fate of this first of his poetic exertions, soon to be followed by two others. Nothing could be done except to swallow his disappointment and turn more than ever to the consolations offered by the "friendship" of Marya Dimitrievna Isaeva. To what extent his feelings were given overt expression at this early period of their relationship remains obscure. All we know is that he became a close "friend of the family," assumed the function of tutor to their son, and, as Wrangel puts it, "spent entire days at the Isaevs."[13] This was the situation when Wrangel appeared on the scene in November 1854 to provide Dostoevsky with closer friendship, and more powerful patronage, than any he had been able to acquire so far.

CHAPTER 14

An Influential Friend

During the agonizing twenty minutes to a half-hour that Dostoevsky stood on the scaffolding in Semenovsky Square, his eyes may well have turned from time to time to the massed crowds surrounding the spectacle and looking on silently. Held back at a respectful distance by the cordon of troops, they could only be seen as a vague, looming presence on the far edges of the adjacent streets. But if Dostoevsky had been able to distinguish one person from another and to examine facial expressions, he would surely have been struck by one young man—just barely seventeen years of age, and wearing the three-cornered hat and uniform overcoat of the elite Alexander Lyceum located at Tsarskoe Selo—who was watching the proceedings with a deep and sorrowful air of concern. The name of this young man was Baron Alexander Yegorovich Wrangel, and he belonged to one of those Russian-German aristocratic families of Baltic origin which, under Nicholas I, staffed the higher echelons of the bureaucracy and the Army and continued to do so, to a large extent, under Alexander II as well.

The young Wrangel had not been involved in the Petrashevsky affair in any way; but he had seen Petrashevsky, Nikolay Speshnev, and several of the others who stood on the scaffolding, when they had come, as they frequently did, to visit the Lyceum where they had once been students. Nor had the shock waves caused by the arrest of the Petrashevtsy spared the sacrosanct precincts of this exclusive institution, which Nicholas feared—and not without some reason—had become a hothouse for fledgling conspirators. A search was accordingly carried out in the student quarters to see if any "subversive" literature would be turned up. But the students were warned in advance, Wrangel hastily hid his copy of the poems of Pushkin [!] under his mattress, and the occasion passed without incident.

Wrangel had also heard conversations about the case at home—and conversations that were much more than idle salon chatter. One of his great-uncles had been a member of the General-Auditoriat; and a close friend of the family, a member of the Senate, was officially kept abreast of the results of the inquiry. The young man listened to everything he heard with avid interest, and pricked up his ears particularly when the name of Dostoevsky was mentioned. For he had just read *Poor Folk* and was reading *Netotchka Nezvanova* with great admiration. Any information concerning the fate of the gifted and unfortunate Dostoevsky aroused his intensest curiosity, although he took care not to reveal in public a literary taste that would have been considered politically suspect in his milieu.

On the day of the mock execution, Wrangel had noticed the unusual parade of closed carriages filing mysteriously through the streets accompanied by armed cavalry. While he was still gazing out of the window, an uncle arrived to explain the significance of the stately procession. This uncle, an officer in a regiment of the Horse Grenadiers, was on his way to join the troops assigned to take part in the solemnities. Hastily throwing on his overcoat and seizing his hat, Wrangel accompanied his uncle to Semenovsky Square. There he joined the rather desultory crowd of lookers-on, who, unlike himself, had no notion whatever of why the ceremony of punishment and execution was taking place. Another officer and relative of the young man, recognizing him in the crowd, flew into a rage and told him he would get into terrible trouble—might even be expelled from the Lyceum—if his superiors learned that he had come voluntarily to watch the punishment of the Petrashevtsy. But to slake his curiosity, and hasten his departure, the officer revealed that no executions would really take place: the original sentences of death were to be commuted at the last moment. Despite this reassuring news, Wrangel stayed to the very end of the macabre comedy and only left when the crowd dissolved, "crossing themselves and blessing the mercifulness of the Tsar."[1]

Several years later, after graduating from the Lyceum and dying of boredom in the Ministry of Justice, Wrangel decided to join a number of his classmates in applying for a post in Siberia. He was just twenty-one years old and, by his own admission, totally devoid of any practical experience of the world; his duties hitherto had consisted of signing papers concerning matters about which, for the most part, he knew little and cared less. All the same, he was appointed to the post of public prosecutor of the region that included Semipalatinsk and began to make preparations for his departure. He obviously had met Mikhail Dostoevsky on some occasion in Petersburg and speaks of having known him quite well (Dostoevsky's letters to Mikhail suggest, however, that the acquaintance could hardly have been more than perfunctory). In any case, Wrangel was only too happy to call on Mikhail just before beginning his lengthy journey and to receive from him letters for Feodor Dostoevsky from his family, some clothes, books, and 50 rubles. Wrangel also paid a visit before his departure to Apollon Maikov, whom Dostoevsky had once tried unsuccessfully to recruit for the Speshnev secret society; and he carried another letter to the exile from this old friend, now recognized as an important poet.

2

Before reaching his final destination, Semipalatinsk, Wrangel stopped in Omsk to pay his respects to the Governor-General, F. X. Gasfort, a former Army comrade of his father's. It was at the home of the Gasforts that he spent an evening with the Ivanovs, and he speaks of Mme Ivanova as "a marvelous, kindhearted woman, highly cultivated, a protectress of unfortunates, especially the politicals."[2] Also of interest are some anecdotes of the journey, which help to justify one of Dostoevsky's most amusing satirical portraits—that of the Russian-German Governor-General von Lembke in *The Devils*. Von Lembke, it will be recalled, takes refuge from the burdens of office by making elaborate cutout toys of remarkable ingenuity. Otherwise, his most notable characteristic is a total and impenetrable obtuseness, which prevents him from understanding the slightest thing about the responsibilities of his government position. Dostoevsky's depiction is so broad and slapstick that one tends to take it as pure caricature; but his imagination may well have been nourished on a solid diet of stories similar to those that Wrangel recounts.

Wrangel's first impression of Gasfort, relayed in a letter to the senior Wrangel, is that the Governor-General "is so empty and stupid that I will not say much about him";[3] and a later episode amply confirms this initial evaluation. Wrangel was impatiently awaiting the arrival of Gasfort in Semipalatinsk in order to speak to him about a new prison to replace the old—its condition had horrified the humane young man when he first paid it a visit—and also about the need for a hospital and a school. "But my disillusion was total," he writes sadly. "The General paid attention above all to his invention—my uniform [a special costume designed by Gasfort himself to impress the natives]. 'It sits well, they really know how to sew in Petersburg,' said the General; 'but the overcoat is three [inches] longer than the regulation—*faites le couper*.' But here, by way of approval, he added, 'Next year I will give all of you [new] regulation snaffles, saddlecloths, and saddles.' "[4] That was the end of the interview, and Wrangel never got an opportunity to talk about the improvements that were so badly needed. Another Russian-German, the military Governor, Major-General Friedrichs, was also an old friend of Wrangel's family; but the young man boldly tells his father that Friedrichs is as "stupid as a post. He listens to reports standing up while he plays the flute. He weighs papers brought to him for signature on a scale, and then boasts of how many pounds he has to sign every week—in a word, my Adam [Wrangel's illiterate Finnish manservant] would be just as good a military Governor."[5]

After this first disillusioning contact with Siberian officialdom, Wrangel pursued his journey and arrived in Semipalatinsk on November 20, 1854. One of the first things he did was to inquire after the whereabouts of

Dostoevsky, and a messenger was sent by the military Governor inviting Private Dostoevsky to take tea with Wrangel the very next day. "Dostoevsky did not know who had summoned him and why," Wrangel recalls, "and, when he came in, was extremely reserved. He was in his gray soldier's overcoat, with a stiff red collar and red epaulettes, morose, his face pale and sickly and covered with freckles. His light-colored hair was cut short, and he was of more than medium height. Intently looking at me with his sharp, gray-blue eyes, it seemed that he was trying to peer into my very soul—now, what sort of a man is he? He admitted to me later that he was very worried when my messenger told him that he was summoned by 'the prosecuting magistrate for criminal affairs.' "[6]

Wrangel's apologies for having summoned Dostoevsky so peremptorily put the latter at ease, and he buried himself in the letters that Wrangel had brought, beginning to sob quietly while reading those written by his brother and sister. Wrangel too had a packet of correspondence awaiting him, and he eagerly turned to them as a relief from the "piercing sadness and loneliness" that had often swept over him during his long months on the road. It was the first time he had really been away from home, and suddenly he too began to sob uncontrollably as memories of his family and friends rose before his eyes. "We both stood there face to face, forgotten by fate, solitary. . . . I felt so distressed that, despite my exalted rank . . . as it were involuntarily, without thinking, I threw myself on the neck of Feodor Mikhailovich, who stood opposite looking at me with a sad and pensive expression."[7] The older man comforted the younger, and the two promised to see each other as frequently as possible.

Despite such an unconventional start, which might have led to mutual embarrassment when the temperature had cooled, Dostoevsky and Wrangel did become fast friends. The difference in age (Dostoevsky was thirty-three) helped to bridge the disparity of social position; and Wrangel had a genuine admiration for Dostoevsky as a writer. The analysis that Dostoevsky gives of his young friend's character, in a letter written after he had known him for about a year, helps to explain why their friendship could become so close and cordial. "He is a very young person," Dostoevsky explains to Mikhail, "very gentle, although with a strongly developed *point d'honneur*, incredibly kind, somewhat proud (but only on the surface, I like that) with some youthful faults, cultivated, but not brilliantly or deeply, likes to study, has a very weak character, is impressionable as a woman, somewhat of a hypochondriac and rather jumpy; what irritates and enrages others distresses him—the sign of an excellent heart. *Très comme il faut*."[8] Dostoevsky's pride and sense of self-respect clearly had nothing to fear from such a person, and he easily learned how to accommodate himself to this scion of an aristocratic milieu for which, at bottom, he had very little sympathy.

7. Baron Alexander
Yegorovich Wrangel

Indeed, the two began to spend so much time together that local tongues
started to wag among what Wrangel calls "the bribetaking bureaucrats"[9]
(his natural enemies in any case), and he noticed that his mail began to
arrive three or four days later than its distribution to others. The military
Governor, considering Wrangel's tender years, felt called upon to warn
him about Dostoevsky and the possible dangers of allowing himself to fall
under the influence of such a notorious revolutionary. Deciding to take
matters into his own hands, Wrangel asked the official in question, with
whom he had become very friendly, to invite Dostoevsky to his home and
judge for himself. After a moment of silence the obliging officer agreed,
and Dostoevsky was asked to come, "without fuss," in his soldier's uniform.
The visit was a great success; the invitation was repeated; and from this
moment Dostoevsky was received, through Wrangel's good offices, in
whatever good society could be found in Semipalatinsk.

Wrangel's appearance on the scene thus did much to ease the difficulties
of Dostoevsky's position, and certainly raised his status in the all-important
eyes of Marya Dimitrievna. He soon began to spend as much time, if not
more, in Wrangel's comfortable quarters than in his own dark and depressing lodgings. Since all his free moments were now divided between
Wrangel and the Isaevs, he tried, without much success, to bring the two
together as much as possible. As Wrangel notes, he "pressingly dragged
me also [to the Isaevs], but I did not like that environment because of her

husband."[10] Just how far Dostoevsky's infatuation with Mme Isaeva had proceeded at this point cannot be stated with certainty; but Dostoevsky's letters a year or so later indicate that they were probably more intimate than Wrangel suspected. "Alas," Dostoevsky wrote to the latter with a sigh, "I never told you: while you were still here I drove her to despair *par ma jalousie incomparable.* . . ."[11] One assumes that if Dostoevsky felt he had the right to be *jealous,* then his relations with Marya Dimitrievna had progressed beyond the point of mere friendship. In the same letter, assuring Wrangel that he knows Marya Dimitrievna loves him and not a rival suitor, he confesses: "My friend! I have never been entirely sincere with you on this matter."[12] Such hints unmistakably suggest that Marya Dimitrievna had responded to Dostoevsky's advances in a manner that made the strength of her attachment perfectly clear.

3

Two months after Wrangel first set foot in Semipalatinsk, an event occurred that shook all of Russia and opened up a new and much more promising perspective on Dostoevsky's future. Nicholas I died suddenly, under mysterious circumstances, on February 18, 1855, and almost a month later the news finally arrived in the distant Siberian outpost. Dostoevsky and Wrangel attended a funeral service at the Russian church, where the atmosphere was reverent and solemn; but only a few grizzled old soldiers wept unashamedly at the demise of their awesome commander-in-chief, struck down while Russia was still engaged in a raging life-and-death conflict. The thoughts of the many political exiles were turned rather to the prospects of amnesty, which traditionally accompanied the installation of a new régime. Moreover, "rumors of the gentleness of character, humaneness, and kindliness of the new Tsar had long since penetrated to Siberia."[13] Dostoevsky shared such general expectations; and now, with the influential Wrangel at his side, whose family had connections with the highest court circles, he had every reason to believe they would be fulfilled.

Less than a month later, Wrangel predictably wrote a letter to his father in which, if we can judge from the context, he speaks of Dostoevsky for the first time. "Fate has brought me together with a rare person as regards both qualities of heart and mind," he says; "he is our young and unfortunate writer Dostoevsky. I am much obliged to him, and his words, advice, and ideas will strengthen me for my entire life." After mentioning that they intended to translate Hegel and Carus together, Wrangel continues: "He is a very devout person, sickly, but with a will of iron." And then he arrives at the crucial issue: "Do you know, dear father, whether there will be an amnesty? So many unfortunates are waiting and hoping, as a drowning person clutches at a straw. Is it possible that the heart of our Sovereign, kind and merciful, does not understand that magnanimity is the best method of conquering ill-wishers?" Two weeks later he sent a letter to his sister, urging her to question their father on the prospects of an amnesty for political prisoners and suggesting that a word might be uttered on Dostoevsky's behalf to Dubelt or to Prince Orlov. "Can it be that this remarkable man will perish here as a soldier? That would be terrible. I am sad and sick about him—I love him like a brother, and honor him like a father."[14]

By the time these letters were written, Dostoevsky and Wrangel had taken up residence together in a *dacha*, affectionately called "Cossack Garden," on the outskirts of town. The climate of Semipalatinsk during the summer months was unbearably hot, and Wrangel decided to escape at the beginning of spring the moment the steppe began to blossom and turn green. He found an empty house on a bank of the river in the midst of luxuriant vegetation, and, since the summer encampment of Dostoevsky's regiment was close by, it was easily arranged for the latter to share his quarters. The picture Wrangel gives of their life together has an idyllic quality that Dostoevsky was not to know again for many years. Wrangel, an enthusiastic and versatile gardener, had determined to show the natives that all sorts of flowers and fruits unknown to the region could be cultivated there, and the work connected with this project "very much pleased and occupied Dostoevsky, [who] more than once recalled his childhood and the farmhouse of his family."[15]

Wrangel gives us such a vivid picture of Dostoevsky as a gardener that one cannot resist transcribing this unusual glimpse of bucolic recreation. "I can still remember very vividly the image of F.M. earnestly aiding me to water young seedlings, in the sweat of his brow, having removed his soldier's overcoat and wearing only a calico, rose-colored waistcoat faded from washing. Around his neck invariably dangled a long native watch chain of small, blue glass beads, once given to him by somebody; on the chain hung a large, onion-shaped silver timepiece. He was usually very absorbed in this task, and obviously found great satisfaction in this pastime."[16] The two friends also made long excursions on horseback to visit Khirghiz encampments in the steppe and sample the hospitality of friendly chieftains (Dostoevsky had not known how to ride, but acquired the knack), fished, and tamed two snakes that lived under the terrace of their house and came to drink milk from bowls at regular hours. One afternoon, the snakes showed up unexpectedly in the presence of some local ladies, who had dropped in, as they often did, to admire the garden—and usually, much to Wrangel's irritation, to strip it bare of flowers as testimony of their appreciation. Panic broke out at the appearance of the snakes, and

8. Chokan Valikhanov

no ladies came to visit the garden for a long time after this untoward, but providential, incident.

Dostoevsky's interest in the life and customs of the local Khirgizes was greatly stimulated by his warm friendship with Chokan Valikhanov (as he was known in Russian), the swarthy, handsome and distinguished descendant of a family of Khirghiz khans and a sultan in his own right. The first of his people to receive a Russian higher education in the Siberian Cadet Corps, Valikhanov was then serving as an officer in the Russian Army. His knowledge of the region made him invaluable to the military authorities; but while providing them with information on hostile border tribes, Valikhanov also had serious scientific interests. He mapped the wild border region between Russia and China and became the first ethnographer of his own people, transcribing their folk epics, legends, and folk songs, and laying the basis for whatever knowledge of Khirghiz culture we have today. In the only surviving letter to him, filled with the most cordial expressions of regard (a regard that was mutual), Dostoevsky urges Valikhanov to make every effort to continue his studies in St. Petersburg and to become his people's *"enlightened* intercessor with the Russians."[17] The value of Valikhanov's work was quickly recognized by Russian Orientalists, and he did reach the capital and eventually Europe as well. His health, however, had been undermined both by the Petersburg climate and by the grueling hardships of his numerous explorations. He went to an early grave in 1865—by which time he had become thoroughly disillusioned with Russian rule because of the persistent mistreatment of the Khirghizes by their despotic overlords.

4

The memoirs of Wrangel are rather pedestrian, and much of his account of Dostoevsky is taken up with the routine incidents of their daily life together. These offer a glimpse of a quotidian Dostoevsky rarely seen elsewhere, and it is useful to be reminded occasionally that he also behaved like any ordinary mortal and did not spend all his time wrestling with the eternal verities. But, intermixed with all sorts of trivialities, there is also happily, if infrequently, information of a more enlightening sort. Whatever material of this kind has not already been gleaned from his pages may be conveniently summarized at this point in our narrative.

With reference to Dostoevsky's involvement in the Petrashevsky circle, Wrangel remarks that "he gloomily refused to talk about his trial, and I did not press the question. I know only, and heard him say, that he did not like Petrashevsky, and had absolutely no sympathy with his tricks. . . ."[18] The passage continues with Dostoevsky's observation, already cited, about a political upheaval being impossible in Russia for the time being, and the ludicrousness of thinking about a "constitution" for Russia on the European model. It was he, the ex-Speshnevist, who had been in favor of an "upheaval" and the legalist Petrashevsky who had desired a constitution and a democratic republic; but both, as Dostoevsky now believed, had been equally deluded in their hopes. Of his old comrades in the Petrashevsky circle, Dostoevsky spoke most often of Durov, Pleshcheev, and Grigoryev.

Much of the talk between the two also focused on the dramatic news of the day, which they followed with both patriotic exaltation and anxiety. Every afternoon, after working in the garden, they sat down on their terrace to drink tea or dine; and then "F.M. and I read the newspapers while smoking our pipes, reminisced about Petersburg and about all those near and dear to us, and also abused Europe. After all, the battle for Sevastopol was still going on, and we were saddened and alarmed."[19] Dostoevsky remembered this moment of nerve-racking trepidation over Sevastopol nearly twenty years later in a letter, where he responds to a newspaper article describing the mood of the Russian intelligentsia at that distant time—quite accurately—as having been defeatist, and even more or less hoping for a victory of the Allies as a blow to the intolerable régime of Nicholas I.

"No, my liberalism did not go that far," Dostoevsky explodes. "I was then still in prison camp [a slight error in dating], and did *not* rejoice at the success of the Allies. Together with my comrades, the 'unfortunates' and the soldiers, I felt myself a Russian, desired the success of Russian arms and—though I still retained a strong dose of the scurvy Russian liberalism propagated by good-for-nothings like those dung-beetles Belinsky and others—I did not consider it illogical to feel myself to be a Russian."[20] This sense of being united by a visceral, emotive bond with the Russian people, mercifully arriving to relieve the isolation and enmity from which he had suffered all through his prison-camp years, powerfully affected the subsequent cast of Dostoevsky's ideas.

Wrangel notes that Dostoevsky very much liked to read Gogol and Victor Hugo; when in a particularly ebullient mood, he loved to recite Pushkin, especially the glitteringly brilliant and sensuous "The Feast of Cleopatra" (part of the unfinished story, *Egyptian Nights*). The irresistible Egyptian queen, in Pushkin's masterpiece, animates a Roman orgy by offering to spend the night with whoever is willing to pay for her favors by the sacrifice of his life. Three enamored swains accept the deadly bargain—but the poem breaks off before the pact is carried through. Dostoevsky's own passion, flaming high at this time, no doubt made him particularly responsive to the poem's theme. As we shall see very shortly, he too was willing to go to an extreme of self-sacrifice—of course not as extreme as in the poem—to demonstrate and express his devotion.

In Wrangel's letter to his father, he speaks of Dostoevsky as being "very devout," and this might be viewed as part of the young man's campaign to persuade his suspicious progenitor that the ex-political prisoner deserved the pardon he was trying to obtain. But his memoirs also depict Dostoevsky as genuinely pious, although at the same time no friend of the official priesthood. His "religion," as Wrangel describes it, seems to have been very personal, vaguely Deistic, and with a touch of pantheism, but Christocentric at the same time.

Dostoevsky liked to lie on the grass at night and "look at the myriads of stars twinkling overhead out of the blue depths of the heavens. Such minutes comforted him. The spectacle of the majesty of the Creator, the all-knowing, all-powerful Divine strength filled us with some sort of tender emotion, the consciousness of our nothingness, somehow it pacified our souls. I rarely talked with Dostoevsky about religion. He was quite devout but rarely went to Church, and did not like the priests, particularly those in Siberia. Of Christ he spoke with rapture."[21] Certainly some part of the sensibility recorded in this passage went into the creation of Alyosha Karamazov, who, at an instant of spiritual crisis in his life, also looked up at the stars shining "vast and fathomless" in the night sky, also felt that "the mystery of the earth was one with the mystery of the stars," and was convinced that, at such a moment, "something firm and unshakable as that vault of Heaven had entered into his soul" (14: 328).

5

Dostoevsky's religious susceptibilities, as we know, had been deeply stirred at the time of his conversion experience; and in all probability they were also immensely enlivened by his epileptic seizures. These have previously been spoken of only in neurological terms, and it has been suggested that they helped to condition the regeneration of his convictions by maintaining his nervous system in a highly impressionable and malleable state of receptivity. There is good reason to surmise, however, that they acted on him in a more specific and determinate fashion as well. To be sure, this is a matter fraught with controversy, and competent neurologists have been unable to agree on the questions raised by Dostoevsky's seizures. The available evidence, though, seems to be clear enough, and is based on three accounts: his own description of the beginning of an attack—what is called the "epileptic aura"—in *The Idiot*; a passage in Strakhov's biography containing his eyewitness account of the effect of such an "aura"; and another passage in the memoirs of Sofya Kovalevskaya, who knew Dostoevsky in the mid-1860s, when she was an adolescent girl and he was courting her older sister.*

* There is, of course, a considerable medical literature regarding Dostoevsky's epilepsy. The best and most complete discussion of the matter for the general reader can be found in the masterly book of Jacques Catteau, *La création littéraire chez Dostoievski* (Paris, 1978), chap. 5 ("La Maladie"). Professor Catteau's book is one of the most important contributions made to Dostoevsky studies in many years, offering illuminating and perceptive discussions, based on a perfect command of the primary and secondary sources, not only on Dostoevsky's epilepsy but on many other issues as well. It is regrettable that this fundamental study is not available in English translation.

For our present purposes, it is only necessary to know that competent modern specialists have diagnosed Dostoevsky's epilepsy as being of a type known as psychomotor-temporal lobe epilepsy, whose cause is frequently found as a focal organic lesion of the brain. This type is distinguished from primary generalized epilepsy, where usually no specific cause can be assigned. The existence of psychomotor-temporal lobe epilepsy was more clearly established in the 1940s thanks to advances in research in the brain. Since that time, Dostoevsky's symptoms, including his description of the "ecstatic aura," have been considered to confirm such a diagnosis.

This conclusion, though, was called into question in 1977 by Dr. Henri Gastaut, a French specialist in epilepsy of worldwide renown, who has had a long-standing interest in Dostoevsky. Indeed, Dr. Gastaut had previously been one of the most forceful advocates of the view he combated. A new examination of the material persuaded him that Dostoevsky suffered from a primary generalized epilepsy; and from a thorough study of the previous literature on "auras," he discovered that, until the publication of *The Idiot*, all medical descriptions of the "aura" had focused on their frightening and terrifying quality. "It can therefore be admitted without any risk of error that at the end of the nineteenth century the most prestigious epileptologists who had collected and categorized thousands of epileptic auras, but who had not yet read the works of Dostoevsky, had complete knowledge of the emotional auras of fear, terror, or anxiety, but did not at all know of the existence of truly euphoric and, by extension, of ecstatic auras."

It was only *after* Dostoevsky's novel entered into the medical literature, at the beginning of the twentieth century, that examples were noted (still quite rare) of pleasurable or euphoric "auras." Dr. Gastaut thus concluded that he himself, as well as many others, had wrongfully accepted the existence of "ecstatic auras" on the basis of Dostoevsky's testimony, even though the evidence for them always had been dubious. Another reason for such acceptance, he suggests, is that the "ecstatic aura" filled an empty place in the classic typology of "auras" first offered by the famous neurologist J. Hughlings Jackson. In Dr. Gastaut's opinion, Dostoevsky's depiction was a transformation of the "few seconds of confused alterations of his

The famous scene in *The Idiot* is the only firsthand depiction of the "aura" that we have from Dostoevsky's pen, and, although he is nominally writing about his character Prince Myshkin, the portrayal is clearly autobiographical. At such moments, Dostoevsky tells us, "his mind and heart were flooded with extraordinary light, all his uneasiness, all his doubts, all his anxieties were relieved at once; they were all merged in a lofty calm, full of serene, harmonious joy and hope, full of knowledge and the ultimate causes of things." Such instants imparted "a feeling, unknown and undivined till then, of completeness, of proportion, of reconciliation, and of ecstatic devotional merging in the highest synthesis of life." Later in the same passage, we are told that Myshkin "had actually said to himself at that second, that, for the infinite happiness he had felt in it, that second really might be worth the whole of life . . . at that moment I seem [Myshkin is talking] somehow to understand the extraordinary saying that *there shall be no more time*. Probably . . . this is the very second which was not long enough for the water to be spilt out of Mahomet's pitcher, though the epileptic prophet had time to gaze at all the habitations of Allah" (8: 188-189).

These words convey the ecstatic heightening of consciousness that swept

---

consciousness in which he became detached from his surroundings into 'several brief instants . . . of perfect harmony with himself and the entire universe.' " In other words, Dostoevsky's "ecstatic aura" was invented in accordance with his own religious ideals and was not an objective datum of the event, though Dr. Gastaut adds that he "believed deeply in the reality of the experiences he described."

But the story does not end here. At a Dostoevsky Congress held in Sophia Antipolis (France) in the summer of 1981, convened to honor the centenary of Dostoevsky's death, the present writer heard Dr. Gastaut, in a still-unpublished paper, reverse himself once again. A renewed reading of Dostoevsky's works had caused him to return to the diagnosis of psychomotor-temporal lobe epilepsy; whether this also re-established the existence of the "ecstatic aura" as well is not clear in my recollection. In any case, this is how the medical discussion stands at the present time.

Dr. Gilbert H. Glaser, Professor of Neurology at the Yale University School of Medicine and one of the leading American experts on epilepsy, has been kind enough to read the above remarks and give me the benefit of his comments on Dostoevsky's case. In his view, "based upon my reading of various descriptions . . . [Dostoevsky's] epilepsy resembled the psychomotor-temporal lobe type more than any other." Also, Dr. Glaser believes, "that aura was *not* incompatible. Many patients I have seen personally, and others, whose records I have reviewed, with definite psychomotor-temporal lobe epilepsy have had that type of aura. I do not deny that it may occur in more generalized epilepsy. Yet, we know that some patients may begin an epileptic seizure with a specific aura like this one, then exhibit signs and symptoms of a psychomotor-temporal lobe seizure and next have a generalized convulsion (i.e., 'secondary generalized epilepsy')."

With reference to Dr. Gastaut's oscillations between one diagnosis and another, Dr. Glaser remarks—and this should always be kept in mind—that "it is difficult to be certain when one does not have an *actual, personal* experience with a patient." But he concludes, all the same, "that the psychomotor-temporal lobe epilepsy category best 'fits the known facts' in this case." (All quotations from a personal communication of Dr. Glaser, July 2, 1982; italics in text.)

For further information, see the book by Catteau mentioned above; T. Alajouanine, "Dostoewski's Epilepsy," *Brain*, 86 (1963), 209-218; Henri Gastaut, "Fyodor Mikhailovich Dostoevsky's Involuntary Contribution to the Symptomology and Prognosis of Epilepsy," tran. Roger Broughton, *Epilepsia*, 19 (1978), 186-201; Gilbert H. Glaser, "Epilepsy: Neuropsychological Aspects," *American Handbook of Psychiatry*, ed. Silvano Arieti, 2nd ed. (New York, 1975) 4: 314-355.

over Dostoevsky at the beginning of his seizures when they occurred in
a state of wakefulness (the majority mercifully took place while he was
sleeping lightly in the early morning hours). When fully aware of them,
he was lifted out of himself into a condition similar to that described by
certain mystics, although he does not attribute any specific doctrinal content to his sensations. Rather, they were one variety of what R. C. Zaehner
has called a "natural" mystical experience, in which the personal ego is
obliterated and fuses into a harmony with the cosmos.[22] This moment of
fusion was further marked in Dostoevsky by the transcendence of time,
more exactly, by the disappearance of any sense of time and by a feeling
of overwhelming happiness at this apprehension of an existence in eternity. Some mystics, on reaching this same ecstatic state, have used it to
affirm the irreality of death and the immortality of the soul; but there is
no attempt by Dostoevsky to make any such affirmation. What predomi-
nates for him is the indescribable bliss of union and reconciliation with
"the highest synthesis of life" and of contact with a realm of being beyond
time and change—a realm whose reality for Dostoevsky had now been
irrefutably confirmed by this tangible evidence of his senses.

The further information provided by Strakhov does not substantially add
to this picture. He tells of a conversation, which he dates approximately
in 1863, that took place on the eve of Easter (this holy day celebrating the
resurrection of Christ plays an extraordinarily symbolic role in Dostoevsky's
life). The two men were engaged in animated conversation on some un-
named subject, and Dostoevsky was walking up and down the room in
Strakhov's apartment in a state of intense excitement. "What he [Dos-
toevsky] said was filled with loftiness and joy," when suddenly he broke
off, as if in search of words, and then, uttering a strange and high-pitched
wail, lost consciousness and collapsed. "Feodor Mikhailovich," Strakhov
writes, "spoke to me several times of the moments of exaltation that preceded a crisis: 'For several brief moments I feel a happiness unthinkable
in a normal state and impossible to imagine by anyone else who has not
lived through it. I am then in perfect harmony with myself and the entire
universe; the sensation is so powerful and so delightful that for a few
seconds of such happiness one would give ten years of one's life, perhaps
even one's entire life.'"[23]

A new element, though, is provided by Kovalevskaya, who supposedly
transmits a story told by Dostoevsky himself in her hearing. Again we are
on the eve of Easter, though the place is now Siberia in the years after
Dostoevsky's release from the prison camp. An old friend of Dostoevsky's
(about whom we hear nothing else from any other source) comes for a
visit, and the two begin to argue about God. The friend is an atheist,
Dostoevsky a believer, and they talk the night through as Russians were
notoriously prone to do about all such "cursed questions" of human life.

Just at the moment when Dostoevsky was proclaiming, in a pitch of feverish exaltation, his belief in the existence of God, "the bells of the neighboring church began to sound the matins for Easter. The atmosphere began to vibrate and to dance. 'And I had the sentiment,' Dostoevsky continued, 'that the heaven had come down to earth and swallowed me up. I really apprehended God and felt him in every fibre of my being. I then cried: Yes, God exists. I remember nothing after that,' " The story concludes with Dostoevsky asserting that, like Mohammed, he had seen Paradise, and that he would not exchange such a moment for all the joys of the world.[24]

If we accept this story as reliable, even though a number of features make it seem rather dubious,* it would indicate that Dostoevsky himself saw some connection between his religious faith and his mystical experiences. It is significant, though, that the experience only comes to *confirm* his belief in God rather than to inspire it. Nor is there any climactic vision of God as in more traditional types of mysticism, but rather a fusion with the "highest synthesis of life," the same unity of heaven and earth that we are already familiar with. It is true that he now designates the moment of ecstasy, marked by the disappearance of time, with the traditional name of "Paradise"; but the reference to Mohammed surely indicates that it had no specific connection with Dostoevsky's own Christianity. His mysticism thus was not theistic in character, but rather what Zaehner calls "pan-en-henistic," that is, the intuition of all-as-being-one typical of most nature-mysticism.[25] From this point of view, Dostoevsky's reveries under the star-filled sky, and the consolation they afforded him, may be seen as attempts to recapture some of the emotional afflatus provided by his "epileptic aura."

Dostoevsky's mysticism, however, possessed one attribute that gave it a tragic rather than a more traditionally sublime character—meaning by "sublime" the triumphant assertion by the human spirit of its capacity to rise above the limitations of time and mortality. His epileptic seizures, being involuntary, contained no such affirmation and were always accompanied by the fear of a plunge into mental degeneracy or of death itself as a result of the physical convulsions caused by the fit. These fears are also embodied in the depiction of Prince Myshkin's meditations about his illness and its contradictory consequences. "Thinking of that moment later [the moment of visionary transcendence], when he was all right again, he often said to himself that all these gleams and flashes of 'the highest sensation of life' and self-consciousness, and therefore of the highest form

---

* Jacques Catteau has printed the account of Kovalevskaya side by side with that of Strakhov and noted some suspicious resemblances of language. Strakhov's account appeared in 1883, and Kovalevskaya began to write her *Memoirs* in 1887. It is possible, of course, that Dostoevsky used many of the same expressions when he told the two stories; but the likelihood of direct influence cannot be ruled out. See Jacques Catteau, *La création littéraire chez Dostoievski* (Paris, 1978), 156-157.

of existence, were nothing but disease, a disruption of the normal conditions; and if so, it was not at all the highest form of being, but on the contrary must be reckoned the lowest."

But Myshkin—and presumably Dostoevsky—came to the "paradoxical conclusion" that the diseased origin of these "moments" did not infirm their supreme value, and "without doubt that moment really was worth the whole of life." Yet doubt persisted all the same, "and he [Myshkin] did not insist on the dialectical part of his argument. Stupefaction, spiritual darkness, idiocy stood before him conspicuously as the consequence of these 'higher moments'; seriously of course he could not have disputed it. There was undoubtedly a mistake in his conclusion—that is, in his estimate of that minute, but the reality of the sensation somewhat perplexed him. What was he to make of that reality?" (8: 188-189) In the absence of other documentation, we may be permitted to take this as an expression of Dostoevsky's own bewilderment and perplexity, which never allowed him to use these flashes of revelation, as other mystics have done, to resolve his religious questionings and achieve some sort of inner peace. But neither could he accept a world in which the reality of these gleams of the absolute, no matter how treacherous and dangerous, was simply negated or denied.[26]

6

The amenities and recreations provided by life in "Cossack Garden" did not, of course, prevent Dostoevsky from continuing to pursue his one all-important goal—the re-establishment of his literary name and reputation. Work on a number of projects went on steadily, although the information provided by Wrangel is regrettably sparse. Still, we hear about early drafts of *House of the Dead* and of what later became Dostoevsky's two satirical novellas, *Uncle's Dream* and *The Village of Stepanchikovo and Its Inhabitants* (better known in English as *The Friend of the Family*). Wrangel recalls Dostoevsky talking of the first of these long stories when, "in an infectiously jolly mood, he guffawed and narrated the adventures of his 'uncle,' humming some snatches of an opera. . . ."[27] Dostoevsky's buoyancy was probably a result of his relations with Marya Dimitrievna, whom he went to visit as often as possible, returning home each time, according to Wrangel, "in some sort of ecstasy, enraptured beyond words, and surprised when I did not chime in."[28] None of these projected works, however, was completed (or probably even near completion) in the spring and summer of 1855; the only composition from Dostoevsky's pen that did not remain in draft was another celebratory poem, "On the First of July, 1855," whose title refers to the birthday of the ex-Empress, the wife of the recently deceased Nicholas I.

Dostoevsky's second poem is much less belligerent than the first and refers to the Crimean War only in passing. "God will decide between them and us!" (2: 408) is the single (and very curt) allusion to the raging battle. Instead, Dostoevsky devotes himself to attempting to console the grieving Empress for her loss, urging her not to give way to despair and to take comfort in the great deeds and accomplishments of her vanished spouse; these continue to exist, not only in the minds and hearts of all Russians, but in the visible monuments to his glory that fill the realm. Some personal touches lacking in the previous poem are present here; and Dostoevsky apologizes for his audacity in daring to address—even more, in presuming to assuage the grief—of so exalted a personage:

> Forgive, forgive me, forgive my wish;
> Forgive that I dare to speak with you.
> Forgive that I dare nourish the senseless dream
> Of consoling your sadness, lightening your suffering.
> Forgive that I, a mournful outcast, dare
> Raise his voice at this hallowed grave.
> But God! our judge from all eternity!
> Thou sent me thy judgment in the disturbèd hour
>   of doubt,
> And with my heart I discovered that tears are—
>   expiation,
> That again I was a Russian, and—again a man!
>
> [2: 407]

If we take these last lines seriously, they would indicate that Dostoevsky had now begun to look on his arrest and conviction as a providential act of God, one that, in causing him to shed tears of expiation, had restored him to the Russian community and thus given him back his self-respect as a man.

CHAPTER 15

"A Knight in Female Clothing"

The idyllic tranquillity of the first months that Dostoevsky spent in "Cossack Garden" provided only a brief respite before he was again plunged into a whirlpool of tormenting emotions. His illicit romance with Marya Dimitrievna, which by this time had probably blossomed into a full-fledged affair, became more and more preoccupying and absorbing; and the need to possess her completely soon drove all other thoughts out of his mind and all other feelings out of his heart. Meanwhile, his struggle for rehabilitation was still going on and, very shortly, became the key to resolving his romantic dilemma.

2

Much to everyone's astonishment, Alexander Isaev actually succeeded in finding another post—a very humble one—in the small town of Kuznetsk, a miserable backwater lost in the depths of the Siberian wilderness. The news struck Dostoevsky like a blow, and suddenly shattered the fragile world of relative contentment he had so laboriously managed to construct. What upset him most was that Marya Dimitrievna, with feminine practicality, had accepted the idea of departure without too much protest. " 'And look, she agrees,' he said to Wrangel bitterly, " 'she doesn't object, that's what's so shocking.' "[1] Such words surely indicate that Dostoevsky had some good reason to believe that Marya Dimitrievna might really have chosen to stay with *him*.

Since the Isaevs were totally destitute, the journey and expenses of moving were completely beyond their means; it was the impoverished Dostoevsky, borrowing some money from the obliging Wrangel, who helped them to scrape together what they needed. The departure took place on a soft May night, bathed in moonlight, and Wrangel and Dostoevsky, according to the Russian custom, accompanied the party on the first leg of the journey after they had paused for a final visit at "Cossack Garden." Wrangel plied the all-too-willing Isaev with champagne until he lapsed into a drunken stupor, and then deposited him in a separate carriage so as to give the two lovers a period of privacy at parting. When the time came to say farewell, Dostoevsky and Marya Dimitrievna embraced, wiped away their tears, and the befuddled paterfamilias was placed back in the open *tarantas* in which the Isaevs were forced to make the journey. "The horses started up, the vehicles began to move, puffs of dust rose from the road, already the cart and its passengers could scarcely be seen, the post bell grew fainter and fainter . . . and Dostoevsky still stood as if rooted to the spot, silent, his head lowered, tears coursing down his cheeks. I went up to him, took his hand—he seemed to wake up after a long sleep, and, not saying a word, got into the carriage. We returned home at daybreak."[2]

Letters immediately began to fly between Semipalatinsk and Kuznetsk at a weekly rhythm, and it is thanks to one of these (unfortunately the only one to survive) that we can obtain some firsthand impression of Dostoevsky's feelings and of the flattering image he had formed of his first great love. The immense importance that Marya Dimitrievna has assumed in his existence becomes perfectly comprehensible in the light of his words. For without her, he says, he feels just as desolate as in 1849, when his arrest and imprisonment had torn him away from everything he had held dear. "I have never considered our meeting as an ordinary one," he writes, "and now, deprived of you, I have understood many things. I lived for five years deprived of human beings, alone, having nobody, in the full sense of the word, to whom I could pour out my heart. . . . The simple fact that a woman held out her hand to me has constituted a new epoch in my life. In certain moments, even the best of men, if I may say so, is nothing more or less than a blockhead. The heart of a woman, her compassion, her interest, the infinite goodness of which we do not have an idea, and which often, through stupidity, we do not even notice, is irreplaceable. I found all that in you. . . ."[3]

Their relationship, it is clear, has already seen some stormy moments, and its tempestuous past hardly augured well for the future. But Dostoevsky chooses to take most of the blame himself ("in the first place I was an ungrateful swine"), and to attribute Marya Dimitrievna's outbursts to a noble nature "offended by the fact that a filthy society did not value or understand you; and for a person with your force of character it is impossible not to rebel against injustice; that is an honest and noble trait. It is the foundation of your character; but life and trouble have of course exaggerated and irritated much in you; but, good God! all this is redeemed with interest, a hundred times over."[4] Dostoevsky would always continue to see Marya Dimitrievna in such a flattering light, as a person whose violent indignation and explosions of temper expressed a noble rage against the injustices of life. One day he was to immortalize this aspect of her personality in the tragically wrathful Katerina Ivanovna Marmeladova of *Crime and Punishment.*

Dostoevsky's separation from Marya Dimitrievna marked the beginning of an agitated and torturing relationship, which at first offered little possibility of any satisfactory outcome. The arrival of each weekly letter, filled

9. Marya Dimitrievna
Isaeva

with accounts of the illness of his beloved, the tedium and loneliness of
her existence, the burdens of caring for her alcoholic husband (whose
health was now failing badly), and of trying to bring up Pasha decently
in the midst of her other woes—all this drove Dostoevsky into a frenzy of
despair. Nor was his anxiety lessened by the increasingly frequent references to a sympathetic young schoolteacher, a friend of Alexander Ivanovich's, who clearly had begun to play the role in her life formerly assumed by Dostoevsky. "With each letter," writes Wrangel, "the utterances
about him became more and more enthusiastic, praising his kindness,
devotion, and nobility of soul. Dostoevsky was torn apart by jealousy; it
was pitiful to observe his gloomy state of mind, which affected his health."5

Indeed, his mood became so downcast that the alarmed Wrangel decided
to arrange a meeting at a town midway between the two localities. He
enlisted the aid of a common friend, a Polish military doctor in exile named
Lamotte, who spread the word that Dostoevsky, suffering from the after-
effects of one of his attacks, was being cared for in Wrangel's quarters;
this precaution was necessary because Dostoevsky did not have official
permission to make the trip. But when the two friends arrived after some
very hard riding, they found, instead of Marya Dimitrievna, a letter explaining that she could not keep the rendezvous because her husband's
condition had worsened. Besides, she lacked sufficient funds to make such
a journey.

A month or two later, in August 1855, Alexander Ivanovich Isaev drew his last breath, leaving Marya Dimitrievna alone, ailing and totally penniless, to struggle along as best she could in the quagmire of Kuznetsk. Frantic on receiving the news, Dostoevsky immediately wrote to Wrangel, then traveling on official business, to send the destitute woman some money if possible. He paints a heart-rending picture of her prostration at having been forced to accept charity, and asks Wrangel to make sure, if he does proffer aid, to do so with particular tact and care; the obligation of gratitude will only make her more sensitive to any undue negligence of tone. No one understood better than the creator of Makar Devushkin in *Poor Folk* the agonies of a cultivated sensibility humiliated by poverty and an inferior social position.

The demise of Alexander Ivanovich made it possible for Dostoevsky to dream at last of possessing, legally and publicly, the lady of his heart; but it was unthinkable to ask for her hand while remaining in his lowly status as a soldier. All this time, to be sure, he had been pulling whatever strings he could reach so as to obtain promotion. Wrangel had asked Governor-General Gasfort, on the occasion of an official dinner, to send Dostoevsky's second poem to the widowed Empress; and it did finally reach her eyes, although just how this was accomplished remains uncertain. There is indisputable evidence that the poem was forwarded by Gasfort; but Wrangel tells a more picturesque story. The piano virtuoso Adolphe Henselt, who had given music lessons to all the Wrangel children, was also an intimate of music lovers in the entourage of the grieving Empress; and he was presumably enlisted to bring Dostoevsky's verses to the attention of the one reader for whom they had been composed.[6]

As a result, Dostoevsky was promoted to the rank of *unter-ofitser* (a noncommissioned grade) in November 1855 and could hope for more important signs of favor in the future. Wrangel left Semipalatinsk a month later for a visit home to St. Petersburg (he expected to return to Siberia, but never did), and while in the capital he intended to devote himself to advancing Dostoevsky's cause. A letter from Dostoevsky around this time to Mikhail pleadingly asks for the dispatch of a hundred rubles to pay his debts (incurred largely for the Isaevs) and to allow him to refurbish his threadbare wardrobe. Another letter, sent with Wrangel, goes into much more detail about his situation and begins by excusing himself to his brother for what may seem his excessive self-preoccupation. But, he explains, there are "two circumstances which compel me to get out of my confined situation and induce such a feverish concern with myself. . . . I wish to write and print. More than ever I know that I have not taken this road [that of prison and exile] in vain, and that it is not in vain that I burden the earth with my person. I am convinced that I have talent and that I will be able to write something good."

The second reason, Dostoevsky continues, is his desire to marry; and since this is the first time he has spoken to his family of his belated romance, he sketches in much of the background we already know. Marya Dimitrievna he describes as being "attractive, very cultivated, very intelligent, good, kind, gracious, with an excellent and generous heart." The travails of life have made her "ill, nervous, and irritable," but Dostoevsky is convinced that "her character at bottom was cheerful and playful." In any event, "if my position improves ever so slightly for the better and positive, I will marry her. I *know* that she will not refuse." And he concludes with the piteous admission that "since the month of May when she left me, my life has been hell."[7]

The anticipation of Wrangel's presence in Petersburg, where he would be able to intercede personally on Dostoevsky's behalf, naturally filled the eager lover with the highest hopes. But his case progressed, if at all, with maddening slowness, and Wrangel was unable to report anything encouraging for a considerable period. "I knew," he writes, "that a manifesto with pardons would be issued at the coronation, but exactly what pardon would be given to the Petrashevtsy nobody of course could predict; even Dubelt . . . as yet knew nothing. This ignorance upset Dostoevsky terribly. His impatience grew, not by days but by hours. He somehow completely failed to realize that I myself, an insignificant Siberian bureaucrat, still wet behind the ears, could not advance his case in an instant; indeed, that many of my relatives, occupying high positions, all the same could do nothing, finally, to speed up his case."[8] A long delay thus occurred between the date Wrangel set foot in the capital and the first letter in which he could give some hope to Dostoevsky, waiting on tenterhooks in his dreary exile for the news that would decide his future.

4

The overwhelming impatience that Dostoevsky displays would have been comprehensible enough even if his relations with Marya Dimitrievna had remained stable and secure; but this was very far from being the case. For she was, as Dostoevsky writes to Wrangel, "melancholy, despairing, constantly ailing, gradually losing faith in my hopes and the successful ordering of our destiny." Inevitably, as an attractive and penniless young widow with a child, she received other offers of marriage. The tone of her letters convinced Dostoevsky that she was concealing something, and rumors reached his ears that she had accepted another suitor. The distraught Dostoevsky sat down to pour out his anguish in a letter, but was interrupted by the arrival of one from her, which lacked, as he tells Wrangel, even "a trace of our future hopes, as if that thought had been completely put aside." And then, finally, came the question he had long feared: what should she do if she received an offer of marriage from a man "of a certain age with good qualities, in the service, and with an assured future? . . ."

Dostoevsky's reaction to this tantalizing missive, with its request for brotherly advice, reveals the melodramatic intensity that will so often mark the love entanglements of his fictional characters. "I was as if struck by lightning, I staggered, fainted, and wept all night. . . . In all my life I have never suffered so much. . . . My heart is consumed by deathly despair, at night there are dreams, shrieks, spasms in my throat choke me, tears sometimes stubbornly refuse to flow, sometimes come in torrents." One can understand why Dostoevsky should exclaim: "Oh! Let God preserve everyone from this terrible, dreadful emotion! Great is the joy of love, but the sufferings are so frightful that it would be better never to be in love."

Worst of all, though, was the moral conflict in which he was plunged by the agonizingly ambiguous situation. Did he really have the right to stand in the way of her making a reasonable marriage when his own prospects were so uncertain? His letter leaves no doubt that he was haunted by the fear of acting selfishly and egotistically, and of injuring the interests of his beloved in the long run. But the vision of someone like Marya Dimitrievna, "ill, nervous, so refined in heart, cultivated, intelligent," burying herself in Kuznetsk forever, and with a husband who perhaps "for his part might consider blows as being perfectly legal in marriage"—this simply drove him out of his mind! He had the eerie sense of living through the pathetic finale of his own first novel, with Marya Dimitrievna cast 'in the situation of my heroine of *Poor Folk*, who marries [the brutal] Bykov (how prophetic I was!)." Moreover, he was certain that she did love him and was thinking of another only out of the direct necessity. "*Mais elle m'aime, elle m'aime*, I know that, I see it—by her sadness, her anguish, her melancholy, by the continual outbursts in her letters, and by much else that I will not write about."9

To assuage his conscience, and sustain his hopes, Dostoevsky asked Marya Dimitrievna to defer any definite decision until September 1856, when she would again be free to marry after the prescribed period of mourning. If, by that time, his future was still so uncertain, then he might agree—though the decision would kill him—that it was necessary to assure her future by a solidly advantageous union. Meanwhile, he appealed to Wrangel, with an urgency verging on hysteria, to redouble his efforts in Petersburg so as to obtain for him a transfer to the Civil Service or a promotion to commissioned rank. Most important of all, what he needed was permission to publish (Dostoevsky claimed that he would have a "novel" and an article completed in September).

He also sent Wrangel, in violation of Army regulations, a personal letter addressed to General E. I. Totleben, already mentioned earlier as having become a national hero because of the brilliant fortifications he had devised for the defense of Sevastopol. Wrangel had already paid him a visit on Dostoevsky's behalf; but it was Dostoevsky's own idea, as a last resort, to appeal directly to the man of the hour and enlist his enormous prestige to accelerate a favorable decision. It would seem unlikely that a letter written specifically to plead for a favor from the mighty, and carefully composed to produce the proper effect, would disclose anything truly revealing about its sender; yet the letter to Totleben turns out to be much more interesting than one might have expected. Perhaps the forlornness of his situation impelled Dostoevsky to disclose at last, in lapidary form, some of those conclusions of his prison-camp meditations that we search for elsewhere in vain. Whatever the reason, there are several passages in which he seems to relax his reticence for the first time, and to offer that glimpse into his consciousness he has so far carefully avoided.

"I was guilty," he admits to Totleben after briefly outlining the facts of his arrest, trial, and conviction. "I recognize it fully. I was convicted of having had the intention (but only that) of acting against the government; I was condemned legally and justly; a long tribulation, torturing and cruel, sobered me up and changed my ideas in many ways. But then—then I was blind, believed in theories and utopias. . . ." And now, for the first time, Dostoevsky attributes his earlier belief in "theories and utopias" to the nervous illness from which he had suffered beginning in the spring of 1846, and which had continued up to the time of his arrest two years later. "Previously, I had been ill for two years running, with a strange, moral sickness. I was a hypochondriac. There were even times when I lost my reason. I was excessively irritable, impressionable to the point of sickness, and with the ability to deform the most ordinary facts and give them another aspect and dimension. But I felt that, even though this sickness exercised a strong and evil influence on my fate, it would have been a very pitiful and even humiliating justification. Yes, and I wasn't even very well aware of it at that time."[10]

Such words bring us to the origin of that connection between mental illness and ideological intoxication which Dostoevsky will so often dramatize in his later portraits of types drawn from the Russian intelligentsia. He had, of course, portrayed mental illness often before, and such deranged characters had even been considered to be his (rather unhealthy) specialty as a writer. But if his characters of the 1840s had broken down and become mentally ill, it was because they lacked the inner fortitude to sustain the struggle of asserting themselves against an overwhelmingly crushing social environment. Now, however, mental illness takes on a new significance and becomes associated—both as cause and as symptom—with specific ideological delusions that exercise "a strong and evil influence" on the destiny of those susceptible to their pernicious appeal.

As Dostoevsky's dossier tortuously wound its way through the Byzantine labyrinth of the Russian bureaucracy, matters went from bad to worse for the two lovers separated by the distance between Semipalatinsk and Kuznetsk. Dostoevsky's frantic and copious letters to his brother and to Wrangel keep us informed of the progress—or rather, what seems to be the impending dissolution—of this harried relationship. To Mikhail, Dostoevsky tries to justify his decision to marry—a decision that, as he is well aware, seemed madness in the eyes of his family, given the precariousness of his situation—and solicits his aid in reassuring Marya Dimitrievna that, if she were to become his wife, the family would give her a warm welcome. With Wrangel, Dostoevsky is much more frank about the difficulties and complexities of his sentimental imbroglio.

The specter of "a man of a certain age having a secure position" had vanished because, it would seem, this worthy gentleman had been invented only to test Dostoevsky's affections; fearing abandonment, Marya Dimitrievna had decided to probe her suitor's devotion. "Basing herself on something that had really happened," Dostoevsky explains, "she wrote to me: 'How should she reply if someone asked for her hand?' If I had answered with indifference, she would have had proof that I had really forgotten her. When I received that letter I wrote a desperate one, terrible, which tore her apart, and then another. She had been ill these last days; my letter really finished her off. But it seems that my despair was sweet to her, although she suffered for me." Dostoevsky excuses this unmistakably sadistic behavior on the part of his beloved because he attributes it to her wounded pride at feeling left in the lurch. "I understand her: her heart is noble and proud," he assures Wrangel.[11]

Despite this soothing explanation, Dostoevsky continues to be uneasy about the future and by no means tranquil about possible rivals. "I am jealous of every name she mentions in her letters," he admits. The plan had been for Marya Dimitrievna to move to Barnaul, the center of the mining district of the Altai region, where Dostoevsky hoped to be employed; but this project had now been called into question because "she is afraid to go to Barnaul, to be accepted there grudgingly and with disdain as a beggar." Instead, Marya Dimitrievna was waiting to hear whether her father wished her to return to Astrakhan; and she had suggested that Dostoevsky write to ask for her hand in marriage, but without revealing the debasing truth about his status and situation. "For me," he confesses to Wrangel, "all this is torment, hell."[12] Even more torment was in store for Dostoevsky than he yet knew, although he may have already suspected something that he stubbornly tried to put out of his mind.

Wrangel's visit to the magnanimous General Totleben, and Dostoevsky's skillful letter, at last succeeded in overcoming the first obstacle to his union. The powerful and influential hero agreed to intervene on Dostoevsky's behalf and to ask the Ministry of War either to promote him to ensign, or to release him to the Civil Service at the lowest rank. In either case, Dostoevsky would also be accorded the right to publish his literary work under the normal conditions of the law. It was this information that evoked Dostoevsky's ecstatic reply of May 23, 1856, to the first affirmative word he had so far been able to obtain from Petersburg. Nothing had yet been decided definitively; but, as Dostoevsky writes, "The affair, if I understand correctly, is on the right path."[13] He is, quite naturally, filled with overflowing gratitude for all those who were helping him to obtain his heart's desire, Wrangel first of all and second the all-important Totleben; he has similar words of praise and thanks for Adolphe Henselt.

Notable too is Dostoevsky's enthusiastic response to what he hears from Wrangel about the new monarch. A month earlier, he had affirmed, "You say that everyone loves the Tsar. . . . As for me, I adore him."[14] On receipt of the good news, Dostoevsky again picks up the refrain: "God grant happiness to the magnanimous sovereign! And so, it's all true, what everyone has said about the ardent love that all feel for him! How happy this makes me! *More faith, more unity, and if there is love as well—then everything can be done!*" (italics added).[15] This last sentence can almost be taken as a statement of the political ideal to which, from this time on, Dostoevsky was to dedicate his life—the ideal of rallying Russia to faith, unity, and love behind and in support of the rule of Alexander II. And while this ideal was certainly inspired by a personal sense of gratitude and devotion, Dostoevsky's words, given the dates of these letters (April and May 1856), unquestionably refer as well to much more portentous events. For in March 1856, speaking before the gentry of Moscow, Alexander II had made his famous declaration: "It is better to begin the abolition of serfdom from above, than wait until it begins to abolish itself from below."[16] Dostoevsky had become a revolutionary *only* to abolish serfdom and *only* after the seeming dissolution of all hope that it would be ended, to quote Pushkin, "by the hand of the Tsar." But now the glorious day had dawned of which Pushkin could only dream, and the Tsar whom Dostoevsky was to support so fervently for the rest of his life was the Tsar-Liberator who had finally decided to eradicate this intolerable moral blight from the Russian conscience.

6

Despite the national and personal good news Dostoevsky had received, his state of mind soon returned to its unalterable gloom; once the first effusions of joy had been uttered, there again appear ominous references to his ill-fated amorous entanglement. "My affairs are going terribly badly," he confides to Wrangel, "and I am almost in despair." Marya Dimitrievna had now flatly refused to go to Barnaul; even worse, although her letters contained "flashes of tenderness," they also suggested "that she could not make me happy, that we are both too unhappy, and that it would be better for us . . ." (at this point, two pages have been ripped from the manuscript of the letter by the vengeful hand of Dostoevsky's second wife). When the letter resumes, we learn that Dostoevsky had decided to go to Kuznetsk and investigate matters for himself. "I am ready to go to jail if only I can see *her*. My situation is critical. We must talk it over and decide everything at one stroke!"[17]

Once on the spot, Dostoevsky's suspicions of having been replaced were amply confirmed. "And so now I can hope with all my strength," he writes bitterly, referring to Wrangel's encouraging words, "but . . . it's too late. My good friend, I have been there, I have seen her. . . . What a noble, what an angelic soul! She cried, she kissed my hands, but she loves another."[18] The other was the young schoolmaster, Nikolay Vergunov, who had befriended the Isaevs on their arrival and whose relations with Marya Dimitrievna had become closer with the passage of time. No doubt Marya Dimitrievna, as Dostoevsky well understood, had begun to lose patience with the slow improvement of his prospects; perhaps she had lost faith in them entirely; and in her recent letters she had been trying gently to disengage herself from a relation that seemed to have little future. A young schoolmaster in hand, even with a pitiable income, was preferable to an even more penurious writer whose glowing anticipations of fame and fortune might never be realized. Dostoevsky himself refuses to utter one word of blame about what he might well have considered a betrayal; and there is no reason for a detached observer, more than a hundred years later, to pass a harsher judgment.

What occurred between the threesome, during Dostoevsky's two days in Kuznetsk, rivals the stormiest scenes of a three-decker novel and was transposed by Dostoevsky a few years later in the pages of his *The Insulted and Injured*. There, to be sure, he depicts himself (or his fictional hero, a young writer who is the author of *Poor Folk*) as retreating helplessly before the infatuation of his beloved for another; but in real life Dostoevsky played quite a different role. He was far from willing to abandon the field without a struggle, and his best weapon turned out to be his imagination as a novelist. For he sketched in, with all the resources of his art, the appalling problems that might arise in the future because of incompatibilities in age and character between Marya Dimitrievna and her young lover (he was only twenty-four). Dostoevsky became so agitated, even in recounting these events to Wrangel, that his handwriting is barely legible;

some passages are difficult to decipher, but the context makes his meaning clear enough.

"How can two such differing characters, with differing views of life, with differing needs, come together in life?" he told Marya Dimitrievna and now repeats for Wrangel. "And [gap in text] will he not later, in several years, when she is still [gap in text], will he not wish for her death? . . . Who knows to what lengths the conflict might go that I inevitably foresee in the future. . . ." Might he not also later reproach her with having calculated on his youth and taken over his life solely to satisfy her voluptuous demands?" "And she, she! pure and beautiful angel, perhaps would have to hear such things!" Naturally, all these agitated premonitions had not been put so bluntly in face-to-face conversation; Dostoevsky had been more subtle and indirect, only sketching his menacing visions as conjectures while maintaining that Vergunov could not possibly behave in such a fashion. "I didn't convince her of anything" he estimates, "but I spread some doubt; she wept and was tormented."[19]

At this point, a peripety occurred that reminds us of those sudden climactic moments in Dostoevsky's work when mutual hostility turns to love. "I felt pity for her, and then she completely came back to me—she felt pity for me! If you know what an angel she is, my friend! You never knew her; at every instant something original, sensible, clever but also paradoxical, infinitely good, truly noble (a knight in female clothing), she has the heart of a knight; she will be her own ruination. She doesn't know herself, but I know her!" Dostoevsky also met Vergunov, who broke down and wept in his presence. "I met him; he cried, but only knows how to cry," he remarks, with a touch of disdain.[20] At Marya Dimitrievna's suggestion, Dostoevsky wrote a letter to Vergunov summing up all the weighty reasons he had advanced against the approaching union of the pair.

It is difficult to repress a smile when Dostoevsky voices some indignation at finding himself in the same situation as Gil Blas (the literary comparison is his own), who loses his lucrative position with the Archbishop of Granada after telling the latter, at his own insistent demand, the awful truth about his sermons. Dostoevsky received the same reward for his candor: both the others turned on him with fury. Marya Dimitrievna, however, kept spinning like a weathervane and told Dostoevsky before his departure: " 'Don't cry, don't grieve, everything is not decided; you and I and nobody else!' These are her exact words," he assures Wrangel. "I don't know how I spent those two days. It was bliss and unbearable torture! At the end of the second day, I left *full of hope*."[21]

Meanwhile, Dostoevsky was continuing efforts to obtain admission for Pasha Isaev to the Corps of Cadets in Siberia, and he asks Wrangel to see if General Gasfort cannot be persuaded to use his influence to help the young petitioner find a place. In addition, he pleads with Wrangel for still another favor involving the Isaevs. "For God's sake, for the sake of heaven's radiance, don't refuse. *She* should not have to suffer. If she marries him, at least let them have some money." And so Dostoevsky urges Wrangel to speak about Vergunov to Gasfort "as a worthy young man with first-rate abilities; praise him to the skies, say that you know him; that it wouldn't be a bad thing to give him a higher post. . . . All this for *her*, for her *alone*. Just so she won't end in misery, that's all!"[22] Such efforts by Dostoevsky to help Vergunov increase his income, and thus indirectly to aid Marya Dimitrievna—efforts later embodied in the compassionate and selfless attitude of the narrator in *The Insulted and Injured* when faced with a similar situation—have been interpreted by Freud as a symptom of repressed homosexuality. But it is permissible to take a less jaundiced view, and to believe that Dostoevsky, who had such an acute personal and literary sense of the aching miseries of genteel poverty, was genuinely moved by the possible future plight of the woman he loved with passion and toward whom he felt an immense debt of gratitude. "She came at the saddest moment of my life," he told Wrangel a few months later, "and she resuscitated my soul."[23]

7

Marya Dimitrievna continued to oscillate during the summer months of 1856, and Dostoevsky continued both to hope and to despair. He wrote one letter to Wrangel in July asking him to help expedite a request for financial aid to which, as a Civil Service widow, Marya Dimitrievna was legally entitled, and also renewed his request to see if something could be done for Vergunov. In early fall, Dostoevsky's promotion was at last officially confirmed, and he became a commissioned officer with a respectable social status and a regular income. His first and only thought on receiving the news was that it would again enable him to visit Marya Dimitrievna. Dostoevsky, now completely obsessed by his all-consuming passion, admitted to Wrangel: "I love her to the point of madness."

His state of mind was indeed lamentable, and he makes no attempt to conceal the ravages of what, as he perfectly well knew, was a pathological fixation. "Don't shake your head, don't condemn me; I know that in many ways I am behaving irrationally in my relations with her, that there is almost no hope for me—but whether there is or is not hope is all the same. I can't think of anything else! Only to see her, to hear her! I am a poor madman. A love of this kind is an illness. I feel it." Marya Dimitrievna, he confides, continues to write letters "full of a sincere, of an extreme devotedness"; even though she often pointedly calls Dostoevsky "brother," he persists in believing that she loves him.[24] Clearly, he was hoping against hope that another visit would have the same rekindling effect as his first.

Consumed with guilt at squandering the money he had begged for so urgently from his brother, he asks Wrangel not to tell Mikhail about his proposed project for a new trip to win over, if possible, his reluctant inamorata.

At the same time, Dostoevsky urges Wrangel to inquire whether it would be possible for him, now that he is an officer, to seek retirement from the Army for reasons of health. This is the first reference in Dostoevsky's correspondence, aside from a casual remark made earlier, to what had become an increasingly worried concern with his physical and mental condition. "If I wish to return to Russia," he says, "it would be solely to embrace those I love, and to see qualified doctors so as to know what my illness is (epilepsy), what these attacks are which always keep recurring, and which each time weaken my memory and all my faculties and which, I fear, may one day lead me to madness. What kind of an officer am I?"[25] Moreover, Dostoevsky had received no word yet as to whether he was permitted to publish, and he appeals to Wrangel for further clarification on this crucial point. Actually, such permission had not been specifically granted with Dostoevsky's promotion; it had been made contingent on his good behavior in the future. A remark in the same letter is prompted by Wrangel's having been recently (July 1856) appointed to take part in a round-the-world expedition organized by the Russian Navy. The important novelist I. A. Goncharov had been named as secretary to the admiral in charge of the squadron to keep the logbook of the journey (he later wrote his own unenthusiastic account of the trip in *The Frigate Pallas*). "Have you met Goncharov?" Dostoevsky asks his friend. "How do you like him? He is a gentleman of the type 'United Society' [a charitable organization], where he is a member, with the soul of a bureaucrat, without an idea, and with eyes like a boiled fish, on whom God, as if for a joke, bestowed a brilliant talent."[26]

A letter to Mikhail, also dated November 9, contains further details about Dostoevsky's literary occupations and a graphic description of the debilitating effect of his attacks. "Yes, my friend," he assures Mikhail, "I know that I will make a career and will be able to conquer an important place in literature. . . . I am tortured by the abundance of what I have to write. . . . I think I can speak about art in a rather remarkable fashion; the entire article is in my head and in the form of notes on paper, but my novel drew me. It's quite a long work. A comic novel that began humorously and became something with which I am satisfied." Dostoevsky wishes to publish finished episodes of this longer work immediately and asks Mikhail to inquire whether this is possible. But if he was optimistic about his literary future, he was deeply troubled about his health. "So far as the fits are concerned," he explains worriedly, "they continue. When I think them ended, they begin again. Each time they cause my courage to sink, and

I feel that because of them I lose my memory and my abilities. Dejection and some kind of morally humiliating condition—that is the result of my seizures."[27]

Dostoevsky, however, did not allow such symptoms to hinder him in the pursuit of Marya Dimitrievna. In December 1856, undertaking the long journey to Kuznetsk again, he finally succeeded in obtaining Marya Dimitrievna's consent. Even so, an air of uncertainty and mystery still continues to hang over this hard-won favorable decision. Dostoevsky tells Wrangel that, "*if a certain circumstance does not prevent it*," the marriage will surely take place, but he never explains what this "circumstance" might be. Still, he is now sure of Marya Dimitrievna's undivided affection. "*What I wrote about last summer* has had very little influence in her attachment for me. She loves me. I know that with certainty. . . . She very quickly lost all her illusions about her new attachment. I already knew that in the summer from her letters."[28]

8
———

All of Dostoevsky's energies were now turned to the task of raising the money necessary for the wedding, which involved a staggering sum for someone who, already up to his ears in debt, could count only on his small salary as an officer. Dostoevsky would have to finance not only another trip to Kuznetsk for himself, but also a return with his new wife and stepson in a closed carriage (it was mid-winter), the transport of their household goods, and the purchase of whatever was necessary to set up housekeeping in a respectable style. On top of all this were the expenses occasioned by his promotion, which required that he outfit himself from head to foot with equipment literally worth its weight in gold in remote Siberia. Luckily, a friendly and prosperous Captain of Engineers attached to one of the mining establishments had offered to advance him 600 rubles as a long-term loan, and one of his sisters had recently sent him 200 rubles as a gift. Since he had unpublished manuscripts worth, by his estimate, about 1,000 rubles, he was sure that once he received permission to publish his troubles would be over. "But if they forbid me to publish for still another year—I am lost." Dostoevsky accordingly renews his plea to Wrangel to communicate to him immediately "the slightest *news concerning permission to publish*." He was so desperate that he affirmed his willingness to publish, if necessary forever, without a signature or under a pseudonym.

The tone of Dostoevsky's references to Marya Dimitrievna now becomes much more matter-of-fact, and the name of Vergunov appears just once more. Dostoevsky unexpectedly says that he is "dearer than a brother," adding that "it would take too long" to explain to Wrangel the complicated story of their relations. It seems likely that Vergunov had accepted Marya

10. Dostoevsky in Uniform, 1858

Dimitrievna's unfavorable decision with equanimity and had behaved, from Dostoevsky's point of view, with some dignity and decency. In any case, he speaks of him to Wrangel as an individual fully worthy of their support: "It is no sin to intercede for Vergunov: *he deserves it.*"[29] Whether anything ever came of Dostoevsky's efforts to obtain promotion for Vergunov, who was about to take an examination for a higher grade, remains unknown.

Two months elapsed before Dostoevsky could complete preparations for the wedding, during which time he wrote a carefully worded letter to his wealthy uncle in Moscow asking for the amount of his loan as a gift. He then departed for a two-week stay at Kuznetsk; and on February 7, 1857, the ceremony was performed in the presence of various local worthies, including Vegunov, who makes his last appearance as a witness at the wedding of the woman he had once loved and the man who had thwarted his suit.*

The honeymoon couple then embarked on the exhausting trip back to Semipalatinsk, breaking the journey at Barnaul to accept the hospitality of Dostoevsky's old friend Count Peter Semenov, an erstwhile occasional visitor to the Petrashevsky circle. More recently, he had been engaged (in company with Chokan Valikhanov) in exploring the Tian-Shan mountain range lying between Russia and the Chinese Empire. What occurred during this stopover cast a pall on Dostoevsky's ill-starred marriage from the very beginning. "On the road home," Dostoevsky writes to Mikhail, "I stopped in Barnaul, at the home of one of my good friends. And then misfortune came my way: totally unexpectedly, I had an attack of epilepsy, which frightened my wife to death, and filled me with sadness and dejection."[30]

Marya Dimitrievna had never before been exposed to the unearthly shriek, the fainting fit, the convulsive movements of the face and limbs, the foaming at the mouth, the involuntary loss of urine that marked Dostoevsky's acute seizures; and she was terrified at discovering that she had unwittingly linked her fate to a husband ravaged by such an illness. Even worse, Dostoevsky now learned, for the first time, the true nature of his malady. "The doctor (well-informed and serious) told me, contrary to everything said previously by doctors, that I had *genuine epilepsy*, and that I could expect, in one of these seizures, to suffocate because of throat spasms

* For the sake of the record, it may be well to include here whatever further information (if it can be called that) about Vergunov exists in the Dostoevsky canon. It comes from the book written about Dostoevsky by his daughter Lyubov, who was eleven years old at his death and thus had no firsthand knowledge of this period of his life. Her book is important for having first disclosed the family tradition about the presumed murder of Dostoevsky's father by his peasants. Otherwise, it is so filled with errors, prejudices, and fantasies that no credence can be given to its assertions unless they receive some support from other sources.

Probably embroidering on what she heard from her mother (Dostoevsky's second wife, who ripped entire pages out of her husband's correspondence with Marya Dimitrievna), Lyubov Dostoevsky first reports what we know: Vergunov had been the lover of Marya Dimitrievna in Kuznetsk before her second marriage. But then she affirms that "even the night before her marriage Marya Dimitrievna had spent with her lover. . . ." Later, Vergunov is supposed to have followed the couple to Semipalatinsk, "and she continued to pay secret evening visits to her little tutor." Dostoevsky is said to have known the young man, "but the handsome youth was so perfectly insignificant that it never entered my father's head to suspect a rival in him." Dostoevsky's letters, of course, prove quite the opposite, and this factual refutation indicates why Lyubov Dostoevsky's book should not be taken as reliable documentation.

Nor can one believe either the further tale that Vergunov had followed the couple to Tver, where, after he finally broke off the liaision, "she confessed everything, describing her love affair with the young tutor in great detail. With a refinement of cruelty she told Dostoevsky how much it had amused them to laugh at the deceived husband, and declared that she had never loved him and had married him for mercenary motives." While it is quite possible that something of this kind may have been said in the course of one (or many) quarrels between the pair, the so-called fact of Vergunov's presence in Tver as lover in residence appears to be a pure invention. See Aimée Dostoevsky, *Fyodor Dostoevsky* (London, 1921), chap. 9.

Lyubov Dostoevsky, who died in Italy in 1926, was a minor and unsuccessful writer of novels and stories, a sickly, neurotic, unhappy woman who spent much of her life in sanatoriums taking cures, and she used her father's life largely as a canvas on which to embroider her own resentments and frustrations.

and would die from this cause. I myself entreated and admonished the doctor, by his reputation as an honest man, to be detailed and frank. In general, he advised me to be careful at the time of a new moon."

If there is reason to suspect that Marya Dimitrievna regretted her recent marriage vows, there is no ambiguity about Dostoevsky's own sentiments. "Now you understand, my friend," he admits to Mikhail, "what desperate thoughts roam through my head. But why talk about it? Maybe it's not true that I have genuine epilepsy. In marrying I completely trusted the doctors who told me they were only nervous seizures, which would pass with a change in the circumstances of my life. *If I had known as a fact that I had genuine epilepsy, I would not have married* [italics added]. For my peace of mind and in order to consult with *genuine* doctors and *take measures*, it is *necessary* to obtain my retirement as quickly as possible and return to Russia, but how can this be done?" Instead of the joyful sentiments of a radiant bridegroom, flushed with the triumph of his conquest after a long and arduous courtship, what Dostoevsky felt on his honeymoon was only sadness at the grim prospect looming ahead, and no doubt also a racking sense of guilt at his involuntary deception of his bride.

The picture that Dostoevsky gives of his first few weeks at home also sounds discouragingly bleak. Marya Dimitrievna had arrived back in Semipalatinsk quite ill herself; and though Dostoevsky had tried to arrange everything in advance, his lack of experience in household matters still left much to be desired and done. Unluckily, a review of the troops occurred at the same time, and "all this has completely worn me out." A remark about Marya Dimitrievna is consoling, but one already senses a certain reserve in Dostoevsky's observations about the unhappy effects left on her character by her difficult past. "She is a good and tender creature, somewhat quick, excitable, extremely impressionable; her past life has left painful traces in her soul. Her impressions change with incredible rapidity, but she never ceases to be noble and good. I love her very much, she loves me, *and for the moment* everything is going along in good order" (italics added).[31] Such words suggest that Dostoevsky had begun to obtain a new insight into just how precarious the emotional equilibrium of Marya Dimitrievna tended to be, and that he was bracing himself against those all too frequent moments when her mood slipped out of balance.

9
—

Once settled in Semipalatinsk, where the newlyweds rented a comfortable four-room apartment, Dostoevsky could at last devote himself seriously, in the time left over from military duties, to pursuing his literary career. But uncertainty continued to hang over his right to publish, and he writes to Wrangel, now back in Petersburg after his round-the-world trip: "Two things torment me, my health and the possibility of publishing."[32] Approximately a year after his marriage, in mid-January 1858, Dostoevsky applied officially for permission to retire from the Army on grounds of disability and in order to be able to consult competent doctors in St. Petersburg about his epilepsy.

Reliable information about the intimate life of the pair is very scarce, although it is obvious that they made every effort to appear in the world as a dignified, united, and contented couple. But we must agree with the judgment of A. S. Dolinin—the editor of the first serious edition of Dostoevsky's correspondence, and one of the greatest Russian connoisseurs of his biography—that "their unhappy family life is hidden in [a] secrecy" that cannot be pierced for lack of evidence.[33] All the same, a close study of Dostoevsky's letters in the two-year period immediately following his marriage reveals traces of discouragement and pessimism which, even if they may be attributed to the uncertainties of his position, form a sharp contrast to the courage and steadfastness he had displayed on earlier occasions and under much harsher circumstances. Such utterances suggest a growing awareness that the union he had pursued with so much passion and persistence had been a grievous mistake.

A month after his marriage, and just as he and Marya Dimitrievna were installing themselves in their new home, Dostoevsky could still write to his brother in the tone of hopefulness that he had managed to retain throughout all his tribulations. "As for the future, I do not know why, I

11. The Dostoevskys' Home in Semipalatinsk

believe in it blindly," he says. "If only God will give me health. It's curious: I have drawn from bitter hardship and bitter experience I do not know what extraordinary vigor and self-confidence."³⁴ One does not hear such words again from Dostoevsky for a very long time; nor do his own comments about his married state indicate any sense of fulfillment or even of satisfaction. Since he knew that his family had looked on his match with disquiet, one might have expected him to refer to it in terms as glowing as possible; but his words create quite the opposite impression. "We are living in a so-so fashion," he writes to his oldest sister, Varvara, just a few weeks after the letter to Mikhail, "do not see many people, skimp on money (though it disappears terribly fast), and count on the future, which will turn out all right if God and the Monarch are willing."³⁵ If Dostoevsky had entertained any expectations that Marya Dimitrievna would be an efficient and economical housekeeper, these seem to have disappeared with the same upsetting rapidity as their scanty resources.

Nonetheless, Dostoevsky manfully acquitted himself of his new responsibilities, managed to place Pasha Isaev in the Siberian Cadet Corps, and wrote dutiful letters to his new father-in-law and his wife's sisters (whom of course he had never met). It may be more than a coincidence that in one such letter to an invisible sister-in-law, almost a year after his marriage, Dostoevsky expresses a world-weariness stemming from a profound sense of disappointment with his life. "Do you know," he remarks strangely, "I have a sort of presentiment, I think that I shall die quite soon. One almost always has such presentiments with a nervous temperament. But I assure you that, in this instance, it does not come from my nervous temperament, and it is quite calmly that I am certain of an imminent death. It seems to me that I have already lived through all that one is required to live through in this world, and that there is nothing to which I can aspire."³⁶ Such words unquestionably have something to do with the fears induced by his epilepsy; but they also express an inner lassitude whose most probable explanation is a desire to escape from the burdens of life in common with Marya Dimitrievna.

References to her disappear almost entirely from the correspondence as time goes on, except for brief remarks that allow us to infer a background of bickering and recrimination. Nor were matters helped by Marya Dimitrievna's resentful conviction that her husband's family regarded her with disapproval. "My wife greets you," Dostoevsky writes Mikhail nine months after the wedding. "She wrote to Varinka and Verochka [Dostoevsky's sisters], but neither replied. This is very bitter for her. She says that this means you are angry with her, and do not desire her in the family. I affirm the opposite, but in vain. . . . She is very unhappy."³⁷ After another year has gone by, Dostoevsky is even more laconic and despairing. "My life is hard and bitter," he confesses to Mikhail. "I shall not write you even a word about it. Perhaps we shall see each other soon."[38]

The most overt reference to Dostoevsky's negative sentiments about his marital misstep may be found in a letter to Wrangel, from whom he had no secrets regarding Marya Dimitrievna, and who, as he knew, had always looked on the older man's infatuation as an unfortunate mishap. Writing two years after his marriage, Dostoevsky says: "If you wish to know what is up with me, what can I tell you? *I have burdened myself with the cares of a family and I pull them along.* But I believe that my life is not yet finished and do not want to die" (italics added).

This image of Dostoevsky harnessed like a beast of burden to the cart of married life can hardly be mistaken in its import; neither can the telltale and spontaneous association between marriage and death, which helps to confirm the interpretation of the quotation in the letter to his sister-in-law. Part of the reason for Dostoevsky's sense of affliction is revealed in the conclusion of this same letter, where he explicitly speaks of Marya Dimitrievna. "She would very much like to see you," he assures Wrangel. And then he adds abruptly: "Always ailing."[39] Marya Dimitrievna was to die of tuberculosis five years later, and the growing ravages of her illness only increased the irritability and irascibility of a character that had so seduced Dostoevsky by its capacity for righteous indignation. And, in all fairness, we must recognize that she herself had good reason to harbor emotions of resentment and betrayal against her second husband, whose promised recapture of fame continued to remain maddeningly problematic, and whose epilepsy kept recurring with alarming frequency and with no hope of relief in sight.

PART IV

A Second Start

CHAPTER 16

A Russian Heart

Dostoevsky's letters during 1855-1856 are, for the most part, either a torrent of words poured out in anguish over the practical problems by which he was beset, or they are devoted to describing, justifying, and furthering his love affair with Marya Dimitrievna. But even amidst this all-absorbing pursuit of what he believed would be happiness, Dostoevsky occasionally turns to other matters and furnishes valuable information about his ideological and spiritual evolution.

There is, in particular, a lengthy letter to Apollon Maikov (January 18, 1856) in which Dostoevsky reveals himself more fully than in any other document of the period. Wrangel had delivered a letter from Maikov on arriving in Semipalatinsk, and this renewal of Dostoevsky's contact with a literary confidant allowed him to feel once again that he was still part of Russian culture. The turbulence of his personal life, however, combined with the difficulties of communication, caused him to delay an answer for over a year. Wrangel's return journey to Petersburg gave him the chance he was seeking; and he now confided himself to paper with more frankness than would have been possible with a less trusted courier. Moreover, Dostoevsky knew that he could rely on the discretion of Maikov, who had scrupulously kept his word not to divulge the existence of his friend's membership in the Speshnev secret society.

Even though Maikov's letter to Dostoevsky has unfortunately been lost, we can catch glimpses of what he said through Dostoevsky's reply; and a further context is provided by Maikov's own social-political evolution in the intervening years. The outbreak of the Crimean War had marked an important date in Maikov's life, which, up to that time, had been that of a progressive Westerner known to be more involved with poetry than politics. The attack on Russia, however, had stirred all his latent patriotic ardor, and he had publicly hailed the conflict as a turning point in Russia's historical destiny. Indeed, Maikov's open letter to the novelist A. F. Pisemsky, published in the St. Petersburg Gazette in 1854 as a cultural-political manifesto, is one of the most important documents recording the upsurge of chauvinistic nationalism (evanescent in most cases, but not his own) that swept over much of literate Russian society at the outbreak of hostilities.

"The present war," he wrote, "is an event in our private lives, in the history of our opinions, just as decisive and as important as in the realm of politics. One must be blind and stubborn, as immovable as a phlegmatic snail, not to respond to that electric spark which has shaken all classes of Russian society. . . . I am ready to prophesy that present events are an enormous step in our development: with them begins a new period in our historical life, if only because they have forced us one and all suddenly to pause and ask, 'Who am I?' And whatever one's education, from whatever source people drew their knowledge and opinions, all with one voice and in one moment had to decide the question, and unitedly, with conscience as their judge, to reply: 'I—am a Russian!' . . . Nothing could suppress in our consciousness that it is perfectly possible to be a learned and educated man and to feel, at the same time, that we are Russian, and that for us, superior to all else, is the single, sacred feeling of love for the fatherland. . . . On us, as writers, lies a great responsibility—to immortalize what we feel along with everyone else. It is our job to illuminate and palpably to delineate that ideal of Russia which is perceptible to everybody."[1]

It is very probable that Dostoevsky had read this declaration of patriotic allegiance in the pages of the newspaper. It is certain—since he declares himself in agreement with its ideas—that he had read Maikov's poem, "The Council of Clermont," written under the inspiration of the mood expressed in the open letter. The poem's title refers to the council convened at Clermont (France) by Pope Urban II in the eleventh century to preach the First Crusade for the rescue of the Holy Land from the Saracen yoke. In a series of striking scenes, Maikov contrasts the behavior of Europe at that distant time, when it sprang to the defense of Christians oppressed by the Mohammedan infidels, with its present conduct in the Crimean War. His general theme—the betrayal of Christ by the European nations allied with Turkey—is the same as that of Dostoevsky's ode "On the Events in Europe in 1854"; but Maikov is a genuine poet, and his verses are much more evocative and pictorial than Dostoevsky's declamatory tirades. Moreover, Maikov depicts Russia as having in the past carried on its own crusade, and as having contributed to the defense of Christian Europe by serving as a buffer against a Mongol invasion of the European heartland. The present ingratitude and treachery of the reigning European powers he attributes to a fear of Russia's growing might:

> On an immeasurable expanse
> We have smoothed the foundation: before it
> Pale the ancient empires,
> And the new force and new glory
> Of the young sun frightens them!

The poem ends with the prediction that out of "icy Russia" will come "a race of giants" with "an unsatisfied thirst for immortality, glory, and goodness"—a race prefigured by that formidable giant Peter the Great, who had also once been nurtured on Russian soil.[2] These texts of Maikov provide part of the background against which Dostoevsky's rather elliptical letter takes on its full significance.

2

Dostoevsky begins by evoking the common life that he and Maikov had shared and his past intimacy with the hospitable and talented Maikov family. Valerian, Apollon's younger brother, had been the center of a small literary circle in the mid-1840s that had played an important role in Dostoevsky's life. Just before his untimely death in 1847, the younger Maikov had defended *The Double* against Belinsky in an extremely perceptive article containing some of the best criticism written about Dostoevsky's early work.[3] At the time of his arrest, a manuscript copy of Valerian Maikov's essays was found among Dostoevsky's papers, and he later asked the authorities to return it to the family. "Has Evgeniya Petrovna [Maikov's mother] received a book—the essays and criticisms that the unforgettable Valerian Nikolaevich published in *Notes of the Fatherland*?" he inquires anxiously.[4] This recollection of the past inevitably leads to thoughts of the great gulf lying between those halcyon days and the present—thoughts that Maikov himself had evidently also expressed. And Dostoevsky replies by striking the note that will resound as a leitmotif throughout the rest of his text: "You say that much time has passed, that many things have changed. Yes! of course. But there is one good thing, *we have not changed as men*. I can answer for myself" (italics added).[5]

It seems clear that Maikov's letter had alluded to the circumstances of Dostoevsky's arrest and conviction, and wondered why he had been singled out for such a harsh blow from the hand of destiny. "You say that you have often thought of me with warmth and asked: why! why! I too remember you warmly, and to your question: why—I will say nothing—it would be superfluous."[6] Of all Dostoevsky's friends who had escaped arrest, only Maikov really knew the answer to the question "why?"; this is the meaning of Dostoevsky's seemingly innocent reference to superfluity. And then, echoing Maikov's statement that he had lived through a good deal, Dostoevsky responds: "I too have thought and lived through a good deal, and there were such circumstances, such influences, that it was necessary to live through, rethink, and digest too much, even more than I could support. Knowing me very well, you will surely do me the justice of believing that I have always followed what I thought was the best and most straightforward path, that I did not play tricks with my heart and that, whatever I gave myself to, I gave myself to with passion. Do not think that these words allude to the reason I am here. I speak now of what followed; this is not the moment to speak of what preceded, *and in any case this was no more than an accident. Ideas change, the heart remains the same*" (italics added).[7] Once again we have the assertion that, however things may appear on the surface, Dostoevsky has not really changed any more than Maikov; both have remained the same men on the level of "the heart," whatever alterations may have taken place in the "ideas" they profess. This serves as a prelude to the important profession of faith that Dostoevsky makes, and which discloses how he had now come to regard his past.

"I have read your letter," he continues, "and have not understood the essential. I mean about patriotism, the Russian idea, the feeling of duty, national honor, everything about which you speak with such enthusiasm. But, my friend! is it possible that you have ever been otherwise? I have always shared exactly these same sentiments and convictions. Russia, duty, honor? Yes! I have always been essentially Russian—I tell you this frankly. What is really new in this movement that you have seen come to birth and of which you speak as a new tendency? I confess that I have not understood you. I have read your verses and find them beautiful; I entirely share your patriotic sentiment about the *moral* liberation of the Slavs. This is the role of Russia, of the noble, great Russia, our holy mother. How beautiful is the end, the final lines of your "Council of Clermont"! Where did you find such a language to express so magnificently such an immense idea? Yes! I agree with you that Europe and her mission will be realized by Russia. This has been clear to me for a long time."[8] Whether the "letter" that Dostoevsky refers to is Maikov's personal communication or the "Open Letter to Pisemsky," there can be no doubt that the "mission" to which Dostoevsky refers is the final accomplishment of the aim of the Christian Crusades—the reconquest of the Holy Land from the unbeliever and the end of Moslem domination over the Orthodox Slavs of Eastern Europe.

A later passage, referring more explicitly to Dostoevsky's past, interprets it in the light of his rooted conviction that nothing had really changed basically, either in himself or in others. "Perhaps, a little while ago, you were still troubled by the influx of French ideas into that class of society which thinks, feels, and studies. True, it was exceptional. But every exception, by its very nature, provokes its contrary. But you will agree yourself that all right-thinking people, that is, those who gave the tone to everything, regarded French ideas from a scientific point of view—no more, and remained Russian even while devoting themselves to the exceptional. In what do you see anything new?"[9] By "French ideas," of course, Dostoevsky was referring to the radical and Utopian Socialist currents of the 1840s, which he denies had had the power to change the Russian character. Even those under their spell still "had remained Russian even while devoting themselves to the exceptional." As in the letter to Totleben, we can note how Dostoevsky's self-interpretation feeds into and anticipates his later creations: time and again he will show in his major characters the persistence of something he considers "Russian," even in those who are most powerfully and corrosively affected by Western European ideas. For Dostoevsky was passionately persuaded (and he accepted his own experience as irrefutable evidence of its truth) that the instinctive sentiments and loyalties of Russians would always break through in some way, no matter how impenetrable might seem to be the overlay of Western European culture in the makeup of their personalities.

As Dostoevsky continues, he further elucidates his rediscovery of himself as a Russian; and now he connects it importantly with the inner transformation of his own attitude in the prison camp. "I assure you," Dostoevsky affirms in a passage already cited in part, "that I, for example, am united to everything Russian to such an extent that even the convicts did not frighten me—they were the Russian people, my brothers in misfortune, and I had the happiness to find generosity more than once even in the heart of a bandit just because, precisely, I could understand him, for I was myself a Russian. Misfortune has led me to understand many things from a practical point of view, and perhaps this practicality has had much influence on me, but I learned one thing practically, that I had always been a Russian at heart. *One may be mistaken in ideas, but it is impossible to be mistaken with one's heart*, and, because of error, to be dishonest, i.e., to act against one's convictions" (italics added).[10]

To be a Russian, then, means to be united with other Russians by a bond that creates and evokes a sense of mutual moral responsiveness; and this bond, stemming from the heart, goes deeper and is much more primary than all the false and mistaken ideas that may distort Russian vision or blunt Russian moral sensitivity. Many Dostoevsky characters, in a few years, will be caught precisely in such an inner struggle between their Russian heart and the evil, corrupting, and amoral power of non-Russian ideas. In other words, as Dostoevsky explores and contemplates his past for the benefit of Maikov, what emerges are the first faint outlines of the rational/irrational dichotomy so characteristic of his post-Siberian creations. And this dichotomy has already begun to take on many of the specific moral, psychological, and ideological connotations to which Dostoevsky will later give such brilliant expression.

3
—————

Dostoevsky's letter to Maikov is thus extremely precious as a source for the analysis of his own personal and artistic evolution. But how are we to evaluate his assertions as statements both about himself and about Russian culture? How much credence can be given to his self-interpretation—his conviction that, in espousing the views he shares with Maikov, nothing in him had really been changed? Should we see this merely as an effort to conceal—a refusal to admit—the betrayal of his old ideals? And how much truth is there in his belief that the Russian intelligentsia as a whole had been only superficially affected by "French ideas"?

So far as Dostoevsky himself is personally concerned, there is a good deal to be said for taking him at his word. A strong streak of xenophobia is manifest in his attitudes from a very early period, and it by no means disappeared at the height of his radical phase. Even while rejecting, in a feuilleton of 1847, the Slavophil idealization of the Russian past, Dostoevsky pours scorn on those Europeans who find it impossible to imagine that Russia could develop along indigenous historical lines and follow a path quite different from the model of Western European nations. And he declares that the absorption of Western European civilization by Russia, rather than destroying Russian nationality, would lead "to the triumph of nationality, which, in my opinion, will not succumb so easily to European influence as many believe" (18: 26). Dostoevsky's heart, as we see, had always been Russian, and had always lived in uneasy tension with the subversive impulses (inspired primarily by hatred of serfdom) that had led him into the ranks of a revolutionary conspiracy. In this sense he might well consider—without necessarily being guilty of a shameful evasion—that his previous crime against the state had merely been an "accident."

With regard to the Russian Westerners, whom Dostoevsky naturally tended to interpret by analogy with himself, the situation is much more complex. One has the impression that Dostoevsky believed them all, or at least a sizable majority, to have come round to accepting the position he now shared with Maikov; in other words, that they too had rallied behind the Tsarist régime in its struggle. This would seem to be the sense of his remark that even those most given to French ideas had still remained Russian at heart. And if this is what he *did* mean, then he was woefully mistaken. For not only the Westerners, but the patriotic Slavophils as well, had been appalled by the corruption, disorder, and incompetence revealed by the régime of Nicholas I during the Crimean War. The majority of the intelligentsia, of whatever political stripe, shared the feelings expressed in the diary of A. I. Koshelev, a relatively liberal Slavophil, who wrote that Russian defeats in the Crimean War "did not distress us [i.e., even the intensely nationalist Slavophils] too much because we were convinced that even the defeat of Russia would be more bearable and more useful than the condition in which it had found itself in recent years. The mood of society and even of the people, if in part unconscious, was of the same nature."[11] Removed as he was from the centers of Russian social-cultural life, and living in a predominantly military milieu unaccustomed (and even hostile to) any independent thinking, Dostoevsky was evidently unaware of such subversive stirrings.

And yet it would be historically inaccurate to say that there is *no* truth in Dostoevsky's words once we consider them outside of a narrowly political context. For if we look at Russian culture as a whole, rather than limiting our view to the problem of support for the régime, then we can see an evolution similar to Dostoevsky's own taking place among the Russian Westerners in the years covered precisely by his arrest and exile. The regeneration of Dostoevsky's convictions has usually been considered only as a purely private event in his personal biography, and a fairly eccentric one at that. In fact, however, it actually anticipates, and then converges with, a massive shift of Russian social-cultural attitudes occurring precisely at this time.

This shift had begun even earlier than Dostoevsky's arrest, and may be dated from a famous article of Belinsky's published in 1847 as a response to Valerian Maikov. For Belinsky, the hitherto immovable Westerner, had declared in this essay that "on this subject [nationality] I am rather inclined to side with the Slavophils rather than to remain on the side of the 'humanistic cosmopolitans.' "[12] Much of what Belinsky says in this article about Russia, and on the possible world-historical role of the Russian people in the future, later turns up in Dostoevsky's own journalism almost word for word; it was a text he knew by heart, and he certainly had it in mind when assuring Maikov that the influence of French ideas had been only a momentary deviation from the true Russian path. Belinsky's article marked the beginning of a trend away from strict Westernism that can also be observed in the Petrashevsky circle a year or two later. Petrashevsky began to speak of the *obshchina* as an embryonic form of the Fourierist phalanstery, while Dostoevsky, along with a few others, maintained that the social institutions of the Russian peasantry provided "more solid and moral foundations" for the solution of Russian social problems "than . . . all the dreams of Saint-Simon and his school."

Such ideas were part of a tendency that P. V. Annenkov noted as coming to the fore in the late 1840s, when "the 'Slavic' party [as he calls the Slavophils], despite all the objections and criticisms made against it, acquired more influence with every passing day and brought under its sway minds of the kind not especially submissive by nature, and did so by preaching about the unrecognized, improperly appreciated and shamelessly disparaged Russian nationality."[13] A rediscovery of "Russianness" in this broad sense had thus begun roughly about the time that Dostoevsky was snatched away from Russian literature; and it continued to flourish and expand in the years that followed. All historians of Russian culture agree that, during the 1850s, the most significant new development was the gradual assimilation of Slavophil ideas by educated opinion as a whole, and the amalgamation of such ideas into a new synthesis with those of the former Westerner party. Since the most important publications in which this synthesis had been worked out were all issued abroad, Dostoevsky could have had no knowledge of them in his Siberian banishment. But his own experiences, indisputably personal though they were, nonetheless coincided with this larger cultural mutation, and the opinions expressed in the letter to Maikov, while erroneous from a strictly political point of view, correctly intuited a more deep-seated and widespread change of sentiment.

4
———

To a great extent, this new synthesis of ideas was devised and propagated by Alexander Herzen, who now occupied for a time the dominating place in Russian culture formerly held by Belinsky in the 1840s. Herzen had gone to live in Europe in 1847; he had been stirred by the intoxicating hopes of the 1848 revolution, whose initial triumphs he had been able to observe in both Italy and France; and he had been horrified at the pitiless repression of the French working-class uprising during the notorious June Days of 1848, when it was crushed by the National Guard at the orders of the bourgeois government of the new French Republic. Herzen poured all his anguish, and his disgusted disillusionment with Western political ideals, into his deeply moving *From the Other Shore*—a work that still retains its force as a profound meditation on the historical destiny of modern Western civilization. His conclusion was that Western Europe would never be able to make the inevitable transition to the new Socialist millennium because the principles of private property, monarchical centralism (ultimately deriving from Roman Catholicism), and obedience to civic authority were too strongly ingrained in the European character to permit a decisive break with the centuries-old past of its tradition.

From the Other Shore is a piercing cry of despair, uttered by Herzen as he saw his old ideals as a Russian Westerner shot to pieces in the fusillades marking the end of 1848 uprisings all over the Continent. It gave no indication as yet of any possible alternative to the blind alley in which, he had become convinced, all of Western civilization was hopelessly entrapped. But, in a series of important utterances in the next few years (*The Russian People and Socialism, On the Development of Revolutionary Ideas in Russia*, and many others less well known), Herzen went from negation to affirmation; and what he now affirmed stood in the very sharpest contrast to what he had formerly believed. For he prophesied that backward Russia, precisely because it had remained outside the main current of European social-historical development, was the chosen instrument of history to lead the world into the new Socialist era. Taking up some of the ideas of the Slavophils and uniting them with those of the Westerners,

Herzen produced a grandiose amalgam that inflamed the Russian imagination and decisively affected the course of Russian social-cultural thought throughout the remainder of the century.

The essence of Herzen's position has been well summarized by the excellent Polish historian of Slavophilism, Andrzej Walicki. "From the Slavophils," he writes, "Herzen took over the view of the village commune as the embryonic stage of a new and higher form of society and the conviction that collectivism (which he called the 'socialist element' or even 'communism') was a national characteristic of the Russian people. . . . Like the Slavophils, Herzen stressed that the Russian people had not been affected by the legacy of Roman law and the individualistic view of property relations connected with it; like them he valued the self-government principle of the communes and the unaffected spontaneity of relations between its members, which were not governed by contracts or codified laws. Finally, like the Slavophils, Herzen believed that the Orthodox faith in Russia was 'more faithful to the teaching of the Gospels than Catholicism,' that religious isolation had fortunately enabled the Russian people to avoid the demoralization of Catholicism and to remain apart from the 'sick' civilization of Europe. Thanks to this isolation—that is, thanks to Orthodoxy—the common people in Russia had been able to preserve its commune . . . had not given way to the authorities, and had 'happily survived to see the emergence of Socialism in Europe.' "[14]

In words that strikingly anticipate those of Maikov and Dostoevsky several years later, Herzen had written in July 1851: "Never have I more clearly felt than in the last years to what extent I am a Russian."[15] And Herzen assigns to Russia the same Messianic mission of world leader as do Maikov and Dostoevsky, although he entertains an entirely different image of the society of the future. When there were rumors of the coming conflict between Russia and Turkey in 1849, for example, Herzen wrote to the Italian revolutionist Giuseppe Mazzini that Russia would probably succeed in taking Constantinople (he did not foresee the intervention of the Western powers), and that this conquest would be the signal for the future worldwide revolution. He imagined that the peasant-soldiers of Nicholas's Army, once victory had been gained, would refuse to return home to serfdom. Calling instead on the other Slavs freed from the Turks to join them, they would lead a general Slav uprising, with Russia at the head of a new Slavic democratic and social federation. "For Russia is the Slavic world organized, the Slavic state. To her belongs the hegemony."[16] Such words illustrate the usually unnoticed convergence between Dostoevsky's new convictions and the dominating trend of Russian culture at the time. For the late 1850s, as D. N. Ovsyaniko-Kulikovsky has remarked in his classic work on the history of the Russian intelligentsia, was a period when Slavophilism "attracted the entire sympathy of the most progressive elements of Russian society."[17]

Herzen went to live in London in 1852 and established there the first Free Russian Press in exile; in the next few years he began to issue his own writings, as well as to found a number of new publications. Among these was an almanac, issued at irregular intervals, called *The Polar Star* (the title of a similar almanac once edited by the Decembrist poet Ryleev), and, most important of all, his famous weekly *The Bell (Kolokol)*. Herzen's ideas, after a few years, began to receive the widest diffusion inside Russia, and *The Bell* was read everywhere (even, rumor had it, in the Imperial Palace itself), despite being banned from the country and available only in copies smuggled across the frontier. By the late 1850s and early 1860s, the basic tenets of Herzen's "Russian Socialism"—with its strong overtones of Messianic nationalism and its positive re-evaluation of peasant life and institutions—had become the general ideology of the Russian Left, even though all sorts of differences soon developed over how these tenets should be interpreted and, particularly, over how they should be applied to the existing Russian social-political situation.

Nonetheless, despite the increasingly vehement quarrels over immediate political issues, a common ideological substratum of idea-feelings about Russia's role in world history, and about the moral-social virtues of the Russian peasant, now had come to unite all factions of the intelligentsia.* And it was the percipient pen of Herzen, writing in 1861 about

---

* E. H. Carr has also noted this same convergence of radical Westerner and Slavophil doctrines in Russia in the aftermath of the revolutions of 1848. "About the time when Bakunin began to proclaim to the world the revolutionary destiny of the Russian people, Konstantin Aksakov, whom he had once met in Moscow, was elaborating a doctrine which, proceeding from the same premises and displaying many of the same features, reached a conclusion diametrically opposite. The Moscow Slavophils, of whom Aksakov was the most important, laid as much emphasis as Bakunin on the peculiar destiny of the Slav race. The communal system of landholding in the Russian countryside belonged to the epoch before Peter the Great had made Russia into a modern state; and this act of Peter, like Rousseau's 'civilization,' was the source of the degeneracy of the modern age. The mission of the Slavs was to combat the materialism of modern civilization, and to bring back Russia (and, through Russia, the world) to that state of primitive perfection which the Slavophils discovered in pre-Petrine Muscovy. The conclusions of Aksakov were reactionary, while those of Bakunin were revolutionary. But the conclusions of both were purely arbitrary, and the teaching of both was identical in its essential features: its romantic theory of the Russian peasant, and its belief in the peculiar world mission of the Slavs." E. H. Carr, *Michael Bakunin* (London, 1973), 180.

This underlying unity of Russian culture during the nineteenth century is usually neglected by historians because of the violence of the more superficial ideological clashes; but it provides the foundation for the great flowering of the arts that occurred at this time. A perceptive book on the 1860s by Abbott Gleason also comments on the same phenomenon. "Despite its intellectual origins in Romantic and counter-revolutionary values, Slavophilism counterposed the Russian people and the Russian state in a provocative fashion that had the profoundest consequences for Russian culture in general and social thought in particular. Since the 1840s, Slavophil ideas have affected all segments of the Russian political spectrum from the extreme Right to the extreme Left." Gleason also remarks that Slavophil ideas are very much alive in the thought of Solzhenitsyn; but he neglects to mention that they probably came through Dostoevsky. See Gleason, *Young Russia* (New York, 1980), 36, and the entire chap. 2 ("Slavophils and Populists").

For a brilliant and imaginative interpretation of the roots of such beliefs in Russian history, or rather in Russian myths about their own history, see Michael Cherniavsky, *Tsar and People* (New York, 1969), esp. chaps. 4-7.

the supposed opposition between the Slavophils and the Westerners, that best defined the unprecedented situation of Russian culture in the 1850s—a situation he had done so much himself to create. "Both they and we," he wrote, "had been from earliest years possessed by one powerful, unaccountable, physiological, passionate feeling, which they took from memory and we from prophecy—a feeling of boundless love, which embraced all of our being, for the Russian people, the Russian way of living, the Russian cast of mind. And like Janus or the two-headed eagle, they and we looked in different directions *while one heart throbbed within us*" (italics added).[18] In this sense, then, Dostoevsky was right in having maintained that a rediscovery of some innate core of "Russianness" had not been merely a revelation vouchsafed to him alone. It was, on the contrary, a much more sweeping phenomenon; and this is why Dostoevsky could later so easily, and so persuasively, transform his personal history into the paradigmatic conflict from which all his greatest work takes its departure—the conflict between Western "ideas" and the Russian "heart." For he had good reason to maintain that such a conflict was continuing to rage—even if, in most cases, unconsciously—in the breast of every educated Russian.

5

Dostoevsky's letter to Apollon Maikov thus provides us with a rewarding glimpse into that psychological-ideological matrix, still in its formative and plastic stage, out of which Dostoevsky's future works would one day emerge. It also contains, more immediately, the most extensive and reliable information we have concerning his literary plans and activities. "During hours when I have nothing to do," he writes, in the first specific reference to *House of the Dead*, "I note certain memories of my life in prison, what was the most curious there. However, there are only a very few personal things in it. If I finish it, and there would be a *very convenient* occasion, I will send you the manuscript as a souvenir of myself."[19]

Such words indicate that Dostoevsky had originally conceived the book as a purely private account of his prison years, written for himself and a few friends. Indeed, the censorship conditions of the time, although they had begun to relax somewhat after the death of Nicholas I, would have made the publication of any such work highly unlikely. Dostoevsky thus refers to his drafts as little more than an absorbing pastime, and, whether or not he nurtured the hope of their eventual appearance, he was clearly not thinking of any kind of "confession" or exploration of his inner life. The impersonality of his project is stressed from the very start, and all future references to it maintain the same focus.

Dostoevsky also confides to Maikov—and to Maikov alone—that he had thought out in his mind during his years in camp what he calls "my grand, definitive story," which unfortunately he had not been able to put down on paper. He had been afraid, he confesses, that as the years passed his passion for the work would grow cold; but he has happily remained just as enthusiastic about it as ever. "The character that I created and which is the foundation of the whole story required several years of development, and I was convinced I would have spoiled it all if I had undertaken it feverishly and without preparation." In veiled terms, Dostoevsky explains that he had not begun to write this "definitive story" on his release because of his love affair with Marya Dimitrievna ("a circumstance, an event, which took a long time to come in my life, and which at last arrived, distracted and absorbed me completely"). As a result, instead of this important work, he undertook something much more relaxing. "I jokingly began a comedy, and jokingly evoked such comic circumstances and so many comic figures, my hero pleased me so much, that I threw out the form of the comedy, even though it was successful, solely for the pleasure of following the adventures of my hero as long as possible and laughing at them myself. This hero somewhat resembles me. In short, I am writing a comic novel, but so far have only written individual adventures of which I have enough; now I am *sewing up* the whole."[20] Whether these words refer to *Uncle's Dream* or *The Village of Stepanchikovo* is not clear; the first seems more likely because of the evident traces in it of the earlier play form.

Even though remarking that "I have read scarcely anything this year," Dostoevsky still imparts some of his impressions of recent literature to Maikov. "It's Turgenev who pleases me the most—only it's too bad that with such *an enormous talent there is such a lack of self-control.*"[21] It is impossible to know which of Turgenev's works Dostoevsky had in mind; but *A Sportsman's Sketches* had been collected in a volume in 1852, plays and stories kept appearing up through 1856, and the first part of *Rudin* began to run in *The Contemporary* the very month Dostoevsky wrote his letter. Dostoevsky always retained his admiration for the work that Turgenev produced during the 1850s (particularly for *A Nest of Gentlefolk*, published in 1859). Nor is this surprising: critics agree that Turgenev, the most impenitent Westerner of all the major Russian writers, was temporarily, like everyone else, going through a strong Slavophil phase at this time.[22]

Dostoevsky also notes that a writer who only signed his work L.T. (of course Tolstoy, just making his literary debut) "pleases me very much," but he goes on to proffer the most monstrously wrong headed literary prediction on record: "In my opinion he will write very little (but perhaps I am mistaken)."[23] Mistaken he was indeed, although the manifestly autobiographical nature of Tolstoy's early work (*Childhood*, *Sevastopol Stories*) may have misled Dostoevsky into believing that the novice lacked the imaginative force to move beyond his own life once that subject had been exhausted. Dostoevsky continues to exhibit interest in Ostrovsky, whom he admits having read only in extracts; but these he evidently finds too external, too much concerned only with reproducing the local color of the Moscow merchant class. "He perhaps knows a certain class in Russia very well, but it seems to me he is not an artist. Moreover, it seems to me that he is *a poet without an ideal*. Correct me please, send me his best works, for God's sake, so that I can know him otherwise than through the critics."[24]

Some appreciative words in the letter are devoted to Pisemsky, whose reputation was then on the rise and whom Dostoevsky finds "clever, kind-hearted and even naive: he knows how to tell a story." But he thinks that Pisemsky writes too hastily; and what Dostoevsky says may well be taken as a melancholy reflection on many of his own efforts in the 1840s. "Ideas flow when one is young, but not every one of them should be caught on the wing and immediately uttered, one should not hurry to speak out. It is better to wait for a larger synthesis—to reflect more, and wait until many small fragments expressing an idea are gathered together into one larger whole, in one image that stands out strongly and in relief, and then express it. Colossal characters, created by colossal writers, often are created and worked over long and stubbornly." Dostoevsky compares Pisemsky to women writers in general, who, he believes, all suffer from a similar lack of patience, and as a result are never truly great artists, "even the unquestionably colossal artist George Sand. . . ."[25] Dostoevsky also remarks appreciatively on the poetry of the great philosophical lyricist F. I. Tyutchev, which had just recently (1854) been collected for the first time by Turgenev and published as a supplement to *The Contemporary*.

Dostoevsky himself was not rushing at this time to complete any of the creative projects on which he was engaged. Continuing his efforts to prove his loyalty to the throne, he wrote another poem, "On the Coronation and Conclusion of Peace," which he dispatched both through General Gasfort and to Wrangel. It contains little of personal interest and is mainly an invocation of the blessings of the All-Highest on the new Tsar and savior of Russia. He had also written, so far as one can judge, the "patriotic pamphlet" already mentioned, but had dropped the idea of attempting to publish it with the end of the Crimean War. Most of all he would have liked to work on a novel, for he was convinced, as he wrote to Wrangel a few months later, that only a novel "will make me a name and attract attention to myself"; but he was also persuaded that permission would not be given him to publish a work of fiction. "The novel up to now has been regarded as an amusement," he writes, anticipating the view of the authorities.[26] What he now pinned his hopes on, above all, was his *Letters on Art*, the work he intended to write (or had partially written) devoted to "the mission of Christianity in art."

Unfortunately, no trace of any such text has turned up among Dostoevsky's papers, although his literary journalism of the early 1860s unquestionably reflects the ideas he was pondering over at this time—that is, the relation of art to a transcendental or supernatural ideal. We know that he was very seriously occupied with the project and had asked Wrangel to consult both Mikhail and Maikov about a possible place of publication. "*The Contemporary* has always been hostile to me," he observes in this connection, "and so has *The Moscovite* [the Slavophil publication]. *The Russian Messenger* has published the introduction of Katkov to his study of Pushkin, and his ideas are quite the opposite of my own. Only *Notes of the Fatherland* remains, but what has become of *Notes of the Fatherland*?"[27] Katkov's article had expressed the position that "poetry in essence is the same as cognitive thinking, the same as knowledge, the same as philosophy,"[28] and we may assume that Dostoevsky rejected any such identification; the essence of art for him could in no way be assimilated to "cognitive thinking," since art expressed aspects of life inaccessible to rational thought and far beyond its grasp.

So far as *The Contemporary* was concerned, Dostoevsky's reference to it was inspired by a recent renewal of the old hostility toward him that it had shown in the late 1840s. For at the exact moment that he was wracking his brains over the best way to bring his name back into literary circulation, the task of reminding the cultural world of his existence was accomplished for him with no special effort on his part—but in a fashion that aroused his indignation rather than his gratitude. In the issue of *The Contemporary* dated December 1855, a sketch by I. I. Panaev (part of a series entitled "Notes of the New Poet on Petersburg Life") contains a section obviously alluding to the critical excitement caused by *Poor Folk* as a result of Belinsky's praise, and then, with the ensuing collapse of the author's momentary fame, his abandonment by all those who had previously trumpeted his glory. No names were mentioned (the young writer in question is merely called *kumirchik*, or the "little idol"), and it is quite possible that uninformed readers, out of touch with the ins and outs of Petersburg literary gossip, would not have caught the reference to Dostoevsky. But all the people who counted for him—all the former members of the Belinsky *pléiade* with whom he had once been friendly, and all his literary colleagues and rivals—would have been perfectly well aware at whom Panaev was poking fun.

The sketch, entitled "Literary Idols, Dilettantes, etc.," begins with Panaev gently mocking his own propensity to celebrate and glorify literary notorieties—a trait, he confesses, characteristic of him since earliest youth. This inclination has occasionally gotten him into trouble, since "my nature required authorities, Carlyle's heroes, adoration—and, in the absence of genuine heros, I bowed down to little idols created by people close to me whom I trusted and respected [i.e., Belinsky]. One such, created in this manner into an idol, we almost drove out of his mind by our incense and reverences before him." Panaev describes how he and his group carried this "little idol" through the streets on their shoulders, shouting to the public: "Here is our little genius who has just been born, and who with time will kill with his works all of past and present literature. Bow down! . . ." These words manifestly satirize the extravagant praise that was lavished by Belinsky on Dostoevsky's book and instantly parroted everywhere by his circle.

Panaev then goes on to tattle about how the "little idol"—presented at an elegant ball to a young and beautiful society belle "with luxuriant curls"—fainted dead away from an excess of emotion (the incident actually occurred to Dostoevsky). As a result, the "little idol" refused to return to the party out of embarrassment, going home instead to dream of a love scene between himself and the beauteous aristocratic damsel irresistibly attracted by his fame. But when he wakes to realize that it is all only a dream, he clutches his head and sobs in despair. The next moment, rushing off to the printer who is scheduled to include his great work in an anthology, he insists that it be separated from the other contributions by a golden border around each page and also by being placed as the final item in the book. Impressed by the fame of the "little idol," the printer agrees—giving his answer in verse and citing a stanza from a satirical poem written by Turgenev and Nekrasov in 1846 to ridicule Dostoevsky. Ever since that time, Panaev writes, "our little idol started to talk absolute nonsense and was quickly removed by us from his pedestal and completely forgotten. Poor fellow! We killed him, we made him ridiculous. It was not his fault. He could not maintain himself at the height on which we had placed him."[29]

Panaev's attack, aimed at a man who had spent four long years in prison camp for a political crime and was still serving out his sentence in the Russian Army, was a distinctly vicious and underhanded blow. How can we explain such unprovoked aggressiveness? Surely not simply as a residue of Dostoevsky's old quarrel with the Belinsky *pléiade* and with *The Contemporary*, now being run by Nekrasov and Panaev. No, the reason is that, in the narrow little world of St. Petersburg journalism, where editors and writers rubbed elbows every day with high officials of the bureaucracy, rumors about Dostoevsky's two poems—and particularly of the second, read by the widowed Empress herself—had filtered down and led to a revival of all the antipathy against him that had once been so widespread. Dostoevsky read this insulting little lampoon, and we can deduce his outrage from a remark in a letter of Aleksey Pleshcheev. "I told him [Nekrasov] frankly," he writes to Dostoevsky in April 1859, "that you had decided not to turn to him [i.e., his journal] except in case of extreme need because they treated you badly; Nekrasov, after hearing me out, said that if really in fact [?] *The Contemporary* spoke shamefully of you while you were in exile, then that was very disgusting; he admits it himself."[30]

7

Nekrasov's evasiveness in response to Pleshcheev's accusations, and the uneasiness evident in his words, could well have been caused by a work of his own that Dostoevsky never saw. This mysterious text, finally published in 1917, is obviously a satirical account of the story that Dostoevsky himself was to tell many years later in his *Diary of a Writer*—the story of how Nekrasov had brought the manuscript of *Poor Folk* to Belinsky, of how the great critic, at first skeptical, had hailed the work as a masterpiece, and of how Nekrasov had awakened Dostoevsky in the middle of the night to tell him the good news. All this is slightly transposed and presented as fiction—Belinsky is called Mertsalov, Dostoevsky is Glazhievsky, Nekrasov is Chudov, and *Poor Folk* is retitled *A Stony Heart*—but there can be no mistaking the originals. The fragment is evidently part of a larger whole, portraying, in a far from flattering light, the life and inner workings of the Belinsky *pléiade*. Only a section of the extant text is devoted to Dostoevsky, and its date of composition remains unknown; but a consensus of the best scholarship, assigning it to the same years as the Panaev *feuilleton*, suggests that the withering depiction of Dostoevsky it contains was a similar response to his efforts to achieve rehabilitation.*

The fragment begins with an affectionate portrait of Belinsky, who is painted as an inflammable personality always being swept away by gusts of uncritical enthusiasm and, although vainly struggling to control his excesses, reacting in all too typical fashion after reading the manuscript of *Poor Folk*. To be sure, Nekrasov had called the work to his attention and obviously appreciated its merits; but there is a clear implication that he believes the critic to have flown off the handle again when Mertsalov declares: " 'I tell you, Chudov . . . I would not exchange all of Russian literature for *A Stony Heart*.' "[31]

Much the best part of the fragment is the image of Dostoevsky that it offers—an image which, for all its elements of caricature, is more sensitive

---

* There has been considerable scholarly discussion as to whether this fragment, first printed as *A Stony Heart*, is or is not part of a larger, completed work entitled *How Great I Am!*, published independently in an extremely small edition. Eyewitness reports exist of such a work, but a copy has not been found up to the present time. For more information, including questions of dating, see the commentary in N. A. Nekrasov, *Polnoe Sobranie Sochinenii i Pisem*, ed. V. K. Evgeniyev-Maksimov, A. M. Kroliva, K. I. Chukovsky, 6 vols. (Moscow 1950), 6: 573-578.

than Panaev to the genuine tortures caused Dostoevsky by his mixture of excruciating shyness and inordinate vanity. Delighted at the news of his success, Dostoevsky agrees to meet Nekrasov the next day and visit Belinsky; but he fails to show up for the rendezvous. The impatient Nekrasov finds him at home still in bed, terrified to meet Belinsky. "The great man [as Dostoevsky is ironically called] was not yet dressed; his countenance bore the traces of lengthy hesitations, a conflict with himself, and weakness." From Dostoevsky's broken phrases, Nekrasov infers that he is afraid his personal appearance will somehow counteract the effect produced by his work; and there is a cruel comment, crossed out in the manuscript but still legible: "Chudov smiled involuntarily, understanding what was the trouble: . . . still, such a fear was perfectly justified."[32]

Exasperated by such indecision and quitting the apartment, Nekrasov is stopped in the street a moment later by Dostoevsky's manservant asking him to wait; and the two young writers proceed together to Belinsky's flat. The same comedy, so reminiscent of *The Double*, is repeated here: Dostoevsky has not the strength to ring the doorbell and retreats back down the staircase; but when Nekrasov remarks that Belinsky might be displeased, he returns in a flash and the two enter. The delineation of Dostoevsky as he sidles into Belinsky's chambers to receive the critic's accolade, even if exaggerated, testifies to Nekrasov's powers of portraiture, and to the mixture of sympathy and derision with which he regards his erstwhile friend.

Chudov [Nekrasov] only then understood all the irresolution of Glazhievsky [Dostoevsky] when he saw to what an astonishing degree the author of "A Stony Heart" quailed before the threatening eyes of the critic. At moments of intense timidity he had the habit of squeezing himself together, of retreating into himself to such an extent that ordinary shyness cannot convey the slightest idea of his condition. It could only be characterized by the very word he had invented himself, *stushevatsa*, to vanish, disappear, efface oneself, which now came into Chudov's head.* Glazhievsky's entire face suddenly became crestfallen, his eyes vanished under his brows, his head went into his shoulders; his voice, always muffled, lost all its clarity and freedom, sounding as if the man of genius had found himself in an empty cask inadequately supplied with air; and meanwhile his gestures, disconnected words, glances, and the continuous trembling of the lips, ex-

---

* Dostoevsky did not invent the word itself, but he did give it the nuance of meaning noted by Nekrasov. In the definitive dictionary of the Russian literary language, the first reference given for this word in the sense of "slipping away unobserved, to disappear" is a citation from Dostoevsky's *The Double. Slovar Sovremmenogo Russkogo Literaturnogo Yazhika*, 17 vols. (Moscow-Leningrad, 1950-1965), 14: 1116.

pressing suspicion and fear, had something so tragic about them that it was not possible to laugh.[33]

This picture unquestionably captures one aspect of Dostoevsky's character, and is the most vivid evocation we have of some of the impressions he created on others in the 1840s. It also, as K. I. Chukovsky has noted, anticipates some aspects of the underground man several years before Dostoevsky himself created this character. But it would be a mistake to imagine the real Dostoevsky any longer behaving in this fashion; the figure created by Nekrasov no longer existed at the time *A Stony Heart* was presumably written. For Dostoevsky had sloughed off completely his crippling insecurity and hypochondria in the prison camp. "If you believe there is still anything remaining in me of that nervousness, that apprehensiveness, that tendency to suspect that I had every conceivable illness, as in Petersburg," he tells Mikhail, "please change your mind, there is not a trace of that, as of many other things."[34] Dostoevsky had been steeled by suffering. And when, on returning from exile, he began to take up the polemical cudgels against *The Contemporary* a few years later, the once ridiculous and timorous "little idol" at whom it had been so easy to sneer proved to be a redoubtable antagonist.

CHAPTER 17

"Weak" and "Strong" Types

Eager as he was to make his re-entry into the literary life, Dostoevsky felt very acutely the disadvantages of his distance from the centers of Russian culture. Books and magazines reached remote Siberia only after long intervals and delays, and facilities such as a library were virtually unknown. He complains bitterly, in one of his letters to Mikhail, of the difficulties of keeping in touch with the literary-cultural scene and of grasping, in the distant confines of his exile, all the nuances of what was taking place at home. "You cannot possibly know, brother," he writes, "what it means to talk about (let's say) literary matters blindly, to write—and not to have even the most necessary books and journals at hand. I would have liked, under the title of 'Letters from the Province,' to begin a series of articles about contemporary literature. A good deal had accumulated within me on that score which was written down, and I know that I would have attracted attention. And what happened: for lack of material, i.e., the journals of the last ten years—I gave it up. And that's how everything goes to pieces for me, my literary ideas and my literary career."[1]

Any letter such as the one from Apollon Maikov, which afforded Dostoevsky a firsthand glimpse into the cultural ambience from which he had been so forcibly severed, was thus immensely valuable to him. And, in this respect, none of his correspondents during these years served him better than his old friend Aleksey Pleshcheev, the lively, engaging, and fervently idealistic young poet who had been among his closest intimates in the past. Both men had belonged to the same circles; both had stood side by side on the scaffold during the mock execution ceremony; and the moment before Dostoevsky (as he believed) was to be led to the stake of execution, Pleshcheev was one of the two people he had embraced in a last farewell.

Like all the Petrashevtsy, Pleshcheev too had been formally condemned to death; but this sentence was commuted by Nicholas I to service in the Russian Army as a private, and he was dispatched to the Orenburg garrison in the southern Urals. His first year or two had been difficult, but nothing compared with the hardships of those who, like Dostoevsky, had been sentenced to hard labor. His lot had also been considerably eased by the pleas and petitions of his mother, the widow of a major-general in the Russian Army. After taking part in an expedition against the Khirghizes

12. Aleksey Pleshcheev

in 1853 and distinguishing himself in combat, Pleshcheev was promoted to noncommissioned rank. Two years later, after the death of Nicholas, he received the commission of ensign and then, by special permission of Alexander II, was allowed to resign from the Army and take a post in the Civil Service.

Pleshcheev began his correspondence with Dostoevsky at the end of 1856, and, after a few months' delay—this was in the agitated period just before Dostoevsky's marriage—the latter replied very warmly. Naturally, he had many good reasons for doing so; and to these was now added the tempting prospect of publication. The ever-generous Pleshcheev, already in contact with editors and publishers, was eager to aid his old comrade, who had complained about his financial straits. "Send me everything that you write, dear friend," Pleshcheev urged him. "Be certain that it will be printed with joy. I vouch for it."[2] Also living in Orenburg at that time was M. L. Mikhailov, soon to be one of the leaders of radical agitation in the early 1860s. Mikhailov was, Pleshcheev happily informed his correspondent, in touch with all the journals and anxious to obtain manuscripts that would be paid for in hard cash.

All of Dostoevsky's letters to Pleshcheev have unfortunately been lost; what remains are only the latter's replies, which at first sight seem of

minor importance and have accordingly attracted little attention. But
Pleshcheev's letters contain a good deal of valuable material that easily
allows us to reconstruct some of Dostoevsky's views on the literary-cultural
scene of the late 1850s, and to catch the first crystallization of certain
attitudes soon destined to clash with influential left-wing trends. Much
more in sympathy with such trends, Pleshcheev serves as an excellent
foil for Dostoevsky because their long-standing intimacy allows him to
express disagreement with no inhibition. In order to understand the issues
at stake between them, however, it will first be necessary to outline the
background of Russian culture against which the two friends were carrying on their amicable disputes.

2

Literary criticism in Russia had always been used, to a certain extent, as
a way of circumventing the ban on the discussion of social-political matters.
And the first signs of a revival of liberal and progressive thought in the
late 1850s—the first signs of recovery from the arrests of the Petrashevtsy
and the severe censorship crackdown after 1848—accordingly appeared
in the form of articles on literary and aesthetic matters. Many of these
came from the pen of N. G. Chernyshevsky, who, as a student in St.
Petersburg in the late 1840s, had become converted to Socialism.* The
son of an Orthodox priest, he was first tutored at home by his father, a
member of the lower provincial clergy unusually open to the modern world
and whose library contained works by Herzen, Dickens, and George Sand.
Chernyshevsky was later placed in a theological seminary; and after grad-
uation, rather than continuing to study for the priesthood, he entered the
university as a pious, hard-working, and owlishly solemn student of Slavonic philology and literature. There he met people who brought him into
contact with the ideas current in the Petrashevsky circle, and he even

---

* Although very little known outside of Russia, N. G. Chernyshevsky is central for any
understanding of nineteenth-century Russian history and culture. Even more, his works are
one of the foundations on which official Soviet Russian culture rests at the present day, though
his ideas have long ceased to have much influence among the intellectually sophisticated and
artistic elite. There is, of course, a vast literature about him in Russia (he has become an
academic industry), but there is no need to clutter up this note with references. A useful, if
now somewhat dated, guide to the literature about him in Russian can be found in M. P.
Nikolaev, *N. G. Chernyshevsky, Seminarii* (Leningrad, 1959).

Luckily, there is a very good book on him in English: William F. Woehrlin, *Chernyshevskii,
The Man and the Journalist* (Cambridge, Mass., 1971). A superb overview of his career from
a social-political perspective can be found in Franco Venturi, *Roots of Revolution* (New York,
1966), chap. 5, and a highly competent, though for my taste too apologetic, treatment is
available in E. Lampert, *Sons Against Fathers* (Oxford, 1965), chap. 3. These should be
enough by way of introduction.

A comically grotesque portrait of Chernyshevsky, based on a wide knowledge of the sources
and with surprising accents of sympathy and tenderness, is given by Vladimir Nabokov, *The
Gift*, trans. Michael Scammell and the author (New York, 1963), chap. 4. Nabokov transforms
Chernyshevsky into a precursor of his immortal Professor Pnin.

became acquainted with two members of Dostoevsky's inner group of friends—P. N. Filippov, a member of the Speshnev secret society, and A. P. Milyukov. It was only a matter of chance, as he noted himself in his *Diary*, that he had not begun to frequent the Petrashevsky circle himself and had escaped the roundup.

After a short stint as a provincial schoolteacher in his native Saratov, Chernyshevsky returned to Petersburg in the early 1850s and began to write for various progressive periodicals. The provocative nature of his articles and reviews soon attracted attention; and his indefatigable pen, as well as his willingness to take on editorial responsibility, quickly made him indispensable to Nekrasov on *The Contemporary*. Very widely read and filled with crusading zeal, Chernyshevsky was primarily interested in politics, economics, and history rather than in literature or philosophy. If he concerned himself with these latter subjects at all, it was only because he could express his radical ideas through them, by an adroit use of Aesopian language, with a little more freedom.

Chernyshevsky's opinions about literature had been formed on the essays of Belinsky's last period, when the powerful critic had been stressing more and more the social function and responsibility of the artist. The young publicist thus discusses writing mainly in terms of social content, evaluating it in the light of his own preference for a literature continuing the Gogolian tradition (as interpreted by Belinsky) of denunciation and exposure of the evils of society. These articles unpleasantly ruffled the sensibilities of the gentry-literati grouped around *The Contemporary*, who did not appreciate either his unceremonious handling of their own works or his sarcastic and jeering tone, which struck them as a breach of good taste. This almost instantaneous objection to Chernyshevsky on grounds of "taste" pointed to a deep cleavage between himself and the others that would have momentous consequences for Russian culture.

The majority of the Russian literati—Nekrasov, Turgenev, Tolstoy, Panaev, Grigorovich, and Maikov, to mention only a few grouped around *The Contemporary*—were all scions of the landed gentry, or at least, like Belinsky and Dostoevsky, had been educated in its cultural traditions. But Chernyshevsky had been educated in a seminary; so had the young Nikolay Dobrolyubov, whom he soon recruited to aid him; so had a good many others who became well-known as writers, journalists, and publicists giving voice to the sentiments of a new generation. They were the first of the *raznochintsy*, the men without official rank or status, who play so dominant a role in Russian culture throughout the remainder of the century. It was they who set the tone that others would follow—a "tone" that instantly aroused the active displeasure of the representatives of the older generation of the 1840s whom they made it their first business to displace.

The differences that quickly began to surface between the two generations can be traced to the gulf created by their class backgrounds and the dissimilarities in their education. The gentry-literati looked down on "the seminarians," as they were called contemptuously, because of their coarseness and lack of breeding.* For their part, the seminarians abhorred (and had no wish to acquire) the easy, elegant manners, the cosmopolitan culture, the reverence for art as a source of wisdom—the last remaining traces of a youthful infatuation with Romantic Idealism—that distinguished the slightly older generation of the 1840s. For Chernyshevsky and Dobrolyubov, such reverence for art still smacked of religion. As the scions of clerical families, both had been intensely religious in their youth; but they had converted to atheism, with equal zeal, under the influence of Feuerbach and his Russian Left Hegelian followers such as Belinsky and, more specifically, Herzen. All the same, the stubborn streak of fanaticism in their makeup, and their supreme contempt for the amenities of culture as shameful frivolities, can plausibly be attributed to the heritage of their clerical ancestry.† In any case, they were—or wished to be—hardheaded materialists and positivists, whose entire energies were devoted to bringing about those radical social changes in which they saw the only hope for the future. The social-cultural influence of the earlier generation, in their view, was one of the major obstacles to a reshaping of the Russian personality along more virile and energetic lines; and such remolding was a necessary precondition for any further progress. A good dose of class antipathy thus envenomed with personal distaste the clashes of opinion that soon began to occur between the two groups. As Herzen once wrote after a jarring encounter with Chernyshevsky—and his words express an extremely prevalent reaction—"They, I mean our jaundiced men, might by their tone drive an angel to fighting and a saint to cursing."[3]

* The memoirs of the period are filled with anecdotes depicting the intimate aversion of the older generation for the younger. A sample from the memoirs of Mme Panaeva, reporting a dinner conversation, can stand for many such entries. "The old contributors [to *The Contemporary*]," she writes, "found that the society of Chernyshevsky and Dobrolyubov brought on a fearful boredom. 'They smack of the grave,' Turgenev found. 'Nothing interests them.' The man of letters [D. V. Grigorovich, known for his nasty tongue] affirmed that he could recognize a seminarian even in the bathhouse, when they were washing; the presence of a seminarian was perceptible by the smell of wood oil and soot, lamps begin to burn feebly because they [the seminarians] attract all the oxygen to themselves and it becomes difficult to breathe." See A. Ya. Panaeva, *Vospominaniya* (Moscow, 1956), 253. The seminarians replied to such private insults by the unutterable disdain they exhibited in public print for the behavior of characters representing the "superfluous men" of the gentry-liberal intelligentsia.
† Abbott Gleason is quite right when he applies to Chernyshevsky and Dobrolyubov the words used by Nicolas Berdyaev to characterize Russian Nihilism in general, even though the term "Nihilism" should properly be limited only to the radical ideology of the mid-1860s after the publication of Turgenev's *Fathers and Children*.
Nihilism, Berdyaev wrote, "grew up on the spiritual soil of Orthodoxy; it could appear only in a soul which was cast in an Orthodox mould. It was Orthodox asceticism turned inside out, and asceticism without Grace. At the base of Russian Nihilism, when grasped in its purity and depth, lies the Orthodox rejection of the world, its sense of the truth that 'the whole world lieth in wickedness,' the acknowledgement of the sinfulness of all riches and luxury, of all creative profusion in art and thought. . . . Nihilism considers as sinful luxury not only art, metaphysics and spiritual values but religion also." See Nicolas Berdyaev, *The Origins of Russian Communism* (Ann Arbor, 1960), 45; cited in Abbott Gleason, *Young Russia* (New York, 1980), 103.

What had been, at the beginning, only a low murmur of discontent turned into a cry of outrage when Chernyshevsky published his doctoral thesis, *The Aesthetic Relation of Art to Reality*, and then reviewed it himself (anonymously) in the pages of *The Contemporary*. Even earlier, Chernyshevsky's public defense of this work, in the amphitheater of the University of St. Petersburg, had taken on the character of a deliberate defiance of the authorities with distinct social-political overtones. For in rejecting the principles of German Idealist aesthetics, he was in effect attacking all attempts to delude mankind into living in a world of imaginary and fictitious pleasures and satisfactions when the real material needs of the vast majority still remained to be satisfied. His philosophical mentor had been Ludwig Feuerbach; and just as Feuerbach had analyzed and debunked God and religion, which he had declared merely supernatural wish-fulfillments of man's own highest attributes and capacities, so Chernyshevsky took on the same task in relation to what he considered the Idealist substitute religion of art. Naturally, no such argument could be made explicitly; but all of Chernyshevsky's readers knew what was involved when, as Marx had already done with Hegel for much the same reasons, he rejected the Idealist point of view and, as it were, brought art back to earth.

Idealist aestheticians (Hegel and F. T. Vischer) viewed art as a function of man's desire to improve the imperfections of nature in the name of the ideal. Chernyshevsky, taking the opposite view, flatly affirmed that "Beauty is Life" and that nature, far from being less perfect than art, was the sole source of true pleasure and infinitely superior to art in every respect. Indeed, art exists only because it is impossible for man always to satisfy his real needs; hence art is useful, but solely as a surrogate until the genuine article comes along. "The imagination builds castles in the air," Chernyshevsky writes sarcastically, "when the dreamer lacks not only a good house, but even a tolerable hut."[4] The function of art is thus to serve as a "Handbook for those who are beginning to study life; [its] purpose is to prepare the student for reading the original sources and later to serve as reference books from time to time."[5] By thus making art subordinate to life and its real demands, Chernyshevsky was obviously telling the artist that his chief task is to fulfill the social needs of the moment—whatever these needs may happen to be in the opinion of the critic. It is also clear that, if Chernyshevsky's ideas are accepted, art is left without any independent value or stature. "Here, surely," as René Wellek has observed, "aesthetics has reached its nadir; or rather it has been asked to commit suicide."[*6]

* Georg Lukács does his formidable best to provide Chernyshevsky's ideas about aesthetics with some intellectual panache; but even he is finally forced to argue that Chernyshevsky

The publication of Chernyshevsky's thesis blew up a storm in the Russian periodical press, and a torrent of criticism hailed down on the head of the audacious young iconoclast. Even the mild-mannered and temperate Turgenev was incensed, and his letters of the time show how disturbed he was at this heavy-handed assault on his artistic pieties (in one he even calls Chernyshevsky "a stinking cockroach" who merits being flayed with the strongest "Hebrew curse").[7] Writing to V. P. Botkin and Nekrasov, he is more restrained in tone: "So far as Chernyshevsky's book is concerned—here is my main objection to it: in his eyes art is, as he expresses it, only a surrogate of reality, life—and in essence is suitable only for immature people. . . . And this, in my view, is nonsense."[8] He also expresses his gratitude to A. A. Kraevsky, the editor of *Notes of the Fatherland*, for having printed a critical onslaught against the book. "Thank you for having manhandled the disgusting book of Chernyshevsky. I have not read anything for a long time that so upset me. *It is worse than an evil book; it is—an evil deed.*"[9]

Dostoevsky had certainly caught echoes of this raging controversy over Chernyshevsky's thesis, whose high point, reached in 1855-1856, set the terms within which the question of art would be debated in Russia throughout the 1860s.* It is likely that Dostoevsky's *Letters on Art*, even though conceived earlier, would have contributed to this polemic. For Dostoevsky would have been as much opposed to Chernyshevsky's ideas, if not more so, than Turgenev, Tolstoy, and all the others who had spoken up with indignation. He would surely have seen such ideas as the unfortunate consequence, the carrying to an extreme, of the position he had challenged long before in his arguments with Belinsky. Had he not accused the latter of wishing, so as to advance the case of social progress, to reduce art only to a depiction of "scandalous occurrences"? One can see how Dostoevsky's defense of the role of Christianity in art would also have met head-on the atheistic implications of Chernyshevsky's rejection of "imagination"; and this will indeed be an important thrust of the attack he will launch, in just a few years, on the Utilitarian aesthetics of the radicals.

4

It was against this background that Dostoevsky and Pleshcheev began their exchange of letters just as the latter was on the point of departing for his first visit home from exile. "I am going to the capital," he informs

---

was "untrue to himself" in giving art only the status of an inferior surrogate for science. "It is clear," he writes, obviously with reluctance, "that here the actual particularity and meaning of the existence of art disappears." Georg Lukács, *Beiträge zur Geschichte der Aesthetik* (Berlin, 1956), 157. See also, for a penetrating discussion of the social-cultural implications of Chernyshevsky's views, Rufus W. Mathewson, Jr., *The Positive Hero in Russian Literature* (Stanford, 1975), 63-83.

* A light-hearted allusion to Chernyshevsky's polemic in favor of nature over art is made

Dostoevsky, ". . . at last I will see Petersburg again—a place which, by the way, does not contain joyous memories for me." Of course he plans to renew his old contacts, but is very much on his guard. "I do not think that literary circles have changed," he tells Dostoevsky, ". . . the same old small beer, cheap conceit, the same intrigues. . . . Just as before, nasty things are being done."[10] Most of all, he is clearly apprehensive about how he will be received at the bureau of *The Contemporary*. "I will visit Nekrasov," he remarks. "But if even one of them [the circle of the journal] addresses me in a high-handed fashion—I will never set foot across his threshold again. Enough! The time is past when one bowed down to great men, who in fact turn out to be complete trash."[11]

Pleshcheev's first few letters, written before his trip, contain a number of disobliging remarks about Nekrasov; and these must certainly have pleased Dostoevsky, still smarting under the insulting *feuilleton* printed about him. Pleshcheev calls Nekrasov "a terrible jobber" so far as money is concerned, citing the example of a young writer in Orenburg who, having published some dramatic scenes in a recent issue of the journal, was hardly paid at all. Nevertheless, he refuses to share what is clearly Dostoevsky's negative appraisal of Nekrasov's poetry. "But still—I do not agree at all with what you say about Nekrasov's talent. . . . In it one finds love, and fellow feeling with everything that is downtrodden and suffers. . . . His latest works especially are penetrated with a much milder, conciliatory feeling."[12] Dostoevsky later came to admire Nekrasov's poetry himself, but at this time was probably put off by the excessive sentimentalism that he mocks, with specific reference to one of Nekrasov's best-known "humanitarian" poems, in the novella he was then writing (*The Village of Stepanchikovo*).

Once Pleshcheev arrived in Petersburg and met Nekrasov face to face, his attitude underwent a notable alteration; and Dostoevsky would have paid close attention to what he reported of his conversation with the powerful editor. On being told that, in view of the remarks printed about him, Dostoevsky would not give his work to *The Contemporary* except in case of utmost need, Nekrasov replied with the words already cited earlier.* But, Pleshcheev adds, "So far as your [Dostoevsky's] particular quarrel with him is concerned, when you were living here [in the 1840s], Nekrasov

in *Uncle's Dream*, though Dostoevsky in other contexts takes the issue very seriously. The decrepit Prince K. of the story, whose sprightly appearance is itself a triumph of craft over the dilapidations of age, tells another character that, having received a tempting catalogue of false beards, he had ordered one for his coachman before recalling that the sturdy peasant already had a flourishing beard of his own. "Of course we were puzzled what to do: to shave his off, or to send back the one they had sent us and let him wear his natural one? I thought and thought about it, and came to the conclusion that it was better for him to have the artificial one." To which his interlocutor jocularly replies: "Probably because art is better than nature, Uncle!" (2: 318; also 517).

* See pp. 237-238.

declared that the cause was our (that is, yours and his) general stubborn-
ness (his words)." It is clear that Nekrasov was being as conciliatory as
possible, and Pleshcheev hastens to reinforce this impression. "Now, I will
only add that he spoke of you with much sympathy; and in general—he
is a person, so it seems to me—really good, although at times his com-
portment may on the contrary repel people." Of I. I. Panaev, the author
of the hostile article on Dostoevsky, Pleshcheev writes consolingly: "Panaev is a hollow shell and nobody here thinks he is worth a penny, but he
knows this himself; and he does not pretend to be an authority. He at
least has the merit of being amusing with his anecdotes."

A sentence or two later, Pleshcheev remarks of Nekrasov that "after
Turgenev (who is sympathetic to the nth degree) and Chernyshevsky—I
prefer him [Nekrasov] to all the others." These "others," among whom
Chernyshevsky is thus not included, are dismissed scornfully and color-
fully as "Lilliputians imagining themselves to be Shakespeares."[13] He had
written earlier that "Turgenev speaks of you [Dostoevsky] with warm concern"; and this news would surely have been flattering to Dostoevsky,
who, before his falling-out with Turgenev in the 1840s, had powerfully
responded to the personal appeal of the latter's worldliness and charm.
Pleshcheev is lavish in his praise of Turgenev's personality, and observes
ironically that "all that clan of Prometheuses standing on pedestals, from
the decaying optimist Druzhinin to the embittered Nekrasov—are not good
enough to clean his boots. It is quite apt that one jester, not long ago,
called Turgenev—a cousin of Jesus Christ! In fact, there is something in
him inexpressibly attaching."[14] Dostoevsky had once voiced much the
same reaction.

Another person expressing a great interest in Dostoevsky, according to
Pleshcheev, was, somewhat surprisingly, the well-known critic and poet
Apollon Grigoryev. There is no evidence that Dostoevsky had been personally acquainted with Grigoryev in the 1840s, and the latter, as a matter
of fact, had been quite uncomplimentary about Dostoevsky's early stories
and the school of "sentimental Naturalism" formed by his followers and
imitators. All the same, Pleshcheev informs Dostoevsky that "there is still
another person inquiring after you with great sympathy, Apollon Grigoryev; he changes his opinions like his linen (by the way, it is doubtful
whether he often changes his linen); but he is an excellent person."[15]
Pleshcheev's comment about Grigoryev's intellectual waywardness anticipates a very important connection shortly to be established between the
two writers. For Grigoryev was destined to become the chief literary critic
of the two magazines published and edited by the Dostoevsky brothers,
and he and Feodor Dostoevsky were to find much in common in their
ideas and values.

Despite the evident amiability of the exchange between Dostoevsky and Pleshcheev, it is perfectly clear, with the benefit of hindsight, that the two no longer saw eye to eye on ideological matters. Not that Pleshcheev, who had suffered exile himself, would have regarded Dostoevsky's efforts to achieve rehabilitation with the authorities as involving any sort of apostasy. He had written a personal letter to Alexander II asking to be transferred from the military to a civilian post, and he strongly advises Dostoevsky to do the same in order to obtain retirement from the Army and permission to reside in St. Petersburg.

No, the ideological divergences between Dostoevsky and Pleshcheev did not involve anything as clear-cut as the question of how to behave vis-à-vis the authorities. Rather, it appears in their differing evaluations of various literary works then being published—works that provided the occasion for additional lines of fracture to appear between the old gentry-liberals of the 1840s and the new generation of *raznochintsy* of the 1860s. Nekrasov's poetry was much admired by Chernyshevsky and his followers, and Dostoevsky's criticism of it is already the indication of such a fissure; but, in this instance, personal motives may have weighed as heavily as artistic-ideological preferences. The two friends ranged themselves on opposite sides, however, in a much more important controversy, actually a new phase of Chernyshevsky's campaign, begun in his treatise on art, to undermine the prestige and spiritual authority of the gentry-liberal intelligentsia. In this case, he singled out an unpretentious little story of Turgenev's, *Asya*, and used it to launch a full-scale onslaught against the lack of strength of character displayed by the "superfluous man"—the cultivated, educated, Russian gentry-liberal, filled with Western humanitarian ideas and dreaming of beneficence for mankind as a whole, but who invariably went down in defeat before the immense stagnation, inertia, and backwardness of Russian life. Such a character, a favorite of Russian writers at least since Pushkin's *Evgeny Onegin*, had been reincarnated by Turgenev in the 1850s with *Rudin* as well as in numerous stories. The main figure of *Asya*, a Russian dilettante idling in Europe, is a minor offshoot of this line.

Told in the first person by such a "superfluous man," the story turns on his love affair with the heroine, whose name gives the work its title. She is traveling with her brother, another young, "superfluous" Russian enamored of European culture, and the narrator meets them in a picturesque little German town on the Rhine. Asya, as it happens, is really the half-sister of her "brother," the daughter of his father and a serf-mother; but she has been recognized and brought up as a member of the family. Her behavior is much freer and more spontaneous than that of a normal girl of her class, and also more erratic, since she is obviously troubled by her ambiguous social status. It is clear that she is in love with the narrator and confesses as much to her brother; persuaded that, because of Asya's birth, the narrator will never marry her, he reveals the situation to him and prepares to depart. At a secret rendezvous, the narrator is swept away momentarily by the purity and ardor of Asya's passion; but he retreats at the last moment, troubled by the difficulties of the situation. When he realizes that he is truly in love with Asya, it is too late; she and her brother have vanished, and he never finds them again.

Chernyshevsky's article, provocatively entitled "A Russian at a Rendezvous," is much more a political diatribe than a piece of literary criticism. He dwells on the hesitations and uncertainties of Turgenev's protagonist, the utter lack of resolution that Chernyshevsky sees as typical of a whole group of characters portrayed by the same author. Without using the specific term, Chernyshevsky makes clear that all these characters belong to the gentry-liberal intelligentsia; and he mercilessly pounds home the point that its members always behave in a similarly pusillanimous fashion when the time comes to take some decisive action. The moment they are faced with the challenge of putting their exalted ideas and feelings to the test of practice, they hesitate, stumble, and fall into confusion. All the same, Chernyshevsky writes, he and others like him, educated to believe that such people had been (and still were) the source of enlightenment in Russian society, have not yet abandoned all hope in them. But "more and more strongly are we gradually beginning to come round to thinking that this opinion about him [the social type of Turgenev's hero] is an empty dream; we sense that we shall not long remain under its influence; that there are people better than he is, namely, those whom he wrongs" (all the other, socially inferior classes of Russian society, especially the *raznochintsy*).[16]

This gauntlet flung in the face of the moral-spiritual hegemony of the gentry-liberal intelligentsia began a polemic that raged all through the 1860s, and to which most of the important representatives of Russian literature (Turgenev, Tolstoy,* Herzen, Chernyshevsky, Dostoevsky) made significant contributions. Turgenev's *On the Eve* and *Fathers and Children*, Herzen's *The Superfluous Men and the Bilious*, Chernyshevsky's *What Is To Be Done?*, Dostoevsky's *Notes from Underground*—all were products of this battle royal, whose opening round was signaled by Chernyshevsky's article. At the end of the decade, the debate was magisterially terminated by Dostoevsky's *The Devils*.

---

* Tolstoy's contribution is a little-known comedy, *Zarazhennoe Semeistvo* (*An Infected Family*), written, like Dostoevsky's *Notes from Underground*, as a satirical response to Chernyshevsky's novel *What Is To Be Done?* (1863). L. N. Tolstoy, *Sobranie Sochinenii*, 20 vols. (Moscow, 1960-1965), 11: 469-508. See also B. M. Eikhenbaum, *Lev Tolstoy*, 2 vols. (Leningrad, 1928-1931), 2: 211-222.

All these works, however, still remained to be written, and the only notable reply to Chernyshevsky at the time was offered by Turgenev's inseparable companion and *alter ego*, the critic P. V. Annenkov. In an article called 'The Weak Person as a Literary Type," Annenkov did not attempt to refute, or even to argue with, Chernyshevsky; rather, he analyzed the problem of why the weak person had become such an important figure in Russian literature. It was true, Annenkov agreed, that Turgenev's character was morally weak and indecisive; poor love-stricken Asya was far better off not to have compromised herself with such a lily-livered swain, incapable of responding to her with the same wholehearted passion that she had displayed herself. But, he continued, if Russian writers show such a preference for the weak person as a literary hero, it is because, as a glance at Russian history will show, the so-called solid (*tselny*) characters in Russia—those who act instinctively and spontaneously—always seem, in doing so, to give free rein to the worst and most egoistic aspects of human nature. The weak person in Russian culture, Annenkov argues, has been made so because he is burdened with the enlightened values of humanity and civilization and is morally torn by the problem of attempting to live up to them. Whatever we may say in criticism of him, "in the nature of this [weak] person there is one outstanding quality: he is capable of understanding himself and, when the occasion demands it, of recognizing the poverty of his moral substance."[17]

Nor is this the only virtue that Annenkov finds in the weak person; whatever his other failings, this type has also played a very important social role. "Was he not, among other things, an early and suspect partisan of many of the ideas of goodness which are now recognized as good unconditionally? Let us agree that he did not know how to manage circumstances, that his footsteps were not firm, and that he resembled a sedentary child never sent to school for exercise; but he was not entirely unequipped. Education endowed him with the capacity promptly to understand suffering in all its aspects, and to experience within himself the misfortune and unhappiness of others. Hence his role as the representative of the deprived, unjustly offended, and the downtrodden; this requires even more than the simple feeling of compassion, it requires a sharp-sighted and humane intuition." Therefore, Annenkov concludes, "We will only say that when we look around at the 'strong' characters of contemporary life, the need to return, for the refreshment of our thought and feeling, to the circle of the 'weak,' becomes a passionate and irresistible need."[18]

6
———

It may be assumed, though it cannot be proven, that Dostoevsky was familiar with this exchange, whose numerous echoes filled the pages of the literary journals of the time. All the more so, since it involved an issue in which he had a keen personal interest. Had not one of his own early short stories been entitled "A Weak [*Slaboe*] Heart"? And had he not, in *The Landlady*, portrayed the relation between "strong" and "weak" characters—even if in hackneyed Romantic terms—as of great significance for Russian culture? Dostoevsky's weak characters had not been the wealthy gentry-liberals whom Chernyshevsky excoriated; but they can be considered a plebeian variation of the same literary type, and their inner impotence illustrates the same dilemma. Indeed, it may well have been Annenkov's article that helped Dostoevsky better to understand some of the larger implications of his own earlier writings. For we find him, approximately a year later, stressing the importance of *The Double* in terms that indicate a new awareness of its social-cultural ramifications. One of his projects for raising money was to revise this novella for a planned republication. "Believe me, brother," he writes Mikhail, "corrected, furnished with a preface, it will be worth a new novel. They will finally see what *The Double* really is! . . . Why lose a remarkable idea, whose social value is considerable, *that I was the first to discover and of which I was the herald*" (italics added).[19] Evidently, Dostoevsky now viewed himself as having created a character-type (the weak and indecisive Golyadkin) whose importance as a symbolic figure in Russian culture had only recently begun to be fully appreciated. One suspects that the preface he mentions would have seen Golyadkin as a character prefiguring the terms of the Chernyshevsky-Annenkov debate, and would have argued that the issues it raised were not limited to the personality traits of the gentry-liberal intelligentsia.

Whatever the value of such a conjecture, there can be no doubt that Dostoevsky's sympathies in this controversy lay with the weak as against the strong. His preference becomes clear in a passage from one of Pleshcheev's letters referring to a disagreement between the two men over Turgenev's new novel, *On the Eve*. Probably in response to Chernyshevsky's criticism of *Asya*, Turgenev's hero is now a "strong" and "solid" character, a Bulgarian revolutionary named Insarov, who places in the shadow all the weak-willed Russians by whom he is surrounded and who succeeds in winning the Russian heroine, Elena, to share his dangerous but ennobling existence. Dostoevsky, however, did not find Insarov inspiring at all, and Pleshcheev's reaction to his remarks allows us to understand why.

"You make me very angry, my friend," he writes Dostoevsky, "by your response to Turgenev's novel. . . . According to that—no artist would dare delineate any type serving to represent a particular species of people, a certain class of society; all would be labels. —And why is life so easy for the Bulgarian—devoting himself to the great work of liberating his country?

I do not know if he finds life so easy—but I would wish to live such a life. An immediate nature, *solid* [*tselny*; italics in text], not subordinated to analysis and the process of reflection, not becoming entangled in various contradictions, may find it easier to live if you wish . . . but when such natures place their lives in jeopardy for the sake of a love for justice—why should they be less worthy of sympathy than Hamlet and the tribe of Hamlets? —And that practical, active natures—do not for the most part love art—that is a fact—continually being repeated in reality. —Turgenev took this fact and was right in so doing. —He did not at all intend to say— that these people *cannot* or *should not* love art. He only showed what is so in fact. Artistic natures for the most part—are not doers."[20]

Dostoevsky had evidently criticized Insarov as a character lacking inner complexity—as being a solid character, undisturbed by doubt and the self-scrutiny of the weak person, and therefore someone for whom life is simple and untroubled. And since one of Insarov's unsuccessful rivals in love is a young Russian sculptor, the unflattering contrast he offers to Insarov— the weighting of the values of the book so that the life of art is shown to be inferior to that of revolutionary action—explains the objection to which Pleshcheev retorts. Dostoevsky may well have seen this treatment of art as too much of a concession to the views that Chernyshevsky had expressed in his thesis, and been upset by this seeming defection of an artist whose talent he admired to the opposing, antiartistic camp (he of course could know nothing of Turgenev's real opinions as expressed in his abusive letters).

Another illustration of the same preference for weak characters may be seen in Dostoevsky's response to Pisemsky's *A Thousand Souls*, which was the literary sensation of 1858. Pleshcheev was enthusiastic about the book and asked Dostoevsky if he had read it; we know that he did from a letter to another Pisemsky enthusiast, his brother Mikhail, to whom he imparted his critical observations. Pisemsky's main protagonist, Kalinovich, a presumably idealistic young man revolted by the corruption of society, makes a wealthy and loveless marriage so as to obtain a position of bureaucratic power from which to initiate reforms. However, his marriage obliges him to abandon his first and only true love, Nastenka, whom he seduces and promises to marry but then knowingly betrays. Dostoevsky, who found such cold-blooded villainy totally unconvincing, thought the book lacked genuine originality. "Is it possible that you find the novel of Pisemsky marvelous?" he asks Mikhail in surprise. "It's really nothing but mediocrity, though gilded. Is there a single new character created in it, one never seen before? All this has already been seen before among our original writers, Gogol in particular. . . . An excellent copy of someone else's model, the work of Sazikov after the drawings of Benvenuto Cellini."

Analyzing Kalinovich in detail for the benefit of his brother, Dostoevsky proceeds to document his judgment that "the end of the second part is absolutely unbelievable and awfully bad. Kalinovich as a self-conscious deceiver is impossible. Kalinovich, as the author has shown him to us previously, should make a sacrifice, offer marriage [to Nastenka], show himself in a favorable light, enjoy his own nobility to the very depths of his soul, and be absolutely certain that he will not deceive. Kalinovich is so vainglorious that even in his heart of hearts he cannot consider himself a blackguard. Naturally he is going to enjoy all that, sleep with Nastenka, and, of course, he will deceive her, but only *afterwards*, when reality compels him, and naturally he will console himself, will say that here too he has behaved nobly."[21] In other words, Dostoevsky thinks that Kalinovich should have been portrayed as essentially a weak person, a prey to his own illusions and self-deceptions—like Golyadkin in *The Double*, or the yet unborn Raskolnikov—rather than as a solid character acting ignobly, and with full awareness, to gain his appointed ends.

Much more to Dostoevsky's taste was another work of Pisemsky's, the play *A Bitter Fate* (1859). "I do not share your enthusiasm for Pisemsky's drama," Pleshscheev writes him, "and I place *The Storm* [by Ostrovsky] incomparably higher."[22] Both works appeared and were performed at approximately the same time, and radical opinion came down forcefully on the side of Ostrovsky. Dobrolyubov was soon to write an impassioned article interpreting (quite tendentiously) the suicide of Ostrovsky's heroine, who refused to return to a husband she could not love, as an act of revolutionary defiance. Pisemsky's play deals with the same theme, conjugal infidelity, but provides a totally different outcome. Here the wife of a proud and independent peasant, in her husband's protracted absence (he is earning their quit-rent in Petersburg), becomes the mistress of their landowner and bears him a child. Her husband is willing to overlook the sin, accept the child as his own, and take the family to the city as a means of burying his disgrace. But the wife, who had married him against her will, prefers the landowner and prepares to move into the manor house to live openly as his mistress. In an access of rage, the furious husband kills the child and then takes refuge in the surrounding woods, where he remains concealed while a farcically corrupt inquiry into the murder is being carried on.

The guilty man has ample money to have fled to Petersburg and vanished for good if he had wished to do so; but he finally gives himself up to the authorities because, it becomes clear, his conscience has forced him to surrender. Even more, he refuses under questioning to exculpate himself in any way by disclosing the real cause of his atrocious crime. When urged to do so as a means of lightening his sentence, he replies: "Even if she [his wife] did do something more to me than I ever dreamed of, it's not for me to be her judge or testify against her: my sin is greater than any

255

of hers, and I don't want to make my sentence a bit lighter."[23] He goes off to prison after asking forgiveness from his fellow villagers and after having embraced and kissed his grieving wife, who falls at his feet in mute despair as he is led away.

It is easy to see why Dostoevsky should have admired Pisemsky's play, which indicated that the moral sensitivity of the weak person—a sensitivity that Annenkov had seen only as the particular attribute of the enlightened "superfluous man"—actually existed as a much more widespread character trait inculcated and fostered by the traditional Orthodox Christianity of the Russian people. And while Dostoevsky did not write about a peasant milieu, his most important creation of this period, *The Village of Stepanchikovo*, also attempted to display the moral pre-eminence of a loving and all-forgiving weak person over a monstrously egoistic strong character consumed by vanity and resentment.

CHAPTER 18

Literary Projects

Dostoevsky's final two years of service in the Russian Army and of life in Semipalatinsk were much more oppressive and exasperating than those he had lived through previously. Whatever his difficulties in the past, he had been sustained by his hopes for the future—and by the reinvigorating power of his love for Marya Dimitrievna. But his new state of wedlock did not bring him the family happiness he had anticipated; and his own anxiety about his health was aggravated by the awareness of his wife's horror at his dread disease. It was to take more than a year before his request for retirement was granted (in May 1859), and he was forced to bide his time, in a frenzy of impatience, while awaiting his release. Many of the people who had helped to make life tolerable for him had either been transferred elsewhere or were no longer alive (such as his amiable battalion commander, Belikhov, who had recently dispatched himself with a bullet). Belikhov's replacement, Major Denisov, was a decent enough fellow, but all the same, as Dostoevsky remarks, "a new commander" means "a new state of affairs."[1] The old, comfortable routine was upset, and it was irksome to have to adjust to unexpected demands and requirements.

Just how deeply Dostoevsky was sunk in depression during this period can be judged from his complaint to E. I. Yakushkin in December 1858 that the one consolation he had had in the past, his literary labors, were now also becoming more of a burden than a blessing. "I live in Semipalatinsk," he writes, "which bores me to death. Life here has become intolerable for me. In a brief letter I cannot explain everything to you. Can you imagine that even literary work has become for me no longer a relaxation, a refuge, but a torture? That's what is worst; the fault lies in what surrounds me and in my sickly condition [his epilepsy]."[2] But he continued to write nonetheless, stubbornly and unflaggingly, in the time left over from his military duties and from the stultifying aftermaths of his epileptic seizures, which always left him feeling sluggish and dull and with his mind refusing to function properly.

2

Once Dostoevsky had received his commission as an officer (March 1857), and once his rights as a nobleman had been restored (May 1857), we hear no more about his *Letters on Art*. Instead, all his energies are now concentrated on the various projects for novels and stories on which he had never ceased to work in the three years since his release from the prison camp. "I will begin with nothing other than a novel or a short story," he roundly declares to Yakushkin (June 1857), "even though I have other things" (presumably his *Letters*).³ He had still not yet obtained any information as to whether he had regained the right to publish; but his correspondents, including his brother, assured him that such a right was implicitly included in those he had been accorded. In any case, other returning Petrashevtsy had begun to appear in public print without apparently endangering their situation. As a result, Dostoevsky decided to go ahead and publish if he could, at first without signature, and see whether this would provoke any untoward reaction on the part of the authorities.

The only work immediately available was the story he had completed in the Peter-and-Paul Fortress, which had been sent to Mikhail on Dostoevsky's departure for Siberia. "Tell me *with exactitude* (this I beg of you) does one seriously wish to publish it?" he asks in March 1857. "If yes, has one tried to or not, and if not, what is the specific reason? I make this request because you suppose that the interdiction to publish has been lifted in my case!"⁴ Dostoevsky, in this instance, obtained quicker action than he thought possible or even than he considered desirable. *A Little Hero*, signed with the initials M.Y., was published in the August 1857 issue of *Notes of the Fatherland*; but on receiving this information, Dostoevsky expressed more regret than satisfaction. "The news of the publication of *A Tale for Children* [his own title] has not been entirely agreeable to me," he explains to Mikhail. "I had thought of redoing it for a long time, and to redo it well, above all to suppress the beginning, which is worthless.* But what can I do? It's published!"⁵ All the same, the appearance of this little work proved that Dostoevsky *could* appear in print, and begin to earn some money from his pen, without bringing down the wrath of either the censorship or the secret police.

3
———

At this time (the summer of 1857) Dostoevsky's literary efforts were concentrated on a work that, as he tells E. I. Yakushkin, was "as bulky as a novel of Dickens" and had occupied him for about a year and a half. "It is a long novel," he writes, "the adventures of the same character, which have a general, unbroken link to each other, but at the same time consist

---

* Dostoevsky here is referring to the frame narrative, written in the high-pitched lyrical and sentimental tone of *White Nights*, which he probably felt—quite rightly—added little or nothing to the effect of the main story and even weakened its impact. He excised this frame in the edition of his work published in 1860, and it was never restored. The omitted fragment can be found in *PSS*, 2: 453-458.

of independent episodes complete in themselves. Each episode is one part. So that, for example, I can very well bring it out by episodes, and each will make up one adventure or story. Naturally, I should like to bring it all out in order." Dostoevsky speaks of a plan containing three books, but "only the first book has been written in 5 parts. . . . All of it is written, but not yet published, and so I will now start to polish it by sections and send the sections to you."[6]

Whether Dostoevsky actually had a manuscript as far advanced as he suggests is highly dubious; he always tended to exaggerate the state of completion of the multifarious plans and projects he mentions, and very probably this idea had not yet proceeded beyond the stage of some preliminary jottings and sketches. In any case, Dostoevsky's words do reveal how early in his post-Siberian phase he began to plan a series of novels about a single central character in various periods of his life. He would return to the same formal ground plan in *Notes from Underground* (which may be considered a miniature realization of this schema) and then, on a larger scale, in the notes for his never-realized five-volume sequence on *The Life of a Great Sinner*. *The Brothers Karamazov*, of course, is the first volume of what was planned to be exactly the same kind of multivolume sequence. Dostoevsky's letter asks Yakushkin to inquire among editors in Petersburg if they would be interested in the first volume and how much they would be willing to pay for it per page.

From a letter to Mikhail a few months later, it is clear that Dostoevsky had hoped to be able to publish in installments as these were completed. Mikhail, however, had evidently told him that such a plan was impractical, and advised his brother to hurry up and complete whatever he was then writing. Dostoevsky's answer comes in the form of an anguished declaration of his refusal to force his literary gifts (as he felt he had too often done in the past). "So far as my novel is concerned," he says, "something unpleasant has happened to it and to me, and this is what it is: I decided, and took an oath on it, that now nothing half-baked, nothing immature, nothing hurried (as before) would I publish solely because I needed money; that one should not trifle with an artistic work, that one should work honestly, and that if I write badly, which probably often happens, it should be because I lack talent to do better and not because of carelessness and giddiness. This is why, seeing that my novel is taking on huge proportions, that it was turning out excellently, and that it was necessary, absolutely necessary (for money) to terminate it quickly—I began to hesitate. Nothing is sadder than such hesitation in the midst of work. Eagerness, will, energy—all sputter out." As a result, Dostoevsky informs his brother that "the whole novel with all its material is now packed in the trunk."[7]

Instead of this major work, Dostoevsky announces that he has decided to concentrate on two other projects. One is a "small story," which, at this time, he intended to send to a relatively new journal, *The Russian Messenger*, edited by Mikhail Katkov. A former member of the Belinsky *pléiade*, and known as a liberal Westerner with Anglophile sympathies, Katkov was soon to evolve in a more conservative direction. Indeed, his journal was destined to become the most important antiradical organ throughout the remainder of Dostoevsky's lifetime, and it also would have the honor of publishing most of the great novels, including his own, that gained for Russian literature of this period its world renown. An invitation to contribute to the journal had been relayed through Aleksey Pleshcheev, and Dostoevsky had indicated his acceptance.

Whether this "small story" is connected with either of the two that Dostoevsky actually wrote between 1857 and 1859 remains unclear; it may be a reference to what later became *Uncle's Dream*. "Having finished that," Dostoevsky continues, "I will write a novel of Petersburg life in the genre of *Poor Folk* (but the idea is even better than *Poor Folk*); both these things have long since been begun and are partly written, they present no problems. . . ."[8] This idea for a novel about Petersburg life no doubt refers to what, five years later, developed into *The Insulted and the Injured*.

All notions of writing a novel of *any* kind had been abandoned by the beginning of the new year because, for financial reasons, Dostoevsky decided to devote himself to shorter works that would bring immediate returns. By this time, he had received an advance from a planned new journal, *The Russian Word* (*Russkoe Slovo*), eager to obtain manuscripts from any writer with a name known to the public. Encouraged by this proof that he did not have to produce a finished text in order to obtain funds, Dostoevsky then wrote to Katkov asking for an advance and proposing his major novel as bait. In fact, as he candidly admits to his brother, he no longer had any intention of writing this novel at all; but he consoles his conscience with reflections on the acute urgency of his needs and the consideration that, in any case, a substantial story would satisfy his obligations. Katkov promptly sent the money, accompanied by an encouraging letter; and Dostoevsky was now committed to writing two shorter works in the immediate future. He makes it clear, however, that he is doing so only under duress and with the greatest reluctance. "My novel (the big one) I will put aside for the time being. I cannot finish it for a deadline! It would only torture me. It has already tortured me enough as it is. I will put it aside until there is some quiet and stability in my life. That novel is so precious to me, has grown into so much a part of myself, that nothing can make me throw it aside entirely. On the contrary, I intend to make it my *chef d'oeuvre*."[9]

Several months later, Dostoevsky explains his situation again to Mikhail and reassures his brother, who had negotiated the advance from *The Russian Word*, that he would not leave this publication in the lurch; to do so would of course have placed Mikhail in an extremely embarrassing position. "Actually, I am working for *The Russian Messenger* (a long story). . . . I will also send something to *The Russian Word* this year. At least I hope so. But not my novel, a story." And then Dostoevsky gives us a glimpse of how he had managed to console himself for having been forced to delay his cherished project. "As for my novel," he goes on, "I will only get down to it on my return to Russia. I can't do otherwise. It contains a rather happy idea, a new character that hasn't yet been seen anywhere. But since such a character is without doubt actually very common in Russia in real life, especially at this moment, if one is to judge by the tendency and ideas everybody is filled with, I am certain that, once back in Russia, I will enrich my novel with new observations."[10]

One should note here the equation of "idea" and "character"—the two are inseparable for Dostoevsky, and he uses the words interchangeably— as well as the ambition to portray a "new character" hitherto unremarked in Russian literature. Such a character would incarnate the ideas "everybody is filled with," in other words, the social-cultural tendencies of this period of ferment in Russian life, just on the eve of the liberation of the serfs and as the country was emerging from its long stagnation under Nicholas I. Dostoevsky had thus already begun to adopt the explicitly "ideological" orientation of all his best post-Siberian creations, and to envisage his creative aim as being the embodiment of character-types representative of these burgeoning tendencies and currents. His early work had also been conceived in terms of the dominating ideas of the decade (the 1840s); but such ideas had already been embodied in a standard repertory of Gogolian figures (the *chinovnik*, or lowly bureaucratic scribe; the Romantic "dreamer"; the unctuous and thoroughly corrupt official representing upper-class "respectability"), which Dostoevsky simply took over and used for his own purposes. Henceforth, he would see his creative task as the depiction of types not yet observed by others or still in the process of formation.

4

When Dostoevsky accepted the offer from *The Russian Word*, he wrote his brother that he had something already prepared that would take very little time to whip into final shape. "In my big novel," he wrote, "there is an episode fully finished and quite good in itself, but which spoils the whole. I want to cut it out of the novel. It's about as long as *Poor Folk*, but comic in content. It has fresh characters."[11] Dostoevsky appears to be referring to the "comic novel" he had mentioned to Maikov as far back as 1856—the work he had begun as a play (*komediya*) but then, because the adventures of the central character pleased him so much, had turned into a novel.

As usual, Dostoevsky underestimated the amount of time it would take to prepare the work for publication, or, perhaps more accurately, he exaggerated the extent to which a creative idea had actually been put into finished literary form. He had hoped to be able to send it off by September 1858, and he apologizes to Mikhail for failing to do so with the explanation that his illness had kept him from his desk. "Last month I had four attacks, which had never happened before—and I almost did not work at all. After my attacks I am for a certain time in a state of despondency and melancholy, and feel completely crushed."[12] Also, work on *Uncle's Dream* was difficult because Dostoevsky wrote it with inner distaste. "I don't like it, and it saddens me that I am forced to appear in public again so miserably. Saddest of all is that I am *forced* to appear this way. . . . But what's to be done? You can't write what you want to write, and you write something that you wouldn't even want to think about if you didn't need money. And because of money I am obliged to *invent stories on purpose*. . . . Being a needy writer is a filthy trade."[13] Strictly speaking, if we are to believe Dostoevsky's earlier letter, *Uncle's Dream* had not at all been invented on the spur of the moment solely to satisfy *The Russian Word*; it had been part of the "comic novel" that he had worked on with so much pleasure. The inconsistency, all the same, reveals how much of a burden the story had become.

Another comment to Mikhail discloses Dostoevsky's reluctance to abandon his more ambitious conceptions. "The story for Kushelev [the financial backer of *The Russian Word*] will be full of comic and even quite passable details," he says hopefully, "but almost unbelievable. What can be done? I would be happy to do better, but all the ideas in my head are for large works, and of smaller size there is only this story."[14] He had promised to have it ready by November, but also failed to meet this deadline because he had put *Uncle's Dream* aside to work on *The Village of Stepanchikovo*. He had agreed, however, to hand it in by the end of the year, and in mid-December announces breathlessly to Yakushkin: "I am writing in post-haste, and have almost completely finished."[15] It was sent off a few days later and published during the spring (March 1859) in *The Russian Word*.

The Village of Stepanchikovo has a more complicated history, and there is some question whether it too originally formed part of the comic novel from which *Uncle's Dream* was taken. Some scholars are inclined to believe so, and the similarity of inspiration in the two novellas is self-evident; but in the same letter referring to *Uncle's Dream* as part of a larger work, Dostoevsky himself seems to speak of his second production as an entirely new creative idea. "Eight years ago I had the idea for a small novel, the size of *Poor Folk*. Recently, I more or less knowingly brought it back to mind, and worked out its plan anew. All this is now ready. I will sit down to this novel and write."[16] It is this idea that, so far as one can judge, became *The Village of Stepanchikovo*, though in a later letter Dostoevsky speaks of having worked on its two main characters "for five years" (which would place it approximately at the time he began to write the play that became his comic novel).[17] In any case, we know that, late in 1857, he began to write something for *The Russian Messenger* that he calls a "small story"; but later allusions show that the work for Katkov has grown in dimension, and the small story originally intended for him was probably shifted over to *The Russian Word*.

At first, Dostoevsky's attitude to his larger story was as negative and resentful as toward *Uncle's Dream*. "The long story that I am writing for Katkov," he tells Mikhail, "displeases me very much and goes against the grain. But I have already written a good deal, it's impossible to throw it away in order to begin another, and I have to pay back a debt."[18] By the time he had sent off three-quarters of the manuscript, though, his opinion had swung round full circle. "Listen, Misha!" he admonishes his brother, "the novel, of course, has very great defects, perhaps especially that it's too long in spots, but what I am as sure of as an axiom is that, at the same time, it has the greatest qualities and is *my best work.* . . . I do not know whether Katkov will appreciate it, but if the public receives it coldly, then, I confess, I may give way to despair. I base all my best hopes on it, and, even more, the consolidation of my literary reputation."[19] To his dismay, Katkov flatly rejected the work and asked the author to return his advance payment; but Dostoevsky did not lose faith in his creation. "Now listen, my dear fellow," he writes Mikhail, "I am convinced that there are many weak and bad things in my novel; but I am convinced—I stake my life on it!—that there are very fine things. They sprang from the heart. There are scenes of high comedy that Gogol would have signed without hesitation."[20]

5

After some deliberation, the two brothers decided to offer the work to Nekrasov, whose friendly disposition had been conveyed by Pleshcheev and who had earlier offered through Mikhail to send Dostoevsky an advance if he were in financial straits. Dostoevsky's standoffish reply to this generous gesture indicates that he had neither forgotten nor forgiven, and that he was still smarting from the old (and not so old) wounds inflicted by *The Contemporary*. "Now they feel sorry for me," he comments to Mikhail. "I am grateful to them for this with all my heart. But I should not like them to think badly of me; all they have to do is promise money, and I leap at it. Perhaps this is false pride—but there it is. And so I prefer to wait, and only as a last—a very last—resort will I become engaged with them financially."[21] Katkov's rejection, however, which required the return of his advance (the sorely pressed Mikhail managed to raise the money somehow), drove Dostoevsky against the wall and left him no recourse but to seize on what seemed the most likely chance to obtain funds immediately.

Nekrasov was handed the manuscript in the first days of September 1859 and hesitated over a month before coming to a decision—a month during which Dostoevsky, on tenterhooks, kept urging his reluctant brother to prod the procrastinating editor. "I have heard that Nekrasov plays cards all the time," he remarks impatiently (Nekrasov was indeed a notorious—and very successful—gambler). "Nor does Panaev either pay much attention to the journal, and if not for Chernyshevsky and Dobrolyubov their whole affair would fall to pieces."[22] Mikhail, however, refused to be rushed, perhaps understanding better than his brother the dilemma in which Nekrasov found himself. On the one hand, he would have wished to aid Dostoevsky as a returning ex-political prisoner and out of the lingering memories of their old friendship. On the other, Dostoevsky's novella contained parodistic thrusts against the Natural School of the 1840s—and thus implicitly against Belinsky—which Nekrasov (not to mention Chernyshevsky and Dobrolyubov) would have found offensive. To make matters worse, these thrusts included a reference to one of Nekrasov's own poems.

Nekrasov, as we now know, did not like the novella at all and expressed himself on the point in no uncertain terms. "Dostoevsky is finished," he is reported to have said. "He will no longer write anything important."[23] But Nekrasov was not one of the most successful editors of his time for nothing, and, rather than reject the story outright, he diplomatically accepted it—but offered to pay so little that no self-respecting author could accept his terms. Both Dostoevsky and Mikhail thought at first that he was bargaining, and the former was very excited at the news that Nekrasov had called on Mikhail without finding him at home. The purpose of this visit, it may be presumed, was to cushion the rebuff by some private conversation; but Dostoevsky hopefully imagined that it signified an eagerness not to let the work slip through his grasp. "If Nekrasov bargains and becomes more *reasonable*, the priority is his whatever happens," he instructs Mikhail. "I regret, I regret extremely that he did not find you at home. . . . You see, it is very important that the novel be published in *The Contemporary*. This journal once sent me packing, and now maneuvers to have my text. This is very important for my literary situation."[24]

Dostoevsky, however, was woefully deceiving himself, and Mikhail soon became aware of the true state of affairs. He offered the work instead to A. A. Kraevsky for *Notes of the Fatherland*, where it was finally accepted after some negotiations and at a higher price per sheet (120 rubles) than Dostoevsky had been willing to accept elsewhere. "That's what it means not to derogate one's dignity," Mikhail writes him triumphantly. He also conveys some literary comments of Kraevsky, a shrewd observer of the literary scene, who particularly liked the main character, Foma Fomich Opiskin, and spotted one of its parodistic sources: "He [Foma] reminded [Kraevsky] of N. V. Gogol in the sorrowful period of his life."

Another remark, this time rather negative, is valuable all the same in helping to define the new tonality observable in Dostoevsky's work—a tonality that put off so many of his old admirers. "You [Dostoevsky] surrender yourself sometimes to the influence of humor and wish to arouse laughter," Mikhail reports Kraevsky as saying. "The strength of F.M. he [Kraevsky] added—lies in feeling, in pathos, here perhaps he had no equals, and so it's a pity that he neglects this gift."[25] Kraevsky was right in detecting, not so much humor, as a new and much sharper satirical edge replacing Dostoevsky's earlier pathos; this is evident not only in the second but also in the first of his Siberian novellas. But it is time now to look at these works more directly and closely.

CHAPTER 19

The Siberian Novellas

The reception accorded Dostoevsky's second literary début stands in sharp contrast to what had occurred when, fifteen years earlier, he had made his first appearance on the literary scene. Then he had created a sensation and become famous overnight; but no such luck attended his renewed try for notoriety and fortune. He was certainly hoping for a similar success, at least with *The Village of Stepanchikovo*, and was pathetically eager to receive some assurance that his hopes were not in vain. At the time Nekrasov was considering his manuscript, with the negative results we know, Dostoevsky wrote his brother: "Note all the particularities and all his words, and, I implore you for God's sake, write me about it in as much detail as you can. For me, you see, it is very *interesting*."[1] Dostoevsky also asked his brother to send him any press comments that might appear after the two works were published; but Mikhail, probably to spare Feodor's sensibilities, remarked that literary journals were no longer reporting on each other to the same extent as in the 1840s. The truth was that *no* reference of any kind appeared in the literary press about either of Dostoevsky's works; they were passed over in complete silence.

2

It is not difficult to understand such a response, or rather, the absence of one, if we glance at the period in which these stories appeared. To mention only the major figures, these were the years in which Turgenev was producing much of his best work and turning out a novel almost annually; Tolstoy had just burst on the scene with his *Childhood, Boyhood, Youth* and *Sevastopol Stories*; Pisemsky's abundant activity has already been documented; and Saltykov-Shchedrin had stirred up a furor with his caustic *Provincial Sketches*, which created a new genre of literary muckraking in Russian writing. Moreover, the whole country was in a fever of anticipation over the forthcoming liberation of the serfs, and the mood of the moment demanded works of literature with solid social-cultural substance. The time-worn plots of Dostoevsky's novellas, however, appeared to involve nothing more momentous than whether one or another character would (or would not) marry the partner of his or her choice. Even worse, *The Village of Stepanchikovo* depicted life on a country estate in which idyllic relations prevailed between the peasants and their warmhearted land-owner; the only conflicts that existed were caused by the excessive good nature of this exemplary proprietor and gave rise to comic situations. Dostoevsky's socially conscious readers, preoccupied as never before with the abuses and injustice of serfdom, could hardly take such a portrayal except as a deliberate slap in the face. As L. P. Grossman has noted, to treat life on a country estate at *that* time in the form of a comic novel was simply to court disaster.[2]

It is thus hardly surprising that Dostoevsky's contemporaries should have failed to respond to these works with any enthusiasm, and took them rather as confirmation of Belinsky's final opinion, uttered just before his death, that Dostoevsky's talent had been considerably overrated. Nor was it only Nekrasov who pronounced a disparaging judgment on Dostoevsky at this moment; even someone as well-disposed as Aleksey Pleshcheev spoke of *Uncle's Dream* as "too farcical," and found that "there was not a single living figure" in *The Village of Stepanchikovo* except for one of the two main characters, Colonel Rostanev. His concluding estimate of this work, which he asked Alexander Milyukov not to convey to Dostoevsky, was that "all this is fabricated, contrived; terribly stilted."[3]

These criticisms, as we see, are not of content but of literary form; and while they probably conceal a judgment of content as well, they are worth considering in their own right. Why should these stories have created such an impression on so well-intentioned a reader? Primarily, in my view, because the technique Dostoevsky used clashed radically with the norms then prevailing in Russian prose. These norms had been established by the dominating influence of the "physiological sketch" during the 1840s (local-color studies of social types), which emphasized character description and portrayal of milieu rather than narrative movement. Most important Russian novelists of the mid-nineteenth century began with such sketches, or were strongly affected by their vogue among the writers of the Natural School who developed under Belinsky's influence. Later, their own novels would continue to have the simplest of plot lines and to retain the emphasis on the portrayal of character through incidents linked together by the largely commonplace events of ordinary social existence. (Even when the circumstances were not at all ordinary, as in Tolstoy's *Sevastopol Stories*, they were treated as if they were with a notable lack of flamboyance.) Dostoevsky's earlier work conformed to this same Russian prose tradition, even though one finds traces of more plot manipulation than customary in some of his stories; and his preference for depicting characters in moments of acute conflict and crisis in their lives always created a certain degree of narrative tension. Yet he himself, in *Poor Folk*, *The Double*, and elsewhere, had parodied the vogue for the tightly plotted and sensational Gothic and adventure novels that the Natural School had displaced.

Dostoevsky's intended comic novel, however, began originally as a dramatic farce (what the Russians call a "vaudeville"). Elaborate plots are traditional in this type of play, and the two long stories that emerged from this original inspiration retain this feature of their gestation. Hence Dostoevsky's stories must have seemed to their first readers as unhappy throwbacks to the superseded manner of the 1830s and a violation of the accepted literary canon. Such readers could hardly have been expected to realize that the use of this technique marks a new departure for Dostoevsky and was not merely an indication of artistic ineptitude.* For all of Dostoevsky's major novels (with the significant exception of *House of the Dead*, which is only semifictional) will employ the same technique and exhibit the same preference for a dramatic plot construction. All will display more or less the same essential features deriving from such a choice of form: an extremely rapid and condensed plot action taking place in a very short space of time; unexpected turns of events that pile up fast and furiously, leaving no room for lulls or breathing spaces; characters who are presented mainly in terms of dialogue and dramatic movement rather than through analytic portraiture or lengthy depiction of consciousness; and climaxes usually taking place amid the tumultuous group scenes that have been labeled "conclaves" and compared with the celebrated finale of Gogol's *The Inspector-General*.[4]

Even though Dostoevsky's two novellas have a distinctly comic surface, this should not at all be taken to mean that they are entirely devoid of serious substance. Quite the contrary is true; and a close reading—one focusing on the allusions embedded in the prose and on the parodistic subtext—discloses as much serious satire in Dostoevsky's pages as light-hearted tomfoolery. Moreover, while the conflicts of his characters appear to involve only picayune problems, there is a notable increase in the range and variety of their types compared with his protagonists of the 1840s. And they are projected with a boldness of contour and a loquacity of self-expression that somehow make them seem to have grown almost physically in size and stature. It is difficult to imagine the Dostoevsky of the

* In truth, this departure was not *entirely* new for Dostoevsky; he had used the same technique in two very minor works during the 1840s—*Another Man's Wife (A Street Scene)* and *A Jealous Husband (An Extraordinary Occurrence)*. Both were later shortened and turned into a single story, *Another Man's Wife, Or the Husband Under the Bed.* As the titles indicate, these stories are comic anecdotes dealing with sexual misconduct, narrative imitations of French bedroom farce, full of fast-and-furious surprises and embarrassing situations.

Dostoevsky wrote these little works only to pick up some extra cash, and they stand out as uncharacteristic trivia among his other stories of the time. What happens now, though, is that he unites the same form with far more serious thematic material—or at least begins to do so in his two Siberian novellas. See my *Dostoevsky, The Seeds of Revolt, 1821-1849* (Princeton, 1976), 330-331; Victor Terras, *The Young Dostoevsky (1846-1849)* (The Hague, 1969), 46-47.

early stories writing the later novels; but the author of these Siberian novellas already gives indications of being able to do so. Finally, whatever the strained high jinks made necessary by his "comic" plots, Dostoevsky has nonetheless already begun to adumbrate the great new theme—it may be called "the critique of ideology," or the conflict defined in his letters as that between "ideas" and "the heart"—which will dominate, in one way or another, all his post-Siberian writings.

Uncle's Dream

The plot intrigue of *Uncle's Dream* may be set down in a few words. "Uncle" is a decrepit but wealthy Russian prince, almost in his dotage, who accidentally arrives in the town of Mordasov one fine day and is immediately taken in tow by the powerful "leading lady" of the environs, Marya Alexandrovna Moskaleva. She conceives the scheme of marrying him to her still unwed twenty-three-year-old daughter Zina, a proud beauty, and expends treasures of ingenuity in carrying out her plan. But it is finally defeated, to the immense joy of her numerous rivals for social supremacy, by the jealousy of a rejected suitor for Zina's hand, a young Petersburg bureaucrat named Mozglyakov, who persuades his distant relative the Prince, quite unable to distinguish between his waking and sleeping states, that the proposal he made to Zina in a drunken stupor had only been "a dream."

Dostoevsky dresses up this anecdote in a faintly mock-heroic style and presents it, in an obvious parody of the title of Balzac's *César Birotteau*, as "the full and remarkable history of the exaltation, glory and solemn downfall of Marya Alexandrovna and all her family" (2: 516). The story is also subtitled "from the annals of Mordasov" (2: 296)—and such epic accents, of course, only underline the insignificance of the events (just a year or two earlier Saltykov-Shchedrin had used the same device in his *Provincial Sketches*, also recounted by a local busybody serving as narrator). This new type of Dostoevskian narrator is a gossip chronicler, as much (if not more) interested in rumor and slander as in what he is able to verify with his own eyes and ears; nor is he ever really certain how to interpret even what he witnesses at first hand. A narrator of this kind is later used by Dostoevsky for other works also set in the Russian provinces, such as *The Devils* and *The Brothers Karamazov*, and he developed this device into a subtle instrument for controlling his narrative perspective. It is particularly valuable in allowing him to portray his main figures against a background of rumor, opinion, and scandalmongering that serves somewhat the function of a Greek chorus in relation to the central action.*

* Traces of the original play form are still evident in *Uncle's Dream*, especially at the beginning of Chapter 3. "Ten o'clock in the morning. We are in Marya Alexandrovna's house

The image given here of provincial life, with its eternal gossip, back-biting, and ruthless struggles for power over trifles, is conveyed with a good deal of mordant humor and insinuating irony, nourished by Dostoevsky's years of enforced observation of such a milieu in Semipalatinsk. But this image only provides the background against which the major figures of the story stand out in sharp relief. And no figure in Mordasov is more major than Marya Alexandrovna—who is even compared to Napoleon and said to be actually *superior* to Napoleon, because, come what may, "her head was never under any circumstances turned," and "she always remained the leading lady in Mordasov" (2: 297).

Marya Alexandrovna openly and frankly exhibits a will to domination that she is hardly entitled to exercise by rank or fortune; and she is the first Dostoevsky character of this type to appear in a work in which the conventions of realism are scrupulously observed. The only previous character of this kind had been the fantastic and mesmeric Murin, who rules over all the others in the highly symbolic *The Landlady*; in other words, Dostoevsky had earlier been able to conceive the psychology of such a figure only in terms of Romantic hyperbole. Now, however, he places such a "strong" personality within the most humdrum of Russian provincial settings, thereby taking his first step toward that re-assimilation of the scope and grandeur of Romantic thematics, and its fusion with Russian social reality, that will distinguish his later work. Indeed, no matter how petty the form taken by such "grandeur" in this instance, the name of Napoleon is enough to alert us to what Dostoevsky will make of such an urge for domination in the future.

Marya Alexandrovna is not averse to exercising her power directly, as she does over her dimwitted and terrified husband, or stooping to fight her feminine rivals in Mordasov with their own weapons of gossip, slander, and, if necessary, a little housebreaking. But her manifest superiority emerges when she is faced with a more difficult and challenging task—that of persuading the proud and high-principled Zina, who has only contempt for her mother's ambitions and machinations, to agree to marry the decrepit Prince. To accomplish her aim, Marya Alexandrovna realizes that she must offer some truly tempting prospect; and the scene in which she brings

---

in the main street, in the very room which the lady of the house calls her *salon*. Marya Alexandrovna has also a boudoir. In this *salon* there are well-painted floors, and rather nice wall-papers that were ordered expressly for the walls. In the rather clumsy furniture red is the predominating color. There is an open fireplace, over the mantelpiece a mirror, before the looking-glass a bronze clock with a Cupid on it in very bad taste" (2: 303). This passage goes on for some time in the same vein and describes the characters as part of the stage scenery.

What we have here are probably the remains of an intermediate draft halfway between stage directions and narrative. It is significant that the chapter begins in the present tense and then shifts, with no explanation, into the narrative past. Dostoevsky at this point would seem to be uncertain about exactly how to handle the transition from the dramatic present of the play form to narrative.

her daughter round, by a masterly deployment of rhetoric, displays a great advance in Dostoevsky's handling of dialogue.

Zina, it should be explained, is in love with an impoverished young schoolmaster dying of tuberculosis, and her mother knows that she has pledged not to marry while he is in the throes of his death-agony. Hence the first approach is to hold out to Zina the hope of escaping from her tormenting situation, while at the same time pretending to sympathize with her grief; "You will leave for ever this detestable little town, full of terrible memories for you. . . . You may even go abroad this Spring, to Italy, to Switzerland, to Spain; to Spain, Zina, where there is the Alhambra and the Guadalquivir, not this wretched, miserable, little river here with its unseemly name . . ." (2: 324).

This appeal to Romantic exoticism, however, has no success, and Marya Alexandrovna is forced to unlimber weapons of heavier caliber. A marriage with the Prince would not be a true marriage at all ("he is not capable of requiring such love"), and in any case, "the Prince will live for a year or two at the utmost, and to my mind it is better to be a (wealthy) young widow than an old maid." The young schoolmaster could not possibly be jealous of the Prince "if he has a spark of common sense," and hence Zina is told to "reflect that you will give him fresh courage and relieve his mind by marrying the Prince!" But Zina sees through her mother's sophistries and pinpoints her strategy with exasperated precision: "I understand you, Mamma, I quite understand you! *You never can resist a display of noble sentiments even in the nastiest action*" (2: 325; italics added). These "noble sentiments" are Marya Alexandrovna's "ideology," and she draws them from the storehouse of commonplaces piled up by the Romantic literature of the 1820s and 1830s both in Russia and Europe.

Realizing that any appeal to enlightened self-interest is doomed to failure, Marya Alexandrovna strikes a higher note—self-sacrifice. Why not think of marriage with the Prince as an act of devotion? "To our minds it is hard to bandage wounds in a hospital; it is revolting to breathe the infected air of the sickroom. But there are angels of mercy who do that and thank God for their vocation. Here is balm for your wounded heart, occupation, self-sacrifice—and you will heal your own wounds. Where is the egoism, where is the baseness?" (2: 326). Dostoevsky, as he will so often do in the future, is not afraid to mock ideas and ideals in which he believes himself when, as in this instance, they are only being used as a screen for selfishness and egoism. Marya Alexandrovna concludes by telling Zina that, if the Prince's wealth bothers her, she can renounce it, give away to the poor all but the barest necessity, and "help him, for instance, that luckless boy lying now on his death-bed" (ibid.).

Here, quite unexpectedly, Marya Alexandrovna strikes a vein of pure gold. As the narrator comments, "An inspiration, a genuine inspiration, dawned upon her," and she realizes that she has found a way of appealing to Zina's authentic idealism: let Zina sacrifice herself by a degrading marriage so as to help her dying beloved. At this point, Marya Alexandrovna pulls out all the stops: "He [the local doctor] told me, in fact, that under different circumstances, especially with a change of climate and surroundings, the patient might recover. He told me that in Spain— . . . that in Spain there is some extraordinary island, I believe it is called Malaga— like some wine, in fact*—where not only persons with weak lungs, but consumptives recover simply from the climate, and that people go there on purpose to be treated. . . . But the magical Alhambra [in Granada, not Malaga] the myrtles, the lemons, the Spaniards on their mules! That alone would make an extraordinary impression on a poetical nature." Once cured— and the Prince conveniently deceased—the lovers could be properly united; or, if not, the schoolmaster will die happily, "trusting in your love, forgiven by you, in the shade of the myrtles and lemons, under the azure exotic sky!" (2: 327). This lengthy tirade, of which only a few samples have been given, is more than Zina can resist; she breaks down and gives her reluctant consent.

Much the same tactic is used with the gullible Mozglyakov, who is persuaded that, although ready to marry the Prince, Zina is actually madly in love with *him* and only testing his character by her decision. If he behaves nobly, thinking only of *her* happiness and the great advantages of such a marriage, his rewards in the future will surpass his most fervid dreams: "For the Prince's health Zina will go abroad, to Italy, to Spain. . . . You will follow her there . . . there your love will begin with irresistible force; love, youth! Spain—my God. Your love of course is untainted, holy. . . . You understand me, *mon ami*" (2: 354). And then, the Prince dead, the wealthy widow Zina will of course marry the man who has proven worthy of her love. Once removed from the spell of Marya Alexandrovna's eloquence, however, Mozglyakov sobers up pretty quickly; it is he who finally ruins the grand design and engineers Marya Alexandrovna's defeat. But even his momentary acceptance of her intoxicating harangue shows the power of her personality and the power of ideology (in this case literary Romanticism) to impose its cloud-capped visions as a substitute for the awful truth.

2

Dostoevsky, it has already been noted, did not think much of *Uncle's Dream* even at the time of writing; fifteen years later his opinion had not changed

* The excited Marya Alexandrovna is confusing Malaga, which is not an island, with Mallorca, whose climate then was reputed to be curative for tubercular patients. George Sand had gone there with Chopin precisely for this reason. An article about their trip had appeared in *The Russian Messenger* in 1856, and Dostoevsky may have gleaned the reference from this source. See *PSS*, 2: 517.

at all. Replying to a correspondent who wished to turn it into a play (at least twenty dramatic versions have subsequently been made), Dostoevsky explains that "I wrote it then in Siberia, just right after *katorga*, solely with the aim of commencing my literary career and in terrible fear of the censorship (as an ex-convict). And hence I wrote a little thing of sky-blue mildness and remarkable innocence." It hardly, he surmises, contains enough substance even to make a "comedy," although it does include the Prince, who is "the single serious figure in the entire story."[5] Dostoevsky here is being unnecessarily severe on himself and on "the leading lady of Mordasov," who is, as we have tried to show, more than simply a figure of farce; but his remark indicates the importance that he continues to attach to his portrait of Prince K.

One reason for this, no doubt, is that he seems to have identified himself with the character in a very intimate fashion. In his letter to Maikov, he remarks that the central figure of his comic novel is "somewhat similar" to himself; [6] and his second wife reports, with some disapproval, that he later enjoyed as a joke assuming the role in real life of an "old man trying to appear younger than he was. He could speak for entire hours in the words and thoughts of his hero, the old Prince of *Uncle's Dream*."[7] Dostoevsky's first serious love affair (with Marya Dimitrievna) occurred much later in his life than was customary, and though not an old man in any literal sense, he could well have imagined himself playing such a role compared with most men of his age. Of course he *was* much older than his second wife, Anna Grigorievna, who probably did not like to be reminded of this fact by his playacting. But such identification could hardly have been the sole reason why Dostoevsky thought Prince K. a "serious" character; the adjective must also have referred to the ideological connotations that he gave to this figure.

Russian scholarship has expended a good deal of time and ingenuity on old Prince K., who tries to conceal his true age with the aid of false hair, false teeth, a false moustache, a glass eye, and other such creations of the cosmetician's art. Indeed, it was "only on closer inspection that you discerned . . . he was a sort of corpse worked by mechanisms," and "was entirely made up of different little bits" (2: 310, 300). Various real-life Russian prototypes have been located who may or may not have been known to Dostoevsky, and it has been noted also that a grotesque character of a similar kind be found in the Russian puppet theater. More relevantly, the burblings and *bons mots* of the Prince have been compared with the lightheaded chatter of Gogol's Khlestakov in *The Inspector-General*; resemblances to traits of his character have also been pointed out in other works of Russian literature—for example, Pushkin's *Count Nulin* and Griboedov's *Woe from Wit*. What gives Prince K. his special stamp, though, is the consistent satire of a certain kind of Russian Westernism that Dostoevsky works into his depiction.

One of the earliest touches of this kind, which sets the tone, occurs in a few sentences that describe the Prince taking a little fresh air. "He was sometimes seen also on foot, wearing an overcoat and wide-brimmed straw hat, with a lady's pink neckerchief round his neck, with an eyeglass in his eye and a wicker-basket for mushrooms, cornflowers and other wild flowers. . . . When he was met by a peasant, who stepped aside, took off his hat, bowed low and said: 'Good-day, Prince, your Excellency, our sunshine,' the Prince promptly turned his lorgnette upon him, nodded graciously and said to him affably: *Bonjour, mon ami, bonjour!*' " (2: 302). The Prince's pastoral get-up and French salutation reveal just how close he is to the realities of Russian peasant life; but, for all his giddiness, he is not unaware of what is going on in the world. He arrives in Mordasov originally because of an accident to his coach, and he assures everyone that the peasant-coachman "was trying to take my life. . . . Only fancy, he has got hold of some new ideas, you know! There is a sort of skepticism in him . . . in short, he is a communist in the fullest sense of the word!" (2: 312).

The Prince's rambling reminiscences are filled with allusions to the Congress of Vienna and Lord Byron, as well as references to his romance with an enchanting French *vicomtesse* whom he lost to a German baron "when I was abroad in the Twenties" (2: 315). The Prince is thus a product of the very same period of literary Romanticism whose productions supply Marya Alexandrovna with her rhetorical arsenal. And even though the addlepated Prince is a figure of comedy, Dostoevsky could not resist evoking, if only for an instant, the grim background against which the cultured Russian of that time was pursuing his carefree European existence. For the Prince recalls "a very poetical [Moscow] lady" he had once met while taking the waters abroad, who had a daughter of fifty, and "she, too, almost talked in verse. Afterwards she had a very unfortunate mishap: she killed one of her serf-girls in a rage and was tried for it" (ibid.). Such a terrifying glimpse of social reality, dropped in a remark made in passing, can easily be overlooked in the comic context; but it explains why Dostoevsky should have insisted that the Prince was really a "serious" character.

3

Two other aspects of the story also call for some comment. One is the deathbed scene of Vasya, the young schoolmaster, which occurs on the day after Marya Alexandrovna's ignominious defeat and deals the final, shattering blow to her prestige. Zina, to the scandalous delight of all Mordasov, rushes to the little hovel in which Vasya is expiring and comforts his last moments. An obvious Dickensian tonality in this deathbed scene might have made it mawkish and cloying; but it is rescued by Vasya's unsparing self-criticism in his last moments. He is, of course, a type that Dostoevsky has treated before—the young *raznochinets* intellectual, like the student Pokrovsky in *Poor Folk* or the "dreamers" of *The Landlady* and *White Nights*. Dostoevsky had depicted this type with respect and tender humor in the 1840s, although he was always somewhat critical of its estrangement from reality; but now his tone is much harsher, and he stresses far more strongly the egoism implicit in the cultural aspirations on which Vasya had nourished his ambitions. "I was proud, I despised the herd," he says; "and in what way was I superior to other people? I don't know. Purity of heart, generosity of feeling? But all that was dreaming, Zina, when we read Shakespeare together . . ." (2: 391).

Vasya, as it turns out, had brought on his own illness out of pique (by swallowing a concoction of vodka and tobacco that affected his lungs) when Zina had asked him to postpone their marriage. "Do you know, Zina," he admits, "I did not understand then what you would be sacrificing in marrying me! I did not even understand that marrying me you might die of starvation. . . . Yes, it is well that I am dying! It is well that you did not marry me! I should have understood nothing of your sacrifice, I should have tormented you, I should have worried you over our poverty; the years would have passed, and who knows!—Perhaps I should have grown to hate you, as a hindrance in my life. . . . Now at least my bitter tears have purified my heart" (2: 391-392). Vasya's merciless self-analysis, for all its hackneyed terms and touches of sentimentality, constitutes a much more hostile exposure of this type than Dostoevsky had ever given before. And this inset episode involving Vasya, so reminiscent of Dostoevsky's previous "sentimental Naturalism," indicates the function that Dostoevsky's earlier thematics will continue to perform in his later work. It will now be relegated to the status of a secondary episode, linked to the main plot line in some significant fashion but no longer providing the focus of the action; this will be centered elsewhere, and involve characters and issues whose moral complexities can no longer be resolved within the limits of Dostoevsky's previous humanitarian ethos.

In conclusion, a word must be devoted to the epilogue of the story, which, as Russian criticism has long been aware, contains a parody of the famous ball scene in the last book of *Evgeny Onegin*. It is the scene in which Evgeny and Tatayana meet again after many years, she no longer the simple country lass but the queen of Petersburg society, he now hopelessly head over heels in love with the girl he had once scorned. Marya Alexandrovna had used this scene earlier to bewitch the bewildered Mozglyakov, holding up before him the vision of a similar encounter with Zina, the wealthy and glamorous widow of Prince K., who falls into his arms in gratitude for his nobility of soul. Three years later, sent to a remote part of the Russian Empire, Mozglyakov meets the Governor-General ("a tall, lean, stern general, an old military man, who had been wounded in battle, and had two stars and a white cross on his breast") and is invited to his wife's name-day ball that very evening (2: 397).

Of course his wife turns out to be the beautiful and imperious Zina, who is said to behave so proudly that she "only danced with generals" and who snubs the bewildered Mozglyakov entirely: "Her eyes glided over his face and at once turned to someone else." Marya Alexandrovna, more gracious, is at the very top of her form; she speaks to him for a few moments, rubs in his social insignificance, and then drops him entirely without breathing a word about the past. Mozglyakov stands around "with a biting Mephisthophelean smile" and in a picturesque attitude, leaning against a column for several hours; but "his disillusioned air and all the rest of it were thrown away. Zina completely failed to observe him." At last, hungry and tired ("as an unhappy lover he could not stay to supper"), he beats a retreat and leaves town the next morning (2: 397-398).

No one seems to have wondered why Dostoevsky should have used Pushkin in this irreverent fashion; but the parody serves several artistic functions. On the level of plot, it confirms Marya Alexandrovna's capacity to survive any disaster and her asserted superiority to Napoleon. It also supplies, on the level of theme, a very suitable conclusion to the attack on literary Romanticism that runs through the work as a subtext. By revealing so glaringly the triumph of "real life," with its necessary limitations and compromises, over an inflated and unworldly idealism nourished on literary stereotypes, Dostoevsky is making a point that he will return to again and again in the future—of course, in relation to other ideologies with far graver consequences when put into practice. But even here, the use of this thematic motif might well be given a greater resonance than it appears to have at first sight. Would not Dostoevsky have tended to see himself as the victim of a similar specious idealism, and had he not learned the human cost of such self-intoxication? Such a deeper note, although it may easily be read into the work, is not really struck by the author; and it would be a distortion to give it greater prominence than Dostoevsky did himself.

The Village of Stepanchikovo

The Village of Stepanchikovo is much more ambitious than *Uncle's Dream*, although pitched at the same level and written in the same key of farcical comedy. Considering it his best work up to that time, Dostoevsky viewed it as an authentic personal expression of his own point of view. "I have put into it my soul, my flesh and blood," he tells his brother. "I do not wish to say that I have expressed myself completely in it; that would be nonsense! There still remains a good deal that I wish to express. Besides, there is not much romantic interest in the novel (i.e., the passionate element, as for example in *A Nest of Gentlefolk*)—but it contains two immensely typical characters, *created and noted down* over a five-year period, worked out flawlessly (in my opinion)—characters entirely Russian and only badly presented up to now in Russian literature."[8] Dostoevsky here is obviously referring to his two main figures, Foma Fomich Opiskin and Colonel Rostanev, whose strange relationship constitutes the heart of his story.

For at least the first of these characters, Foma Fomich (his last name, Opiskin, means a mistake in writing or a slip of the pen), the passage of time has verified Dostoevsky's conviction that he had produced an "immensely typical" figure; no less a judge than Thomas Mann has called him "a comic creation of the first rank, irresistible, rivalling Shakespeare and Molière."[9] Indeed, the name "Foma Fomich" has since become a byword in Russian for any kind of insolent and impertinent hypocrite, toady, and sponger and is used much as the names of Uriah Heep and Pecksniff are used in English. As Mann's mention of Molière suggests, the role Foma Fomich plays in the household of Colonel Rostanev reminds one strongly of Tartuffe in Molière's famous play; and this work is unquestionably one of Dostoevsky's sources. Others of lesser importance have been unearthed (such as a little-known comedy of Turgenev's, *The Boarder* [1848], published in *The Contemporary* in 1857). A possible real-life source, as A. A. Kraevsky suggested immediately, was Nikolay Gogol in his last years, when he lived as a tyrannical and despotic guest who behaved in the most outrageous manner with his hosts. Yuri Tynyanov also established many years ago that much (though not all) of Foma's rhetoric is an explicit parody of excerpts from Gogol's *Selected Passages from My Correspondence with Friends*—a work that Dostoevsky had good reason to remember.

Important as these and others sources may be, however, it is more illuminating to view Foma as a new version of a type that Dostoevsky had often depicted in the 1840s. Like most of the protagonists of these early works, Foma is (or had been) one of the downtrodden, with just enough education to make him feel his obscure social status as a wounding humiliation. In the past, we learn, Foma had tried his hand at everything, once holding a government job (lost, presumably "for a good cause," though this excuse is probably only a self-flattering rumor) and having even taken a stab at literature with a trashy historical novel. At last he finds employment as a reader and paid companion to a vicious general, an invalid who enjoys degrading his flunky for amusement; "there was no ignominy which he had not to endure in return for eating the General's bread" (3: 8).

Previously, Dostoevsky had always treated such characters with a good deal of sympathy, if occasionally also, as in *The Double*, mixed with ironic condescension; but in his very last work before Siberia, *Netotchka Nez-vanova*, there is a significant exception to this rule. There he portrays a vainglorious failed musician, Yefimov, who is convinced that he is a great genius and whose frustrations turn into sadistic abuse of his poor slavey of a wife and emotional exploitation of his innocent little stepdaughter. Dostoevsky carefully emphasizes the lack of any *social* cause for Yefimov's resentment against the world; such resentment springs solely from the unhealthy dilatation of his own Romantic ego, whose claim to superiority he does little or nothing to justify in practice. Yefimov can only respond to his self-induced humiliations by wreaking vengeance on others; and though Dostoevsky makes him pitiable, he is also shown as mean-spirited and contemptible in his total indifference to the fate of his family.

In this unfinished novel, then, Dostoevsky was no longer grounding his psychology, as he had usually done before, primarily in the social situation of the individual. Rather, he was moving toward the placement of moral responsibility squarely on the person himself for the consequences of his actions. But Dostoevsky was still chary, at that time, of breaking too overtly with the philanthropic presuppositions of the Natural School, within whose ranks he had begun his own career and whose values he still accepted. Hence the moral condemnation of Yefimov, who is not at all a victim of society in the strict sense, does not directly clash with the tolerance exhibited by the Natural School toward the failings of those who lived in poverty and suffered from an inferior social status. Moreover, Dostoevsky's harsh treatment of Yefimov also accords with the campaign against Romanticism then being carried on by Belinsky and echoed by younger writers under his influence. With Foma Fomich, however, Dostoevsky firmly and finally confronts the moral assumptions of the Natural School and rejects them out of hand.

Foma Fomich, it is clear, has been forced to endure the most extreme humiliations because of his social inferiority, and his sadistic behavior is directly attributed to his desire to revenge himself on others for what he had suffered himself. But there is no mistaking the indictment that Dostoevsky levels against Foma's conduct when his fortunes are reversed and *he* achieves a position of power. "Well, now imagine," writes the narrator, "what this Foma, who had been all his life oppressed and crushed, perhaps actually beaten too, who was vain and secretly lascivious, who had been disappointed in his literary ambitions, who had played the buffoon for a crust of bread, who was at heart a despot in spite of all his previous abjectness and impotence, who was a braggart, and insolent when successful, might become when he suddenly found himself in the haven he had reached after so many ups and downs, honored and glorified, humored and flattered, thanks to a patroness who was an idiot and a patron who was imposed upon and ready to agree to anything" (3: 13).

What happened is explained without beating around the bush: "He paid us out for his past! *A base soul escaping from oppression becomes an oppressor*" (ibid.; italics added). Nothing that occurred in Foma's past, in other words, can justify or excuse his abhorrent behavior, even though, as the narrator is willing to concede, "his ugly exaggerated vanity" in the present may be "only a false, fundamentally depraved sense of dignity, first outraged, perhaps, in childhood by oppression, poverty, filth, spat upon, perhaps, in the person of the future outcast's parents before his eyes" (3: 12). None of this can absolve Foma Fomich from the onus of being "a base soul," whose definition is precisely the inability to overcome a need to dominate and humiliate others as revenge for one's own humiliation and sufferings.

Foma Fomich is framed in the story by two other characters, whose thematic function has eluded all commentators known to me but who manifestly serve as "quasi-doubles" to highlight this authorial judgment of his baseness. Among the other guests in the hospitable home of Colonel Rostanev is the wealthy heiress Tatyana Ivanovna, whose personal history is an exact parallel to that of Foma's. She too, before inheriting her fortune by a fluke, "in the course of her poor life . . . drained the overfull cup of sorrow, friendlessness, humiliation and reproach, and had tasted to the full the bitterness of the bread of others" (3: 120). All the same, the native sweetness and kindness of her character remains unaltered when her position suddenly changes overnight, even though she does have delusions of grandeur in her own way and dreams of being swept off her feet by a grand Romantic passion. Closer in character to Foma is the clerk Yezhevikin, the impoverished father of the young governess Nastenka with whom Colonel Rostanev is in love. Like Foma, Yezhevikin has a rankling envy of his betters and, while pretending to be "the most abject, grovelling flatterer" (3: 166), clearly is mocking and sneering at those before whom he is verbally subservient. At the same time, though, he is genuinely honest, possessing a "sensitive and touchy" sense of his dignity that does not allow him to exploit others in his own interest or even to accept any but the most essential financial aid offered out of kindness by the Colonel.

That *The Village of Stepanchikovo* explicitly involves some sort of critical revision by Dostoevsky of his own past is also clearly indicated by the narrative perspective. For the story is told by a young man, a nephew of the Colonel, brought up by him and a recent graduate of the University of St. Petersburg. What happens in Stepanchikovo is recounted through his startled and disbelieving eyes; and the change he undergoes is of first-rate thematic importance. Before meeting Foma Fomich in the flesh—and the appearance of the self-proclaimed "great man" is carefully retarded to obtain the maximum dramatic impact—the narrator responds to all the rumors about him in accordance with the humanitarian principles inculcated by his progressive university education. And these principles turn out to be, in a simplified and parodistic form, precisely those which had inspired Dostoevsky's own works in the 1840s. Perhaps, says the young narrator fumblingly, Foma is "a gifted nature" who "has been wounded, crushed by sufferings," and so is avenging himself on humanity. "Do you understand: a man of noble nature . . . perception . . . and to play the part of a buffoon! . . . And so he became mistrustful of all mankind . . . and perhaps if he could be reconciled to humanity . . . he would turn out to be a rare nature, perhaps even a very remarkable one" (3: 29). This point of view is abandoned instantly by the narrator once he sees Foma in action; and his change of heart reveals to what extent Dostoevsky was conscious of having broken with the ideology of his earlier work. From this time on, the social-psychological perspective he had largely maintained throughout the 1840s will be replaced by one in which the moral responsibility of the person takes precedence over all other considerations.

2

As the narrator rightly observes, Foma Fomich could not have achieved the "insolent domination" he exercises at Stepanchikovo if not for the equally remarkable character of the owner of that estate, Colonel Rostanev. No precedent for him really exists earlier, though one may think of the kindhearted General in *Poor Folk*, who gives the tatterdemalion Makar Devushkin one hundred rubles out of the goodness of his heart, or the music-loving Prince X of *Netotchka Nezvanova*, who adopts the heroine as a little orphan and brings her up as a member of his family. Both of these were only shadowy sketches, however, while Colonel Rostanev is a full-length portrait.

No single Dostoevskian character thus anticipates Colonel Rostanev as clearly as Yefimov does Foma Fomich; but the Colonel may nonetheless be linked to a thematic tendency already observable in *Netotchka Nezvanova*. Just as in the case of Yefimov, that is, without overtly clashing with the social-psychological framework of the book, Dostoevsky stressed in that work the need to overcome the instinctive impulse of the humiliated ego to hit back; each important episode illustrates in some way the nefarious moral consequences of a failure to conquer resentment and the ravages of an egoism so self-absorbed as to be incapable of forgiveness or even of mercy. Now, in *The Village of Stepanchikovo*, Dostoevsky essays his first positive embodiment of this thematic motif in a single character, his first attempt to create that ideal of a "perfectly good man" to which he will return repeatedly throughout the remainder of his life. And the juxtaposition and pairing of Foma and the Colonel—the face-to-face opposition of an egomaniacal member of the Russian intelligentsia with a

simple Russian soul, overflowing with charity and love—obviously anticipates a similar pattern in many later works.

Dostoevsky, as we know, had become convinced in Siberia that the moral
qualities of charity and selflessness typical of such a perfectly good man
existed as a moral reality—perhaps concealed from the unobservant eye,
but nonetheless present—at the roots of ordinary Russian life. Such a
conviction had emerged largely as a result of his association with the
peasant-convicts; but those who had helped him most concretely at his
worst moments had been officers in the Army. This may explain why he
presents his first ideal figure in the unlikely guise of such an officer, now
retired to run his estate at Stepanchikovo, who, having spent all his life
in the Army, is not distinguished by any unusual qualities of mind or
education. All the same, while presenting the very image of presumably
self-assertive masculine health and strength, Colonel Rostanev possesses
a moral disposition seraphic in its mildness, amiability, and lack of self-
regard. "He was a perfect child at forty, open-hearted in the extreme,
always good-humored, imagining everybody an angel. . . . He was one of
those very generous and pure-hearted men who are positively ashamed to
assume any harm of another . . . and in that way always live in an ideal
world, and when anything goes wrong always blame themselves first. To
sacrifice themselves in the interests of others is their natural vocation" (3:
13-14).

Colonel Rostanev is thus a "weak" character in the best sense of that
word; and one has the distinct impression that in detailing his qualities,
Dostoevsky is doing so with a side-glance at the Chernyshevsky-Annenkov
controversy. No one seems to have remarked this possibility; but why
otherwise should the narrator have felt called upon to meet the following
objection: "Some people (who?) would have called him (Colonel Rostanev)
cowardly, weak-willed and feeble. Of course he was weak, and indeed he
was of too soft a disposition; but it was not from lack of will, but from fear
of wounding, of behaving cruelly, from excess of respect for others and
for mankind in general. He was, however, weak-willed and cowardly only
when nothing was at stake but his own interests, which he completely
disregarded, and for this he was continually an object of derision, and
often with the very people for whom he was sacrificing his own advantage"
(3: 14).

Foma Fomich obtains his initial hold over the Colonel when he arrives
in the retinue of the Colonel's mother, the widow of the general who had
used (and abused) Foma as his buffoon. Even at this difficult period of
his life, Foma had succeeded in gaining control over this credulous and
superstitious woman, who rivals him in selfishness and self-indulgence
while lacking his cunning and intelligence. "He (Foma) read aloud to
them [*Madame la générale* and her repulsive hangers-on] works of spiritual

edification; held forth with eloquent tears on the Christian virtues; told stories of his life and heroic doings; went to mass and even to matins; at times foretold the future; had a peculiar faculty for interpreting dreams, and was a great hand at throwing blame on his neighbors" (3: 8). As the narrator bitingly remarks: "And this idiot woman my uncle thought it his duty to revere, simply because she was his mother" (3: 14). As a result, the Colonel's reverence for his mother is transferred to Foma, and Foma exploits this filial devotion to turn the Colonel into a plaything at the mercy of the whims of a malicious underling.

Foma, as we are shown at great (too great) length, takes a sadistic pleasure in browbeating and humiliating the Colonel, while the helpless and hapless victim allows himself to be persecuted to an extent that, it must be admitted, strains the limits of credulity. "They began with proving to my uncle at once that he was coarse, impatient, ignorant and selfish to the highest degree. . . . They persuaded my uncle, too, that Foma had been sent by Divine Providence for the salvation of his soul and the sub-duing of his unbridled passions; that he was haughty, proud of his wealth, and quite capable of reproaching Foma Fomich for eating his bread. My poor uncle was very soon convinced of the depth of his degradation, was ready to tear his hair and beg forgiveness" (ibid.). All this is the very opposite of the truth; it is the consummate moral imposter Foma who displays all the sins he imputes to the Colonel; but the latter, incapable of finding fault with others and only too ready to accuse himself, is tre-mendously impressed by Foma's high-minded regurgitations of snippets from Gogol's *Selected Passages* (as well as from several other sources less well-known).

Most of the action is taken up with the various devices invented by Foma, with ingenious nastiness, to harass and mortify the Colonel—all being calculated, at the same time, to exalt the insatiable vanity of the erstwhile flunky. Some are purely on the level of slapstick, such as Foma's insistence that the Colonel address him as "Your Excellency" (a title re-served only for generals) "as a lesson," Foma explains, "not to be in ec-stasies at the sight of generals when there are other people, perhaps, superior to all your generals" (3: 56).

Dostoevsky evidently meant other motifs to be taken as slapstick as well, but in the context of the times they probably gave rise to misunderstanding. Foma decides, for instance, that the Colonel, a kindly and model land-owner, has been neglecting the mental development of his peasants and engages to teach them astronomy and French pronunciation, which are of course no use to them whatsoever. In truth, Foma exhibits the utmost contempt for the peasants, and his so-called concern for their education is only self-glorifying humbug; but Dostoevsky's satire may well have been misunderstood as an attack on the cause of peasant education. Actually, he was always a staunch advocate of such education, while also believing that the acquisition of a superficial smattering of Western ideas would do the Russian peasant more harm than good. To illustrate such a danger, he provides Foma with a refined serf-valet who writes bad poetry and keeps changing his name because the other peasants always find "vulgar" rhymes for each one he adopts. The association of this unfortunate simpleton with Foma, whose vanity and vainglory he seeks to emulate, prefigures the relationship between the valet and cook Smerdyakov with Ivan Karamazov in *The Brothers Karamazov*; and while the tone here is jocular, the poor, misguided house-serf does end in a madhouse.

A more serious level of intrigue involves the plan, concocted by Foma and the Colonel's mother, to force the Colonel into marriage with Tatyana Ivanovna. Actually, he is in love with Nastenka, the poor young governess of his two children by his first marriage. Aware of the Colonel's inclination, Foma and *Madame la générale* persecute Nastenka unmercifully with the aim of driving her away; and the Colonel initially invites his young nephew to Stepanchikovo as a prospective suitor for Nastenka if he can win her consent. Once on the scene, however, the situation becomes clear, and the narrator urges his uncle to defy the plotters and marry Nastenka himself.

The dénouement occurs when Foma finally goes too far, accusing the Colonel in public of having seduced and depraved the young woman. This is too much even for the long-suffering Colonel, who, enraged at the slur on Nastenka's reputation, physically pitches Foma Fomich through a glass door and out of the house. The unbeatable Foma soon returns, bruised and battered, but chastened enough now to realize that he must change his tune. So he blesses the marriage, pretending to have been in favor of it all along, and lives happily ever after in clover with the grateful pair, posing, preachifying, and carrying on much as before, but careful not to overstep the line that finally had been drawn: "She (Nastenka) would not see her husband humiliated and insisted on her wishes being respected" (3: 164).

3

Despite the trite and conventional nature of the plot intrigue, with its well-timed (and, it must be confessed, very satisfying) comeuppance for the odious Foma Fomich, *The Village of Stepanchikovo* is much more than the superficial entertainment it may initially be taken to be. Dostoevsky was speaking quite truthfully when he declared that it had been written with "his flesh and blood"; and one can already see reflected in its pages some of the important artistic consequences of his Siberian years. These consequences are most evident, of course, in Foma Fomich, who surpasses in force and impressiveness all of Dostoevsky's earlier treatments of the psychology of humiliation, and who delineates Dostoevsky's deepened understanding of the explosive power of resentment and frustration simmering in the irrational depths of the human personality. For what had been suggested in Yefimov only as an aberration of the Romantic ego is now presented as a much more widespread human potentiality, which could easily develop in situations of humiliating dependence. Foma's immeasurable vanity, the narrator remarks, may seem a special case, but in fact, "who knows, perhaps in some of these degraded victims of fate, your fools and buffoons, vanity far from being dispelled by humiliation is even aggravated by that very humiliation . . . and being forever forced to submission and self-suppression" (3: 12). Such a comment springs directly from Dostoevsky's indelible recollections of the prison camp, where he had seen the need of the personality to assert itself in some way at all costs.

Indeed, it is possible—though probably a trifle premature—to regard Foma Fomich as a first sketch of the underground man. In general, Foma acts in a perfectly rational manner: everything he does may be inspired by resentment, but ultimately it works to his advantage. His domination of Colonel Rostanev enables him to lead a life of luxurious self-indulgence, which he enjoys to the hilt; and when the benefits of his position are threatened at the climax, he quickly adopts a different tack. Even though his behavior as a whole can thus hardly be compared with the willful self-destructiveness of the undergound man, there is one scene where he does exhibit a willingness to sacrifice immediate self-interest for the sake of an "irrational" ego satisfaction. When the Colonel offers Foma a large sum of money to leave Stepanchikovo and settle in the nearby town, proposing to buy him a house there as well, Foma rejects the inducement with monumental scorn and squeals of outrage that his "honor" is being insulted. Another character comments, on hearing of the incident: "I doubt whether Foma had any mercenary design in it (the refusal). He is not a practical man; he is a sort of poet, too, in his own way. . . . He would have taken the money, do you see, but he couldn't resist the temptation to strike an attitude and give himself airs" (3: 93-94). Such a predominance of emotive impulse over economic calculation is only a momentary velleity in Foma's case; but it does point the way to the future elaboration of his psychology into that of the underground man.*

* Besides the underground man and, in Colonel Rostanev, the future "idiot," we also catch a prefiguration of Raskolnikov in one of the subplots. A seedy young fortune hunter, a cultivated but more craven variation of the Foma-type, persuades Tatyana Ivanovna into a runaway elopement. When caught red-handed and stopped in the nick of time, the culprit turns out to be a Raskolnikov *avant la lettre*, who pleads that he was not inspired by "mercenary motives." "I should have used the money usefully . . . ," he babbles. "I should have helped the poor. I wanted to support the movement for enlightenment, too, and even dreamed of endowing a university scholarship . . ." (2: 123).

The Village of Stepanchikovo is also given depth by numerous literary and ideological parodies, contained primarily in Foma's tirades and occasionally in the reponses of the Colonel. It would be superfluous (and tedious) to go through them all, but they include some sharp digs at *Notes of the Fatherland*, in whose pages the novella appeared; and despite his anxiety to place the work, which had not been originally intended for this journal at all, Dostoevsky was unyielding on the question of retaining his satirical barbs. Some are comic byplay that merely ridicule absurdities and stupidities; others serve to fill out the portrait of Foma, whose literary tastes and preferences reveal the banal shallowness of his mind and the extravagance of his pretentiousness. The work, as we have said, also contains parodistic allusions to Gogol's *Selected Passages*, and it is this feature of the text that has attracted most critical attention.

Whether, as Tynyanov maintained, Foma Fomich was intended as a personal take-off of Gogol, as well as of the rhetoric of his ill-fated book, can only remain a matter for speculation.[10] The attempt to prove that Foma actually resembles Gogol physically, or that his behavior alludes to Gogol's status as a privileged house guest in the home of the Aksakovs, is not supported with very convincing evidence. On the other hand, Dostoevsky had reacted ironically as far back as 1846 to reports of some of the bizarre peculiarities of Gogol's behavior;* he was not averse to employing such purely personal parody; and we know from Kraevsky's remark that contemporaries instantly thought of Gogol when reading the story. One thing, however, is incontestable: Tynyanov amply proves that portions of Gogol's *Selected Passages*, as well as of his earlier *Testament*, are burlesqued in the substance of some of Foma's harangues. Still, Tynyanov's exclusive focus on Gogol's texts is somewhat misleading since several other writers also receive the same sort of irreverent manhandling.

V. V. Vinogradov has righted the balance by describing Foma Fomich, "so long as he has a historically representative character and not simply a human one," as "a collective type of the pretentious literary hack of the 1840s," whose opinions derive from (and burlesque) "the literary activity of N. Polevoy, Kukolnik, and others, and not only Gogol's *Selected Pas-*

---

* "I do not wish to say anything about Gogol," Dostoevsky wrote his brother Mikhail in 1846, "but here are the facts: *The Contemporary* next month will publish an article by Gogol— his spiritual testament, in which he renounces all his works and declares them useless and even worse. He says that he will no longer take up the pen for the rest of his life because his task is to pray; that he agrees with all the criticisms of his adversaries. He orders that his portrait be distributed in an incredible number of copies and that the proceeds be turned over to pilgrims going to Jerusalem, etc. There it is. Draw your own conclusions."
A note of parody and a foretaste of Foma Fomich already creeps into this account, based on a conversation with a close friend of Gogol's, and Dostoevsky does not fail to burlesque a passage from the *Testament* in one of Foma's tirades. F. M. Dostoevsky, *Pisma*, 1: 93; September 5, 1846.

sages."[11] Dostoevsky may originally have been inspired by antipathy to Gogol's book; but he turns Foma Fomich into a more general type and finds other literary instances of the same sort of spiritual humbuggery that he wishes to castigate. The target of the attack is no longer a particular individual or book but Foma's pose of self-glorification and almost self-deification. Such self-inflation, as Dostoevsky had become all too well aware in prison camp, could lead to terrible consequences when a "base soul" such as Major Krivtsov obtained power over others.

The prominence given by Tynyanov to Gogol's notorious text as a parodistic source, however, has led to some misunderstanding of Dostoevsky's own relation to Gogol's values. Most critics regard *The Village of Stepanchikovo* as a total repudiation of Gogol's position; even as acute a reader as K. Mochulsky laments that Dostoevsky "did not appreciate the enormous spiritual and social significance of the *Selected Passages*," which, as he rightly points out, contains much that became "the basis of (Dostoevsky's) world-outlook."[12] But while this regret may seem justified at first glance, it actually overlooks the complex fashion in which Dostoevsky develops his parody.

For it can hardly be true that Dostoevsky meant to repudiate the ideas uttered by Foma Fomich, which contain injunctions and exhortations that certainly speak for his own moral ideals ("Be softer, more attentive, more loving to others," Foma admonishes the Colonel, "forget yourself for the sake of others, then they will think of you. . . . Suffer, labor, pray and hope . . ."; (3: 89). Dostoevsky does not satirize the literal sense of such perfectly respectable Christian counsels, which he had no intention of undermining *in themselves*, but rather their perversion to obtain and justify domination over others. He repudiates Foma, after all, by juxtaposing him with Colonel Rostanev, who is the authentic embodiment of all the moral values that Foma is eternally proclaiming in words and totally ignoring in deeds. A similar technique is used in *Uncle's Dream*, where the attack on literary Romanticism does not touch its genuine values: Zina is ready to sacrifice herself *sincerely* for Vasya, while her mother exalts sacrifice only as a hypocritical screen to obtain the most ignoble ends. One is also reminded of Dostoevsky's initial skirmish with Gogol in *Poor Folk*, where he takes over Gogol's philanthropic appeal in *The Overcoat* and creates a character (Makar Devushkin) more worthy of being regarded with such sympathy and pity than Gogol's doltish Akaky Akakievich.

In each case, Dostoevsky actually *accepts* the values of the parodied source but not the *form* in which they are embodied; hence the character of Foma Fomich does not, in my view, indicate any fundamental repudiation of Gogol's evocation in *Selected Passages* of an ideal Christian Utopia. What Dostoevsky objects to is the distortion and defamation of this ideal by those who abuse or misuse it as a cover for social injustice

(Gogol's defense of serfdom) and personal self-aggrandizement. Such a reading can be supported by a remark, made many years later by Dostoevsky in his notebooks, that reflects his unchanging attitude toward the *Selected Passages*. "The ideal of Gogol is strange," he wrote sometime in 1876-1877; "inwardly it is Christianity, but his Christianity is not Christianity."[13] Dostoevsky created Colonel Rostanev as his first "outward" image of what it meant to be a genuine Christian.

5
———

The question of Dostoevsky's relation to Gogol, however, is only a side issue in the story, or enters as part of the larger theme of his relation to the values of his past. We have already commented on the deflation of the narrator's relatively philanthropic sentiments once he catches sight of Foma in the flesh; and Dostoevsky repeats and reinforces this key motif at the conclusion, where he also adds another important touch to the characterization of the Colonel. For just after Foma has been tamed and placated, the Foma-motif is reiterated in relation to another "great man" and "light of learning"—Korovkin—whom the Colonel has met by chance one day on the high road and invited to Stepanchikovo. This worthy gentleman turns up at the climax, amidst the general rejoicing, attired in greasy rags and dead drunk. The Colonel begins to apologize for him in words almost identical with those earlier used by the narrator about Foma: "You know, he may be an excellent man, but fate. . . . He has had misfortunes. . . . You don't believe it, but perhaps it really is so." At which point the affectionate narrator, to comfort his embarrassed uncle, pretends to agree with him: "And I began fervently declaring that even in the creature who has fallen lowest there may still survive the finest human feelings; that the depths of the human soul are unfathomable; that we must not despise the fallen but on the contrary ought to seek them out and raise them up; that the commonly accepted standard of goodness and morality was not infallible, and so on, and so on; in fact, I warmed up to the subject, *and even began talking about the Natural School.* In conclusion, I even repeated the verses: "When from dark error's subjugation . . ." (3: 160-161; italics added).

The verse in question, taken from a poem by Nekrasov (Dostoevsky will use the same poem, at greater length, in the epigraph to *Notes from Underground*), celebrates the magnanimity of a high-minded "progressive" lover, who, having risen above social prejudice, "redeems" a prostitute by making her his wife. By this time, the narrator regards the words of Colonel Rostanev as typical of the indiscriminately benevolent attitude represented by the poem—the very same attitude he has just managed to slough off himself. He thus cites the poem ironically, as a notorious expression of such well-meant but naive illusions. The Colonel, though, in his entire innocence, takes the narrator's words at face value; but what he says, in supposed agreement, differs significantly from the narrator's progressive litany. " 'My dear, my dear,' he said, much touched, 'you understand me fully, and have said much better than I could what I wanted to express: Yes, yes! Good heaven! Why is it man is wicked? Why is it *I am so often wicked* when it is so splendid, so fine to be good' " (3: 161; italics added).

Dostoevsky, it seems to me, wishes the reader at this point to feel a distinct difference between the effusions of the Colonel and the narrator's tongue-in-cheek recital of his benevolent commonplaces—commonplaces that already have been exploded in the main action involving Foma. But since it is a difference more suggested than articulated, the nuance in their responses has not attracted the attention of commentators. What separates the two attitudes is that, in the Colonel's case, his spontaneous sympathy with his fellow man immediately involves a sense of *his own* weakness and human fallibility. Nothing of the kind can be seen in the humanitarianism of the Natural School, which contains, on the contrary, a latent self-complacency, an implicit posture of superiority to and patronage of the "fallen," who must of course be "sought out and raised up."*

Some additional evidence for such an interpretation can be cited from the brief epilogue, where Dostoevsky comments on the same altruistic position as exhibited by Nastenka. It is she who keeps Foma in check after her marriage with the Colonel; but the narrator remarks that she nonetheless forgave Foma because of her happiness, "and what is more, I believe she seriously with all her heart entered into my uncle's idea that too much must not be expected from a 'victim' who had once been a buffoon, but on the contrary, balm must be poured on his wounded heart. Poor Nastenka had herself been one of the *humiliated*, she had suffered and she remembered it" (3: 164). Once again Dostoevsky emphasizes the *personal* sense of identification with the victim or sufferer—a compassion springing not from any theoretical doctrine of social pity, with its implied

---

* K. Mochulsky has called attention to another facet of the Colonel's reply at this point: his hymn to nature. Just after his remark about his own wickedness, the Colonel continues: "But look, though, what a glorious place this is. . . . What scenery! What a picture! What a tree! Look: you could hardly get your arms round it. What sap! What foliage! What sunshine! How gay everything is, washed clean after the storm! . . . One would think that even the trees understand everything, have feeling and enjoyment of life. . . . Is that out of the question—eh! . . . Marvellous, marvellous is the Creator!" (3: 161).

Mochulsky rightly sees this speech as prefiguring Dimitry Karamazov's "hymn from the underground" in Part IV, Chapter 4 of *The Brothers Karamazov*; and such an "ecstatic" sense of nature does represent an important feature of Dostoevsky's own sensibility. But its use in *The Village of Stepanchikovo* is only incidental, and in my opinion less thematically significant at this stage of Dostoevsky's career than the Colonel's inclusion of himself in the ranks of sinners. K. Mochulsky, *Dostoevsky, His Life and Work*, trans. Michael A. Minihan (Princeton, 1967), 177-178.

sense of distance and hierarchy, but out of a frame of mind and heart placing the forgiver on exactly the same moral-human level as the forgiven.

Erich Auerbach has remarked that Russian Realism, unlike the other European literatures of the nineteenth century, "is based on a Christian and traditionally patriarchal concept of the creatural dignity of every human individual regardless of social rank and position," and "is fundamentally related to old-Christian rather than to modern occidental realism."[14] It may be suggested that, in the passages cited above, we can catch Dostoevsky in the process of discarding his Western-oriented beliefs of the 1840s or, more exactly, transforming the predominantly social emphasis of his earlier commitment to Christian values into one inclining toward a more traditional Christian sense of universal moral culpability and responsibility for evil and sin. It is only a love for one's fellow man springing from *such* a sense, we may interpret him as saying, that can escape the onus of pharisaical pride and insulting condescension and both judge and pardon at the same time.

CHAPTER 20

Homecoming

The publication of Dostoevsky's two Siberian novellas marks the end of his artistic exile and the beginning of his return to the center of Russian cultural life. These works appeared in print during 1859, and at the very end of this year, in mid-December, Dostoevsky finally realized his long-awaited dream of returning to St. Petersburg physically as well. This home-coming, however, did not take place all at once; even after arriving in European Russia, he was forced to stagnate for several months in Tver, a good-sized city on the railroad line between Petersburg and Moscow. He had chosen this place of residence himself when, although granted retirement from the Army for reasons of health, he had been denied the right to live in either of the two cities where he could obtain competent medical treatment. This infuriating ruling seems to have been a bit of bureaucratic bungling inspired by excessive caution. The Ministry of War did not wish to take responsibility for determining Dostoevsky's place of residence and advised him to ask for authorization from the Tsar through the Third Section. Dostoevsky decided that the closer he came to the seat of authority, the better the chance of expediting his affairs; and living in Tver would at least bring him within easy reach of his family in Moscow as well as of the editors and publishers in Petersburg on whom his future livelihood depended.

Accordingly, at the beginning of July 1859, Dostoevsky began the lengthy journey back to Russia, which took about a month and a half and again involved a huge sum of money that he managed to scrape together with the help of a loan from Aleksey Pleshcheev. The party paused at Omsk for a few days to pick up Pasha Isaev, who had been withdrawn from the Siberian Cadet Corps. There Dostoevsky saw old friends, including the humane commandant of the fortress, General de Grave, and Chokan Va-likhanov; the latter had himself been called to Petersburg and was to depart a month later. Dostoevsky's letter describing the trip, written to his former company commander, A. I. Geibovich, is unusually detailed and contains some vivid passages.

A moving moment occurred when the Dostoevsky's *tarantas*, rolling through the Ural Mountains, reached the frontier between Asia and Europe. Ten years before, a prisoner in shackles, Dostoevsky had passed this frontier in the midst of a howling snowstorm; now it was a fine summer afternoon, about five o'clock, when they stumbled on "the handsome column with an inscription, and beside it, in an *izba*, an invalid [i.e., a wounded veteran acting as caretaker]. We got out of the *tarantas*, and I crossed myself; God, at last, had led me to see the promised land. Then we took out our plaited flask full of a tangy wild-orange brandy . . . and we drank our goodbye to Asia with the invalid; Nikolaev [the guide] also drank and the coachman too (and how he drove afterwards)."[1]

The Dostoevsky's were much impressed with the great fair at Nizhni-Novgorod, which was going full blast when they arrived; all the hotels were occupied, and they wandered through the streets for hours before being able to find modest accommodations. The high point of the trip, though, was a nostalgic visit to the monastery of the Trinity and St. Sergey at Zagorsk—the famous place of pilgrimage where, every spring until the age of ten, Dostoevsky had been taken by his mother on an annual outing. One can hardly exaggerate the importance of the impressions gathered by the young boy during these visits to the hallowed shrine, where the glories of the Russian past were inseparably intermingled with the sacred symbols of Russian religious faith. Nor had the monastery ceased to hold its enchantment for Dostoevsky even after these many years; in the midst of complaints about bad roads and greedy guides on the last leg of the journey, he nonetheless adds: "But the monastery of St. Sergey made it all fully worthwhile. I had not been there for 23 years. What architecture, what monuments, what Byzantine chapels, churches! The sacristy amazed us. The pearls in the sacristy (absolutely superb) as heavy as a quarter of a pound, emeralds three inches big, diamonds worth a half-million each. The costumes of several centuries, made by the very hands of Russian Tsarinas and Imperial princesses, the clothes worn at home by Ivan the Terrible, coins, ancient books, all sorts of rareties—there was no end to it."[2]

2

Expecting Tver to be only a very temporary way station on his route, Dostoevsky took furnished lodgings for his family rather than renting a more comfortable apartment and being forced to buy furniture. As usual, however, bureaucratic dilatoriness prolonged his stay for what seemed an eternity; and it was little consolation that the house he occupied had once sheltered the august presence of no less a personage than Pushkin. Life in Tver weighed on him terribly, and he speaks of it, in a letter to Wrangel, as equivalent to a new imprisonment. "Actually, I am locked up in Tver and it's worse than Semipalatinsk. Even though Semipalatinsk, the last year or so, has entirely changed (not one really likable person, nor one happy memory)—but Tver is a thousand times worse. Gloomy, cold, stone houses, no life, no interests—there is not even a decent library. A genuine prison! I intend to get out of here as soon as possible."³ Even the visit of his brother Mikhail and another old friend, Dr. Yanovsky, did not suffice to ease his restlessness. The closeness of Petersburg, where negotiations involving his work were being carried on by proxy, only served to make his location in limbo even more intolerable.

Luckily, his relative social isolation in Tver was ended by the passage of V. A. Golovinsky, an old acquaintance whom Dostoevsky had introduced into the Petrashevsky circle and who, after serving a relatively light sentence in the Russian Army, was on his way to a Civil Service post in Siberia. One of Dostoevsky's closest friends at the time of their arrest, the young man had been not only a fiery partisan of the liberation of the serfs but also one of those who believed, along with Dostoevsky, that "the Slavic principle" of the *obshchina* would "save Russia from the terrible ravages of Socialism." In Tver, Golovinsky introduced Dostoevsky to the Governor-General, Count Baranov, whose wife, as it happened, was a cousin of the writer Count Sollogub, and Dostoevsky discovered he had met her years before in the days of his literary fame. All doors were thus opened to him, and Baranov offered to help Dostoevsky obtain permission to change his place of residence. But he advised him to wait until mid-October, since Prince Dolgoruky, the chief of the Third Section, was at the moment on a voyage with the Tsar and nothing could be done until his return.

Accepting this reasonable advice, but unable to contain his impatience, Dostoevsky then wrote to General Totleben asking him to further his cause with Dolgoruky when the proper time arrived. He also wrote to Wrangel, requesting him to speak to Totleben about the matter in person. But then, unhappily, the imprudent Dostoevsky gave way to what seemed to him an inspiration—why not write directly to the Tsar himself instead of going through his ministers? This inspiration was approved by Baranov, who offered to have his relative Count Adlerberg, known as one of the Tsar's confidants, hand the letter personally to the Sovereign. The letter to the Tsar was dispatched in mid-October, about a week after the one to Totleben, and the letter to Dolgoruky was sent on its way November 4. As he soon realized, however, Dostoevsky had made the fatal mistake of attempting to use two different channels of the same bureaucratic mechanism simultaneously, and the result was only confusion and further delay. No action was possible for Dolgoruky until the Tsar took the initiative, and who could tell if Adlerburg had handed over the all-important letter or when he would deign to do so? Dostoevsky frankly admitted that he had blundered. "I agree with you," he writes Mikhail, "that in this matter I chose the most difficult course. I blame myself every day—and I wait. If only someone reminded Adlerberg of my existence!"⁴

None of these delays, however, dampened the ardor of Dostoevsky's enthusiasm for the new Tsar, which he expressed in accents of the purest devotion in his letter to Geibovich. "There is one unshakable hope: the merciful Sovereign," he tells him. "What a man he is, what a great man he is for Russia, Artemy Ivanovich! Here [in European Russia] everything is clearer and more easily perceptible. I have heard here a good deal. And what obstacles he has to fight against! There are scoundrels who do not like his salutary measures; they are all backward people stuck in the mud."[5] This passage displays Dostoevsky's unquestionably genuine reverence for the Tsar and also, very probably, the effect of his contact in Tver with a liberal social-political milieu. The committee of landowners of the Tver region, then sitting in session to discuss the modalities of the impending liberation of the serfs, was known as the only such committee in Russia with a majority of liberals; and Dostoevsky must have picked up gossip about the opposition they were encountering from dyed-in-the-wool reactionaries.

3

Much of Dostoevsky's energies during the months passed in Tver were taken up with these negotiations over his permission to move to Petersburg; but he was also concerned with his future literary plans. As a "literary proletarian" (he uses the term himself in a letter of October 9, 1859)[6] whose only source of livelihood was his pen, he was constantly turning over ideas for new works and calculating the possibilities of squeezing a little more out of his past publications. Although Mikhail kept supplying him with funds, and even with indispensable clothing (not to mention a new autumn hat for Marya Dimitrievna), Dostoevsky was painfully aware that his brother could not long continue to support such a financial burden.

One of the easiest ways to raise money was to sell the rights of republication to his earlier works; the only problem was to find a buyer willing to reissue them. Mikhail had written Dostoevsky, just before his departure from Semipalatinsk, that copies of *Poor Folk* were now selling secondhand in Petersburg for as high as 15 rubles, and Dostoevsky replies with a sadly disabused comment. "Yes, this [news] would have flattered my vanity and perhaps consoled me a good deal in the past"; but what comes to mind now is the possibility of capitalizing on the information. "If they [copies of the book] are so expensive now, then it would not be a bad idea to republish them when they cost so much."[7] Dostoevsky suggests to Mikhail the idea of a reissue with illustrations to be financed by Count Kushelev, the wealthy Maecenas who had just launched *The Russian Word*. Several months later, this project had developed into a new three-volume edition of Dostoevsky's works (with the exception of *The Double*, which, as we know, he wished to revise and reissue separately, accompanied by a pref-

13. Dostoevsky at the End of the 1850s

ace). The original idea was for the Dostoevsky brothers to publish the edition themselves and reap all the profits; but this old dream once again proved impractical. The works were eventually sold to a publisher named Osnovsky for what Mikhail considered the reasonable sum of 2,000 rubles, and the revised and corrected edition (in two volumes) was published in 1860.

Dostoevsky, however, had no intention of resting on his laurels, especially since he was well aware that those he had acquired in the past had become quite moth-eaten in the eyes of a new generation of readers. Now that his two novellas were out of the way, we find him juggling with a baffling variety of literary projects whose relation to what he actually wrote remains, except in a few obvious instances, extremely conjectural. At the end of August 1859, when Mikhail visited his brother in Tver, Feodor told him about an idea for two novels; what little we know about them comes from a letter of Mikhail's several weeks later. "You are now swinging back and forth between two novels, and I am afraid that you will lose a good deal of time in such oscillations. Why did you narrate the subject for me? Maikov once told me, a long time ago, that you have only to recount a subject never to get down to writing it. My dear fellow, perhaps I am mistaken, but your two large novels will be something on the order of *The Apprenticeship and Wanderings of Wilhelm Meister*."[8]

Nothing more is known of the proposed work to which Mikhail refers; but in a memorandum jotted down in the fall of 1859, which contains the titles of projects to be worked on in 1860, Dostoevsky includes the name Mignon. She is, of course, the mysterious and beautiful young girl in *Wilhelm Meister* who is haunted by the memory of a terrible past and is the inseparable companion of the equally mysterious old man known as the Harper. The character and situation of little Nelly in *The Insulted and Injured* have distinct resemblances with Mignon's, and it is possible that what Dostoevsky spoke of to Mikhail was an early version of this novel. The work may have been planned to stretch over several volumes, and the narrator, a young writer, could well have reminded Mikhail of Goethe's artistically ambitious but personally passive Wilhelm. Other items in the notes refer to the revision of *The Double* and to the future *House of the Dead* (here entitled *Notes of a Convict*). The phrase *Apathy and Impressions* may be the title of an intended article, while the appellation *Fatum* is given to a proposed "tragedy." There is also mention of "a comedy," whose subject would be "a landowner's wife locks up a married tutor just because he is married."[9] This note may be the origin of what became, seven years later, the stormy relation of the tutor Stepan Trofimovich Verkhovensky and his wealthy patroness Varvara Petrovna Stavrogin in *The Devils*.

From Dostoevsky's letters, we gather that he was worried about the lack of what he called "the passionate element" in *The Village of Stepanchikovo*, and he attributed some of his problem in selling the work to this deficiency. Defending it to Mikhail after Katkov's rejection, he nonetheless concedes that "there is very little love interest in the novel (i.e., the passionate element, as for instance in [Turgenev's] *A Nest of Gentlefolk*)."[10] To make up for this failing, we know that Dostoevsky was contemplating a novel in which this type of subject would be abundantly portrayed. "You write . . . that I must hurry," he repeats back to Mikhail, "and get ready for the new year that novel I spoke to you about (with the passionate element) and in this fashion attract attention to myself." Dostoevsky, however, once again refuses to be rushed and, indeed, flatly declares that "this novel has already been eliminated";[11] but some traces of it can be found in the notes that he left for a book to be called *Springtime Love*. Such a title is listed in the memorandum mentioned earlier, and the notes contain phrases that incontestably link his intended heroine with a Turgenev creation that Dostoevsky never ceased to admire: Lisa Kalitina, the quiet, pure-hearted, and self-sacrificing heroine of *A Nest of Gentlefolk*, who retires to a convent when her first and only true love is thwarted by circumstance.

The two main figures of Dostoevsky's plan are a wealthy aristocrat, a prince, and his companion, described as a future writer and sometimes also called "a man of letters" (*literator*). On a journey, the two stop in a small town where the writer's father and family live, and he introduces the Prince to local society. A young girl, engaged to an ignorant bureaucrat, falls in love with the Prince, surrenders to him, and then writes him a letter explaining that she had done so only to escape wedlock with her repugnant fiancé. Dostoevsky could not decide whether or not she would ask the Prince to marry her and includes both alternatives in his notes; her possible reluctance to do so is explained by her lowly birth, the sense of being socially unsuitable for so exalted a personage as the Prince. One variant of the ending sketches the writer discovering the girl's dilemma and marrying her himself. But this variant is only the first version of the idea; more interesting are those that show Dostoevsky's focus turning to the complex repressed antagonism between the Prince and the writer.

He develops the possible relations between his three central figures in various ways (the Prince marries the girl in a noble gesture, or she first gives herself to the writer and only *then* falls in love with the Prince); but what becomes crucial is the rivalry between the two men. "The writer had a moral influence on the Prince and the latter on him physically, financially (and revenges himself unconsciously for the moral influence). In substance, they mutually hate each other, but in fact they even are themselves convinced that they are friends." The secret contest of the two supposed friends over the same woman anticipates a similar situation in *The Idiot*; and there is one passage in the notes that surely points forward to that work. "An important scene: where he [the Prince] offers his hand, and she weeps like a child and says: 'I am not suitable, I am not *worthy*!' But the Prince raises her up, addresses her with a few fervent and persuasive words, and she, meekly submitting to the Prince, understands this completely and takes pride in the Prince and reveals to him that she thought the same herself, but had not dared to speak. . . ."[12] The bold heroine of these notes, who takes her fate into her own hands, obviously raises the issue of the emancipation of women—a very timely topic in Russia at that moment and one which, though in quite a different social setting, Dostoevsky would soon place at the center of *The Insulted and Injured*. The tangled relations between the Prince and the writer seem to have provided a pattern used again in this novel of Petersburg life, where a young writer and the scion of a princely family, even though their amorous rivalry is presented in a very muted fashion, are also competitors in love.

4
———

Dostoevsky's ambition to emulate Turgenev as a portrayer of "the passionate element" was soon swept aside by other plans that he excitedly announces to Mikhail as "definitive," only to sweep them away a few days later for still others. What he wished to hit upon, and desperately needed to find, was an idea that would be certain to create a genuine literary sensation and to attract the public attention that would raise his prestige and financial value. On October 1, 1859, he declares to Mikhail that, "after mature reflection," he has decided to return to the "large novel" he had earlier put aside with so much regret; and he once more stresses its "ideological" character. "It's a novel with *ideas*," he writes, "and will bring me into vogue." The same letter also refers to *The Double* and further illustrates Dostoevsky's frantic eagerness to return to the literary spotlight. "I expect to interest people and even very much so," he says of this plan for revising his old story and republishing it with a preface. "In a word, I am declaring war against everybody (and after all, if I don't revise *The Double* now, when will I revise it?)."*[13]

Nine days later, though, we see him brooding again over the rejection of *The Village of Stepanchikovo* by Katkov and taking a new tack inspired by such reflections. "True, the novel [*Stepanchikovo*] lacks *external* effect," he says, trying to fathom the meaning of Nekrasov's hesitation in accepting it. To remedy this defect, he announces that he has firmly decided to undertake writing the future *House of the Dead* at once—a project whose "external effect" is immediately apparent and which, in addition, would allow him to take advantage of the sympathy inspired in the reading public by a returning political exile. "These *Notes from the House of the Dead* have now taken shape in my mind according to a complete and finished plan. . . . My figure will disappear. These are the notes of an unknown; but I guarantee their interest. The interest will be of the very greatest. There will be the serious and the gloomy and the humorous, and peasant conversation with a particular convict coloring (I have read you several expressions recorded by me *on the spot*), and the

* Why should Dostoevsky imagine that, in revising *The Double* and issuing it with a new preface, he would be "declaring war against everybody"? Such a statement could only refer to what he intended to write in the preface, and its impartial bellicosity would tend to support the speculation ventured earlier (see p. 253). If, as we assume, the preface would have taken up a position in the Chernyshevsky-Annenkov controversy over "weak" and "strong" types, then it would not have agreed with either side. Dostoevsky would have probably favored "weak" types, as did Annenkov, but then also shared Chernyshevsky's scorn of their gentry-liberal incarnation. Hence he would have been declaring "war against everybody" by adopting a wholly independent point of view.

depiction of characters *unheard of* previously in literature, and the touching, and finally, the most important—my name. Remember that Pleshcheev attributed the success of his poems to his name (do you understand?). I am convinced that the public will read this with avidity."[14]

Dostoevsky also mentions two other ideas for works deriving from his prison-camp years, one of which he intends to write in the near future. "In December I will begin a novel (but not the one about the young man who murdered and landed in Siberia). No. Do you recall, I mentioned to you a *confession*—a novel that I wished to write after everything, so to say, that I have had to live through myself. A few days ago I firmly decided to write this right away. It became united with that novel (the passionate element) about which I told you. This will be, in the 1st place, striking, passionate, and in the 2nd, all my heart and all the blood in my body will be poured into this novel. I conceived it in *katorga*, lying on the plank bed, in painful moments of sorrow and self-criticism. . . . The effect will be stronger than *Poor Folk* (and how!) and *Netotchka Nezvanova*. I guarantee . . . that the *Confession* will conclusively establish my name."[15]

This mention of a novel in the form of a confession has often been seen as the original nucleus of *Crime and Punishment*, whose first draft was indeed written in the form of a first-person confession by the murderer (Raskolnikov) and whose last chapter is placed in Dostoevsky's Siberian prison camp. The first sentence of this quotation (frequently omitted when the passage is cited) would seem to exclude such a hypothesis, since the novel about "the young man who murdered" is, clearly, not the "confession." The best recent scholarly opinion regards this latter idea, born "in painful moments of sorrow and self-criticism," rather as the inspiration for *Notes from Underground*, also originally announced under the title of *Confession*.[16] But it would be a glaring anachronism to connect *all* of *Notes from Underground* with Dostoevsky's remark in 1859; in my view, he could have been thinking only of what later became the second part of *Notes from Underground*. For it is in this section that he satirizes the grandiose humanitarian reveries of the 1840s that he had once shared; and one can well imagine him, as he lay on his plank bed, mulling over with bitter self-ridicule the exalted political illusions of himself and his friends—illusions whose abysmal naiveté he was just beginning to understand. The "passionate element" he speaks of as having been combined with the "confession" also fits this second part, which depicts the underground man's relations with the prostitute Liza and reveals his incapacity to respond spontaneously to genuine love.

5

Dostoevsky's letters during this period, in addition to informing us about his abundant plans and intentions for future works, disclose a dialogue being carried on between the two brothers over a joint literary venture. So far, we have seen Mikhail Dostoevsky only as an ex-journalist and minor short-story writer turned cigarette manufacturer, who, out of the goodness of his heart, had supplied his more gifted brother with funds and acted as his literary agent. Mikhail's generosity, however, did not arise from any great affluence or financial success. His cigarette business was a very small affair, largely dependent on the labor of his family; even later, when he launched out into the manufacture of cigars, the enterprise remained on a handicraft level and never yielded any large returns. Some complaints probably made to his brother about the difficulties of his situation elicited from Feodor the following reflections of his own. "You know, I have thought a good deal about your business ventures. Is it possible that they will not compensate you for everything you have given up for them (literature, service [in the Army], occupations more suited to your character)? Here you have had the factory for several years, and is there some positive hope for the future? And meanwhile, time passes, children grow up, expenses increase."[17]

Even though Feodor could hardly have known it at the time, such words struck a very tender nerve in his brother's sensibility. For Mikhail had given up literature only as a result of the direst necessity and had never abandoned the idea of returning to it one day. Just a few months after Feodor's letter, another such epistle, written by the acute liberal historian K. D. Kavelin, describes the new atmosphere in Russia that would ultimately enable Mikhail Dostoevsky to realize this dream. "Here in Petersburg," Kavelin wrote at the beginning of 1856, "public opinion is more and more spreading its wings. It is impossible any longer to recognize the [previous] caravansary of militarism, the cudgel, and benightedness. Everything is talked about, everything is discussed up and down, sometimes stupidly, but all the same discussed and, as a result of this, studied."[18] Under the impetus of this heady sense of freedom (still very relative, to be sure) 150 new newspapers and journals were started in Russia between 1856 and 1860; and on June 19, 1858, Mikhail Dostoevsky submitted to the St. Petersburg Censorship Committee a plan for a weekly "political and literary" periodical to be entitled *Time (Vremya)*. Permission to publish such a journal was granted at the end of October 1858, and the censor appointed to oversee it was none other than I. A. Goncharov.

For reasons that remain obscure, and though he had already been in correspondence with Feodor for several years, Mikhail did not inform his brother of this plan in advance. In one of his letters, though, he remarked vaguely that he would need a story from his brother for the next year, and this called forth an impatient rebuke and rejoinder from Feodor at the beginning of 1858. "I reproach you very much for not writing to me clearly, i.e., what you wish to publish, with whom, and how?"[19] It was only after Mikhail had submitted his proposal in June that, a month later, he explained what he had in mind; and Feodor replied with enthusiasm: "Your newspaper about which you wrote me is a very lovely plan. The thought of such a publication has long been swimming around in my head, but only of a purely literary newspaper. Most important: a literary feuilleton, a critical review of journals, a critical review of what's good and what's mistaken, enmity toward the *mutual back-scratching* now so widespread, more energy, fire, sharpness of mind, firmness—that's what we need now! I speak about all this so *excitedly* because I have written down and sketched out several literary essays along these lines: for instance, *on contemporary poets*, on the *statistical tendency* in literature, on the uselessness of *tendencies* in art—essays written heatedly and even cuttingly, but, most important, readably. But here's the rub: will you be able to edit a newspaper? This won't be an easy job, and with the factory on your hands as well? Take care, brother!"[20]

Even though Dostoevsky tells us nothing more about his proposed essays, it is evident that he is readying himself for a head-on clash with the prevailing emphasis of the radical critics on the importance of "tendencies." The use of the word "statistics" is rather unexpected; but it probably contains an allusion to Chernyshevsky's path-breaking *Essays on the Gogol Period of Russian Literature* (1855-1856). This series of articles, which still offers a valuable survey of what would now be called "the aesthetics of the reception" of Gogol's work, was an important defense of the Gogolian tradition, interpreted, along the lines established by Belinsky, as one of social realism and social satire. Valerian Maikov, in an essay of 1847 comparing Gogol and Dostoevsky, had said that "Gogol's collected works may emphatically be called the artistic statistics of Russia,"[21] and he had argued that Dostoevsky's "psychological" approach penetrated more deeply into the recesses of the human personality. It is likely that in singling out a "statistical tendency," Dostoevsky is referring to this usage, and thus implicitly to Chernyshevsky's efforts to establish such a "tendency" as the only legitimate course for Russian literature to pursue.

Several more years were to pass, however, before Dostoevsky had the opportunity to express such opinions in print. Nothing was done by Mikhail, probably for financial reasons, to get his new publication under way in 1858, and 1859 found it still in the planning stage. The two brothers discussed it during Mikhail's visit to Tver at the end of August 1859, and Pleshcheev was invited to become a contributor in late fall. But Mikhail was still hesitating to take the leap from the relative security of his business, irksome and scarcely profitable as it was, into the unknown of journalism and publishing. "Look at others: neither talents nor abilities, and yet they rise in the world, amass a capital," Dostoevsky writes disconsolately. "And we struggle and struggle. . . . I am convinced, for example, that you and I are much cleverer, more capable, and knowledgeable about affairs than Kraevsky and Nekrasov. Why, they are just peasants [*muzhiky*] about literature. And yet they get rich, and we are strapped for cash." Mikhail, Dostoevsky continues, had just managed to make ends meet with his factory, and the outlook held little promise for improvement. "No, brother, it's necessary to think about it, and seriously; it's necessary to take a risk and engage in some literary enterprise—a journal, for example. . . . Anyway, we'll think about it and talk it over together. It's not too late."[22]

Obviously, things were still very much up in the air more than a year after Mikhail had received the imprimatur of the Censorship Committee for his proposed publication. And we note that Feodor was now thinking, not of a weekly periodical (*gazeta*), but of a monthly "thick" journal (*zhurnal*) that would be able to compete with those of Kraevsky and Nekrasov. Nothing had yet been decided when, in late December 1859, Dostoevsky arrived in St. Petersburg to take up his residence there. His family had rented an apartment for him and his new wife and stepson, furnished it as best they could, and even hired a cook, who eagerly awaited their appearance because it frightened her to live there alone. Other people, more discreetly, were also watching for the arrival of the Dostoevskys: the military Governor-General of Petersburg wrote the Petersburg chief of police on December 2 that, by order of the Tsar, the secret surveillance under which ex-ensign Dostoevsky had been kept in Tver was to be continued on his homecoming to the capital.

6

Dostoevsky's return to the scene of his early literary triumphs caused very little stir and was celebrated only in the small circle of his intimates. Dr. Yanovsky recalled, many years later, that "in Petersburg we all visited him immediately on his arrival; we were at his housewarming: there were Apollon Maikov, Alexander Milyukov, his brother Mikhail with his family, many others, and also Speshnev, who had gotten into Petersburg that very day."[23] Dostoevsky was thus again unexpectedly brought face to face with the man he had once called his "Mephistopheles" and who, in the entourage of the Governor-General of Eastern Siberia, Nikolay Muravyev (like Stavrogin in the entourage of Governor-General von Lembke), had himself just returned from exile. Muraviev was an energetic administrator with liberal pretensions and large political ambitions, who enjoyed rubbing elbows with such political exiles as his second cousin Mikhail Bakunin and Nikolay Speshnev. He had appreciated Speshnev's talent and ability, appointed him editor of a local, government-sponsored journal in Irkutsk, and attached him to his personal staff; during his sojourn in St. Petersburg, Muraviev succeeded in having Speshnev's rights as a nobleman restored.

Bakunin, who by this time had escaped from Siberia largely as a result of Muraviev's laxity, had also been much impressed with Speshnev and communicated his reactions to Herzen. The former conspirator was, he wrote, "a remarkable man" who inspired confidence by his "quiet strength," and he was also "a gentleman from head to foot."[24]

Speshnev had not come to Petersburg merely to renew contact with this old member of his secret society; he also wished personally to examine the leaders of the new radical generation. "Today, on my name day, I was overjoyed not only by your letter," Pleshcheev writes to Nikolay Dobrolyubov from Moscow (February 12, 1860), "but also by the visit of a man very close to my heart—Speshnev; he is traveling from Siberia with Muraviev and will unfailingly be at Chernyshevsky's, whom he wants to meet. I also gave him your address. I recommend him as a person—who, besides a first-rate mind, possesses still another quality—unfortunately quite rare among us: with him the word goes hand in hand with the deed. He has always constantly put his convictions into practice. He is in the highest degree an upright character with a will of iron. It can absolutely be said that, among us all—he was the most remarkable figure."[25]

There is, regrettably, no similar document from Dostoevsky's pen recording his impressions of Speshnev after their long years of separation, nor a more extensive eyewitness account than the fleeting reference of Dr. Yanovsky. We must be content to imagine Dostoevsky's thoughts as he greeted, and probably embraced, the man who had once lured him along the dangerous path of revolutionary adventure. Both would have been able to rejoice, at any rate, that their great dream—the dream of the liberation of the serfs—was on the point of being realized; both could congratulate each other that their sacrifices had not been in vain. Whether they would have agreed on anything else is highly questionable; but in those days of rapturous expectation, when all Russia was poised on the edge of the great new challenge of freedom, it made very little difference.

7

Everything seemed possible then; and for a few years—a very few—all shades of social-political opinion were united as never before by the prospect of impending change. It was not a government sycophant but the intransigent Chernyshevsky himself who had recently declared in *The Contemporary* (February 1858) that "the new life, which now begins for us, will be as much more beautiful, prosperous, brilliant, and happy, in comparison with our former life, as the last one hundred and fifty years were superior to the seventeenth century in Russia."[26] It may be doubted whether Chernyshevsky himself meant such words to be taken with entire literalness; but no matter—they reflect and express a mood prevalent among all sections of the Russian intelligentsia in those glorious days when "bliss was it in that dawn to be alive."

All were joined together in favor of liberation and reform and against the hardened and selfish reactionaries who opposed the beneficent measures proposed by the Tsar to ameliorate the body politic. The little group who came to celebrate Dostoevsky's return all shared in this mood, and there was no sense as yet that the ally of Chernyshevsky and Dobrolyubov could not also, at the same time, continue to remain the friend of Dostoevsky and Maikov. It would take a few short years to bring matters to a head and to make personal relations of this kind, or at least the old cordiality, forever impossible. But tensions had not yet gone that far, and it should be said that Dostoevsky would honestly try in the future, even if unsuccessfully, to keep them from reaching this point of rupture.

A feeling of celebration was thus everywhere in the air at that moment of Russian history; and Dostoevsky had ample reasons of his own for a sense of buoyancy and jubilation. The Siberian cycle of his life, which began when he left St. Petersburg in shackles, had now been completed. Despite his epilepsy and the disappointments of his marriage, he had managed to survive, and even to thrive, in the onerous ten years he had just lived through, emerging from his worst ordeal—the four years in the prison camp—with the conviction that he had acquired new powers there both as a writer and as a man.

He knew he would no longer write "trifles" and that he could face whatever fate had in store for him, if not with serenity, then at least with unflinching courage: he had been tried and not found wanting. He had begun to publish again and never doubted for a moment, whatever the relative failure of his fledgling efforts, that he would once more regain his literary eminence. His head and his notebooks were full of plans for new stories, novels, and essays, and he was certain that his unique experiences had given him invaluable insights into the soul of the Russian people that only he could communicate. As the prospective editor of a monthly journal, he was about to throw himself into the fray at the most exciting and tumultuous moment of Russian culture during the nineteenth century. A new life was just beginning for him—the life of literature, for which he had longed so desperately as a convict and a soldier—and he could hardly wait to roll up his sleeves and get to work.

And work he would, in the next five years, as literary editor and chief contributor to his own journals—reading manuscripts, interviewing and writing to contributors, correcting proof, and, all the while, turning out a flow of copy with a fecundity, a prolificity, an abundance little short of astonishing if we remember that he was incapacitated for days at a time by the constant recurrence of his epilepsy. These were the years in which he wrote two major books (*The Insulted and Injured* and *House of the*

Dead); three short works of fiction (including *Notes from Underground*); a lively series of travel sketches of Europe (*Winter Notes on Summer Impressions*); and produced, in addition, a continual flow of literary essays and polemical journalism.

—But all this takes us into the thick of the next volume, and we should not encroach on it any further. Let us end the narrative of this portion of Dostoevsky's life at the joyous moment when his old friends have gathered round to greet the returning exile and drink his health and happiness. Let us take leave of him before the spontaneous conviviality of this reunion has been fractured by ideological enmity, before the burdens he is about to assume have begun to weigh him down, and while he is still basking in the heady exuberance of his homecoming.

ABBREVIATIONS

Biografiya   Orest Miller and Nikolay Strakhov, *Biografiya, Pisma i Za-metki iz Zapisnoi Knizhki F. M. Dostoevskogo* (St. Peters-burg, 1883). Preceded by the name of the author of the appropriate section.

DMI   *F. M. Dostoevsky, Materialy i Issledovaniya*, ed. A. S. Do-linin (Leningrad, 1935).

DVS   *F. M. Dostoevsky v Vospominaniyakh Sovremennikov*, ed. A. Dolinin, 2 vols. (Moscow, 1961).

DW   F. M. Dostoevsky, *The Diary of a Writer*, trans. Boris Brasol (Santa Barbara and Salt Lake City, 1979).

Pisma   F. M. Dostoevsky, *Pisma*, ed. and annotated by A. S. Dolinin, 4 vols. (Moscow, 1928-1959).

PSS   F. M. Dostoevsky, *Polnoe Sobranie Sochinenii*, ed. and an-notated by G. M. Fridlender et al., 30 vols. (Leningrad, 1972-).

NOTES

CHAPTER 1

1. F. M. *Dostoevsky v Russkoi Kritike*, ed. A. Belkin (Moscow, 1956), 30.
2. Quoted in P. V. Annenkov, *The Extraordinary Decade*, ed. Arthur P. Mendel, trans. Irwin R. Titunik (Ann Arbor, 1968), 150.
3. A. I. Herzen, *Sobranie Sochinenii*, 30 vols. (Moscow, 1954-1961), 7: 122.
4. Quoted in V. I. Cheshikhin, *T. N. Granovsky i Ego Vremya* (St. Petersburg, 1905), 317.

CHAPTER 2

1. Quoted in *Petrashevtsy*, ed. P. S. Shchegolev, 3 vols. (Moscow-Leningrad, 1926-1928), 1: 127.
2. Wiktoria Śliwowska, *Sprawa Pietraszewców* (Warsaw, 1964), 239.
3. Quoted in V. I. Semevsky, "Sledstvye i Sud po Delu Petrashevtsev," *Russkie Zapiski*, 9-11 (1916), 9: 40.
4. *Petrashevtsy*, ed. Shchegolev, 1: 127.
5. Ibid., 128.
6. P. V. Annenkov, *The Extraordinary Decade*, ed. Arthur P. Mendel, trans. Irwin R. Titunik (Ann Arbor, 1968), 241.
7 Sidney Monas, *The Third Section: Police and Society under Nicholas I* (Cambridge, Mass., 1961), 258.
8. Annenkov, *Decade*, 241.
9. *Petrashevtsy*, ed. Shchegolev, 3: 276.
10. Orest Miller and Nikolay Strakhov, *Biografiya, Pisma i Zametki iz Zapisnoi Knizhki F. M. Dostoevskogo* (St. Petersburg, 1883), 90. Cited hereafter as *Biografiya*, preceded by the name of the author of the appropriate section.
11. F. M. *Dostoevsky v Vospominaniyakh Sovremennikov*, ed. A. Dolinin, 2 vols. (Moscow, 1961), 1: 193. Cited hereafter as *DVS*.
12. Ibid.
13. I. Pawlowski, *Russisch-Deutsches Wörterbuch*, 2 vols. (Leipzig, 1974), 2: 1766.
14. A. M. Dostoevsky, *Vospominaniya* (Leningrad, 1930), 192-193.
15. Ibid., 194.
16. Alexander Herzen, *My Past and Thoughts*, trans. Constance Garnett, rev. Humphrey Higgins, 4 vols. (New York, 1968), 2: 447.
17. A. M. Dostoevsky, *Vospominaniya*, 196.
18. Ibid.
19. M. N. Gernet, *Istoriya Tsarskoi Tyurmy*, 5 vols. (Moscow, 1961), 2: 220.
20. A. M. Dostoevsky, *Vospominaniya*, 197.
21. *Petrashevtsy*, ed. Shchegolev, 1: 149.
22. N. F. Belchikov, *Dostoevsky v Protsesse Petrashevtsev* (Moscow, 1971), 244.
23. *Petrashevtsy*, ed. Shchegolev, 1: 149.
24. Belchikov, *Protsesse*, 244.
25. F. M. Dostoevsky, *Pisma*, ed. and annotated by A. S. Dolinin, 4 vols. (Moscow, 1928-1959), 1: 125; August 27, 1849. Cited hereafter as *Pisma*.
26. A. M. Dostoevsky, *Vospominaniya*, 197.
27. Belchikov, *Protsesse*, 215-216.
28. *DVS*, 1: 191.
29. *Petrashevtsy*, ed. Shchegolev, 1: 160-161.
30. Annenkov, *Decade*, 242.
31. *DVS*, 1: 194.
32. Miller, *Biografiya*, 106-107.
33. See the remark in Belchikov, *Protsesse*, 200.

CHAPTER 3

1. *DVS*, 2: 199.
2. Miller, *Biografiya*, 112.
3. For more details, see my *Dostoevsky, The Seeds of Revolt, 1821-1849* (Princeton, 1976), 269-272.
4. *Pisma*, 4: 258-259; June 20, 1849.
5. Ibid.
6. Ibid., 1: 124; July 18, 1849.
7. Ibid., 126; August 27, 1849.
8. Ibid., 124-125; July 18, 1849.
9. Ibid., 127; September 14, 1849.
10. Ibid., 125; July 18, 1849.
11. Ibid., 127; September 14, 1849.
12. Ibid., 124; July 18, 1849.
13. Ibid.
14. Ibid., 125; August 27, 1849.
15. Ibid., 127; September 14, 1849.
16. P. V. Annenkov, *The Extraordinary Decade*, ed. Arthur P. Mendel, trans. Irwin R. Titunik (Ann Arbor, 1968), 243.

17. *Pisma*, 1: 126; August 27, 1849.
18. Ibid., 127; September 14, 1849.
19. Charlotte Brontë, *Jane Eyre* (Harmondsworth, 1980), 344.
20. *Pisma*, 1: 126; August 27, 1849.
21. Ibid., 58; January 1, 1840.
22. Ibid., 127-128; September 14, 1849.

23. V. V. Vinogradov, "Turgenev i Shkola Molodogo Dostoevskogo," *Russkaya Literatura*, 2 (1959), 45-71.
24. *Pisma*, 1: 124; July 18, 1849.
25. Ibid.
26. Ibid., 126; August 27, 1849.

CHAPTER 4

1. F. M. Dostoevsky, *The Diary of a Writer*, trans. Boris Brasol (Santa Barbara and Salt Lake City, 1979), 151. Cited hereafter as *DW*, with the appropriate year.
2. *Pisma*, 1: 178; March 24, 1856.
3. N. F. Belchikov, *Dostoevsky v Protsesse Petrashevtsev* (Moscow, 1971), 95.
4. Ibid.
5. Ibid., 96.
6. Ibid., 265.
7. Ibid., 97.
8. Ibid.
9. Ibid.
10. Ibid., 98.
11. Ibid.
12. Ibid.
13. Ibid.
14. Ibid., 100.
15. Ibid.
16. Ibid., 101.
17. Ibid., 100.

18. Ibid., 101.
19. Ibid., 101.
20. Ibid.
21. Ibid., 101-102.
22. Ibid., 102-103.
23. Ibid., 103-104.
24. Ibid.
25. Ibid., 105.
26. Ibid.
27. Ibid., 105-106.
28. Ibid., 106.
29. Ibid., 109.
30. Ibid., 110-111.
31. Ibid., 111-112.
32. *DVS*, 1: 185.
33. Belchikov, *Protsesse*, 112.
34. Ibid., 86.
35. *Petrashevtsy*, ed. P. S. Shchegolev, 3 vols. (Moscow-Leningrad, 1926-1928), 3: 164.
36. Belchikov, *Protsesse*, 176.

CHAPTER 5

1. V. I. Semevsky, "Sledtsvie i Sud po Delu Petrashevtsev," *Russkie Zapiski*, 9-11 (1916), 11: 26.
2. F. M. Dostoevsky, *Polnoe Sobranie Sochinenii*, ed. and annotated by G. M. Fridlender et al., 30 vols. (Leningrad, 1972-), 11: 189-190. Cited hereafter as *PSS*.
3. Semevsky, "Sledtsvie i Sud," *Russkie Zapiski*, 11: 31.
4. Miller, *Biografiya*, 115.
5. *DVS*, 1: 223.
6. Miller, *Biografiya*, 117.
7. *DVS*, 1: 226.
8. Ibid., 226-227.
9. Ibid.
10. Ibid., 229.
11. Miller, *Biografiya*, 118.
12. *DVS*, 1: 229.
13. *DW*, 152.
14. Miller, *Biografiya*, 118.
15. Ibid., 118-119.
16. F. N. Lvov, "Zapiska o Dele Petrashevtsev," *Literaturnoe Nasledstvo*, no. 63 (Moscow, 1956), 188.
17. Miller, *Biografiya*, 119.
18. F. N. Lvov, "Zapiska," 188.
19. For more details, see my *Dostoevsky,*

The Seeds of Revolt, 1821-1849 (Princeton, 1976), 164-168.
20. *DVS*, 1: 230.
21. Ibid., 231.
22. *Pisma*, 1: 128; December 22, 1849.
23. Ibid., 129.
24. Ibid., 130.
25. Ibid., 129.
26. Ibid., 131.
27. Anna Dostoevsky, *Reminiscences*, trans. and ed. Beatrice Stillman (New York, 1975), 22.
28. *Pisma*, 1: 129.
29. Ibid., 130-131.
30. Ibid., 129.
31. *DW* (1873), 7.
32. *Pisma*, 1: 130.
33. *DVS*, 1: 191.
34. Ibid.
35. Ibid., 192.
36. *Delo Petrashevtsev*, ed. V. R. Leikina, E. A. Korolchuk, V. A. Desnitsky, 3 vols. (Moscow-Leningrad, 1937-1951), 1: 84-85.
37. V. A. Tunimanov, *Tvorchestvo Dostoevskogo*, 1854-1862 (Leningrad, 1980), 149-150.

Chapter 6

1. *DW* (1873), 152.
2. *Pisma*, 1: 133-134; February 22, 1854.
3. Ibid., 134.
4. Ibid.
5. Ibid., 135.
6. Miller, *Biografiya*, 126.
7. Ibid.
8. Ibid., 126-127.
9. *DW* (1873), 9.
10. M. D. Frantseva, "Vospominaniya," *Istoricheskii Vestnik*, no. 6 (1886), 392.
11. *Pisma*, 1: 135.
12. Ibid., 137.
13. Frantseva, "Vospominaniya," 628-629.
14. Leonid Grossman, *Zhizn i Trudy F. M. Dostoevskogo* (Moscow-Leningrad, 1935), 66.
15. *Pisma*, 1: 135-137.
16. Ibid., 138-139.
17. Ibid., 135.
18. This account is contained in a letter of Riesenkampf to Andrey Dostoevsky, partially published in 1881. The relevant extracts are republished in *Literaturnoe Nasledstvo*, no. 86 (Moscow, 1973), 549.
19. *Pisma*, 1: 135.
20. A. E. Wrangel, *Vospominaniya o F. M. Dostoevskom v Siberii* (St. Petersburg, 1912), 14.
21. P. K. Martyanov, "V Perelome Veka," *Istoricheskii Vestnik*, nos. 10-11 (1895), 11: 453.
22. Wrangel, *Vospominaniya*, 37.
23. Martyanov, "V Perelome Veka," 11: 448.
24. Ibid., 456.
25. *Pisma*, 1: 166; January 13, 1856.
26. The letter is included in the article by V. Lyubimova-Dorotovskaya, "Dostoevsky v Siberii," *Ogonek*, no. 46-47 (1946), 27-28.

Chapter 7

1. *Pisma*, 1: 446; July 30, 1854.
2. *DW* (1873), 152.
3. Ibid.
4. *DW* (1876), 184-186; see also my *Dostoevsky, The Seeds of Revolt, 1821-1849* (Princeton, 1976), 70-73.
5. *DVS*, 1: 104.
6. Maxime Leroy, *Histoire des idées sociales en France*, 3 vols. (Paris, 1946-1954), 2: 442.
7. Ibid., 441.
8. See the remark of Pierre Pascal in his excellent French translation, *Récits de la Maison des Morts* (Paris, 1961), 14, n. 2.
9. V. G. Belinsky, *Selected Philosophical Works* (Moscow, 1948), 125.
10. P. K. Martyanov, "V Perelome Veka," *Istoricheskii Vestnik*, nos. 10-11 (1895), 11: 448.
11. Alexander Pushkin, "The Captain's Daughter," trans. Natalie Duddington, reprinted in *The Poems, Prose and Plays of Pushkin*, ed. Avrahm Yarmolinsky (New York, 1936), 741.

Chapter 8

1. *Pisma*, 1: 143; February 20, 1854.
2. Lev Shestov, "Dostoevsky and Nietzsche: The Philosophy of Tragedy," in *Essays in Russian Literature, The Conservative View: Leontiev, Rozanov, Shestov*, ed. and trans. Spencer E. Roberts (Athens, Ga., 1968), 6.
3. Ibid., 68.
4. F. M. Dostoevsky, *The Notebooks for Crime and Punishment*, ed. and trans. Edward Wasiolek (Chicago, 1967), 176. Professor Wasiolek accurately translates the name of "Aristov" found in the text but seems unaware of its relation to Svidrigailov; in one place (67) he gives the name a feminine form. For the connection, see *PSS*, 7: 315, 408.
5. P. K. Martyanov, "V Perelome Veka," *Istoricheskii Vestnik*, nos. 10-11 (1895), 11: 452.
6. *Pisma*, 1: 202; December 14, 1856.
7. Wacław Lednicki, *Russia, Poland and the West* (New York, 1954), 276. Lednicki's book contains a translation of most of the chapter that Tokarzewski devotes to Dostoevsky in his *Siedem Lat Katorgi*.
8. Ibid., 275.
9. Ibid.
10. Ibid.
11. *DVS*, 1: 140-141.
12. Lednicki, *Russia, Poland and the West*, 272-273.
13. *DW* (1876), 187.
14. Ibid., 205-206.

Chapter 9

1. For more discussion of this point, see my *Dostoevsky, The Seeds of Revolt, 1821-1849* (Princeton, 1976), chap. 14.
2. Maxime Leroy, *Histoire des idées sociales in France*, 3 vols. (Paris, 1946-1954), 3: 82.

3. William James, *The Varieties of Religious Experience* (New York, 1929), 172.
4. Ibid., 167.
5. William Sargant, *Battle for the Mind* (New York, 1971), chaps. 1-7.
6. Ibid., 223.
7. Ibid., 130.
8. *DW* (1876), 206.
9. Ibid.
10. Ibid.

11. Ibid.
12. Ibid., 206-207.
13. Ibid., 207.
14. Ibid., 209.
15. Ibid., 210.
16. Ibid.
17. James, *Varieties of Religious Experience*, 242-246.
18. *DW* (1876), 202.
19. *Pisma*, 1: 58; January 1, 1840.

CHAPTER 10

1. Andrzej Walicki, *The Slavophile Controversy* (London, 1975), 417. A passage quoted on the same page gives the general sense of Belinsky's position: "The monotonous form of our modest folk poetry sufficed to express the limited content of the tribal, natural, immediate and semi-patriarchal existence of ancient Russia; but the new content [of modern life] was not suitable to it,

had no room for it; it also required new forms. What we needed was not nationality but Europeanization. . . ."
2. A. E. Wrangel, *Vospominaniya o F. M. Dostoevskom v Siberii* (St. Petersburg, 1912), 35.
3. *Pisma*, 1: 139; February 22, 1854.
4. *PSS*, 4: 289.
5. *Pisma*, 1: 166; February 18, 1856.

CHAPTER 11

1. Ernst Benz, *The Eastern Orthodox Church* (New York, 1963), 18.
2. *Pisma*, 1: 143; February 20, 1854.
3. G. P. Fedotov, *The Russian Religious Mind*, 2 vols. (New York, 1960; Cambridge, Mass., 1966), 1: 341.

4. *Pisma*, 1: 142.
5. Walter Lowrie, *Kierkegaard*, 2 vols. (New York, 1962), 2: 138.
6. Cited in Walter Ruttenbeck, *Sören Kierkegaard, der christliche Denker und sein Werk* (Berlin/Frankfurt, 1929), 225.

CHAPTER 12

1. *Pisma*, 1: 143; between February 20, 1854, and the end of the month.
2. Ibid., 140; February 22, 1854.
3. Ibid., 133.
4. Ibid.
5. Ibid., 138.
6. Ibid.
7. Ibid., 139.
8. A. E. Wrangel, *Vospominaniya o F. M. Dostoevskom v Siberii* (St. Petersburg, 1912), 66.
9. *Pisma*, 1: 140.
10. Ibid.
11. Ibid., 1: 183; April 13, 1856.
12. Ibid, 183-184.
13. Wrangel, *Vospominaniya*, 34.

14. "The prose [of Schiller] is perfectly translated—from the point of view of expressiveness and exactitude," he tells his brother. "You complain about Schiller's language; but note, my friend, that his language could not be otherwise." *Pisma*, 2: 553; summer 1844.
15. Wrangel, *Vospominaniya*, 21.
16. Carl Gustav Carus, *Psyche* (Pforzheim, 1846), 297-298.
17. Ibid., 1.
18. Ibid., 201-202.
19. Ibid., 93.
20. Wrangel, *Vospominaniya*, 53.
21. George Gibian, "C. G. Carus' *Psyche* and Dostoevsky," *American Slavic and East European Review*, 14 (1955), 371-382.

CHAPTER 13

1. *Pisma*, 1: 137; February 22, 1854.
2. *DVS*, 2: 312.
3. Wrangel, *Vospominaniya o F. M. Dostoevskom v Siberii* (St. Petersburg, 1912), 15.
4. George Kennan, *Siberia and the Exile System*, 2 vols. (New York, 1891), 1: 158.
5. *Pisma*, 1: 143; between February 20 and the end of the month.
6. Ibid., 146; July 30, 1854.

7. A. Skandin, "Dostoevsky v Semipalatinske," *Istoricheskii Vestnik*, 91 (1903), 203.
8. *Pisma*, 1: 148; November 1854.
9. Ibid., 2: 560; January 13, 1856.
10. Wrangel, *Vospominaniya*, 38.
11. *Pisma*, 1: 146; July 30, 1854.
12. Wrangel, *Vospominaniya*, 39.
13. Ibid., 39.

Chapter 14

1. Wrangel, *Vospominaniya o F. M. Dostoevskom v Siberii* (St. Petersburg, 1912), 8.
2. Ibid., 13.
3. Ibid., 12.
4. Ibid., 76.
5. Ibid., 12.
6. Ibid., 17.
7. Ibid., 18.
8. *Pisma*, 2: 538; January 13, 1856.
9. Wrangel, *Vospominaniya*, 25.
10. Ibid., 39.
11. *Pisma*, 1: 168; March 23, 1856.
12. Ibid., 170.
13. Wrangel, *Vospominaniya*, 39.
14. Ibid., 34-35.
15. Ibid., 43.
16. Ibid., 44.
17. *Pisma*, 1: 201; December 14, 1856.
18. Wrangel, *Vospominaniya*, 35.
19. Ibid., 45.
20. *Pisma*, 2: 291; October 9/21, 1870.
21. Wrangel, *Vospominaniya*, 52.
22. R. C. Zaehner, *Mysticism: Sacred and Profane* (New York, 1975), 30-49.
23. Strakhov, *Biografiya*, 214.
24. *DVS*, 1: 347.
25. Zaehner, *Mysticism*, 28-29.
26. So far as my reading goes, very little attention has been paid to this aspect of Dostoevsky's seizures. The French neurologist Dr. Alajouanine, however, has sensitively contrasted Dostoevsky's epileptic attacks with the ecstasies of St. John of the Cross. See Théophile Alajouanine, "Littérature et épilepsie," in *Dostoevski, Cahiers de l'Herne*, no. 24, ed. Jacques Catteau (Paris, 1972), 309-324.
27. Wrangel, *Vospominaniya*, 30-31.
28. Ibid., 46-47.

Chapter 15

1. Wrangel, *Vospominaniya o F. M. Dostoevskom v Siberii* (St. Petersburg, 1912), 50.
2. Ibid., 51.
3. *Pisma*, 1: 152-153; June 4, 1855.
4. Ibid., 153.
5. Wrangel, *Vospominaniya*, 64.
6. Ibid., 78-79. See also Leonid Grossman, "Grazhdanskaya Smert F. M. Dostoevskogo," *Literaturnoe Nasledstvo*, 22-24 (1935), 683-692, with the accompanying documents. Dostoevsky firmly believed in the Wrangel version, as can be seen from his letters.
7. *Pisma*, 2: 559-561; January 13, 1856.
8. Wrangel, *Vospominaniya*, 192.
9. *Pisma*, 1: 168-176; March 23, 1856.
10. Ibid., 178; March 24, 1856.
11. Ibid., 184-185; April 13, 1856.
12. Ibid., 186.
13. Ibid., 183; April 13, 1856.
14. Ibid.
15. Ibid., 187; May 23, 1856.
16. W. E. Mosse, *Alexander II and the Modernization of Russia* (New York, 1962), 42.
17. *Pisma*, 1: 188; May 23, 1856.
18. Ibid., 189; July 14, 1856.
19. Ibid., 190.
20. Ibid., 191.
21. Ibid., 189.
22. Ibid., 192.
23. Ibid., 198; November 9, 1856.
24. Ibid., 197-198.
25. Ibid., 198.
26. Ibid., 199.
27. Ibid., 2: 571; November 9, 1856.
28. Ibid., 1: 204-205; December 21, 1856.
29. Ibid., 205-206.
30. Ibid., 2: 579-580; March 9, 1857.
31. Ibid., 580.
32. Ibid., 1: 218; March 9, 1857.
33. Ibid., 2: 517.
34. Ibid., 580.
35. Ibid., 581-582; March 15, 1857.
36. Ibid., 1: 228; November 30, 1857.
37. Ibid., 2: 588; November 3, 1857.
38. Ibid., 596; December 13, 1858.
39. Ibid., 1: 253-255; September 22, 1859.

Chapter 16

1. Cited in Leonid Grossman, "Grazhdanskaya Smert F. M. Dostoevskogo," *Literaturnoe Nasledstvo*, 22-24 (1935), 688-689.
2. A. N. Maikov, *Polnoe Sobranie Sochinenii*, ed. P. V. Bibikov, 3 vols. (St. Petersburg, 1914), 2: 13-20.
3. For more details, see my *Dostoevsky, The Seeds of Revolt, 1821-1849* (Princeton, 1976), chap. 15.
4. *Pisma*, 1: 164; January 18, 1856.
5. Ibid., 163.
6. Ibid., 165.
7. Ibid.
8. Ibid.
9. Ibid., 166.
10. Ibid.
11. Cited in A. A. Kornilov, *Obshchestvennoe Dvizhenie pri Aleksandre II* (Moscow, 1909), 6.
12. V. G. Belinsky, *Selected Philosophical Works* (Moscow, 1948), 371.
13. P. V. Annenkov, *The Extraordinary Decade*, ed. Arthur P. Mendel, trans. Irwin R. Titunik (Ann Arbor, 1968), 159.

14. Andrzej Walicki, *The Slavophile Controversy* (London, 1975), 587.
15. A. I. Herzen, *Sobranie Sochinenii*, 30 vols. (Moscow, 1954-1961), 24: 197; July 26/14, 1851.
16. See Raoul Labry, *Alexandre Ivanovič Herzen, 1812-1870* (Paris, 1928), 356.
17. D. N. Ovsyaniko-Kulikovsky, *Istoriya Russkoi Intelligentsii*, 3 vols. (St. Petersburg, 1909), 2: 4.
18. Alexander Herzen, *My Past and Thoughts*, trans. Constance Garnett, rev. Humphrey Higgins, 4 vols. (New York, 1968), 2: 549.
19. *Pisma*, 1: 164.
20. Ibid., 166-167.
21. Ibid., 167.
22. Henri Granjard calls *A Nest of Gentlefolk* "the most Slavophil work of [Turgenev's] career." See his *Ivan Tourguénev et les courants politiques et sociaux de son temps* (Paris, 1954), 242.

23. *Pisma*, 1: 167.
24. Ibid.
25. Ibid.
26. Ibid., 184; April 13, 1856.
27. Ibid.
28. Cited in Robert Louis Jackson, *Dostoevsky's Quest for Form* (New Haven, 1966), 38-39.
29. I. I. Panaev, *Sobranie Sochinenii*, 6 vols. (Moscow, 1912), 5: 1-11.
30. "Pisma A. N. Pleshcheeva k F. M. Dostoevskomu," in *F. M. Dostoevsky, Materialy i Issledovaniya*, ed. A. S. Dolinin (Leningrad, 1935), 444; April 10, 1859. Cited hereafter as *DMI*.
31. K. Chukovsky, "Dostoevsky i Pleyada Belinskogo," in *N. A. Nekrasov: Stati i Materialy* (Leningrad, 1926), 352.
32. Ibid., 354.
33. Ibid., 356.
34. *Pisma*, 1: 159; August 21, 1855.

CHAPTER 17

1. *Pisma*, 1: 585; November 3, 1857.
2. "Pisma A. N. Pleshcheeva k F. M. Dostoevskomu," in *DMI*, 437.
3. Alexander Herzen, *My Past and Thoughts*, trans. Constance Garnett, rev. Humphrey Higgins, 4 vols. (New York, 1968), 4: 1581.
4. N. G. Chernyshevsky, *Selected Philosophical Essays* (Moscow, 1953), 318.
5. Ibid., 376.
6. René Wellek, *History of Modern Criticism*, 4 vols. (New Haven, 1955-1965), 4: 240.
7. Cited in V. Evgeniyev-Maksimov, *Sovremennik pri Chernyshevskom i Dobrolyubove* (Leningrad, 1936), 22.
8. I. S. Turgenev, *Sobranie Sochinenii*, 12 vols. (Moscow, 1953-1958), 12: 186.
9. Evgeniyev-Maksimov, *Sovremennik*, 21.
10. *DMI*, 439; April 10, 1858.

11. Ibid., 440-441; May 30, 1858.
12. Ibid., 441.
13. Ibid., 444; April 10, 1859.
14. Ibid., 443; February 10, 1859.
15. Ibid., 444; April 10, 1859.
16. N. G. Chernyshevsky, *Izbrannye Filosofskie Sochineniya*, 3 vols. (Leningrad, 1950-1951), 2: 235-236.
17. P. V. Annenkov, *Vospominaniya i Kriticheskie Ocherki*, 4 vols. (St. Petersburg, 1877), 2: 157.
18. Ibid., 164, 167.
19. *Pisma*, 1: 257; October 1, 1859.
20. *DMI*, 451-452; March 17, 1860.
21. *Pisma*, 1: 231; May 31, 1858.
22. *DMI*, 449; December 13, 1859.
23. A. F. Pisemsky, "A Bitter Fate," in *Masterpieces of the Russian Drama*, ed. George Rapall Noyes (New York, 1933), 454.

CHAPTER 18

1. *Pisma*, 1: 277; November 23, 1857.
2. Ibid., 240-241; December 12, 1858.
3. Ibid., 221; June 1, 1857.
4. Ibid., 2: 581; March 9, 1857.
5. Ibid., 1: 231; March 1, 1858.
6. Ibid., 221-222; June 1, 1857.
7. Ibid., 2: 585-586; November 3, 1857.
8. Ibid.
9. Ibid., 589; January 18, 1858.
10. Ibid., 1: 236; May 31, 1858.
11. Ibid., 2: 589.
12. Ibid., 593; September 13, 1858.
13. Ibid., 594-595; December 13, 1858.
14. Ibid., 594.

15. Ibid., 1: 241.
16. Ibid., 2: 589.
17. Ibid., 1: 246; May 9, 1859.
18. Ibid., 2: 593.
19. Ibid., 1: 246.
20. Ibid., 251; September 13, 1858.
21. Ibid., 2: 593.
22. Ibid., 1: 255; October 1, 1859.
23. *DVS*, 1: 323.
24. *Pisma*, 1: 264; October 11, 1859.
25. "Pisma M. M. Dostoevskogo k F. M. Dostoevskomu," in *DMI*, 525; October 21, 1859.

NOTES

CHAPTER 19

1. *Pisma*, 1: 252; September 19, 1859.
2. L. P. Grossman, "Derevnya Dostoev-skogo," in F. M. Dostoevsky, *Selo Stepanchikovo i ego obitateli* (Moscow, 1935), 28. A more recent commentator, raising the same question of the hostile reception accorded Dostoevsky's novella, takes issue with this view. "His contemporaries did not understand Dostoevsky's novel. It is difficult to say exactly why. It can scarcely be that ideological reasons are to blame here, the 'untimeliness' of *The Village of Stepanchikovo*." Unfortunately, no reasons are offered to support this opinion; one would like to know what they might be. See V. A. Tunimanov, *Tvorchestvo Dostoevskogo, 1854-1862* (Leningrad, 1980), 65.
3. Cited in *PSS*, 3: 505.
4. L. P. Grossman, "Dostoevsky—Khudozhnik," in *Tvorchestvo F. M. Dostoevskogo* (Moscow, 1959), 344-348. Grossman begins his analysis of this device by a discussion of *Uncle's Dream* and also calls it *"The Inspector-General* dénouement," locating its source in Gogol's dramatic technique.
5. *Pisma*, 3: 85-86; September 14, 1873.
6. Ibid., 1: 167; January 18, 1856.
7. See *PSS*, 2: 513.
8. *Pisma*, 1: 246; May 9, 1859.

9. See Thomas Mann, "Dostoevsky—in Moderation," printed as a preface to *The Short Novels of Dostoevsky*, trans. Constance Garnett (New York, 1945), xvii. The German text is included in Thomas Mann, *Neue Studien* (Stockholm, 1948). One should note a misdating in Mann's essay. He mistakenly believes that *The Eternal Husband* was written in 1848; in fact it was first published in 1870.
10. Tynyanov's article, which first appeared in 1921, has been reprinted many times. See Yury Tynyanov, "Dostoevsky i Gogol: k Teorii Parodii," in *O Dostoevskom*, ed. with an introduction by Donald Fanger (Providence, 1966), 153-196. Partial translations into English can be found in *Dostoevsky and Gogol*, ed. Priscilla Meyer and Stephen Rudy (Ann Arbor, 1979), 101-117; also *Twentieth-Century Russian Literary Criticism*, ed. Victor Ehrlich (New Haven, 1975), 102-116.
11. V. V. Vinogradov, *Poetika Russkoi Literatury* (Moscow, 1976), 239-240.
12. K. Mochulsky, *Dostoevsky, His Life and Work*, trans. Michael A. Minihan (Princeton, 1967), 177.
13. See "Neizdanny Dostoevsky," *Literaturnoe Nasledstvo*, 83 (Moscow, 1971), 607.
14. Erich Auerbach, *Mimesis*, trans. Willard A. Trask (Princeton, 1968), 521.

CHAPTER 20

1. *Pisma*, 1: 270; October 23, 1859.
2. Ibid., 271.
3. Ibid., 254; September 22, 1859.
4. Ibid., 285; November 12, 1859.
5. Ibid., 272; October 23, 1859.
6. Ibid., 2: 603.
7. Ibid., 597; March 14, 1859.
8. *DMI*, 515; September 21, 1859.
9. *PSS*, 3: 447.
10. *Pisma*, 1: 246; May 9, 1859.
11. Ibid., 2: 605; October 9, 1859.
12. *PSS*, 3: 443-446.
13. *Pisma*, 1: 256-257.
14. Ibid., 2: 605; October 9, 1859.
15. Ibid., 608.
16. See *PSS*, 3: 403.
17. *Pisma*, 1: 157; August 21, 1855.

18. A. A. Kornilov, *Obshchestvennoe Dvizhenie pri Alexander II*, 31.
19. *Pisma*, 2: 591; January 18, 1858.
20. Ibid., 593; September 13, 1858.
21. See my *Dostoevsky, The Seeds of Revolt, 1821-1849* (Princeton, 1976), 206.
22. *Pisma*, 1: 286; November 12, 1859.
23. See the fragment of Yanovsky's unpublished letter to A. G. Dostoevsky in *Literaturnoe Nasledstvo*, no. 86 (1973), 377.
24. *Petrashevtsy*, ed. P. S. Shchegolev, 3 vols. (Moscow-Leningrad, 1926-1928), 1: 92.
25. *DMI*, 490-491.
26. Cited in William F Woehrlin, *Chernyshevskii, The Man and the Journalist* (Cambridge, Mass., 1971), 193.

Library of Congress Cataloging in Publication Data

Frank, Joseph, 1918-
    Dostoevsky, the years of ordeal, 1850-1859.
    Includes bibliographical references and index.
    1. Dostoyevsky, Fyodor, 1821-1881—Biography.   2. Authors,
Russian—19th century—Biography.   3. Soviet Union—
Intellectual life—1801-1917. I. Title.
PG3328.F74   1983   891.73'3 [B]   83-11216
ISBN 0-691-06576-4
ISBN 0-691-01422-1 (pbk.)